D1158334

MONOGRAPHS ON
PHYSICAL BIOCHEMISTRY

GENERAL EDITORS

W. F. HARRINGTON, A. R. PEACOCKE

BIOLOGICAL MACROMOLECULES
AND
POLYELECTROLYTES
IN SOLUTION

BY

HENRYK EISENBERG

PROFESSOR OF POLYMER RESEARCH
THE WEIZMANN INSTITUTE OF SCIENCE, REHOVOT, ISRAEL

CLARENDON PRESS · OXFORD

1976

Oxford University Press, Ely House, London W. 1

GLASGOW   NEW YORK   TORONTO   MELBOURNE   WELLINGTON
CAPE TOWN   IBADAN   NAIROBI   DAR ES SALAAM   LUSAKA   ADDIS ABABA
DELHI   BOMBAY   CALCUTTA   MADRAS   KARACHI   LAHORE   DACCA
KUALA LUMPUR   SINGAPORE   HONG KONG   TOKYO

ISBN 0 19 854612 2

PRINTED BY THOMSON LITHO LTD., EAST KILBRIDE, SCOTLAND

*To the memory of my parents, who
wanted me to study science, and of
Aharon Katzir-Katchalsky, who first
taught me*

PREFACE

THIS book discusses some aspects of biological macromolecules and solution properties of polyelectrolytes. It is based on my work, experience, and predilections and therefore does not claim to cover the entire field of solution studies of charge-carrying macromolecules. References to the literature have been amply indicated to enable the reader to be reliably guided to a wider body of available knowledge.

Part of this book is devoted to an analysis of multi-component solutions of macromolecules, a field of study which has been reviewed by Casassa and myself in *Advances in Protein Chemistry* in 1964. Continued interest in this topic, as well as accumulation of experimental results on solutions of biological macromolecules from various quarters have encouraged me to re-state the analysis. In order to reach a wider audience the discussion here is essentially limited to three-component systems, and the notation is somewhat simplified. But rigour has not been sacrificed for the sake of clarity, and the approximations resulting from some of the simplifications have been clearly indicated. Fundamentals have not been affected in this process. It has been my major objective to emphasize as much as possible the usefulness of properly applied macromolecular science to the progress of biophysics and molecular biology. As such I have stressed the universality of the subject as opposed to the specialization, to enable the subject matter to be profitably studied by physicist, chemist, and biologist. Some of the material is well established, some of it is still controversial, and in some cases I may have erred; criticism leading to correction of the latter will be gratefully appreciated. *Errare humanum est, perseverare diabolicum.*

Work on this book was started while I was a Scholar in Residence, from March to September 1973, at the Fogarty International Center at the National Institutes of Health in Bethesda. I must express my gratitude to the Fogarty Center for enabling me to work on this manuscript in the scholarly loft of Stone House on the NIH Reservation. Continuation of the work was unfortunately interrupted by the Yom Kippur War in October 1973. Thanks are due to the Israeli Defence Forces for enabling me to continue work (in snatches and in unlikely places) on this manuscript while on reserve duty lecturing to the Forces, in the aftermath of the war. My wife, Nutzi, who has steadily supported me throughout this traumatic experience, deserves deep thanks. So also do Claude Cohen, Jamie Godfrey, and Herbert Morawetz, who critically read parts of the manuscript. Last but not least the author would like to thank Mrs. Sylvia Gibraltar for painstakingly typing the final manuscript and many of the innumerable intermediary stages.

Final touches were added while the author was mending his bones at the Max Planck Institut für Biophysikalische Chemie, Göttingen, thanks to the generous hospitality of Manfred Eigen, Eberhard Neumann and many other colleagues, following some non-linear sliding experiments on snow on the occasion of the Tenth Winter Seminar in Zuoz, February, 1975.

H.E.

Rehovot, Israel
June 1975

ACKNOWLEDGEMENTS

I SHOULD like to thank the following Societies and publishers for permission to reproduce figures in this book:

Academic Press for Figs 2.2, 4.1, 4.3, 4.4, 4.5, 5.1, and 5.4.

The American Association for the Advancement of Science for Fig. 1.8, taken from their journal *Science*, © 1965 by the American Association for the Advancement of Science.

The American Chemical Society for Figs 2.1, 5.2, 5.10, 5.11, and 5.12, reprinted with permission from their journal *Biochemistry* and for Figs 5.5 and 6.1 and Tables 6.1 and 6.2 from *The Journal of Physical Chemistry*, © The American Chemical Society.

The American Institute of Physics for Figs 7.7 and 7.8.

ASP Biological and Medical Press for Fig. 5.13(a) and (b).

W. A. Benjamin for Fig. 1.6, © 1970 by J. A. Watson; W. A. Benjamin Inc., Menlo Park, California.

Cold Spring Harbour Laboratory of Quantitive Biology for Fig. 1.7.

Elsevier Publishing Company for Fig. 5.6.

H. R. Lewis and Co. for Fig. 7.2.

Macmillan Journals for Figs 1.4 and 1.9 from *Nature*.

The New York Academy of Sciences for Figs 5.7, 5.8, and 5.9.

Plenum Press for Figs 1.10, 1.11, 1.12, 1.13, and 4.2.

The Rockefeller Institute Press for Fig. 1.15.

The Royal Society for Figs 1.2 and 1.3.

The Weizmann Science Press for Fig. 7.13.

John Wiley and Sons for Figs 1.16, 4.6, 4.7, 7.4, 7.10, 7.11, and 7.14, and Table 5.1.

CONTENTS

LIST OF SYMBOLS AND ABBREVIATIONS

A_2, A_3 virial coefficients, ml mol/g^{-2}; eqn (1.2)

A_{JK} is the cofactor of the element a_{JK} in the determinant $|a_{JK}|$; Section 2.3

B designates position of band in equilibrium sedimentation in a density gradient; Section 5.4

B_2, B_3 virial coefficients; eqn (1.1)

B_J binding of component J, grams per gram of macromolecular component; Section 3.3

C_u concentration, equivalents of charge, or repeating units, per litre; eqn (2.14)

C_J molarity of component J, mol l^{-1} of solution; eqn (2.3)

$C(\tau)$ auto-correlation function; eqn (4.83)

$C_\phi(\tau)$ position auto-correlation function; eqn (4.86)

D relative permittivity

D_t translational diffusion coefficient

D_{ij} diffusion coefficients in multi-component systems; eqn (6.16)

E electromotive force; electric field strength

ES   equilibrium sedimentation

E_J Donnan exclusion of component J, grams per gram of macromolecular component; Section 3.3

$\mathscr{F}$ Faraday electrochemical equivalent

F'_{ik} determinant in eqn (6.19) for diffusion coefficients

F_{ij} frictional force; eqn (6.90)

$F(\tau)$ deformation gradient; Section 7.2

F, F_m shearing stress, maximum shearing stress at capillary wall; Section 7.2

G Gibbs free energy

$G_s(R, \tau)$ self-part of space–time correlation function; eqn (4.87)

I_0 incident light intensity; Section 4.3

I_s light scattered from unit volume; Section 4.3

I_{el} scattering of an electron; eqn (4.52)

J_k, J_{el} flow of component k, of electrical current, per mole; Section 6.3

J^V, J^1 flow with respect to centre of volume, with respect to solvent, component 1; Section 6.3

K optical factor $4\pi^2 n^2 / N_A \lambda^4$; eqn (4.32)

K_{ij} association constants, l mol^{-1}, eqns (5.105) and (5.106)

L length of rod-like particle

LS	light-scattering
L_J	equals $\omega^2(\partial\rho/\partial c_2)_u/2RT$; see eqn (5.35)
L'	equals $-\omega^2 r_B \chi/RT$, eqn (5.80)
L_{ij}, $\mathscr{L}_{ij}$	Onsager phenomenological coefficients on mole basis ($l_{ik} = L_{ik}M_iM_k$)
M	molecular weight, g mol^{-1}
	torque per unit height in Couette flow; eqn (7.64)
M_{app}	apparent molecular weight, eqn (1.3)
M_n, M_w, M_z	number; weight; z-average molecular weights
M_u	molecular weight of equivalent units (M_2/Z)
M_s	equals $M_2(1+\xi_1')$; eqn (5.68)
M_j	j-mers in associating systems; eqns (5.105) and (5.106)
$[M_j]$	activities of components M_j
M_{y1}, M_{y2}, M_{y3}	'ideal' molecular weight moments; eqns (5.120), (5.123), and (5.124)
$\overline{M}_j$	buoyant molecular weights $M_j(1-v_j\rho)$; Section 6.3
M_P^*	molecular weight of macro-ion, including molecular weight of 'bound' counter-ions; Section 6.3
N	number of particles per unit volume; eqn (4.9)
N_A	Avogadro's number
OP	osmotic pressure
$P(q)$	particle interference function $(P(0)=1)$; eqn (4.49)
$P_i(\omega)$	power spectrum; eqn (4.99)
Q	volume discharge in unit time; eqn (7.41)
R	Rayleigh factor, $r^2 I_s/I_0$; eqn (4.9)
R_ρ	density fluctuation part of R; eqn (4.32)
R_g	radius of gyration of particle; eqn (4.59)
(Re)	Reynolds number; eqn (7.78)
S	calibration constant in equilibrium sedimentation in a density gradient; eqn (5.78)
SAXS	small-angle X-ray scattering
S_{12}	shearing stress; eqn (7.1)
$S(t)$	stress tensor; Section 7.2
T	period; eqn (4.84). Extra stress tensor; Section 7.2. Torque; Section 7.2
$\overline{V}_J$	partial molal volumes of component J, ml mol^{-1}
V_m	volume of solution (ml), containing 1 kg of component 1
$\overline{V}_u$	partial molal volume of equivalent units ($\overline{V}_2/Z$); eqn (2.53)
$\overline{V}_2^*$	partial molal quantity defined in eqn (5.17)
X_n, X_w, X_z	Number, weight, and z-average degrees of polymerization
Z	degree of polymerization, or number of charges or of repeating units, per macromolecule. Modified grand partition function; eqn (4.22)

a	force per unit volume in direction of flow; eqn (7.37). exponent in eqns (4.70) and (7.6) identical semi-axes of ellipsoid of rotation; Section 7.3
a_J	activity of component J; eqn (2.15)
a_{JK}	partial derivatives; eqn (2.17)
$|a_{JK}|$	is the determinant of the elements a_{JK}; Section 2.3
b	non-identical axis of ellipsoid of rotation; Section 7.3 designates bottom in ultracentrifuge cell; Chapter 5
c_J	concentration of component J, g ml^{-1}; eqn (2.4)
e	electronic charge
f_j	frictional coefficients of species j; Chapter 6
g	equals Γ_3/Γ_2^2; eqn (1.5)
g_J	grams of component J
i	effective charge parameter; Section 2.4
j_k, j_{ch}	flow of component k, of chemical reaction, on gram basis; Chapter 6
j^V, j^1	flow with respect to centre of volume, to solvent, component 1; Chapter 6
k	association constants, ml g^{-1}; Section 5.5. Huggins constant; eqn (7.7)
$\mathbf{k}$	wave vector $(2\pi n/\lambda)\mathbf{n}$, Chapter 4
l_{ik}	Onsager phenomenological coefficients, on gram basis; eqn (A6.21)
m	subscript, designates meniscus in ultracentrifuge cell; Chapter 5
m_J	molality of component J; mol kg^{-1} of component 1
m_u	molality; moles of repeating unit, or charged groups per kg of component 1; eqn (2.13)
n	refractive index
n_J	mole of component J; eqn (2.1)
p	axial ratio b/a of ellipsoid of rotation; eqn (2.56). Induced electric dipole moment; eqn (4.2).
q	LS parameter $(4\pi n/\lambda)\sin(\frac{1}{2}\theta)$; eqn (4.6)
r	distance between particles; distance from scattering centre to detector. Distance from centre of rotation of ultracentrifuge. Radius of cylinder
r_B	centre of band in sedimentation in a density gradient; Section 5.4
s_j	sedimentation coefficients; eqn (6.21)
$\bar{v}_J$	partial specific volume of component J, ml g^{-1}
$\bar{v}_s$	partial specific volume of 'solvated' macromolecule; eqn (5.62)
v_k	velocity of kth component; Chapter 6

v_2^*	equal to $\overline{V}_2^*/M_2$; eqn (6.45)
v^V	velocity with respect to local centre of volume; eqn (6.78)
w_J, w_J', w_J''	molality of component J. Grams per gram of component 1; eqns (2.2), (3.14), and (3.16)
x	ratio of molecular weights of labelled and natural DNA species; eqn (5.74)
x_J	mole fractions m_J/m_2 of components J composing heterogeneous component 2; Section 5.5
x_k	generalized force on component k; eqn (6.2)
y	activity coefficient on c concentration scale; eqn (1.9)
y_J	weight fractions w_J/w_2 of component J composing heterogeneous component 2; Section 5.5
Π	Osmotic pressure; eqn (1.1)
Γ	half-width of Lorentzian, $D_t q^2$; eqn (4.96)
Γ_2, Γ_3	$A_2 M$, $A_3 M$; eqn (1.4)
$\Gamma, \Gamma', \Gamma''$	membrane distribution parameters; eqns (2.25), (2.71), and (2.75)
Γ^c	Donnan distribution coefficient; eqn (A5.11)
Θ	thermodynamic 'ideal' theta temperature as defined by Flory (1953). Characteristic, or Boyle temperature of a real gas (Appendix 4)
Λ	defines apparent molecular weights $M^* \equiv M\Lambda$ in equilibrium sedimentation; eqn (5.28)
Φ	apparent molal volume; Section (3.1). Dissipation function; eqn (A6.19)
$\Psi_J, \Psi_J^{(c)}$	molal and molar refractive-index increment of component J; eqns (3.28) and (3.31)
Ω	defines apparent molecular weights $M^* \equiv M\Omega$ in light-scattering experiments; eqn (4.43)
Ω_1, Ω_2	angular velocities in Couette flow; eqn (7.62)
α	degree of ionization of macromolecules; eqn (4.77). Polarizability of particle; eqn (4.2)
α_V	volume expansion coefficient; eqn (4.19)
β	$1/kT$. Charge per unit length of cylinder; eqn (A5.1)
β_J	excess chemical potential of component J; eqn (2.15)
β_{JK}	partial derivative; eqn (2.18)
γ_J	activity coefficient of component J on molality scale $(\gamma_J = a_J/m_J)$
δ	$r - r_B$; eqn (5.56)
ε	eccentricity of ellipsoids of rotation; eqn (2.56)
η	viscosity
η_{rel}	relative viscosity η/η^0
η_{sp}	specific viscosity $\eta_{rel} - 1$

$[\eta]$	intrinsic viscosity, $\lim \eta_{sp}/c,\ c \to 0$
θ	scattering angle; Chapter 4. Rotary diffusion constant; Chapter 7
κ	isothermal compressibility; eqn (2.43). Velocity gradient; eqn (7.1)
κ_{DH}	Debye–Hückel screening parameter (inverse radius of ionic atmosphere); eqn 4.1
λ	wavelength *in vacuo*. Charge parameter, $4\pi e^2/DkT$; eqn (A5.5). Equivalent conductivities of ions; Chapter 6
λ_m	wavelength in medium
μ_i	chemical potential of species i
$\tilde{\mu}_i$	total potential of species i; eqn (5.1)
μ_P^*	chemical potential of macro-ion including chemical potential of 'bound' counter-ions; Chapter 6
ν	kinematic viscosity η/ρ. Number of charges αZ per macromolecule; eqn (4.72). Linear frequency of light $(\omega/2\pi)$
ν_{iJ}	number of moles of species i included in 1 mol of component J
ξ	charge density; eqn (A5.1)
$\xi_J,\ \xi_J'\ \xi_J''$	preferential interaction parameters; eqns (3.9), (3.14), and (3.16)
ρ	density
ρ_n	number density of particles; eqn (1.1)
ρ_{el}	density of electron per ml; eqn (4.55)
σ	standard deviation; eqn (5.59). Local entropy production; eqn (A6.8)
$\sigma,(\kappa),\ \sigma_2(\kappa)$	material functions in flow; eqn (7.17)
τ	time delay, s; eqn (4.3)
ϕ	gravitational potential; Section (5.2). Modified pressure; eqn (7.11)
ϕ_J	apparent specific volume; Section (3.1)
ϕ'	apparent quantity in sedimentation equilibrium; eqn (3.12)
ϕ_p	practical osmotic coefficient; eqn (4.72); Appendix 5
ϕ_{app}	apparent fluidity; eqn (7.47)
χ	gradient of density increment $(\partial\rho/\partial c_2)_\mu$ at r_B; eqn (5.57)
ψ	electrostatic potential, Section (5.2). Potential in fluid; eqn (7.10)
$\psi_J,\ \psi_J^{(c)}$	specific refractive-index increment of component J on molal (eqn (3.29)) and molar (eqn (3.32)) scale
ψ_{app}	apparent refractive-index increment; eqn (3.30)
ω	angular velocity; eqn (5.7). Circular frequency of light $(2\pi\nu)$; Chapter 4
ω'	mobility of ions; eqn (6.54)

Subscript s refers to complex solvent mixture, composed of a number of low-molecular-weight diffusible components.

Superscript 0 refers to properties of solution of vanishing concentration of macromolecular component.

Subscript sed indicates constraint to the conditions of sedimentation equilibrium; Section 5.2.

Superscript (r) indicates that the variables depend on position r in the centrifugal field; eqn (5.22).

Primed quantities (m'_y, m'_x) designate concentrations in outer polymer-free solutions in dialysis equilibrium experiment.

Superscripts D and S signify components defined in correspondence with dialysis equilibrium experiment (eqns (2.26) and (2.27)) or according to Scatchard (eqns (2.32) and (2.33) respectively).

Subscripts m, μ signify constancy of all m and μ, except those appearing in the derivative.

1

INTRODUCTION

1.1. Polyelectrolytes

A CONSIDERABLE proportion of the components of the living cell (such as nucleic acids and proteins) are macromolecules, carry electrical charges, and are suspended in aqueous media containing low-molecular-weight ionic and neutral species. In the physico-chemical characterization and the analysis of the behaviour of these large, polyelectrolyte molecules, many problems arise which may be solved by consideration of their special character. Poly-electrolytes (Armstrong and Strauss **1969**)† are long-chain molecules carrying a large number of ionizable sites. These long chain-molecules may exist in solution in either linear open conformation, as do many nucleic acids, for instance, or they may be folded into tertiary structures as are most proteins. In all cases, we should remember that solutions of either nucleic acids or proteins are electroneutral in the thermodynamic sense, and deviations from electroneutrality are extremely rare (Appendix 1). For every charged group fixed to the macromolecule there must therefore exist, somewhere in the vicinity of the macromolecule, a small mobile counter-ion of opposite charge. In the case of an ampholytic protein (a protein which carries both types of positive and negative charges), the mobile ions balance the net charge of positive and negative ions fixed to the macromolecular matrix. Often we shall be interested in the way in which the electrical charges influence the physico-chemical behaviour of these solutions; in many other instances though we shall be satisfied to conclude that if large enough test volumes in our solutions are considered these volumes will contain both many macromolecules and counter-ions and will therefore—for many purposes—be considered electro-neutral phases. To these the laws of thermodynamics (Guggenheim **1967**), pertaining to electroneutral phases, apply *in toto*. It will be important to distinguish when this assumption no longer holds. In such cases we are speaking of electrochemical systems which lie outside the scope of this present text.

1.2. Materials

It may come as a surprising observation that the increase in conceptual

† References indicated in bold numerals refer to books, articles in books, monographs, and reviews, and are collected in part (A) of the Bibliography. Other references are to journals, and are of a less general nature; these are in part (B) of the Bibliography.

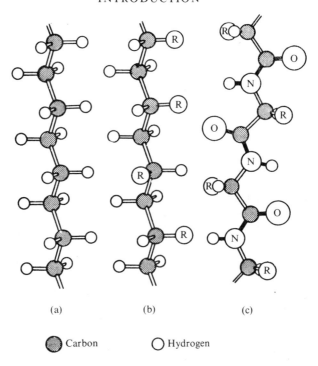

FIG. 1.1 (a) Segment of extended polymethylene chain. (b) Segment of extended vinyl polymer chain. (c) Segment of extended trans-polypeptide chain. (In (a) and (b) of this Figure carbon-backbone atoms are not lying in plane of paper.)

complexity between some well-known synthetic macromolecules and some characteristic biopolymers is rather minor. The very special properties of the latter are often due to some fine details of structure, side-chain composition in particular, and not to the basic features of the macromolecular backbone. We shall, in the following, show how many properties of biological macro-molecules are clearly recognizable in simple synthetic prototype macro-molecules.

Our first example is the simplest member of the class, polymethylene (Fig. 1.1(a)) which can be synthesized by the decomposition–polymerization of diazomethane CH_2N_2. This polymer may be recognized more familiarly as polyethylene, one of the most important modern plastics, more usually obtained by the polymerization of ethylene, $CH_2{=}CH_2$. The polyethylene molecule cannot be drawn totally in the plane of the paper. We can however force the carbon-backbone atoms to lie in the plane of the paper—leading to the extended zig-zag conformation of the polymer. To each carbon are connected two hydrogens, one of which extends above and the other below the plane of the paper, such that the tetrahedral arrangement of substituents around each carbon atom is completed. As both hydrogens are equivalent, stereoisomers do not exist.

An important principle governing macromolecular behaviour (Flory **1953**) is already available in this simplest of all macromolecules, namely, that rotation about carbon–carbon bonds is possible. It is not entirely free, but even hindered rotation allows the polyethylene molecule to assume a huge number of conformations in solution, of which the extended one is only an extreme example of a lone case. Rotation around backbone atoms leads to a large number of possible chain conformations, and forms the basis of rubber elasticity and, with the help of very specific side chain interactions, permits biological macromolecules to fold into a variety of extremely useful shapes. In enzymes for instance, the folded, globular, state is specific and fixed, allowing side groups widely separated along the backbone to be brought into close proximity for concerted action in biological catalytic function. In high concentrations of urea or guanidine-HCl, and usually in the presence of reducing agents (which prevent the formation of sulphur–sulphur cross-bridges between cysteine residues) these native conformations are disrupted and the denatured peptide chains assume random coil conformations. This is the same kind of conformation the polyethylene molecule above would assume if freed from the constraints of the two-dimensional world of the paper or blackboard. The subject of polymer conformation is not within the scope of this book; it has recently been covered in a book by Flory (**1969**), on the statistical mechanics of chain molecules. The classical text (Flory **1953**) by the same author, on the principles of polymer chemistry, should be referred to for all basic aspects related to polymer genesis and behaviour.

A little tampering with the polyethylene chain produces the structure below (Fig. 1.1(b)) in which one hydrogen on every second carbon atom has been replaced by the radical R. Many industrial plastics can now be represented: if R is chlorine, we are dealing with polyvinyl chloride (PVC); if R is a phenyl group, then the chain becomes polystyrene, and so on. All of these polymers are derived from a class of monomers known as vinyl monomers, of the general formula $CH_2{=}CHR$. The genesis and genealogy of these polymers are not relevant to our quest. Very relevant though are features which result from the modification due to the introduction of the radical R. In the first place we notice that distinct stereochemical possibilities are now feasible dependent upon the nature and placement of the group R either above or below the plane of the paper when the backbone is pinned butterfly-fashion, in the plane of the paper, in the extended zigzag two-dimensional array. The radical R is, of course, free to move around as the macromolecule assumes a variety of new conformations but the particular stereochemical arrangement (with R above or below in the sense just described) is built into the structure of the chain and persists with it as long as the chemical bonds joining the backbone atoms remain intact. We owe this realization to Giulio Natta, who in 1955 (see Morawetz **1975**) added a new dimension to the chemistry of synthetic polymers by introducing the iso-, syndio and atactic classes of long-chain polymers. These correspond to all radicals R in Fig. 1.1(b) on one side, alternating, or in random arrangement when viewed along the fully extended zigzag chain. That it has lately become possible to synthesize stereospecific polymers on suitable template catalysts has created a class of molecules with interesting parallel to biological macromolecules. The other important feature introduced by the presence of the side chain R, in addition to the molecular asymmetry, is the fact that it strongly modifies steric hindrances to rotation around bonds and also introduces the possibility of side-chain interactions. These latter may be either attractive or repulsive, weak or strong. Together these two new features help to produce either soft rubbers or tough plastics, low melting waxes or high-temperature-resistant materials, films, and fibres of many kinds, and so on. The radicals R on each chain may be identical or different, and the second hydrogen on the same carbon may sometimes also be substituted by a similar or by a different radical R. There is no end to the ingenuity of the chemist and the materials which can be created starting from, for instance, natural gas. The examples shown are only a fraction of the achievement which started out from pale imitations of natural materials and continued by creating materials which embody structural and functional principles encountered in nature. The synthetic materials may surpass the natural models with respect to single selected properties, although biological functionality and self-replicative character have only been achieved by copying nature in a precise fashion.

Let us now turn to a class of synthetic materials which brings us one step closer to systems of biological interest—polyelectrolytes. All that is required is to introduce charged groups into the molecule by making R in Fig. 1.1(b) equal, for instance, to COOH (polyacrylic acid), $-SO_3^- H^+$ (polyvinylsulphonic acid), $-C_6H_4-SO_3^- H^+$ (polystyrene sulphonic acid), $-C_5H_4N^+ BuBr^-$ (poly-4-vinylpyridinium-N-n-butyl bromide), and so on. Polyacrylic acid is only partially ionized in water, but its state of ionization may be changed by the addition of suitable amounts of sodium hydroxide. The other polymers shown are almost always completely ionized and the counter-ions may often be exchanged with subsequent interesting results. The electrostatic field generated by these changes endows polyelectrolytes with properties interesting *per se*, but which also often help in the understanding of the behaviour of biological macromolecules. Some basic properties of charge-carrying macromolecules have been studied in the analysis of simple polyelectrolyte systems. The theoretical complexities though are enormous, and to the present day our understanding of polyelectrolyte behaviour is incomplete. In the early days of polyelectrolyte research, in the late 1940s and early 1950s, there was hope that a knowledge of polyelectrolyte behaviour

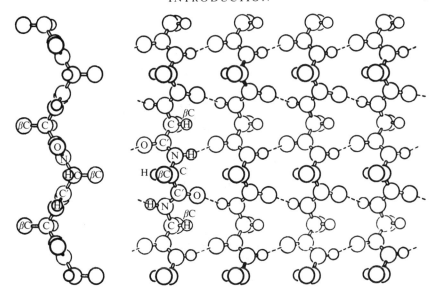

FIG. 1.2. The parallel-chain pleated-sheet structure of polypeptides, according to Corey and Pauling (1953).

would solve many problems related to the behaviour of biological macro-molecules. These latter have proved to be rather more complicated than anticipated, and polyelectrolytes themselves turned out also to be rather complicated. Still a great deal was learned from the study of simple poly-electrolytes, and many new avenues of research were opened (Katchalsky 1971). The principles of the transformation of chemical energy into mechanical work were subjected to close scrutiny—contractile fibres and semipermeable polyelectrolyte membranes were created. Ion exchange is intimately connected to polyelectrolyte theory. Specific interactions of macromolecules with ions and many interesting properties of overwhelming importance to biology can be studied in simple polyelectrolyte systems.

We now come to a brief consideration of the classes of biological macro-molecules of interest to this work. Polymers based on sugars, carbohydrates, cellulose, starches, lipids, etc. will not specifically be considered here, although the methodology developed applies to their behaviour equally well. We shall restrict ourselves to two basic classes, nucleic acids and proteins. The former carry the genetic information, have the capacity for self-replication, and are instrumental in the continued assembly of the macromolecules required by the biological machine, that is, the proteins. Enzymes are created by way of the nucleic acids, and in turn sometimes regulate the activity of the latter. Molecular biology is a fascinating, complex, and fast-moving field of investigation. The reader is referred to the books of Watson (1970) and of

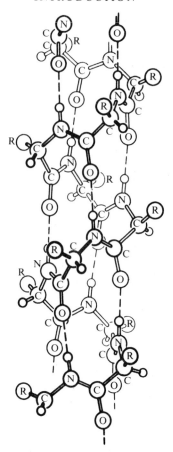

FIG. 1.3. The right-handed α-helix of polypeptides, according to Corey and Pauling (1953).

Kornberg (**1974**) for authoritative exposé of this field of constructive human activity and achievement.

Fig. 1.1(c) shows an extended polypeptide chain in the *trans* configuration (Corey and Pauling 1953). This is not a configuration it likes to maintain. Note the difference between the polypeptide and the synthetic vinyl chain (Fig. 1.1(b)). They share a common appearance, but the details are significantly different. The backbone is not a continuous carbon–carbon chain, but contains the all-important peptide bond, very often so constrained that the peptide grouping CONH (black lines), assumes (as shown by Corey and Pauling) a planar arrangement. The side-chain R groups are drawn from a pool of about 20 different possible l-amino acid residues seemingly randomly dispersed along the backbone. Some are acidic (for example, glutamic and aspartic acids), some are basic (for example, lysine and arginine).

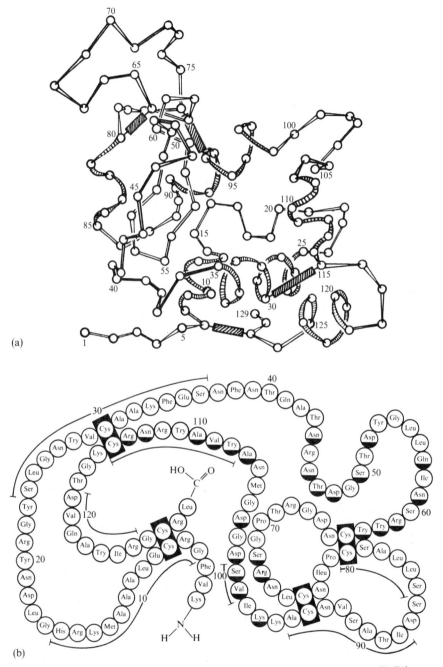

(a)

(b)

FIG. 1.4. (a) Schematic drawing of the main-chain conformation of lysozyme. (b) Primary structure of lysozyme (From Blake *et al.* 1965).

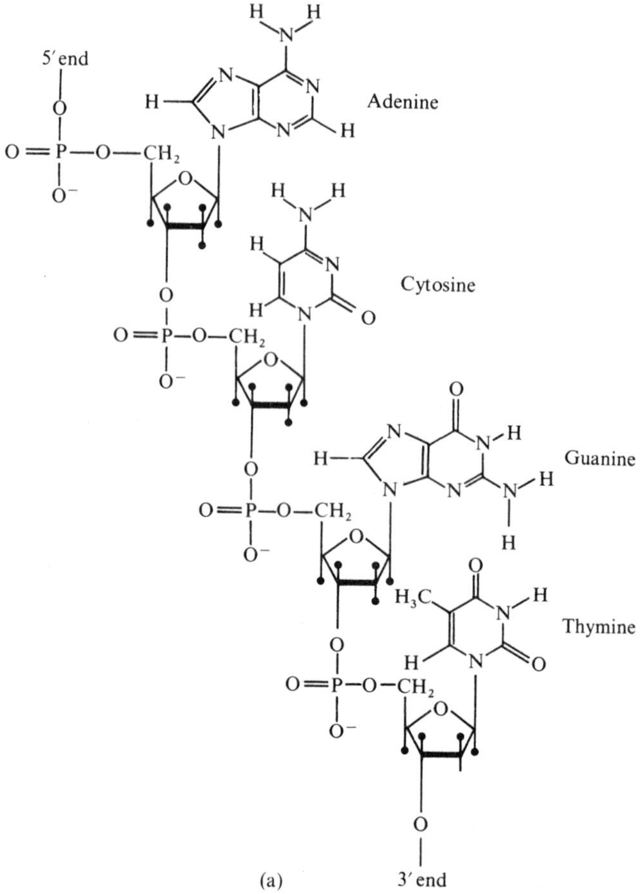

FIG. 1.5. (a) Segment of basic DNA chain.

Many are neutral but still capable of strong or weak interactions with their close or distant neighbours. The polypeptide chain may assume a number of distinct conformations. It may be random, as for instance, in aqueous solutions at high concentrations of guanidine–HCl or urea or at extreme values of the pH. It may be in one of two (parallel or anti-parallel) pleated-sheet structures (Fig. 1.2). These are extended structures in which hydrogen bonds are formed intermolecularly between adjacent polypeptide chains. A well-known structure is the α-helix of Corey and Pauling (Fig. 1.3), in which hydrogen bonds between amino-acid residues thrice removed along the polypeptide chain intermolecularly stabilize a very specific structure. Optical activity is conferred to these organized structures not only because of the intrinsic activity of the asymmetric α-carbon in the naturally occurring

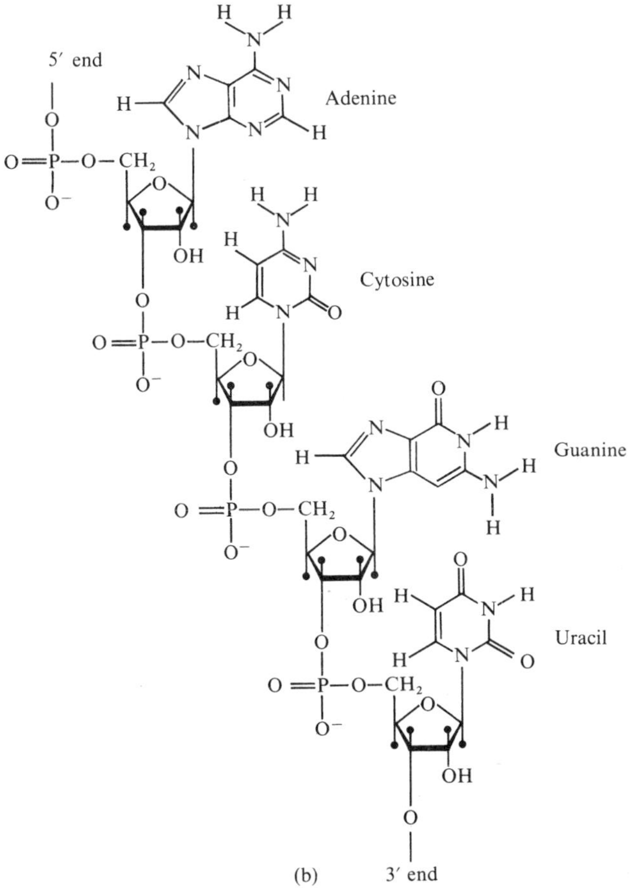

5' end

Adenine

Cytosine

Guanine

Uracil

(b)   3' end

(b) Segment of basic RNA chain.

l-amino acids, but also because of the unique arrangement of the helical form. α-helix stretches as well as intramolecular pleated β-structures are often found in the native structure of globular proteins (Fig. 1.4(a)). This is a somewhat simplified picture of lyzozyme, the structure of which was determined by Phillips and his collaborators (Blake, Koenig, Mair, North, Phillips, and Sarma 1965). We can see five separate stretches of α-helix in the globular protein, as well as four disulphide bridges, which make it easier for the macromolecule to maintain its shape. The primary sequence is shown in Fig. 1.4(b), which also emphasizes the helical sequences in the globular protein and shows that widely separated amino-acid groups congregate to form functional groups within the active binding site. The tertiary globular catalytically active structure is usually (as we know from Anfinsen's work

(**1964**)) uniquely achieved from the preformed polypeptide chain.

Nucleic-acid structures are by and large quite different from those of proteins, although, as we shall see in the case of transfer RNA, structures almost recalling globular proteins are also encountered. The basic structure of the DNA chain is shown in Fig. 1.5(a). In the backbone phosphate and sugar (deoxyribose) residues alternate. The phosphates carry negative charges at neutral pH (therefore the name nucleic *acid*), and to each sugar residue one of the four possible purine and pyrimidine bases are attached. Fig. 1.6 shows the well-known Watson and Crick base pairing arrangement, a schematic model of the DNA double helix, and a possible scheme for DNA replication. In the B-structure of Watson and Crick the parallel-stacked base planes, perpendicular to the helix axis, are 3·4 Å apart. Hydrogen bonding between paired bases is an important factor in stabilizing the structure, but it seems that a large part of the energy which holds the helix together is due to base-stacking interactions directed along the helical axis. The double helix is a formidable and rigid structure. To store the information it carries, its size must perforce be huge, and despite inherent rigidity over short lengths the molecule as a whole is capable of being folded on itself to fit the dimensions of the cell nucleus. In Fig. 1.7 we show an electron micrograph of an intact medium-sized circular DNA molecule, carrying all the information required for the reproduction of a complete virus. The molecular weight of phage DNA may exceed 10^8 daltons, and bacterial and eukaryotic DNA may be orders of magnitude larger still; much smaller DNA is also known. The molecular weight of proteins are much smaller, usually between 10^4 and 10^5 daltons, although notable exceptions exist.

Thus we see that both proteins and nucleic acids originate from linear structures but may assume completely different conformations in space. Physical methods of investigation must therefore be flexible and universal enough to satisfactorily explore both classes of these long-chain molecules.

Ribonucleic acid (RNA) has been much investigated recently, and its basic structure is shown in Fig. 1.5(b). Different functional types of RNA are known and the base sequence of one, transfer RNA, has been determined in some selected cases. A specific example is shown in Fig. 1.8. It is a single chain, but it has a specific secondary 'clover-leaf' structure with the amino acid and codon sites on opposite sides. Recent physico-chemical and X-ray evidence has shown that additional folding is required for efficient protein synthesis. Crystal structures of yeast phenylalanine tRNA at 3 Å resolution have now been reported (Kim, Suddath, Quigley, McPherson, Sussman, Wang, Seeman, and Rich 1974; Robertus, Ladner, Finch, Rhodes, Brown, Clark, and Klug 1974) and, in contrast to DNA, this nucleic acid is quite globular in structure. Robertus *et al.* (1974) have found several interactions which help to maintain the tertiary structure. These are additional base pairs or triples, mostly not of the Watson–Crick type, and also a variety of

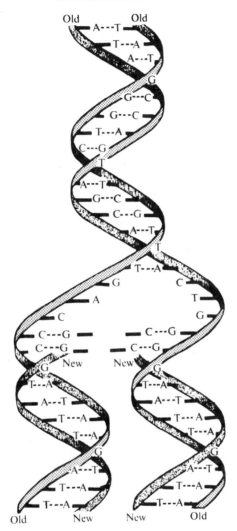

FIG. 1.6. Schematic model of DNA double helix and replication mechanism (From Watson 1970).

stacking interactions. The model, which is shown in Fig. 1.9, is in accord with the chemical reactivity of different tRNAs.

1.3. Methods

It is not possible in a small book on multi-component biopolymer solutions to give a complete discussion on the physical chemistry of macromolecules, involving such diverse aspects as thermodynamics, chain statistics and

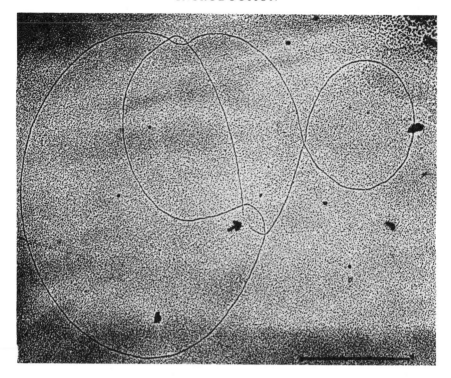

FIG. 1.7. Electron micrograph of circular λ DNA molecule. The contour length is $16\cdot3\,\mu$m (From Ris and Chandler, 1963).

conformation, osmotic pressure, ultracentrifugation, electrochemical phenomena, optical and spectrophotometric properties of various kinds, kinetic aspects, n.m.r., and e.s.r. Here we can only briefly touch on some of the more basic aspects of these methods, and refer for details to other volumes in this series. For a more complete discussion of the physical chemistry of macromolecules see Tanford's text (**1961**), and for some specialized aspects of biophysical chemistry see the work of Edsall and Wyman (**1958**).

We shall, for purposes of classification, divide this book into four major sections which all deal, in one way or another, with (1) the determination of the size and shape of biomacromolecular solutes, and (2) the intermolecular interaction of macromolecules with themselves or with small molecules in solution. This knowledge is required for a fundamental understanding of macromolecular behaviour and phenomena characteristic of multi-component solutions. We shall therefore consider the following.

Thermodynamics, with special reference to thermodynamics of multi-component systems, membrane distribution, and preferential 'binding'

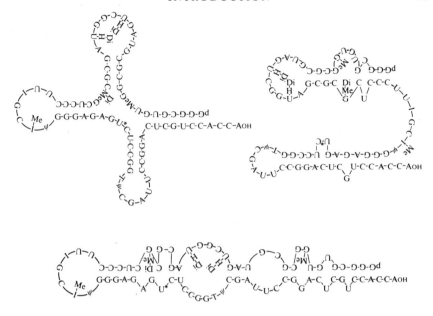

F IG. 1.8. Original report of nucleotide sequence and base-pairing schemes of yeast phenyl-alanine specific tRNA (From Holley, Apgar, Everett, Madison, Marquisee, Merrill, Penswich, and Zamir 1965).

phenomena, osmotic pressure, light-scattering, and equilibrium sedimentation.

Scattering of light and X-rays, for the determination of the size and shape of particles, as well as interactions between them; the recent use of coherent light sources (lasers) and spectral-broadening and frequency shifts of the scattered light.

Hydrodynamics of rigid and flexible particles, with special emphasis on viscosity, diffusion, and sedimentation.

Applications to DNA and enzyme systems.

These categories will not be rigidly adhered to; overlaps in the presentation will occur here and there. In the remainder of this chapter the subject will be introduced in a qualitative way but more precise formulations will appear later. For complete understanding a basic knowledge of thermodynamics, statistical mechanics, differential calculus, and some elementary vector operations is all that will be required.

1.3.1. *Osmotic pressure*
Osmotic pressure is one of the basic phenomena of nature involving solutions separated by membranes, which are 'semipermeable', that is permeable to the solvent and to some of the solutes only. In the laboratory the usual osmotic-

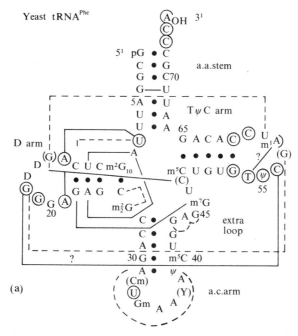

FIG. 1.9. (a) The sequence of yeast tRNA^{Phe} arranged in the clover-leaf formula. An arm of the clover leaf is made up of a double helical stem and a single stranded loop. Bases which are invariant in all tRNA sequences are circled: semi-invariants, that is, purines or pyrimidines exclusively, are bracketed. Nucleotides which are base-paired in the tertiary structure are joined by solid lines, and those which stack on each other by dashed lines. (From Robertus *et al.* 1974.) (b) A schematic diagram of the tertiary structure of yeast tRNA^{Phe}. The ribose–

pressure experiment consists of a thin collodion membrane, separating two liquid phases, permeable to all solutes except the macromolecular component. An equally satisfactory semipermeable membrane, however, is afforded by the air space (or vacuum) in a closed desiccator in an isopiestic distillation experiment (Fig. 1.10). This membrane is permeable only to the principal solvent (usually water), which is allowed to equilibrate between a container holding a protein or nucleic acid solution and another container enclosing a suitable reference solution. Distillation of water proceeds until the vapour pressures of the two solutions are identical. A more general statement for the equilibrium condition requires that the chemical potential μ of all components (taken in neutral combinations) permeable through the osmotic membrane be identical in contiguous phases (see Appendix 2).

The study of osmosis goes back to 1748 when the Abbé Nollet used animal bladders to separate alcohol and water (see Findlay (**1953**) for a historical review of the subject). The role of osmosis with respect to many biological phenomena and transport of materials in the living cell can hardly be over-

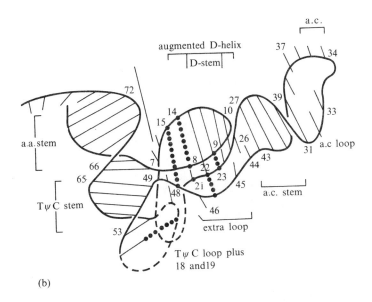

(b)

phosphate backbone is represented by a continuous line, except where there is ambiguity when it is shown dashed. Base pairs in the double helical stems are represented by long, light lines, and non-paired bases by shorter lines. Many of the latter stack as indicated; those which do not are drawn at an angle, for example, 16, 17, and 47. Base pairs additional to those in the clover-leaf formula are indicated by dotted lines. (From Robertus *et al.* 1974.)

emphasized. Brownian motion is due to the thermal motion of the molecules themselves and constitutes (in conjunction with the semipermeable membranes) the basis of osmotic pressure; it was discovered by the botanist Robert Brown in 1827.

The colloidal state of matter was characterized by Thomas Graham in 1854 and the proper theoretical basis of osmosis was provided by J. H. Van't Hoff in 1880. Artificial copper ferrocyanide membranes were introduced by M. Traube in 1864 and extensive osmotic studies are due to W. F. P. Pfeffer in 1877. More recently, mention must be made of Albert Einstein for theories of Brownian motion in 1905, and of fluctuations and viscosity; F. G. Donnan (1911) for interpreting the distribution of ions across semipermeable membrane; Jean Perrin who in 1908 determined Avogadro's number from Brownian motion; Peter Debye for his work on scattering of X-rays in 1915 and of light rays in 1944; The Svedberg who invented the ultracentrifuge in 1925; Herman Staudinger who established in 1920 the concept of macro-molecules (as opposed to the conception of large molecules as being colloidal

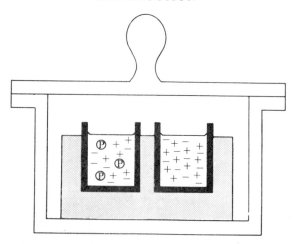

FIG. 1.10. Schematic arrangement in isopiestic experiment. Protein solution containing low-molecular-weight salt is equilibrating in thermostated copper block against solution of low-molecular-weight salt. Solvent molecules which equilibrate across the vapour phase are not indicated (for an experimental study of protein solutions by this method see Hade and Tanford (1967) and for nucleic acids see Hearst (1965)). (From Eisenberg **1974a**.)

aggregates of small molecular entities); and Werner Kuhn who in 1930 laid the foundation for modern macromolecular theory.

A simple osmometer is described in Fig. 1.11. In the simplest case of neutral polymeric solute, which cannot pass through the pores of the semipermeable membrane, there is only solvent on the outside of the compartment enclosed by the membrane, but there is both solvent and polymeric solute inside this compartment; the solvent is free to move across the membrane. In agreement with the practice to be followed later, we call the solvent component 1 and the electroneutral polymeric solute component 2. What happens when the osmometer compartment is introduced into the solvent beaker is easily predictable on thermodynamic grounds. The reader will find kinetic explanations in elementary textbooks, but the thermodynamic explanation is more general and does not depend upon a particular model. For a recent review of applications of osmotic pressure to protein solutions see Guidotti (**1973**) and Tombs and Peacocke (**1974**).

The chemical potential μ_1 of the solvent is lowered in the inner compartment because of the presence of the dissolved component 2. Therefore component 1 will tend to flow from the outer into the inner compartment, from a higher to a lower potential. This process would go on indefinitely were it not for the fact that the influx of solvent raises the solvent level in the measuring capillary and thereby raises the pressure P in the inner compartment. Increase of P raises μ_1 until equilibrium with respect to the chemical potential of the solvent, diffusible through the semipermeable

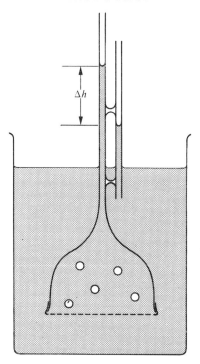

F I G. 1.11. Schematic representation of simple osmometer. (From Eisenberg **1974a**.)

membrane, is achieved and μ_1 inside the osmotic compartment equals μ_1^0 of the pure solvent. The reference capillary takes into account capillary effects. Its radius is identical with that of the measuring capillary and from the height difference Δh at equilibrium, the osmotic pressure Π is determined to be $\Delta h \rho g$ dyn cm^{-2}; here ρ is the density of the solution and g is the gravitational constant. In close parallel to the properties of dilute gas systems (see Appendix 3) it can be shown that the osmotic pressure is closely related to the number density ρ_n of particles per unit volume of solution, and the interaction between them as described by the second (B_2) and higher virial coefficients (B_n)

$$\Pi/\rho_n kT = 1 + B_2 \rho_n + B_3 \rho_n^2 + \cdots. \tag{1.1}$$

Here k is Boltzmann's constant and T the absolute temperature. Osmotic pressure is thus a colligative method and, roughly speaking, counts the number of non-diffusible particles in a given volume. The reason that we usually believe that osmotic pressure gives the molecular weight of the particles is simply related to the fact that we usually convert the number density ρ_n to an experimentally meaningful practical concentration (mass density) unit, say grams per millilitre $(g\,ml^{-1})$ $c = \rho_n M/N_A$, where M is the molecular weight in $g\,mol^{-1}$ and N_A is Avogadro's number. Substitution of ρ_n by c in eqn (1.1) yields the familiar expression

$$\Pi/cRT = M^{-1} + A_2 c + A_3 c^2 + \cdots, \tag{1.2}$$

where M^{-1} is the first virial coefficient A_1, $A_2 = B_2 N_A/M^2$ is the second virial coefficient in familiar units $(ml\,mol\,g^{-2})$, A_3 is the third virial coefficient and R is the gas constant $N_A k$. In the light of later discussion on more complicated systems we should remember that M is a molecular weight expressed in terms of grams of dry material weighed into the solvent† and is therefore completely independent of processes (such as solvation in this simple system) which may occur in solution without a change in number of colloid particles per millilitre. We shall soon see that incomplete understanding of this point has led, and is still leading, to confusion in many instances particularly when more complicated systems are involved.

Thermodynamic non-ideality in macromolecular solutions may be represented in various ways. Based on the osmotic-pressure (OP) eqn (1.2) we may define an apparent molecular weight M_{app},

$$M_{app}^{-1}(OP) \equiv M^{-1} + A_2 c + A_3 c^2 + \cdots \tag{1.3}$$

$$= M^{-1}(1 + \Gamma_2 c + \Gamma_3 c^2 + \cdots), \tag{1.4}$$

where $\Gamma_2 = A_2 M$, $\Gamma_3 = A_3 M$, and so forth. In polymer solutions (Flory **1953**) it is possible to assume a connection between the virial coefficients

$$\Gamma_3 = g\Gamma_2^2, \tag{1.5}$$

and, for the special value of $g = 0.25$,

$$M_{app}^{-1}(OP) = M^{-1}(1 + 0.5\Gamma_2 c)^2, \tag{1.6}$$

if the virial series may be truncated after the third virial term; eqn (1.6) is useful for computational procedures.

We shall see below that, in light-scattering (LS) and equilibrium sedimentation (ES), molecular weights are derived from the derivative of the osmotic pressure (eqn 1.2) with respect to the concentration of the macromolecular component. The concentration-dependence of the apparent molecular weights M_{app} from these measurements therefore is

$$M_{app}^{-1}(LS, ES) \equiv M^{-1} + 2A_2 c + 3A_3 c^2 + \cdots \tag{1.7}$$

$$= M^{-1}(1 + 2\Gamma_2 c + 3\Gamma_3 c^2 + \cdots), \tag{1.8}$$

where the As and the Γs are still the 'osmotic-pressure' virial coefficients, and

---

† The concentration may also be given in terms of some secondary measurement, which relates an optical absorption coefficient for instance or any other analytical elementary determination to a total dry weight.

a different value of $g = \frac{1}{3}$ is now required to complete a perfect square, in analogy to eqn (1.6).

A different way of representing concentration-dependent non-ideality is based on the equation for the chemical potential μ of the macromolecular component

$$\mu = \mu^0 + RT \ln yc \qquad (1.9)$$

where μ^0 is a standard potential (see Appendix 2) and y is an activity coefficient defined on the c concentration scale. Combination of the Gibbs–Duhem equation (A2.6) at constant T and P

$$n_1 \, d\mu_1 + n_2 \, d\mu_2 = 0$$

(where 1 represents the solvent and 2 the macromolecular component) with the differentiated osmotic-pressure equation (A2.10)

$$\bar{V}_1 \, d\Pi = -d\mu_1$$

and some elementary transformations of concentration units lead to

$$\frac{1}{RT} \frac{d\Pi}{dc} = \frac{1}{RT} \frac{d\mu}{dc} \frac{c}{M} = \frac{1}{M} \left(1 + \frac{d \ln y}{d \ln c} \right), \qquad (1.10)$$

the last term arising by differentiation of eqn (1.9); all quantities now refer to the macromolecular component 2. Use of $d\Pi/dc$ from eqn (1.2) in eqn (1.10) and integration of $d \ln y/dc$ leads to

$$\ln y = 2A_2 Mc + \tfrac{2}{3} A_3 Mc^2 + \cdots \qquad (1.11)$$

$$= 2\Gamma_2 c + \tfrac{3}{2} \Gamma_3 c^2 + \cdots . \qquad (1.12)$$

We now have an understanding of how to determine the molecular weights of non-ionic polymers (illustrated in Figs. 1.1(a) and 1.1(b)) dissolved in a single non-ionic solvent. A simple consideration shows that if the polymer is not homogeneous with respect to size, a number-average molecular weight M_n results from the osmotic-pressure measurement.†

Our next question refers to an ionized polymer, in a single solvent, restricted to one side of the semipermeable membrane. This situation, which is described schematically in Fig. 1.12, complicates matters considerably. No longer do we determine the molecular weight of the macromolecular particles. In precise language we can say that, because of the long-range electrostatic interactions between the macro-ions and the small counter-ions,

---

† For a homogeneous solute, at low concentrations c, $\Pi/RT = c/M$. If J macromolecular components, each of molecular weight M_J and at concentrations c_J are present, then the osmotic pressure is given by $\Pi/RT = \sum(c_J/M_J)$, where the sum goes over all components J; furthermore, $\sum c_J = c$, the total concentration.

The number-average molecular weight $M_n = \sum n_J M_J / \sum n_J$, $n_J = c_J N_A / M_J$, therefore $M_n = c / \sum(c_J/M_J)$ and $\Pi/RT = c/M_n$.

INTRODUCTION

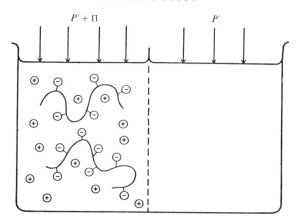

$P' + \Pi$ P'

F I G. 1.12. Schematic representation of osmotic membrane experiment; charged polyelectrolyte molecules are restricted to one side of semipermeable membrane and no low-molecular-weight salt is present. (From Eisenberg **1974a.**)

as well as between the macro-ions themselves,‡ the osmotic pressure cannot be expanded into a virial series, an expansion in powers of the concentration, in which the first virial coefficient is just unity (when the concentration is expressed in particle density units ρ_n (eqn (1.1)) or equal to M^{-1} (with concentration in g ml^{-1}) (eqn (1.2)). If, by some artifice, we could remove the charge from the macro- and counter-ions and still constrain all particles to remain on one side of the membrane (although no longer naturally constrained to it by the requirement of electroneutrality) then we would (in the limit of vanishing concentration c) measure the number-average molecular weight of the dissolved particles—both large and small. Since one of our main aims is to determine the molecular weight of the dissolved macromolecular entities, we must somehow modify the two-component osmotic system. This will be discussed below.

The procedure consists in adding another component, component 3, which is a low-molecular-weight electrolyte. For convenience we choose a salt such that one of its ions is identical (a common ion) with the polyelectrolyte counter-ions. If this condition was not fulfilled we would have four components not three. A typical example of a three-component system is, for instance; component 1, water; component 2, the sodium salt of polystyrene sulphonic acid (or the sodium salt of deoxyribonucleic acid, DNA, for instance); and component 3, sodium chloride at some suitable concentration, say 0·2 M or 1·0 M. Henceforth, we shall deal mostly with such three-component systems. The complications introduced by having not one

‡ Coulombic electrostatic potentials decay with increasing distance r according to r^{-1}, whereas repulsive potentials between neutral particles decay much faster according to r^{-6}, and are therefore of shorter range.

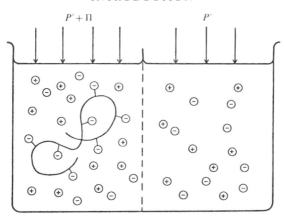

$P' + \Pi$ P'

FIG. 1.13. Same as Fig. 1.12, but low-molecular-weight uni–univalent salt has now been added to system. (From Eisenberg **1974a.**)

low-molecular-weight component 3 but a more complex buffer made up of two or more components (diffusible through a semipermeable membrane) are not too difficult to handle, as will be made clear later on. All macro-molecules (component 2) may be identical (a pure protein, or an intact nucleic acid) or they may be polydisperse with respect to molecular weight but part of a homologous series in which all members are chemically identical (or closely similar) to each other. A more complicated case arises when they cannot be considered identical and some specific properties cannot be evaluated as average properties of the macromolecular component. Such a situation arises, for instance, as a result of density heterogeneity in DNA particles in a method known as equilibrium sedimentation in a density gradient (p. 117). Even more complicated situations arise when mixtures of chemically dissimilar polymers are considered. These are *bona fide* new components and deserve new numbers. As I have already mentioned, we shall here mostly consider only the simplest case of three components. More ambitious readers should consult the monograph of Casassa and Eisenberg (**1964**), in which the thermodynamic aspects discussed in this book are extensively formulated; therein many situations which do or might occur are analysed in exact fashion. Here we shall consider some simpler situations only.

We return to the osmotic system now comprising three electroneutral components (Fig. 1.13). Electroneutral means that components are picked in electroneutral combinations from the ionic species. As we shall see later we can do this in many ways that are different from the present procedure, which actually corresponds to the way components may be stored in bottles and weighed into the solutions.

The fact that an ionized low-molecular-weight component is now present produces a profound change in the nature of the solution. The screening of the fixed charges of the .macro-ion by oppositely charged low-molecular-weight ions, reduces the range of the electrostatic forces.†

At close distances to the macro-ions there are still more counter-ions (ions of opposite charge to the fixed charges of the macro-ion) than co-ions (ions of the same sign as the fixed charges of the macro-ions) but with the electrostatic potential now extending over much shorter range, these differences will average out much closer to the macro-ions. We shall discuss a phenomenon called the Donnan effect which causes some net outflow of the low-molecular-weight salt from the compartment containing the macromolecular component (this outflow may to some extent be counteracted by 'binding' of some of the low-molecular-weight salt to the macro-ion). The over-all result of the addition of the low-molecular-weight salt is to allow now the osmotic pressure to be expanded in a virial series (see Hill **1960**) with eqn 1.2 again applicable. The reciprocal of the molecular weight M^{-1} is indeed obtained in the extrapolation of Π/cRT to $c \to 0$. But note, however, that in an osmotic experiment we actually 'count' molecules or moles (see eqn (1.1)) and molecular weight only appears in terms of any convenient way in which we choose to express concentrations. The question, sometimes asked, whether the weight of counter-ions (or the degree of 'binding' of the counter-ions to the macro-ion) is included in the molecular-weight determination is really irrelevant. ‡

This concludes our preliminary qualitative discussion of the osmotic pressure. All subsequent discussion will in some way be related to the basic ideas introduced above.

1.3.2. *Equilibrium sedimentation*

When a polymeric solution is brought to equilibrium sedimentation in the

---

† A screened electrostatic Debye potential decreases roughly as $\exp(-\kappa_{DH} r)/r$ rather than the Coulombic potential which decreases as r^{-1}. For a recent extensive and readable review of theories relating to polyelectrolyte research see Armstrong and Strauss (**1969**).

‡ Suppose, for instance, that x g of NaDNA are dissolved in a 0·5 M solution of CsCl. Many more caesium than sodium ions will now be surrounding the DNA macro-ion, and to speak of NaDNA in solution will be meaningless. Still the molecular weight of NaDNA will be derived if concentrations are expressed in terms of the x g ml^{-1} of NaDNA originally weighed in; the weight of NaDNA can, of course, be calculated on the basis of a known relation between ultraviolet light absorption under some standard conditions and the dry weight of NaDNA. Should a phosphate analysis be available then a similar procedure can be adopted.

We can, of course, by a simple calculation which takes into account the relative weights of the caesium and sodium ions, also express the molecular weight as that of CsDNA. Or better still, if concentrations are expressed in mol l^{-1} of phosphate, $C_u = 10^3 \times \rho_n Z/N$, then the molecular 'weight' is given in terms of number Z of phosphates (or nucleotides) per macromolecule. This is a very convenient way of representing macromolecular degree of polymerization and is obviously independent of the ionic state or, as we shall see later, of the fact that small molecules may 'bind' to the macromolecules, without change in the number of moles of the latter.

ultracentrifuge (Tanford **1961**; Creeth and Pain **1967**), a concentration gradient is set up, the magnitude of which, quite apart from the physical conditions of the experiments, depends on the component composition of the polymeric solution. We shall be able to show that the work required to set up this gradient is intimately connected with the osmotic work required to produce concentration changes in solution. Thus, from the extrapolation of such results to vanishing concentration, we may determine the molecular weight of the particles,† and from the concentration dependence we may determine the virial coefficients which express interactions between macromolecular solutes. We shall take into account the problems introduced by the multi-component nature of the solutions and modify our procedures accordingly. We should note though, as a general observation, that whereas interactions between macromolecular solutes (short-range interactions in the case of screened potentials) vanish in the limit of low concentrations of macromolecules, interactions between macromolecular solutes and low molecular weight solutes persist at vanishing concentrations of macromolecules but fixed concentrations of solutes of low molecular weight.

1.3.3. *Light-scattering*

Light-scattering is an optical method which can also be related to the osmotic pressure but which, in addition to yielding the molecular weight and the macromolecular solute–solute interactions, provides an entirely new piece of information (see Eisenberg **1971,** for a recent review).

A homogeneous material, such as a perfect crystal, for instance, scatters almost no light, by virtue of the fact that light scattered from any atomic centre undergoes destructive interference with scattered light coming from another centre in the regular crystalline lattice. For destructive interference to be incomplete and therefore for scattering to occur inhomogeneities are required in the material. Many years ago Einstein deduced that the relatively low scattering from pure liquids may be ascribed to density inhomogeneities which result from density fluctuations in the compressible liquids. In the case of solutions, Debye (1947) has shown that here inhomogeneities result from concentration fluctuations in small volumes of the solutions. The ease with which concentration fluctuations are produced depends on the osmotic work required, and this establishes the sought-for connection. Light is only scattered if the local change in concentration is accompanied by a change in refractive index. (Similarly changes in concentration in the ultracentrifuge

---

† The same considerations with respect to defining the particular molecular weight derived apply here (as well as below in light-scattering) as discussed with respect to osmotic pressure. A higher-average molecular weight M_w will usually be derived rather than the number-average molecular weight obtained from osmotic-pressure measurements of polydisperse polymers. The fact that M_n as well as the weight- and z-average molecular weights may also be derived from equilibrium sedimentation experiments makes this method extremely useful in the analysis of interacting systems (Roark and Yphantis 1969).

only occur if accompanied by changes in the density of the solution.) Small-angle X-ray scattering† is essentially equivalent to light-scattering and depends upon changes in electron density consequent upon fluctuations in concentration.

The additional information available from measurements of the angular dependence of scattering relates to parameters characteristic of the shape and size of the particles. Here low-angle X-ray scattering and light-scattering are beautifully complementary methods, and together provide a wide range of interesting information.‡

With the advent of the laser a new dimension is being added to the investigation of solutions of biopolymers by the study of scattered light (Peticolas **1972**; Ford **1972**; Chu **1974**). Whereas classical light-scattering is wholly based on the study of the total intensity of the elastically scattered light (in elastic scattering the frequency of the scattered beam equals that of the incident light), scattering of coherent monochromatic laser radiation enables the study of the quasi-elastic frequency-broadened (or shifted) scattered components. From these types of study it is possible to derive conveniently information about motion of the macromolecules as a whole or internal flexing, and in particular, the translational and, sometimes, the rotational diffusion coefficients can be determined. This is an exciting new field and now in full development.

1.3.4. *Transport methods*

Transport methods are, in general, not subject to the complete, unequivocal interpretation applicable to equilibrium studies. However, they are useful in many instances—both for the speed and ease with which experiments can be undertaken and the small amounts of valuable materials which are needed. Thus, with the use of absorption and interference optics in the ultra-

---

† The recent development of a new position-sensitive detector for X-ray crystallography (Gabriel and Dupont 1972; Dupont, Gabriel, Chabre, Gulik-Krzywicki, and Schechter 1972) has made it possible to reduce the time required for these experiments by 2 orders of magnitude, thereby enabling experiments, not previously considered to be rewarding, to be performed with biological material.

‡ Recently it has also been possible to study successfully by neutron small-angle scattering the conformation of polymer chains in the bulk state (Kirste, Kruse, and Schelten 1972; Ober, Cotton, Farnoux, and Higgins 1974; Cotton, Decker, Benoit, Farnoux, Higgins, Jannink, Ober, Picot, and des Cloizeaux 1974) and selected properties (such as the radius of gyration, inter-particle effects, particle volumes, and hydrogen–deuterium exchange) of haemoglobin in solution (Schelten, Schlecht, Schmatz, and Mayer 1972). Neutron scattering at small angles, of biological macromolecules in solution has been reviewed by Stuhrmann (**1974**), and current experimental techniques and applications have been discussed by Schmatz, Springer, Schelten, and Ibel (**1974**). High-flux neutron reactors were used and advantage was taken of the large difference of the coherent scattering cross-sections of hydrogen and deuterium. The scattering contrast in solution can readily be varied by adjusting the H_2O–D_2O ratio of the solvent over a wide range of compositions. Neutron scattering is sufficiently different from X-ray scattering to envisage obtainment of many interesting new results by clever design of experiments and powerful modern techniques.

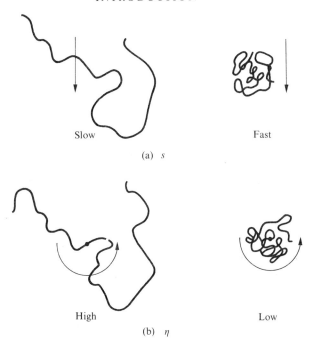

Slow   Fast

(a) *s*

High   Low

(b) *η*

F I G. 1.14. Schematic representation of resistance to sedimentation (a) and viscous flow, (b) for expanded and coiled chain molecules.

centrifuge, experiments with micrograms of materials can be undertaken (Creeth and Pain **1967**).† Sedimentation velocity depends on the size and shape of the particles, but not in a sensitive way. For a rod-like particle sedimentation velocity depends, to a first approximation, on M/L, where L is the length (a linear dimension) of the rod. If for some reason (let us say because of the melting of an ordered structure) the rod shrinks, then the sedimentation coefficient s increases, that is, the particle sediments faster (Fig. 1.14(a)). The excess viscosity due to the rod-like particle cannot be measured quite so easily with as small amounts of material as the sedimentation velocity, but it is much more sensitive to particle dimensions (Zimm **1971**; Uhlenhopp and Zimm **1973**). The intrinsic viscosity $[\eta]$ (which is due to the energy dissipated in rotational motion of the particles) depends, to a first approximation, on L^3/M (L^3 is roughly the hydrodynamically effective volume of the particle) and, unlike sedimentation, $[\eta]$ decreases when the particle shrinks (Fig. 1.14(b)).

† By light-scattering with coherent light it is now also possible to determine the translational diffusion constant D_t conveniently with micrograms of materials, therefore the M of scarce biological materials can be determined from the Svedberg equation (Svedberg and Pedersen **1940**) from the sedimentation velocity and the diffusion constant.

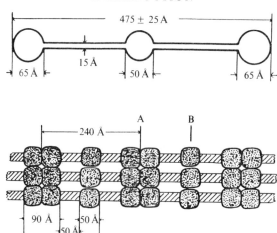

F IG. 1.15. Fibrinogen model of Hall and Slayter (1959) and mode of association to fibrin.

No single physical method is capable of completely and unequivocally describing the properties of a particle or system of particles in solution. Consistent conclusions from different methods are usually required to increase confidence in our deductions. We should like to conclude this qualitative introduction with a specific example demonstrating that, even if a particle is visualized in the electron microscope, conflicting conclusions may be reached. It is necessary to avoid both errors in experimentation and interpretation in physical studies in solutions as well as artefacts of one kind or another in direct visualization in electron microscopy. Fibrinogen, and a model for its association to fibrin, have been described by Hall and Slayter (1959) on the basis of electron microscopy studies. The triple-dumbbell model (Fig. 1.15) was found to disagree to some extent with physical studies in solution. Koeppel (1967) re-investigated fibrinogen by electron microscopy and reports a structure completely different (Fig. 1.16) from the Hall and Slayter model. He concludes that fibrinogen is an essentially hollow pentagon dodecahedron with the triple helical peptide chains along the edges of the structure the interior of which is filled with solvent. It was claimed (see Lederer and Finkelstein 1970; Lederer and Schurz 1972) that this model fits known facts, physical and chemical, about fibrinogen, including the hydrodynamic behaviour (diffusion coefficient, sedimentation coefficient, intrinsic viscosity) and the well-known polymerization to fibrin which is involved in blood-clotting. Light-scattering data cannot distinguish between the various models since the molecular dimensions are too small compared to the wavelength of the light; however, small-angle X-ray scattering which appeared to have promise in deciding among the various models, was unable to provide the

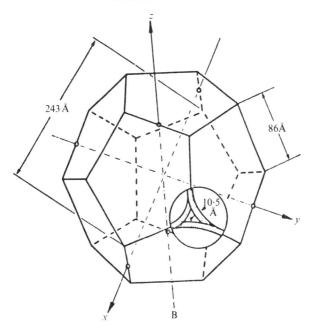

FIG. 1.16. Schematic representation of fibrinogen structure according to Koeppel (1967). (From Lederer and Finkelstein 1970.)

definitive evidence (Lederer 1972). We will not enter into a discussion on the merits of the two profoundly conflicting structures. The dissimilarity may be due to differences in isolation procedures or in the way in which the material is deposited on the electron-microscope grid.[†] Whereas physical solution methods may be interpretable in terms of more than one model, the choice can be narrowed down considerably by judicious application of a variety of methods and exclusion of structures which are not consistent with all methods. Electron microscopy provides additional direct information, but may be subject to artefacts of preparation. Michael Faraday is reported (Scatchard **1966a**) to have said that he would like to hold his theories at his finger tips so that the least breeze of facts may blow them away; George Scatchard, much later, added that, whereas for Faraday facts were the exclusive result of first-hand observation by skilled observers, in our own times they more often are obtained second-hand from books or journals; Scatchard continues, 'so now I try to be ambidextrous, holding theories at the

[†] Comparison of predicted scattering curves for the well-known crystal structures of haemoglobin with small-angle neutron scattering results and considerations referring to the structure of the protein in the dissolved state are due to Schelten *et al.* (1972). A similar comparison for myoglobin by small-angle X-ray scattering was made by Stuhrmann (1973). Further work on the structure of fibrinogen by Lederer and by Stuhrmann, and their collaborators, is in progress.

finger-tips of one hand and facts at the finger-tips of the other ready to have either carried away.' We conclude now by saying that henceforth our efforts must be bent towards establishing the kind of experimental facts and theory that will withstand unscathed the most violent storm.

2

BASIC THEORY OF MULTI-COMPONENT SYSTEMS

2.1. Concentration scales

HERE we shall use, to a large extent, the symbolism introduced by Scatchard and his co-workers (Scatchard 1946; Scatchard, Batchelder, and Brown 1946; Scatchard **1966b**). Components are designated by upper-case subscripts and ionic species, from which the components are formulated in electroneutral combinations, by lower-case subscripts. In the fundamental thermodynamic derivations concentrations will usually be given as weight molalities m, referred to a kilogram mass of the principal solvent (usually water), designated as component 1. Component 2 is the macromolecular component, and component 3 is a low-molecular-weight diffusible salt, having an ion in common with the macromolecular component. The general expressions applicable to any number of components will be found in the article of Casassa and Eisenberg (**1964**). Here we shall mostly refer to a three-component system.

In addition to the molality (moles of component J per kilogram of component 1)

$$m_J = 10^3 n_J / n_1 M_1 \tag{2.1}$$

we can also define weight molalities

$$w_J = m_J M_J / 10^3 = n_J M_J / n_1 M_1 \tag{2.2}$$

in grams of component J per gram of component 1; n_J and M_J are the number of moles and molecular weight respectively.

Alternatively we may define two comparable concentration measures on a volume basis (V is the volume in millilitres): C_J, the molarity, that is, the number of moles per litre of solution

$$C_J = 10^3 n_J / V \tag{2.3}$$

and

$$c_J = C_J M_J / 10^3 = n_J M_J / V \tag{2.4}$$

in grams of component J per millilitre. The two schemes are related by

$$C_J = 10^3 m_J / V_m \tag{2.5}$$

and

$$c_J = 10^3 w_J/V_m, \tag{2.6}$$

where

$$V_m = 10^3 V/n_1 M_1 \tag{2.7}$$

is the volume of the solution in millilitres containing 1 kg of component 1. If we use the definition of the volume

$$V = \sum n_J M_J/\rho \tag{2.8}$$

(where ρ is the density of the solution) and eqn (2.7) then, for three components,

$$V_m = (10^3 + M_2 m_2 + M_3 m_3)/\rho. \tag{2.9}$$

Furthermore, substitution of eqn (A2.5) in eqn (2.7), use of eqn (2.2), and the definition of partial specific volumes,

$$\bar{v}_J = \overline{V}_J/M_J, \tag{2.10}$$

yields

$$V_m = 10^3 (\bar{v}_1 + \bar{v}_2 w_2 + \bar{v}_3 w_3). \tag{2.11}$$

It will be useful to remember for practical calculations that from eqns (A2.3), (2.2), and (2.7)

$$\overline{V}_J = (\partial V_m/\partial m_J)_{P,T,m}, \quad J \neq 1, \tag{2.12}$$

where subscript m signifies constant molality of all other components except component J.

Advantages or disadvantages in the use of the various concentration scales depend upon the character of the experiment under consideration (Casassa and Eisenberg 1964). The molality units are independent of temperature and pressure and, in a closed system, addition of one component does not change the concentration of the others. Preparation of solutions by weight ensures the highest accuracy. Molarity scales are more convenient when volumetric manipulations are involved. Redistribution of diffusible components in a dialysis process complicates the use of the molality scale. For proteins and nucleic acids concentrations are often easily determined on a volume-based scale without interference from other components, by elementary (nitrogen, sulphur, phosphorus) analysis or ultraviolet absorption, provided the necessary conversion factors are available. If, for example, the amino-acid composition of a protein is known exactly, the amount of nitrogen or sulphur per mole (as a submultiple of a mole) is thereby known, and the molecular weight can be arbitrarily defined on the basis of molecular formulae of the constituent amino acids, for example, the total molecular weight of the macromolecule with no side groups ionized, or of the sodium salt corresponding to complete ionization of all carboxylic or phosphate groups (in the case of nucleic acid), and so on. Ambiguities associated with 'dry weights' are in this way eliminated, as well as conceptual difficulties connected with unknown degrees of association, contributions from counter-ions, or contributions from other 'bound' low-molecular-weight materials (salts or neutral molecules) to the molecular weight.

It is often convenient to use, instead of molal units m_J or molar units C_J, units

$$m_u = m_J Z \qquad (2.13)$$

or

$$C_u = C_J Z, \qquad (2.14)$$

where Z is the number of ionizable groups, or residues per macromolecule, or the degree of polymerization; m_u and C_u are therefore 'equivalent' concentrations of a conveniently determined element or functional group. The practical advantage of these latter units derive from the fact that neither m_u nor C_u depend on the ionic state (for example, pH, sodium or caesium salt) or on interaction of small molecules (ligands) with the macromolecular species.

2.2. Definition of components

The activity a_J (eqn (A2.9)) of any solute component J is given by

$$\mu_J = \mu_J^0 + RT \ln a_J$$
$$= \mu_J^0 + RT \sum_i v_{iJ} \ln m_i + RT\beta_J, \qquad (2.15)$$

in which μ_J^0 is the chemical potential in the standard state at 1 atm, and $RT\beta_J$ is the excess chemical potential or RT times the logarithm of the activity coefficient γ_J ($a_J = \gamma_J m_J$) for component J. In the reference state with all m_J at infinite dilution, γ_J approaches unity; the β_J and γ_J are, in general, functions of pressure, temperature, and all the concentrations.

The number of moles of species i included in a mole of component J is v_{iJ}, hence

$$m_i = \sum_J v_{iJ} m_J. \qquad (2.16)$$

We wish the concentrations of components to be independent thermodynamic variables, and so require that the v_{iJ} be taken in electrically neutral combinations. Beyond this stipulation the definition of a component in the expression of thermodynamic relations is a matter determined by convenience and simplicity only. The derivatives a_{JK} (or sometimes $\mu_{JK} = RTa_{JK}$)

defined by

$$a_{JK} \equiv \left[\frac{\partial \ln a_J}{\partial m_K}\right]_{P,T,m} = \left[\frac{\partial \ln a_K}{\partial m_J}\right]_{P,T,m} \qquad (2.17)$$

$$= \sum_i \frac{v_{iJ}\, v_{iK}}{m_i} + \beta_{JK} \qquad (2.18)$$

will be encountered below. The subscript m, as before, signifies constancy of all concentrations m_J, except that indicated in the differentiation.

We now specify a mole of the non-diffusible component so as to contain 1 mol of the non-diffusible species and just enough low-molecular-weight ionic species to achieve electroneutrality, and limit the lower-case subscripts to diffusible species. All definitions of components used in this book, unless specifically indicated, will follow this convention. This will be illustrated for the three component case of particular interest in this book. We have

$$a_{22} = \frac{1}{m_2} + \sum_i \frac{v_{i2}^2}{m_i} + \beta_{22}, \qquad (2.19)$$

$$a_{23} = \sum_i \frac{v_{i2}\, v_{i3}}{m_i} + \beta_{23}, \qquad (2.20)$$

$$a_{33} = \sum_i \frac{v_{i3}^2}{m_i} + \beta_{33}. \qquad (2.21)$$

These 'simple' definitions agree with the definitions of Lewis and Randall (**1961**) in the treatment of low-molecular-weight electrolytes (see Table 2.1, row one). If a salt XY_Z dissociates according to

$$XY_Z = X^{Z+} + ZY^-,$$

then $v_+ = 1$ and $v_- = Z$; $m_+ = m_3$, $m_- = Zm_3$, and β_3 represents $(v_+ + v_-)\ln \gamma_\pm = \ln \gamma_3$, where $\gamma_\pm$ is the mean ionic activity coefficient.

If the component 3 is a 1–1 electrolyte XY (for example, NaCl) and component 2 is a Z-valent ion P along with its complement of Z univalent counter-ions X, then

$$\ln a_2 = \ln m_2 + v_{X2} \ln m_X + v_{Y2} \ln m_Y + \beta_2,$$
$$\ln a_3 = v_{X3} \ln m_X + v_{Y3} \ln m_Y + \beta_3.$$

For the uni–univalent supporting electrolyte $v_{X3} = v_{Y3} = 1$ and

$$m_X = m_3 + v_{X2} m_2,$$
$$m_Y = m_3 + v_{Y2} m_2.$$

According to our definition of components $v_{Y2} = 0$ (the species Y is not represented in component 2) and $v_{X2} = Z$; therefore $m_X = m_3 + Zm_2 =$

TABLE 2.1

Composition of components in a three-component system

Component	1	2	3
Original 'simple' definition	H_2O	PX_Z	XY
Dialysis equilibrium	H_2O	$X_{(1+\Gamma)Z} PY_{\Gamma Z}$, or $PX_Z(XY)_{\Gamma Z}$	XY
According to Scatchard (1946)	H_2O	$X_{Z/2} PY_{-Z/2}$, or $PX_Z(XY)_{-Z/2}$	XY

$m_3 + m_u$ ($m_u = Zm_2$ is the polymer molality per equivalent charge) and $m_Y = m_3$;

$$\ln a_2 = \ln m_2 + Z \ln(m_3 + Zm_2) + \beta_2,$$

$$\ln a_3 = \ln(m_3 + Zm_2) + \ln m_3 + \beta_3,$$

and

$$a_{22} = \frac{1}{m_2} + \frac{Z^2}{m_3 + Zm_2} + \beta_{22}, \tag{2.22}$$

$$a_{23} = \frac{Z}{m_3 + Zm_2} + \beta_{23}, \tag{2.23}$$

$$a_{33} = \frac{1}{m_3 + Zm_2} + \frac{1}{m_3} + \beta_{33}. \tag{2.24}$$

Alternative definitions of components are sometimes convenient. As an example we may (Scatchard and Bregman 1959; Casassa and Eisenberg 1960) establish the composition of components defined in correspondence with the equilibrium dialysis experiment (outer polymer-free solution components in the dialysis equilibrium experiment are designated by primes). At dialysis equilibrium $m_Y \neq m'_Y$. We define components by setting m_3 equal to m'_Y at dialysis equilibrium

$$m_3 = m'_Y = m'_X$$

Electroneutrality in the case of a uni–univalent component 3 (XY) requires

$$m_X = m_Y + Zm_2 = m_Y + m_u.$$

We express the equilibrium distribution of the co-ion in terms of a distribution parameter Γ defined as

$$\Gamma \equiv (m_Y - m'_Y)/m_u, \tag{2.25}$$

and calculate the composition of component 2 consistent with this definition. Component 3 is 'rejected' and therefore $\Gamma < 0$ for a simple Donnan distribution (p. 41).

We evaluate v_{X2} and v_{Y2} from

$$m_X = m_3 + v_{X2} m_2$$

and

$$m_Y = m_3 + v_{Y2} m_2 .$$

We find

$$v^D_{X2} = (1 + \Gamma)Z \tag{2.26}$$

and

$$v^D_{Y2} = \Gamma Z , \tag{2.27}$$

where Γ is unequivocally given in terms of experimental quantities by eqn (2.25); superscript D signifies component 2 defined in correspondence with the dialysis equilibrium experiment. Considering that for a Donnan distribution Γ is negative, v^D_{Y2}, according to eqn (2.27), is also negative and component 2^D contains a negative amount of the ionic species Y. We now write down the values of the a_{JK} eqns (2.19) to (2.21) for components defined as in rows 2 and 3 of Table 2.1.

$$a^D_{22} = \frac{1}{m_2} + \frac{(1+\Gamma)^2 Z^2}{m_3 + (1+\Gamma)Zm_2} + \frac{\Gamma^2 Z^2}{m_3 + \Gamma Zm_2} + \beta^D_{22}, \tag{2.28}$$

$$a^D_{23} = \frac{(1+\Gamma)Z}{m_3 + (1+\Gamma)Zm_2} + \frac{\Gamma Z}{m_3 + \Gamma Zm_2} + \beta^D_{23} . \tag{2.29}$$

In the limiting case $Zm_2 \ll m_3$

$$a^D_{22} = \frac{1}{m_2} + \frac{(1 + 2\Gamma + 2\Gamma^2)Z^2}{m_3} + \beta^D_{22}, \tag{2.30}$$

$$a^D_{23} = \frac{(1+2\Gamma)Z}{m_3} + \beta^D_{23} . \tag{2.31}$$

In accordance with the definition m_3 constant and equal to m'_Y at dialysis equilibrium $(\partial m_3 / \partial m_2^D)_\mu = 0$; therefore, as will become apparent in the next section a^D_{23} is also equal to zero up to inconsequential terms (see eqn (2.65) below). The special case when $\Gamma = -0.5$ defines the components according to the original definition of Scatchard (1946) (see row 3 of Table 2.1); in the limit $Zm_2 \ll m_3$,

$$a^S_{22} = \frac{1}{m_2} + \frac{Z^2}{2m_3} + \beta^S_{22}, \tag{2.32}$$

$$a^S_{23} = \beta^S_{23} . \tag{2.33}$$

The value of a_{33} is not affected by the two definitions given above.

The physical consequences of the definition of the composition of components consistent with dialysis equilibrium are immediately obvious. With the salt XY at equal concentrations m_3, on both sides of a semipermeable membrane, addition of 1 mol of component 2 thus defined to one side involves addition of 1 mol $X_Z P$ and removal of ΓZ moles of XY; thus no net flow of XY occurs across the membrane and the original distribution of component 3 is not disturbed. (The amounts of low-molecular-weight species which would be required to flow across the membrane subsequent to the addition of the macromolecular species are included in the definition of component 2.) The system may, therefore, be regarded formally as behaving like a two-component system, water and salt constituting the 'solvent'. For practical purposes it is useful if, at low concentration of component 2 ($m_u \ll m_3$), the composition of component 2 thus defined is independent of m_u. In that case dialysis may be performed by preparing the solution with the highest concentration of component 2; dilutions are then obtained at constant μ_3 by simply mixing the polymer with variable amounts of the dialysate solution.

Scatchard's original intention in equating Γ to -0.5 was to define components in such a way that addition of a macromolecular component to a solution containing component 3 should reflect mostly effects due to the addition of the macro-ion, and not the large number of small co-ions (by his definition he adds $1 + Z$ particles for each mole of macromolecules, and removes $2(Z/2) = Z$ small particles). We usually prefer the more general definition consistent with the requirement of osmotic equilibrium. It must be emphasized, however, that these definitions are merely formalistic devices based on simple intuitive ideas and that no actual gain in the thermodynamic information is implied. We shall therefore put the greater emphasis on a rigorous thermodynamic analysis which does not involve a particular definition of components and does lead a little more elegantly to results of slightly greater generality (Eisenberg 1962).

2.3. Osmotic pressure

We proceed to a quantitative derivation of the osmotic-pressure equation. The complete basis for the derivation of the osmotic pressure equation is contained in the work of J. Willard Gibbs (see Guggenheim **1936**). Later, F. G. Donnan (1911) derived equations for ideal solutions for the osmotic pressure and distribution of ions across membranes permeable to some solutes, but impermeable to others. In 1946 Scatchard derived equations for the osmotic pressure and distribution of ions in non-ideal multi-component protein solutions. The following derivation follows a slightly different course, but the result is in the main equivalent to Scatchard's expressions. We shall consider the outer polymer-free solution, the dialysate, to be at fixed atmospheric pressure P' with the equilibrium pressure acting on the polymer solution equal to $P = P' + \Pi$; Π is the osmotic pressure. A three-component system only will be considered.

The condition for osmotic equilibrium is that

$$d\mu_1 = d\mu_1' = 0$$

and

$$d\mu_3 = d\mu_3' = 0$$

for the diffusible components, if both the pressure and the composition in the outer phase are maintained constant. The Gibbs–Duhem equation (A2.6) then reduces, at constant temperature to

$$V\,dP = n_2\,d\mu_2.$$

For the change of pressure with number of moles n_2 of the non-diffusible species, and after conversion to molal concentrations, we obtain

$$V_m\,(d\Pi/dm_2) = m_2\,(\partial\mu_2/\partial m_2)_\mu, \tag{2.34}$$

where $d\Pi/dm_2 \equiv (\partial P/\partial m_2)_\mu$, and the subscript μ signifies constancy of the chemical potentials of the diffusible components 1 and 3. Henceforth we shall sometimes omit the subscript T, as constant temperature will usually be maintained in all that follows.

We next express the total variation $d\mu_2$ in terms of the partial derivatives a_{JK} previously defined

$$d\mu_2 = (\partial\mu_2/\partial P)_m\,dP + RTa_{22}\,dm_2 + RTa_{23}\,dm_3. \tag{2.35}$$

The first term on the right-hand side of eqn (2.35) equals the partial molal volume $\overline{V}_2$ by eqn (A2.4). Thus

$$\left(\frac{\partial\mu_2}{\partial m_2}\right)_\mu = \overline{V}_2\frac{d\Pi}{dm_2} + RTa_{22} + RTa_{23}\left(\frac{\partial m_3}{\partial m_2}\right)_\mu \tag{2.36}$$

From

$$d\mu_3 = \overline{V}_3\,dP + RTa_{23}\,dm_2 + RTa_{33}\,dm_3, \tag{2.37}$$

derived in similar fashion to $d\mu_2$ above, we obtain for the change in molality m_3 with change in m_2

$$\left(\frac{\partial m_3}{\partial m_2}\right)_\mu = -\frac{a_{23}}{a_{33}} - \frac{\overline{V}_3}{RTa_{33}}\frac{d\Pi}{dm_2}. \tag{2.38}$$

Substitution of eqn (2.38) into (2.36) and the latter into (2.34) yields

$$\frac{V_m - \left(\overline{V}_2 - \dfrac{a_{23}}{a_{33}}\overline{V}_3\right)m_2}{RTm_2}\frac{d\Pi}{dm_2} = a_{22} - \frac{a_{23}^2}{a_{33}}. \tag{2.39}$$

It is useful, in particular for more complex systems, to write the right-hand side of eqn (2.39) in the form $|a_{JK}|/A_{22}$, where $|a_{JK}|$, or $|a|$, is the determinant

$$\begin{vmatrix} a_{22} & a_{23} \\ a_{32} & a_{33} \end{vmatrix}$$

of the coefficients a_{JK}, and $A_{22} = a_{33}$ is the cofactor of the element a_{22} of the determinant $|a_{JK}|$, or $|a|$, for short.

In the limit of infinite dilution of component 2, $m_2 \to 0$, eqn (2.39) conforms to van't Hoff's law (superscripts zero indicate the limiting case)

$$(d\Pi/dm_2)^0 = RT/V_m^0 . \tag{2.40}$$

This follows because, according to eqns (2.22) to (2.24),

$$RTm_2\left(a_{22} - \frac{a_{23}^2}{a_{33}}\right)$$

equals RT when $m_2 \to 0$; V_m^0, according to eqns (2.9) or (2.11), equals $(10^3 + M_3 m_3)/\rho$ or $10^3(\bar{v}_1 + \bar{v}_3 w_3)$ respectively.

To obtain $d\Pi/dm_2$ in eqn (2.39) in terms of quantities at infinite dilution of component 2, we expand V_m in Taylor's series about the limiting value V_m^0 at fixed potential of diffusible components

$$V_m = V_m^0 + (\partial V_m/\partial m_2)_\mu^0 m_2 + \cdots . \tag{2.41}$$

We express V_m as a function of the concentrations m_2, m_3, and pressure,

$$dV_m = \bar{V}_2 \, dm_2 + \bar{V}_3 \, dm_3 - V_m \kappa \, dP , \tag{2.42}$$

where κ denotes the isothermal compressibility

$$\kappa = -(d \ln V_m/dP)_{T,m} . \tag{2.43}$$

At constant potentials μ of diffusible solutes, combination of eqn (2.42) with eqn (2.38) yields

$$\left(\frac{\partial V_m}{\partial m_2}\right)_\mu = \bar{V}_2 - \frac{a_{23}}{a_{33}}\bar{V}_3 - \left(\frac{\bar{V}_3^2}{RTa_{33}} + V_m \kappa\right)\frac{d\Pi}{dm_2} . \tag{2.44}$$

By use of eqns (2.40) and (2.44) in eqn (2.41) we obtain

$$V_m - \left(\bar{V}_2 - \frac{a_{23}}{a_{33}}\bar{V}_3\right)^0 m_2 = V_m^0\left\{1 - \left(\frac{\bar{V}_3^2}{a_{33}V_m^2} + \frac{\kappa RT}{V_m}\right)^0 m_2 + \cdots\right\}. \tag{2.45}$$

We would like, henceforth, to drop terms which are inconsequential in relation to the best experimental accuracy which can be attained. The term in braces on the right-hand side of eqn (2.45) equals unity to better than 1 part in 10^6 within this approximation; this may be verified by noting that $\bar{V}_3$ is about 25 ml, a_{33} equals $2/m_3$ to a first approximation (see eqn (2.24)), V_m is about 10^3, and κ for aqueous solutions is about 5×10^{-5} atm^{-1}, m_2 for a protein of molecular weight 10^4 at 10 mg ml^{-1} is about 10^{-3}. We can thus write eqn (2.39) in the simpler limiting form (we shall use the approximate-equality symbol to indicate dropping of inconsequential terms as discussed above),

$$\frac{V_m^0}{RT}\frac{d\Pi}{dm_2} \approx \left(a_{22} - \frac{a_{23}^2}{a_{33}}\right)m_2 + \cdots,\tag{2.46}$$

or, with the use of eqn (2.19),

$$\frac{V_m^0}{RT}\frac{d\Pi}{dm_2} \approx 1 + \left(\sum_i \frac{v_{i2}^2}{m_i} + \beta_{22} - \frac{a_{23}^2}{a_{33}}\right)m_2 + \cdots,\tag{2.47}$$

which may be compared with the virial expansion eqn (1.2) in the differential form

$$\frac{1}{RT}\frac{d\Pi}{dc_2} = \frac{1}{M} + 2A_2 c_2 + \cdots.\tag{2.48}$$

The second virial coefficient

$$2B_2^{(m)} \approx \left(\sum_i \frac{v_{i2}^2}{m_i} + \beta_{22} - \frac{a_{23}^2}{a_{33}}\right)^0\tag{2.49}$$

of eqn (2.47) is related to A_2 of eqn (2.48) by

$$B_2^{(m)} = \frac{M_2^2 A_2}{V_m^0} - \frac{1}{V_m^0}\left(\frac{\partial V_m}{\partial m_2}\right)_\mu^0,\tag{2.50}$$

where $(\partial V_m/\partial m_2)_\mu^0$ is derived from eqn (2.44). We may approximate $(\partial V_m/\partial m_2)_\mu^0$ by $\bar{V}_2 - (a_{23}/a_{33})\bar{V}_3$, on the basis of considerations given above. We may not, on the other hand, neglect the second term on the right-hand side of eqn (2.50) with respect to the first term. The reader may easily convince himself that if A_2, for proteins for example (Reisler and Eisenberg 1971), equals about $10^5 \text{ mol ml g}^{-2}$ and for $(\partial V/\partial m_2)_\mu^0$ we assume approximately $\bar{v}_2 M_2 \approx 0.75 M_2$, then this is indeed so.†

---

† To transform from volume concentrations c_2 to molalities m_2, $c_2 = m_2 M_2/V_m$, we use

$$\left(\frac{\partial c_2}{\partial m_2}\right)_\mu = \frac{M_2}{V_m}\left\{1 - \frac{m_2}{V_2}\left(\frac{\partial V_m}{\partial m_2}\right)_\mu\right\}\tag{2.51}$$

to evaluate $d\Pi/dm_2 = (d\Pi/dc_2)(\partial c_2/\partial m_2)_\mu$; similarly (see p. 42) for evaluation

$$\left(\frac{\partial C_3}{\partial C_u}\right)_\mu = \Gamma\left(\frac{\partial C_3}{\partial m_3}\right)_\mu\left(\frac{\partial m_u}{\partial C_u}\right)_\mu\tag{2.52}$$

and related quantities, we use $C_3 = 10^3 m_3/V_m$,

$$\left(\frac{\partial C_3}{\partial m_3}\right)_\mu \approx \frac{10^3}{V_m} - \frac{C_3}{V_m}\left(\bar{V}_3 + \frac{\bar{V}_u}{\Gamma}\right),\tag{2.53}$$

where $\bar{V}_u \doteq \bar{V}_2/Z$ is the partial molal volume of equivalent units, $C_u = 10^3 m_u/V_m$, and

$$\left(\frac{\partial C_u}{\partial m_u}\right)_\mu^0 = \frac{10^3}{V_m^0}\tag{2.54}$$

in the limit $m_u \to 0$.

2.3.1. *Second virial coefficients*

Second virial coefficients may depend on molecular size and asymmetry. Ishihara and Hayashida (1951) have calculated the virial coefficients for various geometrical forms and in particular for cylindrical shapes. These calculations take into account positive deviations from ideality due to geometric-volume exclusion only and not the more complicated excluded-volume problem (Berry and Casassa **1970**) in which attractive or repulsive forces between molecules are taken into account as well. It is demonstrated in Appendix 4 (p. 230) that for a hard-sphere gas at high temperatures B_2 due to volume exclusion only is just 4 times the molecular volume V of the gas $(A_2 = 4N_A V/M^2)$; B_2 may be reduced, or even made to vanish, if attractive forces exist. Eqn (2.49) shows that, for ionized particles dissolved in a solvent containing an additional low-molecular-weight salt, there are additional contributions to the virial coefficient due to ionic charge and unequal distributions of ions.

For geometric-volume exclusion of ellipsoids of rotation of axial ratio $p = b/a$ ($a, a,$ and b are the semi-axes of the ellipsoids). Ishihara and Hayashida (1951) find for both prolate $(p > 1)$ and oblate $(p < 1)$ ellipsoids of volume V

$$A_2 = \frac{4N_A V}{M^2}\left[\frac{1}{4} + \frac{3}{16}\left(1 + \frac{1}{\sqrt{(1-\varepsilon^2)}}\frac{\sin^{-1}\varepsilon}{\varepsilon}\right)\left\{1 + \frac{1-\varepsilon^2}{2\varepsilon}\ln\left(\frac{1+\varepsilon}{1-\varepsilon}\right)\right\}\right], \quad (2.55)$$

where ε is the eccentricity

$$\varepsilon^2 = 1 - p^{-2}, \quad p > 1; \quad \varepsilon^2 = 1 - p^2, \quad p < 1. \quad (2.56)$$

For a cylinder of radius r and length L, they find

$$A_2 = \frac{4N_A V}{M^2}\frac{\pi r^2 + (\pi + 3)rL + L^2}{8rL}, \quad (2.57)$$

where $V = \pi r^2 L$ is the volume of the cylinder; eqn (2.57) becomes independent of M for long cylinders of constant radius, because L is proportional to M,

$$A_2 = \frac{\pi N_A rL^2}{2M^2}, \quad (2.58)$$

a result already found by Zimm (1946).

For protein molecules of asymmetric shape and near the isoelectric point (low charge density) the major contribution to A_2 may indeed be due to volume exclusion. Fig. 2.1 shows calculated values for A_2 of an enzyme, glutamate dehydrogenase, which associates to form linear rods; the values of A_2 for various degrees of association have been calculated (Reisler and Eisenberg 1971) eqn (2.57); they are temperature independent and correspond approximately to the experimental values. In highly charged nucleic acids or polynucleotides (Eisenberg and Felsenfeld 1967), on the other hand, a strong positive contribution to A_2 derives from electrostatic charge and

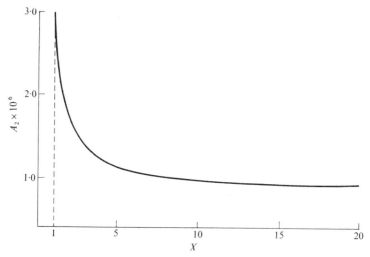

FIG. 2.1. Calculation of second virial coefficient A_2 versus degree of stacking X of circular cylinder of length $l = 133$ Å, constant radius $r = 46 \cdot 3$ Å, and molecular weight $M = 312\,000$, according to eqn (2.57) (Ishihara and Hayashida 1951). (From Reisler and Eisenberg 1971.)

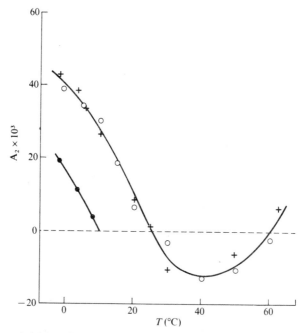

FIG. 2.2. Second virial coefficient A_2 (from light-scattering) of polyriboadenylic acid (poly A) at neutral pH, as a function of temperature; $+$, $Z_w = 1740$, $1 \cdot 0$ M NaCl; $\bigcirc$, $Z_w = 1462$, $1 \cdot 0$ M NaCl; $\bullet$, $Z_w = 1740$, $1 \cdot 3$ M NaCl; Z_w is the weight average degree of polymerization (nucleotides per macromolecule). (From Eisenberg and Felsenfeld 1967.)

unequal distribution of diffusible components (see eqn (2.81) below for the result of a simple calculation of this contribution) sometimes compensated by negative contributions due to strong intermacromolecular attractions. In this case A_2 may depend both on concentration of component 3 and on temperature (Fig. 2.2); it may vanish, and even assume negative values, which is strongly reminiscent of the behaviour of the real gas of Appendix 4 (curve (d), Fig. A4.1). The increase of A_2 in this system at higher temperatures is discussed in the original publication.

2.4. Distribution of diffusible components

We have seen that when an ionized macromolecular component 2, PX_Z, is added to a solution of a low-molecular-weight-salt component 3, XY (having an ion in common with component 2) in a solvent, component 1, the chemical potential μ_3 is raised if no other additional molecular mechanism such as ion-'binding', occurs. If the solution containing all three components is in equilibrium across a semipermeable membrane, with a solution containing the diffusible components 1 and 3 only, then the situation discussed in the previous section will be realized at osmotic equilibrium; in particular the chemical potentials of the diffusible components will be identical on both sides of the membrane. This corresponds to the classic Donnan equilibrium and the unequal distribution of ions across the membrane is known as the Donnan distribution. We generally require, in a membrane-equilibrium electroneutrality,

$$m_u + m_Y = m_X,$$
$$m'_Y = m'_X,$$
(2.59)

and equality of the activities of diffusible components, rather than of the ionic species, in the inner and outer phases,

$$a_X a_Y = a'_X a'_Y = (a'_3)^2.$$
(2.60)

We use the equivalent molal concentration $m_u = m_2 Z$ (eqn (2.13)) of charges for the macromolecule carrying Z negatively charged groups. We calculate first the 'ideal' Donnan distribution, identify the activities with concentrations and use eqn (2.59) and $m'_X = m'_Y$ to obtain

$$m_Y(m_Y + m_u) = (m'_Y)^2.$$
(2.61)

We may solve this quadratic equation for m_Y,

$$m_Y = -\tfrac{1}{2}m_u + m'_Y\left(1 + \frac{m_u^2}{4m'^2_Y}\right)^{\frac{1}{2}}$$
(2.62)

and expand the square-root for low concentrations m_u to obtain an expression for Γ (eqn 2.25)

$$\Gamma \equiv \frac{m_Y - m_Y'}{m_u} = -\tfrac{1}{2} + \frac{m_u}{8m_Y'} - \frac{m_2^3}{128m_Y'^3} + \cdots \qquad (2.63)$$

(the Donnan distribution Γ is often defined with the opposite, positive, sign; we prefer the above definition to consistently define salt-rejection as a negative and salt-binding as a positive contribution).

When $m_u \to 0$, $\Gamma \to -0.5$ (recall Scatchard's definition of components on p. 34) and $m_Y' > m_Y$; component 3 is therefore 'rejected' from the solution compartment. In the non-ideal case the value of Γ will not be equal to -0.5; it may be larger or smaller or even positive (if ion-binding is involved). It has been customary, in polyelectrolyte studies, to account for non-ideality by assuming that the macromolecule carried an 'effective' charge iZ (where i varies from zero to unity), that $1 - i$ counter-ions are 'bound' to the macromolecule, and that i counter-ions are 'free' and behave 'ideally' (theoretical models for formulations of this concept have been advanced (see Appendix 5) (Gross and Strauss **1966**; Katchalsky, Alexandrowicz, and Kedem **1966**; Manning 1969a). The value of Γ in the limit $m_u \to 0$ is then $-\tfrac{1}{2}i$, and it varies between zero (for $i = 0$, all counter-ions 'bound') and -0.5 (for $i = 1$, all counter-ions 'free'). Within the more thermodynamic context of this book I wish to consider Γ as a 'preferential' interaction (or distribution) parameter, the value of which is obtained as an experimental quantity. We shall see in later chapters that it is usually not possible to associate unique molecular mechanisms with these distribution parameters and the measured value usually reflects, in addition to the Donnan mechanism discussed above, salt-binding (of component 3) and/or solvation (binding of component 1).

We would like to connect Γ with the differential distribution parameter $(\partial m_3 / \partial m_2)_\mu$ of eqn (2.38) and in conjunction with the original 'simple' definition of components (see Table 2.1).

From the expansion, at low concentration m_u ($m_3^0 \equiv m_3'$),

$$m_3 = m_3^0 + (\partial m_3 / \partial m_u)_\mu^0 m_u + \cdots, \qquad (2.64)$$

we find

$$\Gamma^0 = (\partial m_3 / \partial m_u)^0 = Z^{-1}(\partial m_3 / \partial m_2)_\mu^0.$$

The limiting value $(\bar{V}_3 / a_{33} V_m)^0$ of the second term on the right-hand side of eqn (2.38) equals approximately 0·01 mol of salt per mole of component 2 and therefore it can be neglected, and to a good approximation,

$$\Gamma = \left(\frac{\partial m_3}{\partial m_u}\right)_\mu \approx -\frac{1}{Z}\frac{a_{23}}{a_{33}}. \qquad (2.65)$$

The distribution parameter Γ thus reflects the change in activity of component 3 with change in concentration of component 2, as well as with change in its own concentration.

In an experiment in which components are allowed to equilibrate it is necessary to determine concentrations of diffusible components precisely by analytical methods. Thus, for instance, if the diffusible component is an alkali halide, halide-ion concentration must be determined on both sides of the membrane. It is the usual procedure to determine volume concentrations, and therefore a distribution coefficient $\partial C_3/\partial C_u$ is likely determined rather than Γ. The connection between the two quantities, at vanishing concentration C_u, is easily derived by proper manipulation of some molar and molal concentration units (see eqns (2.52)–(2.54)) to yield (in the limit of vanishing concentration of component 2),

$$\left(\frac{\partial C_3}{\partial C_u}\right)_\mu = \Gamma - 10^{-3}C_3\,(\bar{V}_u + \Gamma\,\bar{V}_3) \tag{2.66}$$

or

$$\left(\frac{\partial c_3}{\partial c_2}\right) = \xi_3 - c_3(\bar{v}_2 + \xi_3 v_3), \tag{2.67}$$

where $\xi_3 = (\partial w_3/\partial w_2)_\mu = (M_3/M_u)\Gamma$ and $M_u = M_2/Z$ is the weight of equivalent units.

Thus if Γ or ξ_3 be positive, because of ion-binding the expression for $(\partial C_3/\partial C_u)_\mu$ or $(\partial c_3/\partial c_2)_\mu$ may incur a reversal of sign with increasing concentration of salt, an effect easily visualized as a dilution of the salt on a volume basis by the addition of space-filling macromolecular material, even though the amount of salt per mass of component 1 is actually increased in the presence of component 2. The difference increases with increasing c_3 because the more of component 3 is excluded in the volume $\bar{v}_2$ occupied by unit weight of component 2, the more of component 3 there is in unit volume.

2.4.1. *Electromotive-force determinations*

Distribution coefficients of diffusible components can also be obtained by two additional experimental methods of universal applicability, which do not require the analytical determination of concentration of component 3 across a semipermeable membrane. We refer first (Imai and Eisenberg 1966) to the determination of the activity of simple electrolyte in cells without liquid junction, by use of a cation-sensitive glass electrode and a suitable electrode reversible to the anion. Although we found the method to be rather exacting and time-consuming we now wish to recommend it in view of recent advances in electrode technology and in the precise measurement of small electromotive forces. A large number of highly selective electrodes reversible to ions, to neutral molecules (see Durst **1969**), and to biological materials *in* *vitro* and *in vivo* (Rechnitz **1975**) are now available. The method is free from any arbitrary assumption in the interpretation of the experimental data.

Consider a reversible electrochemical cell, without liquid junction, of the type

$$Cu|X(s)| \text{ aqueous } XY, PX_Z|AgY|Ag|Cu,$$

where Cu stands for the metallic copper terminals, $X(s)$ is a cation-specific (glass) electrode reversible with respect to X ions (for example, K^+), and for Y^- we use a reversible silver–silver halide electrode (if Y^- is Cl^- or Br^-, for example). The chemical change for a flow of 1 faraday in the above cell is given by

$$X(s) + AgY(s) \rightarrow Ag(s) + X^+ + Y^-,$$

and is accompanied, at constant temperature and pressure, by a change ΔG in Gibbs free energy,

$$\Delta G = \mu_{Ag}^s + \mu_{XY} - \mu_X^s - \mu_{AgY}.$$

The electromotive force E of the cell is therefore given by

$$-\mathscr{F}E = \Delta G = \text{constant} + \mu_3,$$

where $\mathscr{F}$ is the Faraday electrochemical equivalent and $\mu_3 = \mu_{XY}$; from the definition of $a_{JK} = \mu_{JK}/RT$ of eqn (2.17) we find

$$-(\partial E/\partial m_2)_{P,T,m_3} = RTa_{23}/\mathscr{F} \tag{2.68}$$

and

$$-(\partial E/\partial m_3)_{P,T,m_2} = RTa_{33}/\mathscr{F}. \tag{2.69}$$

It is thus seen that, by determining the electromotive force of the electrochemical cell as a function of m_2 (at constant m_3) and as a function of m_3 (at constant m_2, or in the limit $m_2 = 0$) we can evaluate the partial derivatives a_{23} and a_{33} of the activity of component 3.

If we divide eqn (2.68) by eqn (2.69) we can define a new quantity Γ' thus:

$$\Gamma' \equiv -\frac{(\partial E/\partial m_u)_{P,T,m_3}}{(\partial E/\partial m_3)_{P,T,m_u}} = -\frac{1}{Z}\frac{a_{23}}{a_{33}}. \tag{2.70}$$

The quantity Γ', as is shown below, is directly related to the distribution of diffusible ions across a semipermeable membrane in a dialysis experiment, where the non-diffusible component 2 is restricted to one side of the membrane only.

From eqn (2.37) we find immediately

$$\Gamma' \equiv \left(\frac{\partial m_3}{\partial m_u}\right)_{P,T,\mu_3} = -\frac{1}{Z}\frac{a_{23}}{a_{33}}, \tag{2.71}$$

which relates Γ' to the change in molality m_3 of diffusible solute with change in molality m_u of the non-diffusible component. The quantity Γ' is, strictly speaking, not a measurable quantity in a membrane experiment as, at constant P, flow of component 1 will proceed indefinitely across the membrane. At osmotic equilibrium, which is the only true equilibrium possible in the membrane system, we have seen that $d\mu_1 = 0$ and $d\mu_3 = 0$. We therefore have, from eqn (2.38) and the definition of Γ and Γ',

$$\Gamma = \Gamma' - \frac{\bar{v}_3}{RTa_{33}}\frac{d\Pi}{dm_u}. \tag{2.72}$$

We have already shown, in the considerations leading to the approximate expression eqn (2.65), that under most conditions of experimental interest the second term on the right-hand side of eqn (2.72) is negligible, and therefore

$$\Gamma \approx \Gamma'.$$

Eqn (2.65) is approximate because of the subscript μ. Eqn (2.71) is exact (subscripts P, T, μ_3) because of the restriction constant P; this term is eliminated from eqn (2.37). We find therefore that essentially the same information with respect to distribution coefficients is obtained from two widely different experimental methods, dialysis equilibrium on the one hand and electromotive-force measurements on the other hand.

2.4.2. Isopiestic distillation

Whereas membrane distribution experiments are naturally analysed in terms of a distribution coefficient based on the analytically determinable distribution of component 3, there exists another type of experiment, isopiestic distillation (see Robinson and Stokes (**1959**) for a detailed discussion of isopiestic distillation in simple electrolyte solutions), which is usually interpreted in terms of a distribution coefficient of component 1.

We turn to an analysis of the isopiestic-distillation (Fig. 1.10, p. 16) experiment and its relation to membrane dialysis. Such experiments have been performed by Hearst (1965) with DNA solutions and by Hade and Tanford (1967) in the study of interaction parameters of guanidine–hydrogen chloride–protein solutions. In this experiment identical amounts of dry salt (component 3) and water (component 1) are introduced into two vessels; to one of the vessels a weighed amount of component 2 is added and isopiestic distillation allowed to proceed until equilibrium is achieved. The final difference in water weight between the two vessels, divided by the weight of component 2, is identified as 'net hydration' and usually found to increase with increasing salt concentration (we shall have occasion to discuss 'net' or 'preferential' hydration in later chapters). With equal justification though these experiments can be interpreted (Cohen and Eisenberg 1968) in terms of the change of the molality of component 3, with change in molality of component 2, at constant pressure P and chemical potential μ_1.

A thermodynamic analysis of the isopiestic experiment leads to the following results (Cohen and Eisenberg 1968). We may describe the variation of the chemical potential μ_3 of component 3 in terms of the molalities m_2 and m_3 and the pressure P by eqn (2.37), and for the variation of μ_1 of component 1 we write (at constant temperature)

$$d\mu_1 = \mu_{12}\, dm_2 + \mu_{13}\, dm_3 + \overline{V}_1\, dP. \qquad (2.73)$$

In equilibrium dialysis (μ_1 and μ_3 constant) eqn (2.38) applies, or, in a less familiar form,

$$\Gamma \equiv \left(\frac{\partial m_3}{\partial m_u}\right)_\mu = -\frac{a_{12}}{Za_{13}} - \frac{\overline{V}_1}{RTa_{13}}\frac{d\Pi}{dm_u}. \qquad (2.74)$$

With the restrictions pertaining to isopiestic distillation (μ_1 and P constant) eqn (2.73) yields

$$\Gamma'' = \left(\frac{\partial m_3}{\partial m_u}\right)_{P,\mu_1} = -\frac{1}{Z}\frac{a_{12}}{a_{13}}. \qquad (2.75)$$

Substitution of eqn (2.75) in eqn (2.74) yields

$$\Gamma = \Gamma'' - \frac{\overline{V}_1}{RTa_{13}}\frac{d\Pi}{dm_u}. \qquad (2.76)$$

To see how Γ is related to Γ'' we must evaluate the second term on the right-hand side of eqn (2.76). For vanishing polymer concentration and uni–univalent added salt this term is approximately equal to $-1/2Z$ ($(d\Pi/dm_u)^0 \sim RT/V_m^0 Z$; from eqn (A2.10) and the fact that component 3 dissociates into two ions, $\mu_{13} = RTa_{13} = -2RT\overline{V}_1/V_m^0$). For low-molecular-weight sonicated DNA, for instance ($Z \sim 2000$ nucleotides per DNA chain) this is about 2.5×10^{-4}, which is a negligible quantity when compared with Γ, which is about 0·1 to 0·7. Thus, for all practical purposes we can neglect the difference between Γ and Γ'' and obtain the useful conclusion that

$$(\partial m_3/\partial m_u)_\mu \approx (\partial m_3/\partial m_u)_{P,\mu_1}. \qquad (2.77)$$

The data from isopiestic experiments often given in terms of a distribution coefficient of the volatile component 1 (water) can be, as will be shown later, re-calculated into the distribution coefficient Γ for component 3.

2.4.3. Ideal distribution

From considerations on the ideal distribution of a uni–univalent electrolyte component 3 across a semipermeable membrane, it is possible to arrive at a simple expression for the osmotic pressure. We assume all deviations from electroneutrality to be due to unequal distributions of ions. From van't Hoff's law $\Pi = \Delta\rho_n kT$ we find, in terms of molality, $\Delta m = \Delta\rho_n V_m/N_A$,

$$V_m \Pi/RT = \Delta m, \tag{2.78}$$

where Δm signifies differences in molality across the semipermeable membrane. In the particular instance, and in the limit of low concentrations m_2,

$$V_m^0 \Pi/RT = (m_2 + Zm_2 + 2m_3) - 2m_3',$$

or, with the definition of Γ, eqn (2.63),

$$V_m^0 \Pi/m_2 RT = 1 + Z + 2Z\Gamma. \tag{2.79}$$

Substitution of the expansion of Γ in powers of molality (eqn (2.63)) leads to

$$V_m^0 \Pi/m_2 RT = 1 + (Z^2/4m_Y')m_2 - (Z^4/16m_Y'^3)m_2^3 + \cdots. \tag{2.80}$$

We see that the second virial coefficient, in this simple derivation, equals

$$B_2^{(m)} = Z^2/4m_3 \tag{2.81}$$

(from $B_2^{(m)}$, A_2 may be derived by eqn (2.50)).

Alternatively consideration of eqn (2.50) shows that for the 'simple' definition of components (see Table 2.1, p. 33)

$$2B_2^{(m)} \approx \frac{Z^2}{m_3} + \beta_{22} - \left(\frac{a_{23}^2}{a_{33}}\right)^0. \tag{2.82}$$

Use of eqns (2.23) and (2.24) for a_{23}^0 and a_{33}^0, and disregard of all non-ideality corrections β_{22}, β_{23}, and β_{33} shows that B_2 is identical with the value given in eqn (2.81). This proves the identity of the two schemes.

It is interesting to note from eqn (2.80) that if component 3 is a uni–univalent electrolyte, there is no contribution due to the unequal distribution of ions to the third virial coefficient $B_3^{(m)}$; the next ionic contribution is the fourth virial coefficient

$$B_4^{(m)} = Z^4/16m_3^3. $$

This explains why in most polyelectrolyte solutions in uni–univalent electrolytes a plot of Π/c versus c, at low concentrations c is usually linear; the only contributions to $B_3^{(m)}$ derive from the terms for the non-ionic non-ideality interactions. In non-ionic solutions these are the only contributions to the virial coefficients and curvature in the plots is usually observed.

3

PARTIAL VOLUMES, DENSITY, AND REFRACTIVE-INDEX INCREMENTS

PARTIAL volumes and refractive-index increments are of fourfold interest in the study of multi-component biopolymer solutions for the following reasons.

1. We shall see, in Chapters 4 and 5 of this book, respectively, that refractive-index increments are required in the evaluation of light-scattering experiments and partial volumes in the evaluation of sedimentation measurements in the ultracentrifuge. Hence knowledge of them is required to obtain molecular weights and thermodynamic interactions between macromolecules by these techniques.
2. A more trivial application is as calibration constants that sometimes permit conversion of observed density or refractive-index changes into measurement of concentration—thus, for instance, refractive-index differences are used in the determination of concentration gradients in the ultracentrifuge.
3. Considered as independent measurements, changes in refractive index and partial volumes yield evidence for physical effects in solution; for instance, changes of volume or of index upon denaturation of a globular protein, or melting of a DNA double helix, changes in hydration or electrostriction of solvent by charged solutes.
4. Finally we shall see that if density or refractive-index changes are determined both at constant composition and at constant potential of diffusible solutes, interaction parameters reflecting the distribution of diffusible solutes may be conveniently derived.

3.1. Partial volumes

In Appendix 2 (p. 227) the partial specific volumes $\bar{v}_J$ are discussed and their relationship to the experimentally accessible apparent specific volume,

$$\phi_J \equiv \Phi_J/M_J = \Delta V/g_J,$$

is shown, where ΔV is the volume change upon addition of g_J g of component J to a solvent mixture of volume V_s (at constant P, T, and composition); ϕ_J may be derived in various ways, but it is well worth noting that in protein and nucleic-acid solutions, and at low concentrations of the macromolecular component 2 in particular, ϕ_2 is found to be independent of concentration of component 2 and may therefore be identified with the partial specific volume $\bar{v}_2$. If we now differentiate eqn (2.9) and use eqns (2.10) and (2.12) we find

$$\left(\frac{\partial \rho}{\partial m_2}\right)_{P,m} = \frac{M_2}{V_m}(1 - \rho \bar{v}_2). \tag{3.1}$$

From $c_2 = m_2 M_2 / V_m$ we derive

$$\left(\frac{\partial c_2}{\partial m_2}\right)_{P,m} = \frac{M_2}{V_m}(1 - c_2 \bar{v}_2), \tag{3.2}$$

and therefore

$$\left(\frac{\partial \rho}{\partial c_2}\right)_{P,m} = \frac{1 - \rho \bar{v}_2}{1 - c_2 \bar{v}_2}. \tag{3.3}$$

At low concentrations c_2, $(\partial \rho / \partial c_2)_{P,m}$ equals $\Delta \rho / c_2$, where $\Delta \rho = \rho - \rho^0$ represents the increase in solvent-mixture density ρ^0 upon addition of component 2, at constant composition of the solvent mixture. At the low concentrations of component 2 with which we are dealing another justified simplification is possible. We may write

$$\rho = \rho^0 + \left(\frac{\partial \rho}{\partial c_2}\right)_{P,m} c_2, \tag{3.4}$$

and substitute into eqn (3.3) to obtain

$$\left(\frac{\partial \rho}{\partial c_2}\right)_{P,m} = 1 - \rho^0 \bar{v}_2, \tag{3.5}$$

which is a particular simple expression for obtaining $\bar{v}_2$ from the measured values of $(\partial \rho / \partial c_2)_{P,m}$, or more simply $(\Delta \rho / c_2)_{P,m}$.

A major problem arising in the determination of the partial specific volume $\bar{v}_2$ in multi-component solutions derives from a practical consideration. Whereas in solutions of simple low-molecular-weight salts of polyelectrolytes it is a reasonably straightforward procedure to dissolve materials dried to constant weight into appropriate solvent mixtures, the delicate nature of biopolymer solutes, and the sometimes prolonged solution process, vitiates this procedure (even synthetic polyelectrolytes may often not be satisfactorily freed from water of hydration and the solution process is rather slow). This is the reason why true partial volumes have in the past been rarely obtained. More often biopolymer solutions are prepared by dialysis against the appropriate buffer solutions and density increments $(\partial \rho / \partial c_2)_\mu$ measured under these conditions are not appropriate for substitution in eqn (3.5) for the calculation of partial specific volumes. In the process of dialysis redistribution of diffusible components occurs (see Chapter 2) and the density increments measured contain a contribution due to this redistribution; this is clearly not related to a volume change at constant composition, as required from the definition of the partial volume.

It is possible, with reasonable effort, to measure density increments both at constant chemical potentials of diffusible solutes, as well as at constant composition of the solvent mixture. At constant chemical potential this increment is derived by measuring the density differences between a solution of component 2 in dialysis equilibrium with a solution of low-molecular-weight solutes. The measurement of the latter quantity is a little more involved in view of the difficulties mentioned above. We have devised an appropriate procedure and applied it to the determination of partial specific volumes of both nucleic acid (Cohen and Eisenberg 1968) and protein (Reisler and Eisenberg 1969) solutions. The procedure consists in preparing a solution of component 2 in either water or very dilute salt. The concentration of this solution can be accurately determined by either ultraviolet absorption, dry-weight determination, or elementary analysis (of phosphorus, nitrogen, or any other suitable chemical element or group). Next a dry amount of low-molecular-weight component 3 is weighed into the above solution of component 2 in water or very dilute salt.† The constituent weights of components 2 and 3 and 1 (water) in the resulting solution are now well known and therefore the molality of components 2 and 3 are properly defined; the concentration in volume concentration units may be calculated from the molalities (see p. 29) because the density of the solution is precisely known (for density determination we recommend a recently developed method (Kratky, Leopold, and Stabinger, 1969) by which densities are determined by measuring the resonant frequencies of a capillary tube bent into U-shape in which the solutions are enclosed). To obtain the proper reference solution at the same composition (molality of component 3) dry component 3 is weighed into an appropriate weighed quantity of water (or very dilute salt, if such a solvent was used), and the density of a series of such closely similar solutions is determined. The density of the solution at the precise molality required for the determination of the density increment $\Delta\rho$ at constant composition is obtained by interpolation to appropriate solvent molality. The procedure is straightforward and permits the determination of reliable well-defined partial specific volumes in multi-component solutions by use of eqns (3.3) or (3.5). Classically, densities were determined by pycnometry. Recently, density determinations have been greatly facilitated, by the mechanical oscillator technique of Kratky, Leopold, and Stabinger (**1973**), and can now be rapidly undertaken with small amounts of valuable materials.

† It is sometimes necessary to use a dilute salt solution rather than pure water to prevent denaturation of the biopolymer solute; thus 10^{-3} M NaCl is usually sufficient to prevent denaturation of DNA. Alternatively, if the DNA solution is handled at low temperatures only, pure distilled water or much more dilute salt may be used.

3.2. Density increments and 'preferential' or 'net' interaction parameters

We now turn to some theoretical considerations of density increments and analysis of the information which can be derived from such studies.

Below is presented an analysis of a system in which, in addition to the three components considered hitherto, a low-molecular-weight neutral component 4 has been included. The latter may be sucrose or glycerol, for instance; these are sometimes added to protein solutions on the assumption that whereas they affect the density of the solutions, they do not by themselves interact with the protein or affect interactions between components 1 and 2 and 3 and 2. We are not concerned now with the validity of this assumption but rather with the consequences which result from it in the attempt to derive information on true physical ion-binding or solvation from the measurement of preferential interactions.

We may write for the dependence of the density upon composition and pressure P in the four-component system,

$$\mathrm{d}\rho = \left(\frac{\partial \rho}{\partial m_2}\right)_{P,m} \mathrm{d}m_2 + \left(\frac{\partial \rho}{\partial m_3}\right)_{P,m} \mathrm{d}m_3 + \left(\frac{\partial \rho}{\partial m_4}\right)_{P,m} \mathrm{d}m_4 + \left(\frac{\partial \rho}{\partial P}\right)_{m} \mathrm{d}P, \quad (3.6)$$

$$\left(\frac{\partial \rho}{\partial m_2}\right)_{\mu} = \left(\frac{\partial \rho}{\partial m_2}\right)_{P,m} + \left(\frac{\partial \rho}{\partial m_3}\right)_{P,m}\left(\frac{\partial m_3}{\partial m_2}\right)_{\mu} + \left(\frac{\partial \rho}{\partial m_4}\right)_{P,m}\left(\frac{\partial m_4}{\partial m_2}\right)_{\mu} + \kappa\rho\,\frac{\mathrm{d}\Pi}{\mathrm{d}m_2}, \quad (3.7)$$

where we have used the isothermal compressibility coefficient

$$\kappa = (\partial \ln \rho / \partial P)_m.$$

With the help of equations similar to eqns (2.11) and (2.51), eqn (3.7) transforms exactly into

$$\left(\frac{\partial \rho}{\partial c_2}\right)_{\mu} = \frac{(1 - \bar{v}_2\rho) + \xi_3(1 - \bar{v}_3\rho) + \xi_4(1 - \bar{v}_4\rho)}{1 - (\bar{v}_2 + \xi_3\bar{v}_3 + \xi_4\bar{v}_4)c_2} + \kappa\rho\,\frac{\mathrm{d}\Pi}{\mathrm{d}c_2}, \quad (3.8)$$

where the interaction parameters ξ_J defined by

$$\xi_J \equiv (\partial w_J/\partial w_2)_{\mu} = (M_J/M_2)(\partial m_J/\partial m_2)_{\mu} \quad (3.9)$$

indicate the change in molality of component J, with change in molality of component 2, required to maintain μ_1, μ_3, and μ_4 constant. The density increment $(\partial \rho/\partial c_2)_{\mu}$ is, as has been mentioned before, the determining quantity required for the evaluation of equilibrium and velocity sedimentation, equilibrium sedimentation in a density gradient, and small-angle X-ray scattering (Timasheff **1963**; Eisenberg and Cohen 1969) experiments in multi-component systems. For these methods $(\partial \rho/\partial c_2)_{\mu}$ may, as a rule, be obtained as an experimental quantity, and a decomposition into the quantities appearing on the right-hand side of eqn (3.8) is not required. Our main interest though in the discussion below will centre on the decomposition of $(\partial \rho/\partial c_2)_{\mu}$ into the quantities of which it is composed.

We shall make two approximations which are inconsequential in relation to the principles involved, but lead to a highly simplified presentation. We make the reasonable assumption (as above in eqn (3.4)) that the density of the solution, at low concentrations of component 2, is linear in c_2

$$\rho = \rho^0 + (\partial \rho / \partial c_2)_\mu^0 c_2.$$

We furthermore neglect the compressibility term in eqn (3.8), which is due to the fact that the equilibrium osmotic pressure has to be maintained (this term is equal to $\kappa \rho RT/M_2$ at low protein concentrations and is negligible in aqueous solutions, in most cases of practical interest). With the above assumptions eqn (3.8) simplifies to the much more attractive form

$$(\partial \rho / \partial c_2)_\mu = (1 - \bar{v}_2^0 \rho^0) + \xi_3 (1 - \bar{v}_3 \rho^0) + \xi_4 (1 - \bar{v}_4 \rho^0) \qquad (3.10a)$$

or

$$(\partial \rho / \partial c_2)_\mu = (1 + \xi_3 + \xi_4) - \rho^0 (\bar{v}_2^0 + \xi_3 \bar{v}_3 + \xi_4 \bar{v}_4). \qquad (3.10b)$$

Here $\bar{v}_2^0$ is the partial specific volume at vanishing protein concentrations, and $\bar{v}_2$ and $\bar{v}_4$ are the corresponding quantities for components 3 and 4 at their finite, specified concentration (in the absence of component 2).

To determine all the quantities in eqns (3.10a, b) for a given system we consider first the case in which component 4 is absent; from the experimental values of $(\partial \rho / \partial c_2)_\mu$, $\bar{v}_2^0$ and $\bar{v}_3$ it is then possible to calculate the interaction parameter ξ_3. If component 4 is present then it is necessary to determine in addition at least one interaction parameter ξ_3 or ξ_4, by way of the evaluation of, for instance, the concentration difference of either component 3 or 4 across a semipermeable membrane. If, as may usually be the case, volume concentrations are determined, one may apply (at vanishing polymer concentration) the connection analogous to eqn (2.67) between, for instance, the interaction parameter $(\partial c_3 / \partial c_2)_\mu$ on the concentration scale and ξ_3 on the molality scale

$$(\partial c_3 / \partial c_2)_\mu = \xi_3 - c_3 (\bar{v}_2^0 + \xi_3 \bar{v}_3 + \xi_4 \bar{v}_4). \qquad (3.11)$$

If component 4 is volatile (glycerol, for instance, may be evaporated under relatively mild experimental conditions along with component 1, water, in a high vacuum and at suitably high temperatures) then ξ_3 may be evaluated from the difference in weight between dried aliquots of the macromolecular and dialysate equilibrium solvent solutions. All the quantities in eqns (3.10a, b) can thus be derived from well-defined experimental procedures.

The value of $(\partial \rho / \partial c_2)_\mu$ is often expressed in analogy to simple two-component systems by introducing (Casassa and Eisenberg **1964**) an apparent quantity ϕ' defined by

$$(\partial \rho / \partial c_2)_\mu \equiv 1 - \phi' \rho^0, \qquad (3.12)$$

which, in contradistinction to Φ_2 or ϕ_2, is not a molal or specific apparent volume because it includes contributions due to redistribution of components; it does not correspond in form to either eqn (3.10a) or eqn (3.10b). We shall see that ϕ' increases significantly at high concentrations of component 3, presumably because of solvent redistribution, both in the case of DNA in simple salt solutions as well as in the case of proteins at high concentrations of guanidine hydrochloride (GuHCl). Nevertheless eqn (3.12) is useful because ϕ' is a slowly changing parameter only and is useful if we want to evaluate $(\partial\rho/\partial c_2)_\mu$ in a given system, say nominally at 6 M GuHCl (but not exactly 6 M GuHCl) in a solution the density of which is precisely known. It is also in keeping with one of those customs which are hard to eradicate, namely, that buoyancy terms of the form $(1 - \bar{v}_2\rho)$ appearing in two-component systems in sedimentation equations are persistently expressed in this form even in systems containing more than two components, rather than in the more natural formulation of density increments.

Whereas the basis for the molality in the definition of ξ_3 and ξ_4 was component 1, water, the symmetry of the system requires that the reduced density increments (due to addition of component 2) may be expressed to within the same assumptions as embodied in eqns (3.10a, b), in two equivalent forms

$$(\partial\rho/\partial c_2)_\mu = (1 - \bar{v}_2^0\rho^0) + \xi_1'(1 - \bar{v}_1\rho^0) + \xi_4'(1 - \bar{v}_4\rho^0), \qquad (3.13)$$

where

$$\xi_1' = (\partial w_1'/\partial w_2')_\mu \quad \text{and} \quad \xi_4' = (\partial w_4'/\partial w_2')_\mu \qquad (3.14)$$

and the primed quantities

$$w_J' = n_J M_J / n_3 M_3$$

represent weight molalities gram of component J per gram of component 3. We may also write

$$(\partial\rho/\partial c_2)_\mu = (1 - \bar{v}_2^0\rho^0) + \xi_3''(1 - \bar{v}_3\rho^0) + \xi_1''(1 - \bar{v}_1\rho^0), \qquad (3.15)$$

where

$$\xi_3'' = (\partial w_3''/\partial w_2'')_\mu \quad \text{and} \quad \xi_1'' = (\partial w_1''/\partial w_2'')_\mu \qquad (3.16)$$

and the double-primed quantities $w_J'' = n_J M_J / n_4 M_4$ represent weight molalities grams of component J per gram of component 4. No basic advantage accrues from the use of either eqn (3.15) or (3.13) over eqn (3.10a). Sometimes though a given set of parameters may be preferable to another set under conditions of a specific experiment. The connection between the various phenomenological interaction parameters in eqns (3.10a), (3.13), and (3.15) is easily established by the use of a procedure suggested by Hade and Tanford

(1967). It is based on the fact that, independent of any definition of the molality scale, the proportionality

$$1:w_2:w_3:w_4 = w_1':w_2':1:w_4' = w_1'':w_2'':w_3'':1$$

must hold; more simply we may use (Cohen and Eisenberg 1968), for the case of vanishing macromolecular concentration

$$c_1 + c_3 + c_4 = \rho^0 \quad \text{and} \quad c_1 \bar{v}_1 + c_3 \bar{v}_3 + c_4 \bar{v}_4 = 1, \tag{3.17}$$

to give

$$c_1(1 - \bar{v}_1 \rho^0) + c_3(1 - \bar{v}_3 \rho^0) + c_4(1 - \bar{v}_4 \rho^0) = 0. \tag{3.18}$$

Comparison of eqns (3.10a), (3.13), and (3.15) in pairs and substitution of eqn (3.18) yields the set of connections

$$\frac{\xi_1''}{c_1} = -\frac{\xi_4}{c_4}; \quad \frac{\xi_3''}{c_3} = \frac{\xi_3}{c_3} - \frac{\xi_4}{c_4}, \tag{3.19}$$

$$\frac{\xi_1'}{c_1} = -\frac{\xi_3}{c_3}; \quad \frac{\xi_4'}{c_4} = \frac{\xi_4}{c_4} - \frac{\xi_3}{c_3}. \tag{3.20}$$

The weight molalities are related to the volume concentrations by

$$w_J = c_J/c_1; \quad w_J' = c_J/c_3; \quad w_J'' = c_J/c_4.$$

The ξs, as well as the primed and the double-primed parameters are operational quantities and do not reflect any specific molecular mechanism *per se*. They are sometimes called 'preferential' or 'net' interaction parameters, but this may be a misleading designation because of the intuitive tendency to associate a positive value of the parameter with 'physical binding' of either component 1, 3, or 4 to the macromolecular entity. Positive ξ_3, for instance, may indicate salt-binding, but this does not lead to partial or complete exclusion of other solute components from the surface of component 2. Negative values of ξ_3 (with the sign as defined here) may indicate salt-rejection, which usually results from an electrostatic Donnan mechanism. This may be equivalent to 'net' or 'preferential' water-binding (Ifft and Vinograd 1966) (positive ξ_1', see eqn (3.20)) and cannot easily be distinguished from it. The connection between interdependent interaction parameters has been given before (Cohen and Eisenberg 1968; Lauffer 1964; Timasheff and Inoue 1968; Bull and Breese 1970; Timasheff **1970**), but we feel that the present exposition is simpler and more rigorous than previous derivations, and, moreover, can easily be extended to concentrated solutions and to solutions containing any number of independent components.

3.3. A model for physical binding

We may now proceed one step further and devise a scheme to evaluate the phenomena described in terms of a realistic physical model (see also Inoue and Timasheff 1972; Eisenberg **1974**). To do this we perform the following thought experiment (Fig. 3.1).

To 1 ml of a mixed solvent s of density ρ^0, containing components 1, 3, and 4 we add, in step I, c_2 g of component 2; in step II we mix, let counter-ions dissociate and allow binding of components 1, 3, and 4 to component 2 (if appropriate) to occur—at this stage volume expansion or contraction may come about, but the total composition (on a weight molality basis) remains

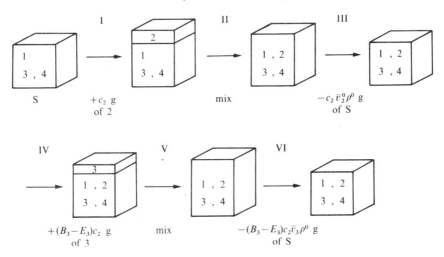

FIG. 3.1. Schematic representation of addition (I) of component 2 to 1 ml of solvent mixture S, mixing (II); restoration of original volume by removal (III) of solvent mixture S; addition (IV) of component 3; mixing (V) and removal (VI) of solvent mixture S to restore original volume of 1 ml. Steps IV–VI are designed to restore original value μ_3 in solvent mixture S; μ_3 was disturbed by addition of component 2 in steps I–III. Similar procedures with respect to components 1 and 4 are not indicated in diagram. See text for further details.

unchanged. The volume occupied by component 2 is now $c_2 \bar{v}_2^0$ and the partial specific volume $\bar{v}_2^0$ takes into account all processes having occurred on a molecular scale, without change in solvent composition. To restore the volume to 1 ml, we remove in step III $c_2 \bar{v}_2^0 \rho^0$ g of the original solvent mixture s.

In the next steps of our imaginary process we aim to restore the values μ_1, μ_3, and μ_4 disturbed by the addition of component 2, to their original values, by appropriate modification of solvent composition. We define the quantities B_3 and E_3 as binding of component 3 (salt) and electrostatic (Donnan) exclusion of the same respectively, as well as B_1 and B_4 as binding of component 1 (water) and the neutral component 4 respectively; all these above quantities are expressed in grams per gram of the macromolecular component 2. To the millilitre of solution we add in step IV $(B_3 - E_3)c_2$ g of component 3 to allow for salt-binding and Donnan exclusion ($(B_3 - E_3)c_2$ may represent a negative amount of component 3 if the Donnan exclusion term E_3 is larger than the salt-binding term B_3); in step V we mix all components and in step VI we remove $(B_3 - E_3)c_2 \bar{v}_3 \rho^0$ g of the original solvent mixture S. The last step brings the volume back to 1 ml and $\bar{v}_3$ corresponds to the value for the solvent mixture (at the proper concentration of component 3 in the absence of component 2) because the change in volume inherent in the physical binding process has already been absorbed in the experimental value of $\bar{v}_2^0$. To account for binding of components 1 and 4 we proceed by similar arguments which will not be developed here in detail. We have tacitly assumed that the proper consideration of binding and Donnan exclusion restores the original values of the chemical potentials of the solvent components to their original values.†

In mathematical terms the total change in density is given by

$$\Delta\rho = \text{I} + \text{II} + \text{III} + \text{IV} + \text{V} + \text{VI} + \ldots$$

$$\Delta\rho = c_2 - c_2 \bar{v}_2^0 \rho^0 + (B_3 - E_3)c_2 - (B_3 - E_3)c_2 \bar{v}_3 \rho^0 + B_1 c_2 - B_1 c_2 \bar{v}_1 \rho^0 + B_4 c_2 - B_4 c_2 \bar{v}_4 \rho^0$$

or

$$(\partial\rho/\partial c_2)_\mu = (1 - \bar{v}_2 \rho^0) + (B_3 - E_3)(1 - \bar{v}_3 \rho^0) + B_1(1 - \bar{v}_1 \rho^0) + B_4(1 - \bar{v}_4 \rho^0). \quad (3.21)$$

Substitution of $(1 - v_1 \rho^0)$ from eqn (3.18) and $w_J = c_J/c_1$ yields

$$(\partial\rho/\partial c_2)_\mu = (1 - \bar{v}_2 \rho^0) + (B_3 - E_3 - w_3 B_1)(1 - \bar{v}_3 \rho^0) + (B_4 - w_4 B_1)(1 - \bar{v}_4 \rho^0). \quad (3.22)$$

Thus, by comparing with eqn (3.10a),

$$\xi_3 = (B_3 - E_3) - w_3 B_1, \quad (3.23)$$

$$\xi_4 = B_4 - w_4 B_1. \quad (3.24)$$

Both ξ_3 and ξ_4 are, as we have seen above, experimental quantities which may be used to estimate the binding and exclusion parameters in eqns (3.23) and (3.24) without assuming (as is usually done) constancy of binding or exclusion parameters with changing solvent composition. A practical necessity though is the requirement for finding a neutral component 4 so that B_4 is zero or close to zero. This might permit evaluation of B_1 by eqn (3.24) and $(B_3 - E_3)$ by eqn (3.23). It is not possible to separate unequivocally the contribution due to the binding of component 3 from Donnan exclusion of the same component. The term E_3 cannot be disregarded in highly

---

† In the establishment of the original values of the chemical potentials we have neglected the effect on the density of the system of the small pressure application (the osmotic pressure-term) necessary to fully restore the chemical potential μ_1 subsequent to introduction of component 2; this neglect is inconsequential in dilute aqueous macromolecular solutions in its effect on these parameters.

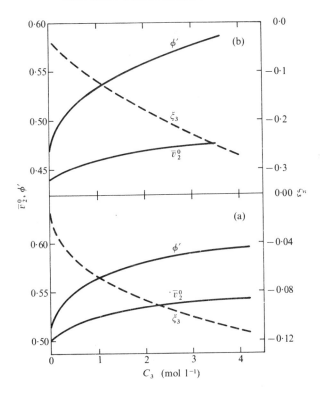

FIG. 3.2. Specific volumes ($\bar{v}_2$ and ϕ') and preferential interaction parameters ξ_3 in DNA solutions: (a) NaDNA in sodium chloride; (b) CsDNA in caesium chloride. (From Cohen and Eisenberg 1968; see Eisenberg **1974**.)

charged polyelectrolytes such as DNA or other polynucleotides; its effect can be considerably reduced in protein solutions by working close to the isoelectric point. It can sometimes be evaluated on the basis of electrostatic statistical-mechanical calculations. In nucleic acids ξ_3 (defined as a 'binding' and not as an exclusion parameter) is negative and becomes more negative with increasing salt concentration (Cohen and Eisenberg 1968). Salt-binding B_3 is presumably negligible and ξ_3 decreases with increase in w_3 because of the last term in eqn (3.23). In the case of proteins in GuHCl solutions ξ_3 is positive but decreases strongly with increasing w_3 (Reisler and Eisenberg 1969; Reisler, Haik, and Eisenberg, to be published). Values of $\bar{v}_2^0$, ϕ', and ξ_3 are summarized in Fig. 3.2 for nucleic acid–simple salt solutions and in Fig. 3.3 for bovine serum albumin in GuHCl solutions. For a detailed recent discussion of hydration of proteins and polypeptides refer to Kuntz and Kauzmann (**1974**).

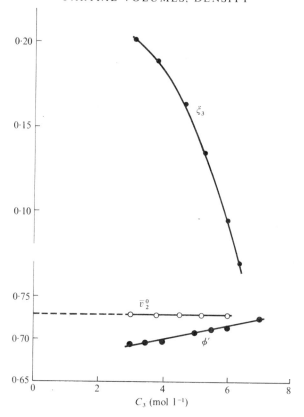

F IG. 3.3. Specific volumes ($\bar{v}_2$ and ϕ') and preferential interaction parameters ξ_3 in bovine serum albumin solutions at various concentrations of GuHCl (From Reisler, Haik, and Eisenberg, to be published).

We note that the belief sometimes expressed that a linear decrease of $(\partial\rho/\partial c_2)_\mu$ with ρ^0 indicates that the values of the interaction parameters are independent of w_3, is not well-founded (Reisler and Eisenberg 1969). A fortunate choice of an additional component to change ρ^0 without affecting other interactions in solutions may sometimes prove to be felicitous, but success cannot be predicted *a priori*. Edelstein and Schachman (1967) and Thomas and Edelstein (1971) have used solvents in which ρ^0 was varied by using the light and heavy isotopes of oxygen and of hydrogen in equilibrium sedimentation (Chapter 5) studies; the main advantage of their method resides in the minute quantity of protein required for the experiments but the accuracy of the results is not very high. Stevens and Lauffer (1965) and Jaenicke and Lauffer (1969) have described a novel, if protracted, method of measuring $(\partial\rho/\partial c_2)_\mu$ by determining the buoyant weight of a dialysis bag enclosing protein solution, in equilibrium with suitable reference solutions containing a low-molecular-weight salt and sometimes also varying amounts of glycerin.

We would also like to dispel the notion, sometimes met, that if we extrapolate $(\partial\rho/\partial c_2)_\mu$ measured at finite salt concentrations to zero salt concentration (which corresponds to ρ^0 equal to unity in aqueous solutions), $(\partial\rho/\partial c_2)_{P,m}$ (from which $\bar{v}_2$ can be calculated) is obtained. This idea is based on the fact that, in a three-component system, eqn (3.13) reduces to

$$(\partial\rho/\partial c_2)_\mu = (1 - \bar{v}_2^0\rho^0) + \xi_1'(1 - \bar{v}_1\rho^0). \tag{3.25}$$

It is claimed that as w_3 tends to zero, ρ^0 tends to unity and therefore with $\bar{v}_1$ equal to unity $(1 - v_1\rho^0)$ vanishes. On the other hand, by eqns (3.20) and (3.23),

$$\xi_1' = -\xi_3/w_3 = B_1 - (B_3 - E_3)/w_3. \tag{3.26}$$

The value of ξ_1' for finite values of $(B_3 - E_3)$ goes to infinity for vanishing w_3. The second term on the right-hand side of eqn (3.25) therefore does not usually vanish when w_3 goes to zero, unless the Donnan exclusion term E_3 is strictly absent; it is probably safe to assume that $B_3 \to 0$ with $w_3 \to 0$. At any rate, for low salt concentrations w_3 it appears preferable to evaluate

$$(\partial\rho/\partial c_2)_\mu = (1 - v_2^0\rho^0) + \xi_3(1 - \bar{v}_3\rho^0), \tag{3.27}$$

which avoids the above-mentioned catastrophe. When $w_3 \to 0$, ξ_3 tends to $(B_3 - E_3)$ (eqn (3.23)) or more likely to $-E_3$, as B_3 may be assumed to vanish under these conditions; $-E_3$ can be calculated if the charge of the protein or nucleic acid is known.

3.4. Refractive-index increments

Refractive-index increments of component 2 may be obtained at fixed pressure, temperature, and composition of all the other components, or at constant chemical potentials of diffusible components. This is quite analogous to the density increments discussed above and the discussion may proceed along similar lines. We define the molal refractive increment of a component J by

$$\Psi_J \equiv (\partial n/\partial m_J)_{P,T,m}, \tag{3.28}$$

in conformity with the concentration scale defined earlier in the thermodynamic derivations. We shall, as before, omit subscript T because constancy of temperature is implied throughout. The specific refractive-index increment on the molal scale is

$$\psi_J = (\partial n/\partial w_J)_{P,m} = 10^3\,\Psi_J/M_J. \tag{3.29}$$

In practice, we determine an apparent increment $\psi_{app} = \Delta n/w_J$, where Δn is the difference in refractive index between a solution containing all components and the solution without component J; the apparent increment is related to ψ_J by

$$\psi = \psi_{app} + w_J(d\psi_{app}/dw_J). \tag{3.30}$$

It is usually found that Δn for polymers, proteins, and nucleic acids is much more nearly proportional to concentration on the c scale rather than on the w scale; therefore specific increments are generally given in volume units. For a multi-component system we keep the composition (molality) of all components except component J constant and write

$$\Psi_J^{(c)} \equiv (\partial n/\partial c_J)_{P,m} \tag{3.31}$$

and

$$\psi_J^{(c)} \equiv (\partial n/\partial c_J)_{P,m} = \Psi_J^{(c)} \times 10^3/M_J. \tag{3.32}$$

It is usually not possible to discern variation by differential refractometry of $\Psi^{(c)}$ or $\psi^{(c)}$ with concentration up to several per cent. The connection between the molal and molar units is easily obtained with the use of eqn (3.2),

$$\Psi_J = \psi_J^{(c)}(1 - c_2 v_2)M_J/V_m. \tag{3.33}$$

In the multi-component systems of interest here we are usually concerned with the refractive-index increment for a single macromolecular solute (component 2) in a multi-component system of low-molecular-weight species, or with the increment for mixed macromolecular components all of which have the same increment ψ or $\psi^{(c)}$). The specific increment is found to be independent of chain length in the case of nucleic acids, for instance, and dependence upon base composition in a typical DNA is very slight. In a similar way the dependence of the specific increment in the case of protein solutions is found to be essentially independent of the state of aggregation of the protein. Altogether, $\psi^{(c)}$ is not a very sensitive quantity for most proteins or nucleic acids, under a given set of experimental conditions. To overcome the experimental difficulty of adding a dry bio-macromolecular component 2 to a mixed solvent system, for the determination of $\psi^{(c)}$, we may proceed by the same procedure of preparing solutions and reference solvents as described in the case of partial volume measurements on p. 50.

In multi-component solutions we may vary the concentration of the macromolecular component 2 at fixed chemical potentials of the components diffusible through a dialysis membrane; at dialysis equilibrium we may define an increment $(\partial n/\partial m_2)_\mu$, which is related to the Ψ_Js by

$$\left(\frac{\partial n}{\partial m_2}\right)_\mu = \Psi_2 + \Psi_3\left(\frac{\partial m_3}{\partial m_2}\right)_\mu + \left(\frac{\partial n}{\partial P}\right)_m \frac{d\Pi}{dm_2}. \tag{3.34}$$

in the case of the three-component system discussed in Chapter 2. Eqn (3.34) is easily extended to include the four-component system discussed in Section 3.2 by addition of a term $\Psi_4(\partial m_4/\partial m_2)_\mu$ on the right-hand side of the equation.

We shall see in Chapter 4 that the increment required in the interpretation of light-scattering experiments is $(\partial n/\partial m_J)_{P,\mu(d)}$, where the $\mu(d)$ are the chemical potentials of all diffusible components except component 1; in the particular case of the three-component system under discussion this is given by

$$\left(\frac{\partial n}{\partial m_2}\right)_{P,\mu_3} = \Psi_2 + \Psi_3 \left(\frac{\partial m_3}{\partial m_2}\right)_{P,\mu_3} \qquad (3.35)$$

In practice it is found that $(\partial n/\partial m_2)_\mu$ and $(\partial n/\partial m_2)_{P,\mu_3}$ are not experimentally distinguishable. For water, dn/dP is about $1.5 \times 10^{-5}\,\text{atm}^{-1}$; hence, for aqueous systems, the last term on the right-hand side of eqn (3.34) is about 4×10^{-4}. In aqueous nucleic acid and protein solutions $\psi_2^{(c)}$ is about 0.2; therefore, by eqn (3.33) Ψ_2 is roughly $2 \times 10^{-4} M_2$, and the effect of pressure in the eqn (3.34) can be neglected for molecular weights larger than 2000, and certainly in the range of commonly encountered molecular weights (the precision with which the increments can be determined does not exceed 0.2 per cent).

For the practical evaluation of light-scattering experiments we are interested in the increments $(\partial n/\partial c_2)_{P,\mu(d)}$ which, to within the inconsequential neglect of the pressure effect, are equal to $(\partial n/\partial c_2)_\mu$. We use eqns (2.43) and (3.2) and a similar expression for component 3 to transform eqns (3.34) or (3.35) to the c scale,

$$\left(\frac{\partial n}{\partial c_2}\right)_\mu \approx \frac{\psi_2^{(c)}(1-c_2\bar{v}_2) + \psi_3^{(c)}(1-c_3\bar{v}_3)\xi_3}{1 - (c_2/M_2)(\partial V_m/\partial m_2)_\mu} \qquad (3.36)$$

and $(\partial V_m/\partial m_2)_\mu$, according to eqn (2.44) is given, to a similar approximation by

$$\left(\frac{\partial V_m}{\partial m_2}\right)_\mu \approx \bar{V}_2 - \frac{a_{23}}{a_{33}}\bar{V}_3 \qquad (3.37)$$

and

$$(\partial V_m/\partial m_2)_\mu/M_2 \approx \bar{v}_2 + \xi_3\bar{v}_3. \qquad (3.38)$$

In the limit of low concentrations c_2 we can write eqn (3.36) in the much simpler form

$$(\partial n/\partial c_2)_\mu^0 \approx \psi_2^{(c)0} + \psi_{3,m_2=0}^{(c)}(1-c_3\bar{v}_3)\xi_3. \qquad (3.39)$$

If the various refractive-index increments in eqn (3.39) are determined, ξ_3 may be evaluated. This is similar to eqn (3.10a) derived for density increments. Should an additional, diffusible, component be present, it is necessary to add a term

$$\psi_{4,m_2=0}^{(c)}(1-c_4\bar{v}_4)\xi_4$$

to eqn (3.39). Further considerations are then similar to the procedures developed with respect to the density increments.

3.5. Variation of refractive increment with refractive index of solvent

The refractive-index increment is obviously a function of the refractive index of the solvent. In the usual circumstance addition of the organic solute to the aqueous solvent system raises the refractive index; the index increment is positive. Raising the refractive index of the solvent by addition of large amounts of inorganic salts or organic components lowers the increment due to the macromolecular solute. It may vanish (iso-index solutions), or it may even become negative (we shall see that in light-scattering the square of the index increment determines the amount of light scattered, and this quantity is then independent of the sign of the index increment).

The variation of the refractive index with solvent index is analogous to the variation of the density increments with solvent density (see Section 3.2). The density increments may be positive or negative or the solutions may be isopycnic, when the density increments vanish for a suitable value of ρ^0. Iso-index and isopycnic solvents do not usually have identical composition. In the case of density increments, the variation of these with ρ is usually accounted for in terms of the partial specific volumes (see eqn (3.5), for instance). The situation is more complex in the case of multi-component solutions. Still we may always characterize the density of a solution in terms of partial specific volumes and specific interaction parameters, and it is more convenient to refer to these rather than to much more variable density increments. No similar device exists for the corresponding case of the refractive-index increments, and we therefore require a way to express these increments as a function of the solvent index. An approximate expression for this will be given below with the warning that, if precise refractive-index increments are required, they should always be determined for the particular solvent system for which they are needed.

Specifically it is assumed (Casassa 1956) that

$$n = \sum n_J \bar{v}_J c_J, \tag{3.40}$$

where the summation extends over all components and the n_J do not necessarily correspond with the actual refractive indices of the pure components. In the three-component system of primary interest to us here

$$n = n_2 \bar{v}_2 c_2 + n_s v_s c_s, \tag{3.41}$$

where

$$n_s = \frac{n_1 \bar{v}_1 \bar{c}_1 + n_3 \bar{v}_3 c_3}{\bar{v}_1 c_1 + \bar{v}_3 c_3} \tag{3.42}$$

and

$$\bar{v}_s c_s = \bar{v}_1 c_1 + \bar{v}_3 c_3. \tag{3.43}$$

From the fundamental property of the partial volume,

$$\bar{v}_2 c_2 + \bar{v}_s c_s = 1,\tag{3.44}$$

we obtain the relation

$$n = n_s + (n_2 - n_s)\bar{v}_2 c_2.\tag{3.45}$$

For a solvent of fixed composition differentiation of eqn (3.45) yields

$$\psi_2^{(c)} = (n_2 - n_s)\bar{v}_2.\tag{3.46}$$

We would like to apply the very approximate eqn (3.46) to the specific case in which we calculate on the basis of a known refractive increment $\psi_{2a}^{(c)}$ in one mixed solvent (a), the increment $\psi_{2b}^{(2)}$ in another mixed solvent (b); we assume n_2 is the same in the two solvents with respective refractive indices n_a and n_b, and eliminate n_2 by applying eqn (3.46) to both the solvents. Thus

$$\psi_{2b}^{(c)} = \psi_{2a}^{(c)} - \bar{v}_2(n_b - n_a).\tag{3.47}$$

In view of the assumptions involved in the derivation of eqn (3.47) it should be used only with caution in all cases in which estimates of index increments are to be made. Quite obviously, the considerations with respect to the optical properties relating to the refractive index are not as well based as the more precise statements which can be made with respect to density and density increments. A more detailed discussion is given in Casassa and Eisenberg (**1964**).

4

LIGHT AND SMALL-ANGLE
X-RAY SCATTERING

4.1. Introduction

MOST physical measurements from which information about the properties
of molecular or electronic systems, solutions, or suspensions is derived are
based on the interaction between an externally applied field and the system
which is being studied. Pressure, temperature, centrifugal, or electric fields,
for instance, can be used in one of three ways. In the more classical sense
the systems under investigation are allowed to come to equilibrium conditions and the characteristic properties determined in relation to the values
of the externally applied parameters. Sometimes the systems are not in
equilibrium but rather in a stationary state, dissipating energy at a constant
rate, such as, for example, in a hydrodynamic field, in a viscosity study, or
in a centrifugal field in a sedimentation-velocity experiment. Finally, a great
deal of information may be obtained in a relaxation experiment in which
the external field is used (such as in the well-known temperature-jump
experiment of Eigen and de Maeyer **1973**) to quickly disturb a state of
chemical equilibrium and then to follow the relaxation of the system to a
new equilibrium state characteristic of the modified experimental conditions.
It is of course required that the state of the system be affected by the
application of the external field and that a suitable probe (change in light-
absorbing properties, for instance) be available to monitor the change. A
more classical relaxation process is a diffusion process in which diffusion
proceeds as a natural process tending to equalize the concentration of a
solute component across a concentration gradient boundary artificially
established. To follow a classical electrophoretic mobility experiment it is
also necessary to observe the motion of an artificially established boundary
(see Tanford (**1961**) for a discussion of these various experimental techniques).

The interaction of radiation with matter is one of the most useful tools
in the armamentarium of the physical chemist and has led to a variety of
spectroscopic methods such as absorption of light of various frequencies,
optical rotation, fluorescence, X-ray diffraction, n.m.r., Rayleigh, Brillouin,
and Raman scattering, and others. Whereas in most experimental techniques
in which the interaction between radiation and matter is probed equilibrium
properties are investigated, it is well known that relaxation phenomena can
be related to the frequency-broadening of spectral lines as in n.m.r. exper-

iments (see, for instance, Grunwald, Loewenstein, and Meiboom 1957; Loewenstein and Meiboom 1957; Meiboom, Loewenstein, and Alexander 1958). We shall now indicate that, with the advent of monochromatic coherent laser radiation, it has become possible to extend classical light-scattering, which yields time averaged properties of macromolecular systems, to a study of time-dependent relaxation properties of these systems.

When a beam of light interacts with a molecular system secondary dipole centres are formed radiating energy in all directions. The classical calculation is due to Rayleigh (1871) who evaluated the scattering from a collection of independent particles in a dilute gas. Molecular crystals, on the other hand, scatter very little light because of destructive interference between rays of scattered light originating from the ordered scattering centres. Pure liquids scatter light rather poorly, because of the short-range molecular order in these fluids. To calculate the scattering from pure liquids Einstein (1910) abandoned the approach via a detailed molecular calculation requiring complete information about the position and motion of all the molecules in the fluid, and introduced the concept of scattering due to spontaneous density fluctuations in small volume elements of the fluid. Scattering in liquids is attributed to the fact that because of fluctuations of density in volume elements small with respect to the wavelength λ, yet containing many molecules, a time-averaged contribution to the optical polarizability of these volume elements persists. Similarly Debye somewhat later (1944) ascribed light-scattering from macromolecular solutions to time-averaged fluctuations in the number densities or concentrations, of the macro-molecular solute particles. In these measurements the total intensity[†] of the scattered light is determined. In recent years the availability of mono-chromatic coherent laser sources made possible the measurement of the spatial and temporal evolution of the fluctuations, rather than their time-averaged values only. Motion of the scattering particles leads to 'flickering' in the intensity of the scattered light and the analysis of the phenomenon can be related to the over-all motion or internal flexing of the dissolved particles. By present-day modern techniques statistical fluctuations in the intensity of the scattered light can be directly evaluated by constructing the intensity auto-correlation function from the time-dependence of the intensity of the scattered light; this is known as intensity-fluctuation spectroscopy (Foord, Jakeman, Oliver, Pike, Blagrove, Wood, and Peacocke 1970; Cummins and Pike **1974**). More conventionally it has been customary to measure the frequency-broadening, the spectrum of the scattered beam. This is the Fourier transform of the correlation function, and the two quantities

---

† We are using the term 'intensity' of the incident and scattered beams in rather loose fashion. Purists (Kaye and Havlik 1973) prefer the terms irradiance and radiant intensity respectively, and the reader is referred to specialized texts for the definition of the optical beam in precise terms in relation to the classical photomultiplier detecting devices.

are related by the Wiener–Khinchine theorem (Davidson **1962**). In view of the very small Doppler spectral-broadening (from a few Hz to a few kHz as compared to the frequency (10^{14} Hz) of the optical carrier wave) special techniques known as optical mixing spectroscopy (Benedek **1969**; Cummins and Swinney **1970**; Pecora **1972**; Chu **1974**) had to be developed. These may be compared to heterodyne detection, for instance in the analysis of modulated radio waves, where the acoustic signals are extracted from the high-frequency carrier wave by the method of beats.

For a summary of theoretical aspects and various application of laser-light scattering to solutions of biological macromolecules we refer to the articles of Peticolas (**1972**), Ford (**1972**), and Cummins (**1974**); a very extensive general bibliography is given in a review of Fleury and Boon (**1973**).

From both intensity fluctuation spectroscopy or optical mixing spectroscopy translational and rotational diffusion coefficients, internal motion and flexibility, or electrophoretic mobility in an external electrical field (Ware and Flygare 1972) may be determined. The advantage of these methods is that artificial concentration gradients required in the conventional experiments do not have to be established.

The classical study of the angular dependence of the integrated time averaged intensity of the scattering of electromagnetic radiation constitutes a powerful method in the study of the properties of macromolecules in solution. Scattering by visible light is limited in that the spectral region accessible to experimentation extends over a relatively narrow range of frequencies only. The ultraviolet part of the spectrum is not suitable for scattering studies because solutions of biopolymers absorb radiation in this range; similar reasons, and also the fact that scattering strongly decreases with increasing wavelength, prevent the use of the low-frequency visible and near-visible spectrum. The essential complementarity of small-angle X-ray scattering (SAXS) and visible-light scattering (LS) provides a convenient way of extending the range accessible to either method. The scattering of light and X-rays as applied to solutions of nucleic acids has recently been reviewed by Eisenberg (**1971**); various aspects particular to scattering from solution of proteins have been reviewed by Timasheff and Townend (**1970**), Pessen, Kumosinski, and Timasheff (**1973**), and Pittz, Lee, Bablouzian, Townend, and Timasheff (**1973**).

From the frequency-unshifted elastic scattering of electromagnetic radiation in solutions of high-molecular-weight materials we derive information on three parameters relevant to the solute: (1) the molecular weight of the particles; (2) the interaction between particles as manifested in the second and higher virial coefficients; and (3) information on the distribution of mass and the volume of the particles. From the shape of the angular dependence of the scattering curve it is possible to characterize the particle in terms of a globular, random or worm-like coil, or rod-line structure. Most aspects of scattering were analysed by Debye less than 30 years ago (see McIntyre and Gornick **1964**), when he showed that the determination of Rayleigh scattering could provide an absolute measurement of molecular weights of polymeric substances, the usefulness of the method exceeding by far the limited range of osmotic-pressure determinations. In this book we shall be interested mainly in the thermodynamic aspects of the phenomenon, as derived from the statistical theory of time-averaged fluctuations. Physically we can visualize random thermal forces acting upon a microscopic part of a system, containing a fixed mass of one component, to produce fluctuations in density of this component and in concentrations of the other components (Stockmayer 1950). With these fluctuations are associated variations in refractive index from the macroscopic average, the effect of which is to cause scattering of incident radiation, as predicted by electromagnetic theory. Since the production of fluctuations requires work against gradients of chemical potentials, the methods of statistical thermodynamics can be used to derive the dependence of the observed electromagnetic effect upon the thermo-dynamic properties of the system. We shall mostly consider the particular aspects which derive from the fact that the systems of interest to us in this work contain more than two components (most of the discussion as before will be limited to an analysis of three-component systems) and that we are dealing with ionic species. The latter fact may pose certain limitations with respect to the condition of electroneutrality of microscopic fluctuating volumes in the systems. The phenomena associated with scattering of coherent laser-light and molecular motion lead to a convenient way of evaluation of diffusion coefficients and will therefore be briefly considered in relation to our discussion of transport phenomena.

For studies of dilute solutions of macromolecules, the equations for both LS and SAXS can be deduced from the Rayleigh–Debye–Gans approxi-mation (see Chapter 8 of Kerker **1969**) for scattering from an assembly of optically isotropic particles.† If the particles are non-interacting, then the total scattering from the system is the sum of the scattering from the individual particles. For interacting particles we will derive the total scatter-ing intensity on the basis of the Einstein–Debye treatment of fluctuations (under suitable thermodynamic restrictions) of density and concentrations. Whereas for two-component systems and short-range interactions, mutual interactions between macromolecules are eliminated at high dilutions, prefer-ential interactions between macromolecular solute and solvent persist in mixed multi-component solvent systems at the limit of vanishing solute concentrations. Solutions of biological macromolecules, more often than

---

† It is required that the particles do not distort the field of the incident beam. For very large particles of refractive index different enough from that of the medium, this condition may fail seriously. For most proteins and other biological materials the error is probably insignificant.

not, contain additional salts of low-molecular weight salts or buffer components. They therefore constitute mixed solvent systems to which these
considerations are applicable. Although the theoretical analysis of scattering
from multi-component systems was essentially carried through by Zernicke
(1918) many years ago, his work remained virtually unknown until similar
further developments made independently by Brinkman and Hermans (1949),
Kirkwood and Goldberg (1950), and more recently Shogenji (1953) and Ooi
(1958) finally provided relations free of inadequate approximations suggested
by the much simpler treatment of two-component systems. In the theoretical
derivation, we shall follow Stockmayer (1950), and in the formulation of
practical aspects of the problem, the work of Casassa and Eisenberg (1960,
1964), and note that an equivalent treatment has independently been derived
by Vrij and Overbeek (1962). Basic aspects of light-scattering are very
clearly presented by Tanford (**1961**).

4.2. The effect of charge

Scattering theory in charged systems faces a difficulty in that, in low-ionic-
strength solutions (less than 10^{-3} M) the range of electrostatic forces becomes comparable to the wavelength of the light. In these cases interparticle
interference effects occur (Doty and Steiner 1952) and fluctuation theory,
which assumes that fluctuations in neighbouring volumes are independent,
becomes inadequate (Hermans 1949). Only electroneutral fluctuations are
taken into account in the theory to be developed below. We must therefore
attempt to state the conditions under which electroneutral fluctuations are
deemed adequate to describe the scattering phenomena in the sense that
the macromolecular particles plus their complete surroundings are the
scattering units. We shall see that we can account for solute–solvent interaction, negative absorption due to Donnan effects and specific binding of
low-molecular-weight components as long as deviations from electroneutrality may be disregarded.

   Following Vrij and Overbeek (1962), we divide a scattering solution into
volume elements dV (Fig. 4.1). Fluctuation theory may apply to these volume
elements if, on the one hand, they are small enough, with respect to the
wavelength of the light, to keep phase differences negligible; on the other
hand they must be large enough to make concentration fluctuations in a
given volume element independent of those in the neighbouring volume
elements (Hermans 1949). The maximum phase difference of light rays (with
wavelength λ_m in the medium) scattered under an angle θ by the volume
element is equal to $(2d/\lambda_m)\sin(\frac{1}{2}\theta)$, where d is the thickness of the volume
element. To satisfy the first of our conditions this quantity must be small
with respect to unity. To satisfy the second of our conditions the size of
the particles and the range r of the intermolecular forces should be small

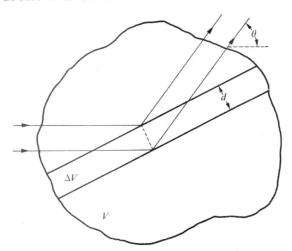

FIG. 4.1. Light scattered by the element ΔV, of thickness d, has a maximum phase difference $(2d/\lambda_m)\sin\frac{1}{2}\theta$. (From Vrij and Overbeek 1962.)

with respect to the thickness d of the volume element $(r \ll d)$. This can be achieved at all scattering angles for short-range forces and visible light. For long-range forces though it is necessary to reduce θ considerably so that $(2r/\lambda_m)\sin(\frac{1}{2}\theta)$ becomes small with respect to unity.

In systems which contain charged particles such as nucleic acids, proteins, polyelectrolytes, and simple electrolytes a measure of the range of electrostatic forces is provided by the thickness κ_{DH}^{-1} of the Debye–Hückel ionic atmosphere;

$$\kappa_{DH}^2 = (4\pi e^2/DkT)\sum v_i^2 \rho_i, \tag{4.1}$$

where D is the relative permittivity of the medium, k is the Boltzman constant, e is the electronic charge, and v_i and ρ_i are the valency and number density respectively of the ith ionic species. For a $0.1\,M$ solution of a uni–univalent electrolyte κ_{DH}^{-1} equals $10\,\text{Å}$ and for a $10^{-3}\,M$ electrolyte solution κ_{DH}^{-1} equals $100\,\text{Å}$. According to Hermans (1949) non-electroneutral fluctuations may be neglected relative to electroneutral fluctuations in volume elements whose linear dimensions exceed κ_{DH}^{-1}. For deviations to be less than 1 per cent, $(2/\kappa_{DH}\lambda_m)\sin\frac{1}{2}\theta$ should be about 0.05, which is a condition easily met in scattering with visible light when the ionic strength is $10^{-3}\,M$ or larger, at all scattering angles. Conditions in small-angle X-ray scattering (see p. 81) may be more restrictive in view of the much smaller value of the wavelength ($\sim 1.5\,\text{Å}$) used in these studies.

4.3. Basic equations for LS in multi-component systems

Light incident on a sample from which scattering is to be observed subjects the sample to an electromagnetic alternating field with a frequency in the range of 10^{14}–10^{15} Hz. In response to this field the electrons in the sample become a source of secondary dipole radiation. The induced electric dipole moment p may be expanded in terms of the electric field. We write, in somewhat simplified fashion,

$$p = \alpha E_0, \tag{4.2}$$

where E_0 is the field strength of the incident field and α is the polarizability of the particle. In more precise fashion we should note the particles under study may be optically anisotropic and that both p and E_0 may depend on direction. Therefore for α we should substitute components of a nine-component tensor; also higher terms in the field may appear, in particular with the use of powerful laser sources. For our present discussion eqn (4.2) is quite adequate.

A volume of solution containing N identical scattering particles is illuminated with a plane-polarized monochromatic radiation of circular frequency ω (v is the linear frequency and $\omega = 2\pi v$). The light (see Fig. 4.2) is propagated along the y-axis and polarized along the z-axis. Scattering is observed in the x, y-plane only, at distance r from the scattering sample; θ is the scattering angle formed by the y-axis and the direction of scattering. For forward scattering $\theta = 0°$, and $\theta = 90°$ corresponds to scattering along the x-axis. The field of the incident light is given by

$$E_0 = A_0 \exp i(\mathbf{k}_0 . \mathbf{r} - \omega_0 t), \tag{4.3}$$

where $\mathbf{r} = 0$ is an arbitrary reference point and the wave vector $\mathbf{k}_0$ of the incident light is given by

$$\mathbf{k}_0 = (2\pi n/\lambda)\mathbf{n}_0 .$$

$\mathbf{n}_0$ is a unit vector in the direction of the incident beam, n is the refractive index of the medium, and λ is the wavelength of the light *in vacuo*. The incident beam arrives at plane I with all rays in phase. Each scattered ray though will arrive at the detector with a phase depending on the distance travelled by it. If $\mathbf{n}_s$ is a unit vector in the direction of the scattered beam then the angle between $\mathbf{n}_0$ and $\mathbf{n}_s$ is the scattering angle θ.

The field observed at r due to the jth scatterer is given by

$$E_j = A_j \exp i(\phi_j - \omega_0 t). \tag{4.4}$$

If the position of the jth scatterer is r_j and the phase ϕ is chosen zero for a scatterer at the origin then

$$\phi_j = (\mathbf{k}_0 - \mathbf{k}_s) . \mathbf{r}_j = \mathbf{q} . \mathbf{r}_j . \tag{4.5}$$

For slowly moving scatterers $|\mathbf{k}_0| \approx |\mathbf{k}_s|$ and we define $\mathbf{q}$ as

$$q \equiv |\mathbf{q}| \approx 2|\mathbf{k}_0|\sin{\tfrac{1}{2}\theta} = (4\pi n/\lambda)\sin{\tfrac{1}{2}\theta} . \tag{4.6}$$

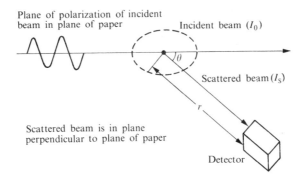

Plane of polarization of incident
beam in plane of paper

Incident beam (I_0)

Scattered beam (I_s)

r

Scattered beam is in plane
perpendicular to plane of paper

Detector

FIG. 4.2. Geometry of light-scattering experiment.

For the total scattered field at the detector we have

$$E_s = \sum_{j=1}^{N} E_j = \sum_{j=1}^{N} A_j(t) \exp \mathrm{i}(\mathbf{q}.\mathbf{r}_j - \omega_0 t), \tag{4.7}$$

and A_j may be time-dependent with changing orientation of the scatterers. The intensity of the scattered radiation is given by the time-averaged square of the amplitude of the scattered light

$$I_s = \langle E_s . E_s^* \rangle, \tag{4.8}$$

and the asterisk refers to the complex conjugate of the electromagnetic field. For an assembly of N small particles which are not correlated with respect to position of motion, the intensity reduces to N times the square of the scattered amplitude A. Following the classical analysis by Lord Rayleigh of the scattering from a dilute gas (see Tanford **1961**) the amplitude A is proportional to $\mathrm{d}^2 p/\mathrm{d}t^2$ and p is proportional to E_0 by eqn (4.2). We readily obtain Rayleigh's equation for I_s, the light scattered from unit volume, in the plane defined by the direction of propagation and perpendicular to the direction of polarization of the incident radiation (see Fig. 4.2)

$$R = 16\pi^4 \alpha^2 N/\lambda^4, \tag{4.9}$$

where R, equal to $r^2 I_s/I_0$, is known as the Rayleigh factor (the dimensions of R are cm^{-1}). The value of R in this experiment with vertically polarized incident light is independent of the scattering angle θ. With non-polarized incident radiation an angular-dependence factor (symmetric around $\theta = 90°$) must be considered (Tanford **1961**).

At the other extreme to the ideally non-interacting gas we find the perfect crystal, from which scattering does not occur, because of destructive interference of light at all scattering angles. Bragg's condition $\sin \theta = \lambda/2d$ (where d is a distance between scattering points, of the order of molecular dimensions) which leads to constructive interference in the case of X-ray diffraction for a small number of selected angles, is not satisfied in the present situation because usually $\lambda \gg d$. For pure liquids and for macromolecular solutions Einstein and Debye respectively approached the problem by dividing the solution into a large number of volume elements containing many molecules, but with linear dimensions small with respect to the wavelength λ. The polarizability α of each volume V element fluctuates at each moment around its equilibrium value and is therefore given by $(\alpha + \Delta\alpha)$. The mean-square time-averaged value $\overline{(\alpha + \Delta\alpha)^2}$ equals

$$\overline{(\alpha + \Delta\alpha)^2} = \alpha^2 + 2\alpha\overline{\Delta\alpha} + \overline{(\Delta\alpha)^2}. \tag{4.10}$$

The equilibrium value α is equal for all scattering volumes and the time-averaged fluctuation $\overline{\Delta\alpha}$ is equal to zero; therefore, in eqn (4.10) above only the mean-square-average fluctuation $\overline{(\Delta\alpha)^2}$ contributes to the scattering. We assume the system to be stationary and ergodic and therefore substitute the ensemble average $\langle(\Delta\alpha)^2\rangle$ for the time average $\overline{(\Delta\alpha)^2}$. We therefore obtain, for vertically polarized incident radiation,

$$R = (16\pi^4/\lambda^4 V)\langle(\Delta\alpha)^2\rangle, \tag{4.11}$$

where V^{-1} is the number of volume elements per millilitre and the remaining problem becomes the evaluation of $\langle(\Delta\alpha)^2\rangle$. For particles much smaller than λ, R is independent of the scattering angle θ, and for particles whose linear dimensions l are larger than or equal to $\lambda/20$ approximately, we determine $R(q)$ at finite scattering angles and extrapolate to $R(0)$ (which is equal to the value given by eqn (4.11)) by plotting (in general) $R(q)$ against q and extrapolating to the forward-scattering direction to $q = 0$ (Zimm 1946; Tanford 1961). The Rayleigh criterion for scattering requires $\lambda \gg l$; if this condition is not met but the refractive index (n_2) of the solute is close to that (n_0) of the solvent then the weaker Rayleigh–Gans criterion

$$2|k_0|l(n_2 - n_0) \ll 1$$

applies (Kerker 1969).

Changes in polarizability in the volume element exposed to an external radiation field are related to changes in refractive index n of the solution by the formula

$$(n^2 - n_0^2) = 4\pi\alpha/V, \tag{4.12}$$

from which we derive

$$\Delta\alpha = (nV/2\pi)\Delta n. \tag{4.13}$$

Substitution of $\Delta\alpha$ of eqn (4.13) into eqn (4.11) yields

$$R(0) = (4\pi^2 n^2 V/\lambda^4)\langle(\Delta n)^2\rangle, \tag{4.14}$$

where $\langle(\Delta n)^2\rangle$ is the mean-square refractive-index fluctuation.

For systems with no angular scattering disymmetry we may write for the turbidity τ,

$$\tau \equiv \ln(I_0/I) \tag{4.15}$$

(where I is the attenuated emergent beam intensity in the direction of the incident beam after passing through 1 cm of solution),

$$\tau = (16\pi/3)R. \tag{4.16}$$

In view of the set of thermodynamic variables to be used ultimately Stockmayer (1950) considered the fluctuation of index in a portion of solution containing a constant mass of one of the components. The choice of this component is arbitrary, but for dilute solutions it is convenient to choose the solvent, component 1, and to fix its quantity as 1 kg; the numbers of moles of component 2 and 3 are then expressed as weight molalities (mol kg^{-1} of component 1). The refractive index n is expressed as a function of temperature T, pressure P, and the molalities m_2 and m_3. We have

$$dn = \left(\frac{\partial n}{\partial T}\right)_{P,m} dT + \left(\frac{\partial n}{\partial P}\right)_{T,m} dP + \left(\frac{\partial n}{\partial m_2}\right)_{T,P,m_3} dm_2 + \left(\frac{\partial n}{\partial m_3}\right)_{T,P,m_2} dm_3. \tag{4.17}$$

On the assumption that n, at constant composition, is uniquely a function of density ρ eqn (4.17) may be written as

$$dn = (-\alpha_V dT + \kappa dP)(\partial n/\partial \ln \rho)_m + \Psi_2 dm_2 + \Psi_3 dm_3, \tag{4.18}$$

where α_V is the volume expansion coefficient

$$\alpha_V = -(\partial \ln \rho/\partial T)_m. \tag{4.19}$$

Application of the thermodynamic relationship

$$dV_m = \alpha_V V_m dT - \kappa V_m dP + \bar{V}_2 dm_2 + \bar{V}_3 dm_3 \tag{4.20}$$

yields

$$dn = (\partial n/\partial \ln \rho)_m (\bar{V}_2 dm_2 + \bar{V}_3 dm_3 - dV_m)/V_m + \Psi_2 dm_2 + \Psi_3 dm_3. \tag{4.21}$$

The aim of the calculation will now be to derive fluctuations of volume and of the m_i for a system in statistical equilibrium with surroundings in which constant values of T, P, and chemical potentials μ_2 and μ_3 are maintained; the quantity m_1 is fixed. The modified grand canonical partition function $Z(\beta, P, \mu_2, \mu_3)$ for this system (see Appendix 3, eqns (A3.6) and (A3.7)) is

$$Z = \exp(-\beta\mu_1 m_1) = \sum_{U,V,m_2,m_3} \Omega \exp\{-\beta(U + PV - \mu_2 m_2 - \mu_3 m_3)\}. \tag{4.22}$$

The desired fluctuations are obtained by appropriate differentiation of Z.

For instance,

$$(\partial Z/\partial \mu_2)_{T,P,\mu_3} = \sum \beta m_2 \Omega \exp\{-\beta(U+PV-\mu_2 m_2-\mu_3 m_3)\}$$
$$= \beta Z \langle m_2 \rangle \qquad (4.23)$$

and

$$(\partial Z/\partial \mu_3)_{T,P,\mu_2} = \beta Z \langle m_3 \rangle. \qquad (4.24)$$

By a second differentiation

$$(\partial^2 Z/\partial \mu_2 \partial \mu_3)_{T,P} = \beta^2 Z \langle m_2 m_3 \rangle. \qquad (4.25)$$

But from the last term of eqn (4.23) we can also obtain

$$(\partial^2 Z/\partial \mu_2 \partial \mu_3)_{T,P} = \beta \langle m_2 \rangle (\partial Z/\partial \mu_3)_{T,P,\mu_2} + \beta Z (\partial m_2/\partial \mu_3)_{T,P,\mu_2}$$
$$= \beta^2 Z \langle m_2 \rangle \langle m_3 \rangle + \beta Z (\partial m_2/\partial \mu_3)_{T,P,\mu_2}. \qquad (4.26)$$

In the derivative $(\partial m_2/\partial \mu_3)_{T,P,\mu_2}$, $\langle m_2 \rangle$ has been identified with the thermo-dynamic variable m_2. A comparison of eqns (4.25) and (4.26) yields

$$\beta \langle \Delta m_2 \Delta m_3 \rangle = \beta \langle m_2 m_3 \rangle - \beta \langle m_2 \rangle \langle m_3 \rangle$$
$$= (\partial m_2/\partial \mu_3)_{T,P,\mu_2} = (\partial m_3/\partial \mu_2)_{T,P,\mu_3}. \qquad (4.27)$$

Similarly one may derive the other fluctuations

$$\beta \langle \Delta V^2 \rangle = (\partial V_m/\partial P)_{T,\mu}$$
$$= \kappa V_m - \bar{V}_2 (\partial m_2/\partial P)_{T,\mu} - \bar{V}_3 (\partial m_3/\partial P)_{T,\mu} \qquad (4.28)$$

and

$$\beta \langle \Delta m_i \Delta V \rangle = (\partial V_m/\partial \mu_i)_{T,P,\mu} = (\partial m_i/\partial P)_{T,\mu}. \qquad (4.29)$$

Squaring eqn (4.21) and averaging, using eqns (4.27)–(4.29) for the fluctuations, we obtain

$$\beta \langle (\Delta n^2 \rangle = (\partial n/\partial \ln \rho)_m^2 V_m^{-2} \{ \sum \sum \bar{V}_i \bar{V}_j (\partial m_i/\partial \mu_j)_{T,P,\mu} + \kappa V_m + \sum \bar{V}_i (\partial m_i/\partial P)_{T,\mu} \}$$
$$+ 2(\partial n/\partial \ln \rho) V_m^{-1} \{ \sum \bar{V}_i \Psi_i (\partial m_i/\partial \mu_j)_{T,P,\mu} + \sum \Psi_i (\partial m_i/\partial P)_{T,\mu} \}$$
$$+ \sum \sum \Psi_i \Psi_j (\partial m_i/\partial \mu_j)_{T,P,\mu}. \qquad (4.30)$$

The summations extend over components 2 and 3. The last expression, because of $\bar{V}_i = (\partial \mu_i/\partial P)_{T,m}$ and

$$\left(\frac{\partial \mu_i}{\partial P}\right)_{T,m} \left(\frac{\partial m_i}{\partial \mu_j}\right)_{T,P} = -\left(\frac{\partial m_i}{\partial P}\right)_{T,\mu},$$

simplifies to

$$\beta \langle (\Delta n)^2 \rangle = \{ \kappa (\partial n/\partial \ln \rho)_m^2/V_m \} + \sum \sum \Psi_i \Psi_j (\partial m_i/\partial \mu_j)_{T,P,\mu}. \qquad (4.31)$$

The contribution from density fluctuations at constant composition is seen to be independent of the concentration fluctuations and is given by the well-known Einstein–Smoluchovski formula. Considering that corrections for scattering of the solvent are always made, this term will not be emphasized from now on. We therefore have, combining eqns (4.14) and (4.31), and writing R_ρ for the density fluctuation term,

$$R(0) = R_\rho + KV_m RT \sum \sum \Psi_i \Psi_j / (\partial \mu_i / \partial m_j)_{P,T,\mu}, \qquad (4.32)$$

where K denotes $4\pi^2 n^2 / N_A \lambda^4$ and V_m, the volume of solutions in millilitres containing 1 kg of principal solvent (component), has been chosen consistent with the molality units (mol kg^{-1} of component 1) used for the concentrations.

The optical factor K is proportional to the square of the refractive index of the solution, and it is therefore imprecise to regard it as a constant. Over the range of concentrations of macromolecular solutes ordinarily utilized for light-scattering measurements, however, the variation is very small. It should also be mentioned that, to a good approximation, changes in K are compensated by the change with refractive index of the irradiated volume 'seen' by the usual detector optical systems (Hermans and Levinson 1951), and therefore, for all intents and purposes, variations in K need not be of major concern.†

The partial derivatives $(\partial \mu_i / \partial m_j)_{P,T,\mu}$ in eqn (4.32) can be identified, on the strength of simple arguments similar to considerations presented on p. 36, with

$$(\partial \mu_i / \partial m_j)_{P,T,\mu} = RT |a_{ij}| / A_{ij}, \qquad (4.33)$$

and therefore, finally,

$$R(0) = R_\rho + KV_m \sum \sum \Psi_i \Psi_j \quad A_{ij} / |a_{ij}|. \qquad (4.34)$$

4.4. Practical equations for LS in a three-component system

Equ (4.34) can be immediately written down for the special case of the three-component system which is our main concern here,

$$R(0) = R_\rho + KV_m (\Psi_2^2 a_{33} - 2\Psi_2 \Psi_3 a_{23} + \Psi_3^2 a_{22}) / |a_{ij}|. \qquad (4.35)$$

The above equation can be rearranged by algebraic manipulations to the equivalent form

$$R(0) = R_\rho + KV_m \frac{\{\Psi_2 - (a_{23}/a_{33})\Psi_3\}^2}{a_{22} - a_{23}^2/a_{33}} + KV_m \frac{\Psi_3^2}{a_{33}}. \qquad (4.36)$$

---

† This conclusion has been challenged in a number of publications and no final conclusion may be reached with respect to the dependence of scattering on refractive index (see Wallace, Volosin, Delumyea, and Gingello (1972) for a summary of these studies). This uncertainty may affect the absolute values of scattering by a few per cent, which is probably inconsequential in most applications, considering other errors in the absolute calibration of scattering values.

The Rayleigh ratio for the solvent mixture (components 1 and 3 only) is given by

$$R^s(0) = R_\rho + (KV_m \Psi_3^2/a_{33})_{m_2=0} . \tag{4.37}$$

If we now deduct eqn (4.37) from eqn (4.36) and agree that whatever differences may exist between the scattering contributions of component 3 (the last terms on the right-hand sides of these equations) in the presence and absence respectively of component 2, is a negligible quantity as compared to the major term, we obtain for $\Delta R(0)$

$$\Delta R(0) \equiv R(0) - R^s(0) = KV_m \frac{\{\Psi_2 - (a_{23}/a_{33})\Psi_3\}^2}{a_{22} - a_{23}^2/a_{33}} . \tag{4.38}$$

By eqns (3.35) and (2.71)

$$(\partial n/\partial m_2)_{P,T,\mu_3} = \Psi_2 - (a_{23}/a_{33})\Psi_3 . \tag{4.39}$$

We substitute this equation and eqn (2.39) into eqn (4.38), transform to the c concentration scale by use of eqn (2.44),

$$(\partial V_m/\partial m_2)_{P,T,\mu_3} = \bar{V}_2 - (a_{23}/a_{33})\bar{V}_3 , \tag{4.40}$$

and eqn (2.51), to find, to a very good approximation,

$$\left(\frac{\partial n}{\partial c_2}\right)_{P,T,\mu_3}^2 \frac{Kc_2}{\Delta R(0)} \approx \frac{1}{RT}\frac{d\Pi}{dc_2} , \tag{4.41}$$

which shows the direct relationship between the light scattered and the osmotic work required to produce a change in concentration. For a more precise formulation the right-hand side of eqn (4.41) should be multiplied by a term

$$1 + \left(\kappa RT + \frac{\bar{V}_3^2}{V_m^0 a_{33}}\right)\frac{c_2}{M_2}$$

which reappears in the linear term in the concentration if the osmotic pressure is expanded in a virial series in powers of c_2 (eqn (1.2)),

$$\left(\frac{\partial n}{\partial c_2}\right)_{P,T,\mu_3}^2 \frac{Kc_2}{\Delta R(0)} = \frac{1}{M_2} + \left(2A_2 + \frac{\kappa RT}{M_2^2} + \frac{\bar{V}_3^2}{V_m^0 a_{33} M_2^2}\right)c_2 + \dots . \tag{4.42}$$

The correction term to $2A_2$ in eqn (4.42) is negligible in all situations of practical interest; it may be of some importance when M_2 is small, or when the second virial coefficient is made to vanish, for instance, in experiments in which the light-scattering technique is to be used for the precise location of the Flory temperature (Flory **1953**). But experiments may not be accurate enough to warrant this application (the value of a_{33} can be estimated by substituting for it its ideal value $1/2m_3$).

The major significance of eqns (4.41) and (4.42) lies in the restrictions specifying the refractive-index increment $(\partial n/\partial c_2)_{P,T,\mu}$. Thus, up to minor correction terms, these equations for multi-component systems formally represent the chemical equations for a two-component system, with the proviso that refractive increments be measured at constant chemical potentials of added electrolyte. This conclusion can also be reached by way of suitable definitions of components (Eisenberg and Casassa 1960), but the thermodynamic derivation is more general.

We now ask what error is committed if instead of the appropriate refractive-index increment $(\partial n/\partial c_2)_{P,T,\mu}$ in eqn (4.41) the conventional increments $\psi_2^{(c)}$ (eqn (3.32)) are used. We have by eqn (3.39), at vanishing concentration c_2,

$$(\partial n/\partial c_2)^0_\mu \approx (\partial n/\partial c_2)_{P,T,\mu_3} \approx \psi_2^{(c)0}\Omega = \psi_2^{(c)0}\left\{1 + \frac{\psi_{3,m_2=0}^{(c)}}{\psi_2^{(c)0}}(1 - c_3\bar{v}_3)\xi_3\right\}. \quad (4.43)$$

The magnitude of the correction term Ω thus depends on the ratio $\psi_3^{(c)}/\psi_2^{(c)}$, on the value of the preferential absorption parameter ξ_3, on salt concentration c_3, and on partial volume $\bar{v}_3$.

Acceptability of the assumption, sometimes made injudiciously in the past, that Ω is equal to unity within limits of experimental precision will depend on the system under study and definitions of components adopted explicitly or implicitly. In solutions of biological materials exhibiting typically low charge densities (such as proteins close to the isoelectric point) in the usual aqueous buffers, differences between $M_2\Omega^2$ and the molecular weight of component 2 defined without inclusion of interacting species (except for counter-ions required for electroneutrality) are likely to be rather small, though not entirely negligible. Casassa and Eisenberg (1961, **1964**) calculated from refractive-index data of Perlmann and Longsworth (1948) of iso-ionic serum albumin in 0·1 M NaCl, that the error in molecular weight would be only 0·5 per cent but would increase roughly to 5 per cent in 1 M NaCl; considerable errors may arise in the case of proteins in special solvents, such as 6 M GuHCl or urea, for instance, and in highly charged mixed solutions of nucleic acids and simple salts. Membrane distribution studies have shown strong interactions in nucleic acid solutions (Shack, Jenkins, and Thompsett 1952); hence, in solutions of polynucleotides equations for light-scattering have to be handled carefully. Similar conclusions apply to small-angle X-ray scattering (Section 4.7).

In solutions of highly charged synthetic polyelectrolytes, effects of preferential interactions with diffusible solute can be quite marked. Strauss and Wineman (1958) found Ω^2 for sodium polyphosphates (with the component defined 'simply' by the stoichiometric composition) to be 0·78 in 0·1 M and 0·71 in 0·4 M NaBr solution; similarly, Strauss and Ander (1962) found values of 0·625 and 0·424 for lithium polyphosphates, in 0·9 and 1·8 M LiBr respectively. Reasonably, these large effects may be supposed to be associated with the high charge densities of the macro-ions. Solutions of uncharged synthetic polymers in mixtures of two organic solvents have also been studied (Ewart, Roe, Debye, and McCartney 1946) in which preferential interactions between the polymers and one of the solvents, together with a non-vanishing value of Ψ_3 lead to apparent molecular weights grossly different from the true values. Even in solutions exhibiting strong preferential interactions, experimental conditions can, in principle and sometimes in practice (for example, Vrij and Overbeek 1962), be achieved to make Ω equal to unity. Eqn (4.43) indicates that in order to achieve this it is necessary to have $\psi^{(c)}_{3,m_2=0}$ equal to zero or, at suitable concentration c_3, $c_3 \bar{v}_3$ should be equal to unity.

Eqn (4.42) is the basis for unambiguous determination of molecular weight by light-scattering without the requirement of full knowledge of refractive increments and thermodynamic interactions for all solutes. A plot of the reciprocal scattering function versus concentration must extrapolate to an intercept $1/M_2$ and from the limiting slope of the linear plot A_2 is obtained directly (trivial approximations involving the compressibility of the solutions or the conversion of concentration units may affect the value of A_2 in a negligible way).

Questions sometimes arise as to which molecular weight is determined by light-scattering in multi-component systems, in particular cases. We recall a similar argument with respect to osmotic pressure on p. 22. Examination of eqn (4.42) shows that these questions, which have led to a great deal of confusion in past studies, are really quite irrelevant. Light-scattering is a colligative method, connected to the osmotic-pressure derivative and 'counts' rather than 'weighs' molecules. Molecular weights enter only because weight concentrations are being used. The molecular weight M_2, in the limit of vanishing concentration of component 2, is unambiguously defined in terms of the weight of material included in the definition of c_2. Eqn (4.42) shows that, in the limit $c_2 = 0$, multiplication of both c_2 and M_2 by an identical scale factor, leaves the equation unchanged. As long as the refractive-index increment has been measured under the proper restrictions $(\partial n/\partial c_2)_{P,T,\mu}$ binding of any low-molecular-weight component (diffusible through a semipermeable membrane) to the macromolecular species (without change in the molarity of the latter) does not change this result. The quantity $(\partial n/\partial c_2)^2_{P,T,\mu} c_2 M_2$ which appears in this combination in eqn (4.42) easily transforms (by substitution of eqn (2.4)) into the more basic (but less practical) expression $10^3(\partial n/\partial C_2)^2_{P,T,\mu} C_2$, or, by further substituting eqn (2.14) into the more useful form

$$10^3(\partial n/\partial C_u)^2_{P,T,\mu} C_u Z.$$

According to the latter result we have, in the limit $C_u = 0$,

$$10^3 \left(\frac{\partial n}{\partial C_u}\right)^2_{P,T,\mu} \frac{KC_u}{\Delta R(0)} = \frac{1}{Z}. \tag{4.44}$$

We can therefore reach the practical conclusion that if c_2 g of NaDNA, for instance, have been weighed into a millilitre of mixed solvent, and the concentration is expressed in these units, then the molecular weight will be given in (by eqn (4.42)) units of grams of NaDNA per mole. More likely concentrations will be measured in terms of an optical absorption coefficient which, in some way, can be related to the dry weight of a well-defined species. If C_u represents the number of moles of nitrogen atoms per litre (in a protein solution) then Z is the number of molecules of nitrogen per protein molecule. Or if C_u is the number of moles of phosphate atoms per litre (in a nucleic-acid solution) then Z is the number of nucleotides per nucleic acid macromolecule.

The practical application of this scheme for avoiding explicit measurements of Ω depends on the availability of a membrane permeable to all species except the macromolecular one. If dialysis is not possible, as for instance in soap micelles in equilibrium with unassociated monomer able to pass through the membrane, only the refractive-index increments at fixed pressure and composition can be measured, and hence additional measurements to determine Ω are ordinarily necessary. Vrij and Overbeek (1962) suggested a procedure to evaluate correct molecular weights, without resorting to equilibrium dialysis. They demonstrated the validity of their method for half-neutralized polymethacrylate acid in $0 \cdot 1$ M sodium-halide solutions. The polymethacrylate is a negatively charged macro-ion which attracts positive counter-ions and repels negatively charged co-ions. It is thus a fair assumption that these latter ions influence the preferential absorption coefficient ξ_3 to a lesser extent then the positively charged counter-ions which abound in the close vicinity of the macro-ion. Vrij and Overbeek therefore assume that the preferential absorption of the four sodium halides is the same for all co-ions (F^-, Cl^-, Br^-, and I^-). They show (Fig. 4.3) that a plot (see eqn (4.43)) of $(\partial n/\partial c_2)_\mu$ versus $\psi_3^{(c)}$ is linear and from the slope the preferential absorption coefficient may be derived (the term $(1 - c_3 \bar{v}_3)$ is rather close to unity in $0 \cdot 1$ M salt solution). In a different type of plot $(M_2^*)^{1/2} \equiv M_2^{1/2} \Omega$ experimentally obtained from

$$\psi_2^{(c)2} \frac{Kc_2}{\Delta R(0)} = \frac{1}{M^*}. \tag{4.45}$$

in the limit of $c_2 = 0$ is plotted (Fig. 4.4) against $M_3 \psi_3^{(c)}$ for the various salts. The correct value of M_2 (see eqn (4.44)) is obtained when these data are linearly extrapolated to $\psi_3^{(c)} = 0$. While this kind of consideration is useful for certain applications (see the work on reversible micelles, for instance; Overbeek, Vrij, and Huisman, **1963**; Kratohvil and DelliColli, 1970) it

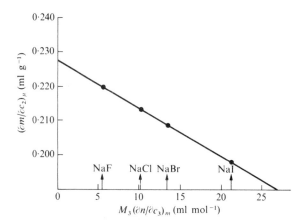

FIG. 4.3. Refractive-index increment at constant chemical potential of solution of Na–poly-methacrylate in 0·1 M simple salt, plotted against molar refractive-index increment of the salt. (From Vrij and Overbeek 1962.)

implies an empirical assumption, and the reader should distinguish carefully between certain approximations, which introduce errors the magnitude of which can be evaluated, and *ad hoc* assumptions which are often necessary, but the validity of which cannot *a priori* be established.

One final remark with respect to dialysis. While according to eqn (4.42) the refractive-index increments $(\partial n/\partial c_2)_{P,T,\mu_3}$ or $(\partial n/\partial c_2)_{T,\mu}$ derived from equilibrium dialysis are the quantities prescribed, the solutions used in the light-scattering experiments proper do not have to be dialysed, should this be inconvenient or not advisable because of scarcity of the biological macro-molecule. At low concentrations of component 2 $m_3 \approx m_3'$ and it is of relatively minor consequence whether the scattering occurs at concentrations m_3 or m_3' of component 3. The relevant argument is that, as described earlier in this chapter, fluctuations occur at constant P, T, and μ_3, from which we have derived that $(\partial n/\partial c_2)_{P,T,\mu}$ is the appropriate increment. The scattering though in dilute solutions with respect to component 2 is essentially unaffected whether or not the polymer solutions are prepared by dialysis.

We conclude this section with a brief remark with respect to polydispersity characterized by a common index increment for all macromolecular species, independent of molecular weight. Consider a collection of particles char-acterized by identical refractive-index increment but dissimilar in size (for the usual DNA, for instance, $(\partial n/\partial c_2)_{T,\mu}$ is not sensitive to composition— GC content—in a significant way). We have (for $c_2 \to 0$)

$$R(0) = K' \sum c_i M_i, \qquad (4.46)$$

where $K' \equiv K(\partial n/\partial c_2)^2_{P,T,\mu}$ and the summation is over all species i, and

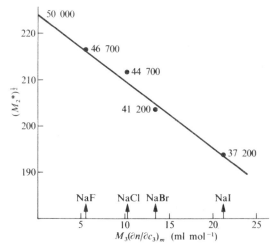

FIG. 4.4. Square-root of the apparent molecular weight M_2^* of Na–polymethacrylate plotted against molar refractive-index increment of salt. (From Vrij and Overbeek 1962.)

$\sum_i c_i = c_2$, the total concentration. The weight-average molecular weight is given by

$$M_w = \sum c_i M_i / c_i$$

and substitution into eqn (4.46) shows that indeed M_w is obtained

$$\{K'c_2/R(0)\}_{c_2 \to 0} = 1/M_w. \tag{4.47}$$

This is the usual result in light-scattering of polydisperse particles. The virial coefficient A_2 in a polydisperse system is biased toward contributions from species of higher molecular weight and exact expressions can be specified (Casassa and Eisenberg **1964**). For other related phenomena such as optical anisotropy or information to be derived from the angular dependence of scattering we refer to Tanford (**1961**), Timasheff and Townend (**1970**), and Eisenberg (**1971**).

4.5. Small-angle X-ray scattering (SAXS) in multi-component systems, and the angular dependence of LS and SAXS

The essential complimentarity of SAXS and scattering with visible light provides a convenient way of extending the range accessible to either method (Timasheff **1963**; see also Finch and Holmes **1967**, Kratky and Pilz **1972**, and Pessen, Kumosinski, and Timasheff (**1973**) for recent reviews of the subject). SAXS, as well as LS, can be deduced from the Rayleigh–Gans approximation for scattering from an assembly of optically isotropic particles (see Guinier and Fournet **1955**; Beeman, Kaesberg, Anderegg, and Webb

1957). The analysis of SAXS, as well as that of classical Rayleigh scattering with visible light (p. 75), must take proper account of the problems earlier discussed in the thermodynamics of multi-component systems. To determine the angular dependence of scattering intensity we return to eqn (4.7) for the scattered field E_s and eqn (4.8) for the total intensity I_s, but now consider all correlated scattering elements to be part of a single macromolecule, fixed in space for the present moment. From eqns (4.7) and (4.8) we now have

$$I_s = A^2 \left\langle \sum_{j=1}^{N} \exp(i\mathbf{q}.\mathbf{r}_j) \sum_{j=1}^{N} \exp(-i\mathbf{q}.\mathbf{r}_l) \right\rangle$$

$$= A^2 \sum_{j=1}^{N} \sum_{l=1}^{N} \exp\{-i\mathbf{q}.(\mathbf{r}_l - \mathbf{r}_j)\}, \qquad (4.48)$$

where both $\mathbf{r}_l$ and $\mathbf{r}_j$ are independent of time. For $q = 0$, $I_s = A^2 N^2$, and we define a function

$$P(q) \equiv I(q)/I(0) = \frac{1}{N^2} \sum_{j=1}^{N} \sum_{l=1}^{N} \langle \cos \mathbf{q}.\mathbf{r}_{jl} \rangle \qquad (4.49)$$

where $\mathbf{r}_{jl} = \mathbf{r}_j - \mathbf{r}_l$ and eqn (4.49) has been obtained by taking only the real part of eqn (4.48) and assuming that the average of the sum is equal to the sum of the average. For freely rotating scatterers Debye averaged over all angles (see Tanford **1961**) and obtained

$$P(q) = \frac{1}{N^2} \sum_{j=1}^{N} \sum_{l=1}^{N} \frac{\sin \mathbf{q}.\mathbf{r}_{jl}}{\mathbf{q}.\mathbf{r}_{jl}}, \qquad (4.50)$$

which can be evaluated for various shapes. The reader can easily verify that $P(0)$ equals unity, as expected. For all other values of q, $P(q)$ determines the factor by which the scattering is reduced because of destructive interference for particles with non-negligible dimensions as compared to λ. To analyse SAXS we return to the fundamental equation (4.11), but introduce the function $P(q)$ to take into account the dependence of I_s on q.† We have (subscript s is dropped henceforth)

$$\frac{I(q)}{I_0} = \frac{16\pi^4}{r^2\lambda^4 V} \langle (\Delta\alpha)^2 \rangle P(q). \qquad (4.51)$$

Only in some occasions, in SAXS studies, in the case of rather small macro-molecules, is it possible to extrapolate to $q = 0$, and in most cases the investigation of the angular dependence of scattering at finite values of q is the major object in SAXS. In distinction from light waves, X-rays travel through matter in practically straight lines (Prock and McConkey **1962**) and

---

† In SAXS studies, the scattering angle is usually designated 2θ and $i_n(q)$ is the factor represented by $P(q)$ in light-scattering studies. We shall adhere to uniform notation (corresponding to light-scattering notation) in this book.

the refractive index for X-rays is very close to unity. The scattering I_{el} of an electron is given by

$$I_{el}/I_0 = (16\pi^4/r^2\lambda^4)\alpha_{el}^2,$$ (4.52)

where α_{el} is the polarizability of an electron, and combination of eqns (4.52) and (4.51) yields

$$I(q) = (I_{el}/V\alpha_{el}^2)\langle(\Delta\alpha)^2\rangle P(q).$$ (4.53)

We disregard temperature and pressure fluctuations and consider concentration fluctuations only

$$d\alpha = \sum_i \left(\frac{\partial\alpha}{\partial m_i}\right)_{P,T,m} dm_i$$ (4.54)

and

$$\left(\frac{\partial\alpha}{\partial m_i}\right)_{P,T,m} = \left(\frac{\partial\rho_{el}}{\partial m_i}\right)_{P,T,m} \rho_{el} V_m,$$ (4.55)

where ρ_{el} is the density in electrons per millilitre and we consider scattering from a volume V_m containing a fixed number of electrons of component 1.

Substitution of eqn (4.55) into eqn (4.54), squaring and taking the average $\langle(\Delta\alpha)^2\rangle$ and introducing into eqn (4.53) leads to

$$I(q) = I_{el} V_m \left\{ \sum\sum \left(\frac{\partial\rho_{el}}{\partial m_i}\right)_{P,T,m} \left(\frac{\partial\rho_{el}}{\partial m_j}\right)_{P,T,m} \langle\Delta m_i \Delta m_j\rangle \right\} P(q).$$ (4.56)

We now introduce the concentration fluctuation as derived in eqn (4.27) and obtain, together with eqn (4.33)

$$I(q) = (I_{el} V_m/N_A) \left\{ \sum\sum \left(\frac{\partial\rho_{el}}{\partial m_i}\right)_{P,T,m} \left(\frac{\partial\rho_{el}}{\partial m_j}\right)_{P,T,m} \frac{A_{ij}}{|a_{ij}|} \right\} P(q).$$ (4.57)

We follow arguments analogous to the considerations developed in Section 4.4 and reach the final result, after transformation from molalities to volume concentrations, and in the limit $c_2 = 0$,

$$\frac{I_{el}}{N_A}\left(\frac{\partial\rho_{el}}{\partial c_2}\right)_{P,T,\mu}^2 \frac{c_2}{\Delta I(q)} = \frac{1}{M_2 P(q)}.$$ (4.58)

$\Delta I(q)$ means that we have corrected for the scattering of the solvent and the electron density increment $(\partial\rho_{el}/\partial c_2)_{P,T,\mu}$ is completely analogous to the refractive-index increment at constant chemical potential of diffusible solutes, of eqn (4.42). We can of course easily extend the validity of eqn (4.58) to finite concentrations by addition of virial coefficients in powers of c_2.

Before proceeding further we must qualify the range within which the treatment based on the assumption of independent electroneutral fluctuations is valid for SAXS in solutions of ionized macromolecules. We have seen in Section 4.2, based on the discussion of Hermans (1949) and Vrij and Overbeek (1962) that, in order to keep deviations below 1 per cent, q/κ_{DH} (where κ_{DH}^{-1} is the thickness of the Debye–Hückel atmosphere) should be smaller than 0·05. In solutions of 1:1 electrolytes in water at 25 °C, κ_{DH}^{-1} equals $3·043 \times C_3^{-0·5}$ Å; C_3 is the concentration of electrolyte, in mol l^{-1} (see Harned and Owen **1958**). Thus in 10^{-3} M and 10^{-1} M NaCl, for instance, q should be smaller than 0·0005 or 0·005, respectively. This, as we have already seen, is easily realized for light-scattering with visible light at all scattering angles (for a maximum scattering angle of 180° and $\lambda = 5460$ Å, $q \approx 0·00049$). On the other hand, for SAXS ($\lambda = 1·54$ Å for Cu $K\alpha$ radiation) and in 10^{-1} M 1:1 electrolyte solution, the scattering angle should not exceed 0·008 rad ($\sim 0·45°$), for q to stay below 0·005. This is a fairly serious restriction in terms of the fluctuation theory developed above and the absolute scattering at higher resolution is not easily predictable.

Problems related to the angular dependence of scattering are beyond the fundamental subject matter of this book and will not be treated extensively. The problem though is so basic to the methods of LS and SAXS that we will briefly compare here the range of q in which these two methods are applicable, as well as the information which can be obtained by either method. This is best seen by examination of Fig. 4.5, taken from Finch and Holmes (**1967**). In the forward direction of scattering ($q = 0$) interference effects are eliminated ($P(q)$ is equal to unity). In scattering at all other angles interference occurs for a solution composed of 'large' particles. In a diffraction experiment on randomly oriented dissolved particles we record, in the limit of vanishing concentration $c_2 \to 0$ the spherical average of the square of the Fourier transform per particle. Fig. 4.5 shows the origin peak of the particle transform (actually the normalized function $P(q)$) for two particles: (1) a small spherical particle of radius 100 Å; and (2) a rod-like particle of length 3000 Å and diameter 150 Å, corresponding, respectively, to a globular protein and a molecular similar to tobacco mosaic virus. The regions explored by either LS or SAXS are shaded.

The wavelengths most commonly used in LS are the mercury lines at $\lambda = 4358$ Å and 5461 Å (presently the use of laser beams has extended this range over almost the whole visible spectrum), and the scattering angles explore the angular range from about 10° to 150°; the corresponding quantities in SAXS are $\lambda = 1·54$ Å for Cu $K\alpha$ radiation, and scattering angles as low as 0·0015–0·00015 rad. In both instances upon extrapolation of the scattering intensity to $q = 0$ and $c = 0$, the true molecular weight is obtained (eqns (4.42) and (4.58)). The scattering intensity extrapolated to $q = 0$ is independent of the shape of the particles and depends on molecular weight only; both $\Delta R(0)/(\partial n/\partial c_2)^2_{P,T,\mu} K c_2$ and $\Delta I(0) N_A/(\partial \rho/\partial c_2)^2_{P,T,\mu} I_{el} c_2$ equal M_2 in the limit $c_2 = 0$.

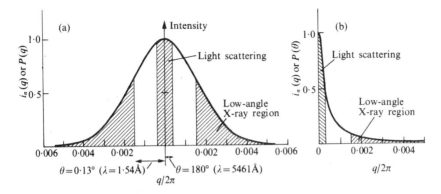

F I G. 4.5. Comparison of LS and SAXS, according to Finch and Hólmes (**1967**). Particle scattering factor versus $q/2\pi$: (a) Small spherical particle (radius 100 Å); (b) Rod particle of length 3000 Å and diameter 150 Å. This corresponds to tobacco mosaic virus particle. With modern techniques the range of SAXS may be extended lower, to overlap with the LS range.

For molecular-weight determinations it is necessary to have an absolute calibration (possibly in terms of a secondary standard) of the scattered intensity, and the values of the refractive-index and electron-density increments. The shape of the origin peak in Fig. 4.5 around $q = 0$ is (when $c_2 = 0$) independent of the shape of the particle and depends on the distribution of mass in the particle only. Guinier's (1939) approximation yields $-R_g^2/3$ as the limiting slope in the plot of either $\ln \Delta I(q)$ or $\ln \Delta R(q)$ against q^2; R_g^2 is the mean-square radius (of gyration) and is independent of the exact nature of the particle shape. For rigid particles or for a given fixed conformation of a flexible particle

$$R_g \equiv \left(\sum m_i r_i^2 / \sum m_i\right)^{\frac{1}{2}}, \tag{4.59}$$

where we consider m_i mass elements each located at distance r_i from the centre of the mass. Thus the interecpt of a plot of $\ln \{\Delta R(q)/(\partial n/\partial c_2)_{P,T,\mu}^2 K c_2\}$ or of $\ln \{\Delta I(q) N_A/(\partial \rho_{el}/\partial c_2)_{P,T,\mu}^2 I_{el} c_2\}$ against q^2 yields $\ln M_2$, and the limiting slope of these plots equals $-R_g^2/3$. Neither absolute scattering values nor the values of the constants or the refractive-index or density increments are required for the determination of R_g.

In LS it is customary to use the Zimm (1948) plot for the double extrapolation to zero angle and zero concentration. The method is equivalent to Guinier's method, if the exponential in

$$\Delta R(q)/\Delta R(0) = \exp(-R_g^2 q^2/3) \tag{4.60}$$

is expanded for small enough values of q. It is usually customary to use Guinier's plot in SAXS and Zimm's plot in LS.

With increasing values of q more detailed information about the shape and the size of the particles may be obtained.† A suitable model must be assumed. For the sake of an example we chose a model appropriate to an idealization of DNA molecules, namely a cylinder of length L and radius r; for this model

$$R_g^2 = \tfrac{1}{2}r^2 + \tfrac{1}{12}L^2. \tag{4.61}$$

Here $\tfrac{1}{2}r^2$ is equal to r_g^2, the mean-square radius (of gyration) of the cross-section.

The complete particle scattering factor $P(q)$ for N scattering elements was derived by Debye (1915) (eqn (4.50)) and correctly yields Guinier's (or Zimm's) approximation, when expanded for low values of the argument $\mathbf{q} \cdot \mathbf{r}_{ij}$. For long, thin rods the particle scattering factor was obtained by Neugebauer (1943) to be

$$\frac{2}{qL} \int_0^{qL} \frac{\sin w}{w}\,dw - \left(\frac{\sin \tfrac{1}{2}qL}{\tfrac{1}{2}qL}\right)^2. \tag{4.62}$$

For values $qL \gg 1$ (but $\mathbf{q} \cdot \mathbf{r} \ll 1$) we have

$$\frac{q\Delta I(q)N_A}{I_{el}(\partial \rho_{el}/\partial c_2)^2_{P,T,\mu}c_2} = \frac{q\Delta R(q)}{K(\partial n/\partial c_2)^2_{P,T,\mu}c_2}$$

$$= \frac{M_2}{L}\left(\pi - \frac{2}{Lq}\right), \tag{4.63}$$

which asymptotically approaches $\pi M/L$ with increasing values of q. This (see Fig. 4.5(b)) is the range in which (for elongated particles) SAXS is particularly useful, but asymptotic extrapolation of LS to high angles may also yield M/L (see Eisenberg 1971). Sometimes (Sadron, Pouyet, Freund, and Champagne 1965) in LS the asymptotic behaviour is plotted in the form

$$\left(\frac{\partial n}{\partial c_2}\right)^2_{P,T,\mu} \frac{Kc_2}{\Delta R(q)} = \frac{2}{\pi^2 M_2} + \frac{L}{M_2}\frac{q}{M_2}. \tag{4.64}$$

Thus the plot of $(\partial n/\partial c_2)^2_{P,T,\mu} Kc_2/\Delta R(q)$ against q yields a straight line with the slope L/M_2 and the intercept is equal to $2/\pi^2 M$. If the particle is not rigidly rod-like, or has flexible joints, the intercept may become negative and interesting information with respect to DNA structure and flexibility may in principle be obtained. For the determination of the mass per unit length M/L absolute calibration of the scattered intensity and values for the other constants are required.

---

† We refer to Chapter 8 in the work of Kerker (1969) for a more detailed critical discussion of size parameters which can be obtained from the analysis of Rayleigh–Debye scattering from solutions of macromolecules. Kerker also reviews LS of multi-component solutions (Chapter 9) and problems raised by optical anisotropy (Chapter 10) in the absence and presence of external fields.

With q increasing even further the asymptotic expression becomes sensitive to r and for the right-hand side of eqn (4.63) it is possible to write

$$(\pi M_2/L)\exp(-r_g^2 q^2/2). \tag{4.65}$$

This region is beyond the resolution of LS but is accessible to SAXS— provided that, in charged systems, the values of q correspond to volume elements which are large enough for independent electroneutral fluctuations. In the case of DNA solutions this restriction has not yet been convincingly tested. Again, for the determination of r_g, absolute calibration and the value of the various constants is not required.

Whenever LS and SAXS are discussed together, contributions relating to the size and shape of the particles, coming from the origin peak only, are considered. With increasing values of q, additional, much weaker side bands and maxima may appear. For systems extending over molecular and macromolecular dimensions, these are seen with SAXS only. A detailed analysis of the shape of the SAXS curve may be quite rewarding in the case of nucleic acid, ribosome, and protein systems. SAXS may provide information, for example, on the volume of the particles, or inhomogeneities in the distribution of the mass. For the most recent comprehensive reviews of this field we refer to Kratky and Pilz (**1972**) and Pessen et al. (**1973**).

To average the root-mean-square radius R_g in a polydisperse system we write, at $c_2 = 0$,

$$\Delta R(q) = (\partial n/\partial c_2)^2_{P,T,\mu} K \sum c_i M_i P_i(q), \tag{4.66}$$

and obtain at low angles, with the use of Guinier's law, or Zimm's expansion

$$(\partial n/\partial c_2)^2_{P,T,\mu} K c_2/\Delta R(q) = \sum c_i/\{\sum M_i c_i - \tfrac{1}{3}q^2 \sum M_i(R_g^2)_i c_i\}, \tag{4.67}$$

which is transformed to

$$(\partial n/\partial c_2)^2_{P,T,\mu} K c_2/\Delta R(q) = M_w^{-1}(1 + \langle R_g^2 \rangle_z \tfrac{1}{3}q^2), \tag{4.68}$$

where

$$\langle R_g^2 \rangle_z = \sum M_i c_i (R_g^2)_i / \sum M_i c_i \tag{4.69}$$

is the z-average of the mean-square radius; $(R_g^2)_i$ is for chain-like molecules, proportional to M_i^{2a}, where a increases from $a = 0.5$, for random coils, without excluded volume, to $a = 1$ for rigid rods. These are two extreme cases which may be consistent with very-long or very-short linear DNA, respectively. Thus, an experimentally determined R_g corresponds to an average molecular weight defined by

$$\langle M \rangle_{R_g} = (\sum c_i M_i^{1+2a}/c_i M_i)^{1/2a}; \tag{4.70}$$

for $a = 0.5$ this is the z-average molecular weight M_z and for $a = 1$ this is $(M_z M_{z+1})^{\frac{1}{2}}$.

For polydisperse rod-like particles the intercept in the asymptotic plot against q (eqn (4.64)), yields the number-average molecular weight M_n. Owing to deviations from this limiting model of ideal rods, it is not believed that M_n can be obtained with any degree of accuracy. In the case of polydisperse large gaussian chains M_w and $\langle R_g^2 \rangle_z$ are obtained from the analysis at low angles ($qR_g \ll 1$), whereas at high angles ($qR_g \gg 1$) the analysis, in principle, leads to M_n and $\langle R_g^2 \rangle_n$ (see Shultz and Stockmayer 1969).

4.6. Scattering in salt-free systems; the osmotic coefficient in polyelectrolyte systems

Even in the early days of polyelectrolyte research it had already been established that the properties of polyelectrolyte solutions in the absence of added simple salts are not simply explained in terms of the properties of single macromolecules. In salt-free aqueous solutions electrostatic forces are long-range and extend over large distances. It is thus more appropriate to consider the properties of the solutions as those of a system rather than as representative of the properties of the constituent molecules. Under those conditions we will obtain neither the molceular weight nor the dimensions of the simple particles. This situation has already been referred to on p. 19, where it was stated that the osmotic pressure may not be expanded in a virial series under these conditions. A particular striking illustration of this point is exemplified by the dependence of the reduced specific viscosity η_{sp}/c_2 upon c_2; the specific viscosity η_{sp} equals $(\eta - \eta^0)/\eta^0$, where η and η^0 are the viscosity of the solution and the solvent, respectively (see Chapter 7). In non-ionic polymer solutions $[\eta]$, which is the limit of η_{sp}/c_2 at $c_2 \to 0$, is a measure of the volume of the macromolecular coils (Flory **1953**, Tanford **1961**), and η_{sp}/c_2 increases moderately with increasing c_2. In the case of polyelectrolyte solutions, in the presence of high enough concentrations of salt, this behaviour is still observed (Armstrong and Strauss **1969**), in spite of the coil-expansion which occurs as a result of electrostatic repulsion in polyelectrolyte coils. In aqueous solution though, in the absence of salt, the behaviour is quite different and coil-expansion ceases to be the main factor responsible for the increase of η_{sp}/c_2 (see Fig. 4.6, taken from Eisenberg and Pouyet 1954); η_{sp}/c_2 increases with decrease in c_2, attains a maximum, and decreases with decreasing c_2 only at very low concentrations c_2 (in this range we expect the equivalent polyelectrolyte charge concentration to fall below the concentration of residual simple salt, which can never be completely eliminated from an aqueous solution). In the complete absence of salt we would expect η_{sp}/c_2 to increase to infinity with decreasing c_2: for polyelectrolytes in salt-free systems η_{sp}/c_2 does not converge, and properties of the coils, such as M_2 and coil dimensions, cannot be derived. (It is known that in simple electrolytes (Harned and Owen 1958) $\eta_{sp}/c_2^{\frac{1}{2}}$ is the proper

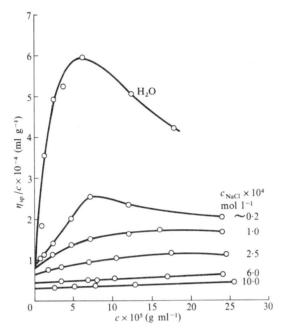

FIG. 4.6. Reduced specific viscosity η_{sp}/c of aqueous solutions of partially quaternized poly-vinylpyridine butyl bromide as a function of polymer and sodium chloride concentration. (From Eisenberg and Pouyet 1954.)

quantity to plot in this case.) Very low concentrations of simple electrolytes affect this situation drastically (Fig. 4.6). Already at a simple-salt concentration of 10^{-3} M NaCl most of the 'abnormal' effect has disappeared and the extrapolation to $c_2 = 0$ is easily performed. At 10^{-3} M NaCl (which we have shown in Section 4.2 to be a high enough simple-salt concentration to permit independent electroneutral concentration fluctuations in LS experiments) the long-range electrostatic interactions have completely disappeared and η_{sp}/c_2 increases linearly with c_2 over a wide range of concentrations.

After this diversion on the viscosity behaviour of polyelectrolyte solutions in salt-free systems we now return to an analysis of LS in these systems. We consider the system to be two-component and write, in analogy to eqn (4.41),

$$\left(\frac{dn}{dC_u}\right)^2_{P,T} \frac{KC_u}{\Delta R(0)} = \frac{1}{RT} \frac{d\Pi}{dC_u}. \tag{4.71}$$

The new feature is that, contrary to the non-ionic two-component systems, we are not allowed to expand the osmotic-pressure derivative in this expression into a virial series. An alternative approach must be found, and we shall refer to the experimental results and the analysis of Alexandrowicz

(1959, 1960) (see also the review of Katchalsky *et al.* (**1966**)). The osmotic pressure was formally written as

$$\Pi = 10^{-3} \times RTC_2(1 + v\phi_p), \tag{4.72}$$

where each polymeric chain carries v charges and ϕ_p is a practical osmotic coefficient (the one poly-ion has been taken here to be ideal and deviations from ideality have been ascribed to the v counter-ions; this formulation refers to the case of vanishing concentrations C_2, when poly-ion–poly-ion interactions can be neglected). Since, for highly charged polyelectrolytes $v\phi_p$ is much larger than unity it is usually possible to write that

$$\Pi = 10^{-3} \times RTC_2 v\phi_p, \tag{4.73}$$

and therefore

$$\phi_p = \Pi/\Pi_{\text{ideal}}, \tag{4.74}$$

where Π_{ideal} is the ideal osmotic pressure, which would obtain in the absence of electrostatic interactions. From polyelectrolyte theory, which we discuss in Appendix V (p. 232), it is possible to show that, for some molecular models,

$$\phi_p = -2\Gamma_3, \tag{4.75}$$

provided that Γ_3, which is equal to $(M_2/M_3)\,\xi_3$, is due to Donnan exclusion E_3 only.

If we now differentiate eqn (4.72) with respect to C_u and introduce the value for $d\Pi/dC_u$ into eqn (4.71) we find

$$10^3 \times \left(\frac{dn}{dC_u}\right)^2_{P,T} \frac{KC_u}{\Delta R(0)} = \frac{1}{Z} + \alpha\phi_p, \tag{4.76}$$

where

$$\alpha = v/Z \tag{4.77}$$

is the fraction of the Z repeating units which are ionized (generally, for charged poly-ions $\alpha\phi_p \gg 1/Z$). From eqn (4.76) ϕ_p can be evaluated. Alexandrowicz (1959, 1960) could show that, if sufficient care is taken in the LS and osmotic-pressure measurements the osmotic coefficients, in solutions of salts of polymethacrylic acid at various degrees of ionization, can be consistently obtained from both these experimental methods (Fig. 4.7). This is an important result in terms of relating the validity of fluctuation theory (as followed by optical probes in the LS experiments) to the derivative of the osmotic pressure with respect to poly-ion concentration. Earlier attempts (Oth and Doty 1952) to determine the rather low scattering of salt-free polyelectrolyte solutions had not been so successful. It was found by Alexandrowicz and other workers that for a given system ϕ_p is independent of molecular weight and only slightly dependent on concentrations. The

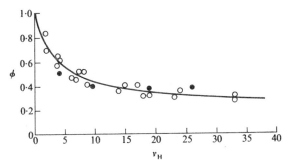

F I G. 4.7. Osmotic coefficient ϕ of bovine serum albumin as a function of protein charge ν_H, determined by light-scattering (open circles) and by osmotic (filled circles) measurements. (From Alexandrowicz 1959.)

primary factor determining the magnitude of ϕ_p is the charge density along the polymeric backbone, with the value of ϕ_p decreasing rapidly with increasing charge density. In vinylic polymers such as polyacrylic and polymethacrylic acids the value of ϕ_p drops to about 0·12–0·15 for $\alpha = 1$, indicating that only 12–15 per cent of the counter-ions are osmotically active. Similar considerations apply to highly charged nucleic acids chains and structures at neutral pH (Eisenberg **1974**).

In conclusion, we have shown in this section that, in the case of highly charged polyelectrolytes in salt-free solutions, osmotic coefficients rather than molecular weights are determined in osmotic pressure and LS experiments (we shall see, in the following chapter, that similar conclusions result from sedimentation experiments in the ultracentrifuge). A different phenomenon, in which charge fluctuation become important in determining colligative properties of proteins in salt-free solutions at the isoelectric point will be discussed in the following section.

4.7. Scattering due to charge fluctuations

In the preceding section we have seen that, in the case of salt-free systems, the scattering is much reduced, the osmotic pressure cannot be expanded in a virial series, and molecular weights are not obtained. In this section we shall show that a mechanism exists (first described by Kirkwood and Shumaker (1952) and by Timasheff, Dintzis, Kirkwood, and Coleman (1955)) in which charge fluctuations lead to increased scattering in salt-free systems compared to aqueous solutions of macromcolecules having a net zero charge (proteins at the isoelectric point, for instance). These charge fluctuations, to be described below lead to attractive forces between particles, and therefore to increased scattering. Both van der Waals and electrostatic repulsive potentials lead to positive virial coefficients, and therefore to a reduced intensity of scattering. An extreme case of molecular attraction can result in the association of biological macromolecules (with subsequent strong increase of scattering) and examples of this will be discussed in Chapter 7.

The work of Kirkwood and Shumaker (1952) was first concerned with the influence of dipole-moment fluctuations on the dielectric increments in proteins in solution. Proteins contain a number of neutral and negatively charged basic sites such as $-NH_2$ and $-CO_2^-$, for instance, to which protons are bound rather loosely; a mechanism of charge fluctuation may be provided by the migration of the small ions within the macromolecule. Except in highly acid solutions, the number of basic sites exceeds the average number of protons bound to the molecule, and many possible configurations of the protons exist, differing little in free energy. Fluctuations in the configurations of the protons have been associated with a non-vanishing mean-square electric charge, even in the case (at the isoelectric point) when the mean charge is zero (the theory is more general and molecules with a permanent charge may also be considered).

In the special case of a solution of macromolecules of average net charge $\bar{v}$ equal to zero, there will be macromolecules carrying one or two more charges of both signs as a result of charge fluctuations, and the mean-square net charge

$$\langle v^2 \rangle = \sum c_i v_i^2 / \sum c_i \qquad (4.78)$$

will be different from zero. Inter-ionic attraction results from the fact that the system is composed of both positive and negative macro-ions. The Debye–Hückel limiting theory of simple electrolytes (see Harned and Owen **1958**) can be used to evaluate the influence of $\langle v^2 \rangle$ on the free energy (and quantities derived thereof) of the system, because large fluctuations from zero charge are not likely to be encountered (Timasheff *et al.* (1955) found $\langle v^2 \rangle^{\frac{1}{2}}$ to be equal to 3·5 electronic charge units in solutions of bovine serum albumin).

From the limiting Debye–Hückel theory the excess chemical potential $kT \ln y$ per molecule of the macromolecular component is given by†

$$kT \ln y = -\tfrac{1}{2}\kappa_{DH} \langle v^2 \rangle e^2 / D, \qquad (4.79)$$

where the Debye–Hückel characteristic radius κ_{DH}^{-1} is given by eqn (4.1). Differentiation of

$$\mu = \mu^0 + RT \ln c + RT \ln y$$

---

† Compare eqn (2.15) for the formulation of the excess chemical potential but note that y is defined on the volume concentration rather than on the molality scale (both Harned and Owen (**1958**) and Robinson and Stokes (**1959**) present detailed definitions of activity coefficients and interconversion relations).

leads to

$$\left(\frac{da}{dc}\right)_{T,P} \equiv \frac{1}{RT}\left(\frac{d\mu}{dc}\right)_{T,P} = \frac{1}{c}\left(1 + c\frac{d\ln y}{dc}\right)$$

$$= \frac{1}{c}\left\{1 - \left(\frac{\langle v^2\rangle e^2}{DkT}\right)^{\frac{3}{2}}\frac{\pi N_a}{M_2}c^{\frac{1}{2}}\right\} \tag{4.80}$$

if the value of κ_{DH} is introduced into eqn (4.79) and the differentiation of eqn (4.80) is performed. For the two-component system of interest we can further rewrite eqn (4.38) as

$$\Delta R(0) = KV_m\Psi_2^2/a_{22},$$

or, in volume concentration units,

$$\left(\frac{dn}{dc_2}\right)_{T,P}^2\frac{K}{\Delta R(0)} = \frac{1}{M_2}\left(\frac{da_2}{dc_2}\right)_{T,P},$$

and finally, neglecting inconsequential terms,

$$\left(\frac{dn}{dc_2}\right)_{T,P}^2\frac{Kc_2}{\Delta R(0)} = \frac{1}{M_2}\left\{1 - \frac{1}{2}\left(\frac{\langle v^2\rangle e^2}{DkT}\right)^{\frac{3}{2}}\left(\frac{\pi N_A}{M_2}\right)^{\frac{1}{2}}c_2^{\frac{1}{2}}\right\}. \tag{4.81}$$

Thus, at low concentrations c_2, the reciprocal reduced scattering function should correctly extrapolate to M_2^{-1} as c_2 vanishes, but should then decrease linearly with $c_2^{\frac{1}{2}}$. With further increase in concentration it is expected that a positive term in c_2 arising from other types of interactions previously discussed will appear. Eqn (4.81) has been tested by Timasheff et al. (1955) in salt-free de-ionized solutions of bovine serum albumin, and the expected behaviour has indeed been observed (Figs 4.8 and 4.9). From the slope of the line in Fig. 4.9, $\langle v^2\rangle$ has been calculated to be 3·5 elementary charge units, in good agreement with an evaluation from potentiometric titration work. In another contribution, Kirkwood and Timasheff (1956) account for the effect of increasing ionization on the LS or isoionic proteins with progressive dilution; this effect leads to corrections at very low protein concentrations, which are discussed by the authors.

4.8. Analysis of time-dependent fluctuations by scattering of coherent radiation

This important topic, as we have already mentioned above, has recently come to the fore as a result of the use of coherent laser radiation and sophisticated spectral and time-correlation techniques. It will only be mentioned briefly in the present context as it is still rapidly evolving, encompasses difficult problems and merits a much more extensive discussion. Briefly, we return to eqn (4.7), but now we assume that the vectors $\mathbf{r}_j$ are time-dependent quantities.

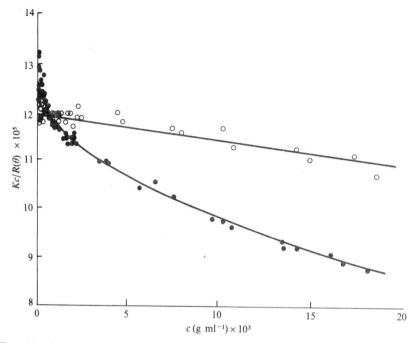

F IG. 4.8. Light-scattering of bovine serum albumin: (filled circles, isoionic salt-free aqueous solutions; open circles, solution in 0·001 M NaCl. (From Timasheff *et al.* 1955.)

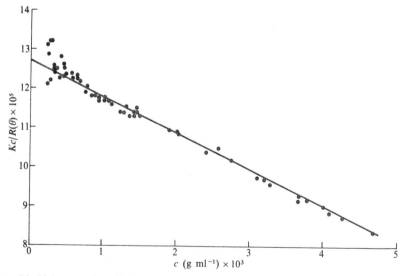

F IG. 4.9. Light-scattering of isoionic bovine serum albumin; square-root of concentration plot. (From Timasheff *et al.* 1955.)

In order to compute the spectrum of the scattered light we follow the discussion of Cummins, Carlson, Herbert, and Woods (1969) applied to the very simple case of statistically independent, spherical, isotropic scatterers only. As a result of the motion of the macromolecules the scattered field fluctuates. We apply the Fourier transform known as the Wiener–Khinchine theorem (Davidson 1962) for the intensity spectrum $I(\omega)$ of the scattered light,

$$I(\omega) = \frac{1}{2\pi} \int_{-\infty}^{+\infty} C(\tau) \exp(i\omega\tau) \, d\tau, \qquad (4.82)$$

where the auto-correlation function $C(\tau)$ is defined by

$$C(\tau) = \langle E_s^*(t) E_s(t+\tau) \rangle \qquad (4.83)$$

and is therefore the time-averaged quantity relating the amplitude of the optical field at time t to the amplitude of the field τ seconds later (the asterisk refers to the complex-conjugate quantity).

$$C(\tau) \equiv \lim_{T\to\infty} \int_{-\frac{1}{2}T}^{\frac{1}{2}T} E_s(t+\tau) E_s^*(t) \, dt, \qquad (4.84)$$

where T is one period. Frequency shifts in the spectrum between 10 Hz to 10^5 Hz correspond to scattered-light amplitude correlation between 10^{-1} s and 10^{-5} s. Combining eqns (4.7) and (4.83), and using the simplifying assumptions introduced above, we find

$$I(\omega) = N|A|^2 \frac{1}{2\pi} \int_{-\infty}^{+\infty} \exp\{i(\omega-\omega_0)\tau\} C_\phi(\tau) \, d\tau, \qquad (4.85)$$

where $C_\phi(\tau)$ is the position auto-correlation function as the scattering amplitude which, in our case, is independent of the orientation of the scatterers

$$C_\phi(\tau, \mathbf{q}) = \langle \exp[-i\mathbf{q} \cdot \{\mathbf{r}(t) + \mathbf{r}(t+\tau)\}] \rangle. \qquad (4.86)$$

Subscripts to the position vectors $\mathbf{r}$ are not required since we are dealing with the correlation functions for a single particle only. To connect the field correlation function $C_\phi(\tau, q)$ with molecular properties of the system we use the 'self' part $G_s(\mathbf{R}, \tau)$ of the space–time correlation function of Van Hove, which is the conditional probability, averaged over the ensemble, that the centre of mass of a particle located at the origin at time $t = 0$ will be (in a unit volume) at $\mathbf{R}$ at time τ

$$C_\phi(\tau, \mathbf{q}) = \int G_s(\mathbf{R}, \tau) \exp(i\mathbf{q} \cdot \mathbf{R}) \, d\mathbf{R}. \qquad (4.87)$$

We are interested in the 'self' part of this function only, that is, in correlation of the motion of a single particle, as the motion of the particles are considered to be uncorrelated. To analyse the light scattered from moving particles it is thus necessary first to construct the space–time correlation function $G_s(\mathbf{R}, \tau)$. Evaluation of the integral eqn (4.87) yields the auto-correlation function $C_\phi(\tau, \mathbf{q})$ which, in principle, can be measured directly. If the spectrum $I(\omega)$ is required this can be obtained by use of the Wiener–Khinchine theorem (eqn (4.82)). Cummins *et al.* (1969) have analysed this problem for three simple cases, and their result will now be presented.

Case (a): fixed scatterers

For fixed scatterers the probability distribution

$$G_s(\mathbf{R}, \tau) = G_s(\mathbf{R}, 0) = \delta(\mathbf{R}) \tag{4.88}$$

is a delta function, and its integral over all space,

$$C_\phi(\tau) = \int \delta(\mathbf{R}) \exp(i\mathbf{q} \cdot \mathbf{R}) \, d\mathbf{R} = 1, \tag{4.89}$$

equals unity. The spectrum, by eqn (4.85),

$$I(\omega) = N|A|^2 \left(\frac{1}{\pi}\right) Re \int_0^\infty \exp\{i(\omega - \omega_0)\tau\} \, d\tau$$
$$= N|A|^2 \delta(\omega - \omega_0), \tag{4.90}$$

which indicates that for fixed scatterers the scattered light is unshifted in frequency (see Fig. 4.10).

Case (b): scatterers moving with constant velocity
In this case

$$\mathbf{r}(\tau) = \mathbf{r}(0) + \mathbf{v}\tau, \tag{4.91}$$

so that $\mathbf{R} = \mathbf{v}\tau$ and $G_s(\mathbf{R}, \tau) = \delta(\mathbf{R} - \mathbf{v}\tau)$; the auto-correlation function $C_\phi(\tau)$ is given by

$$C_\phi(\tau) = \int \delta(\mathbf{R} - \mathbf{v}\tau) \exp(i\mathbf{q} \cdot \mathbf{R}) \, d\mathbf{R}. \tag{4.92}$$

The spectrum $I(\omega, q)$ corresponding to this case,

$$I(\omega, q) = N|A|^2 \delta(\omega - \omega_0 + \mathbf{q} \cdot \mathbf{v}) \tag{4.93}$$

is a simple Doppler shift (Fig. 4.10). The most interesting case within the self-imposed limits of our discussion corresponds to case (c).

Case (c): scatterers undergoing Brownian motion
Here the time-evolution of the distribution function G_s is governed by the macroscopic diffusion equation

$$\partial G_s / \partial t = D_t \nabla^2 G_s, \tag{4.94}$$

where D_t is the translational diffusion coefficient. The solution of this

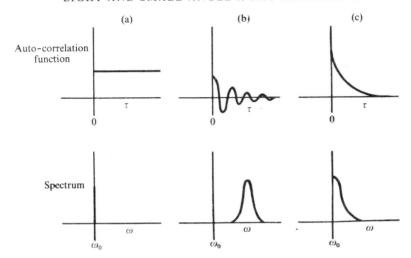

FIG. 4.10. Schematic results for the auto-correlation functions and the spectra of light for three typical cases: (a) fixed scatterers; (b) scatterers moving with constant velocity v (this case is experimentally realized by light-scattering from solutions of charged particles under the influence of electric fields (see Ware and Flygare 1972); (c) scatterers subject to Brownian motion.

equation is

$$G_s(\mathbf{R}, \tau) = (4\pi D_t \tau)^{-\frac{3}{2}} \exp(-R^2/4D_t\tau), \qquad (4.95)$$

with G_s at $\tau = 0$ equal to the delta function $\delta(\mathbf{R})$. Introduction of this equation into eqn (4.87) yields

$$C_\phi(\tau, q) = \exp(-\Gamma\tau), \qquad (4.96)$$

where $\Gamma \equiv D_t q^2$ and the auto-correlation function therefore exponentially decreases with increasing time-shift τ. The translational diffusion constant D_t can therefore be derived from this plot. The intensity spectrum $I(\omega, q)$ is given by

$$I(\omega, q) = N A^2 \left(\frac{1}{\pi}\right) Re \int_0^\infty \exp\{i(\omega - \omega_0)\tau\} \exp(-\Gamma\tau)\, d\tau$$

$$= N A^2 \frac{\Gamma/\pi}{(\omega - \omega_0)^2 + \Gamma^2}, \qquad (4.97)$$

and is therefore represented by a normalized Lorentzien centred at $\omega - \omega_0$, with half-width at half-maximum equal to Γ (see Fig. 4.10).

In more sophisticated applications it may be possible to determine electrophoretic mobility superimposed on Brownian motion (Ware and Flygare 1972), rotational diffusion of asymmetric molecules (Schurr and Schmitz 1973), and internal motions (Pecora 1968; Fujime 1970), as well as chemical kinetics (Yeh and Keeler 1969; Berne and Giniger 1973). Magde, Elson, and

Webb (1972, 1974), and Elson and Magde (1974) have measured the chemical rate constants and diffusion constants for binding of ethidium bromide to DNA by determining the temporal correlation of thermodynamic concentration fluctuations as followed by fluorescence correlation spectroscopy of the fluorescent reaction product.

In practice the evaluation of the light-scattering experiments is not as simple as may appear from the equations above. Neither $I(\omega, q)$ nor the amplitudes $E(t)$ are experimentally accessible quantities. What can be determined is the photocurrent $i(t)$ of the photomultiplier detector, which is proportional to the square of the optical field, and therefore to $I(t)$, the intensity of the scattered light, as a function of time. We can therefore determine the current auto-correlation function

$$C_i(\tau) = \langle i(t)i(t+\tau) \rangle \qquad (4.98)$$

and the power spectrum $P_i(\omega)$ by a different form of the Wiener–Khinchine theorem,

$$P_i(\omega) = (2\pi)^{-1} \int_{-\infty}^{+\infty} \exp(i\omega\tau)C_i(\tau)\,\mathrm{d}\tau. \qquad (4.99)$$

The relation between the experimental second-order intensity and the optical first-order field-correlation functions is straightforward only for optical fields obeying gaussian statistics; a detailed analysis entails a fair amount of complexity (Oliver, Pike, and Vaughan **1973**) and will not be dealt with here.

4.8.1. *Experimental techniques*

The more conventional approach entails the measurement of spectral-broadening and Doppler shifts. Fabry–Perot interferometers (filters) are not extremely useful in Rayleigh spectroscopy because we are required to determine line-widths of the order of 10–10^5 Hz at optical frequencies of about 10^{14} Hz. The experiment is therefore performed by a method adapted from radio-wave analysis, by allowing the modulated scattered wave to beat with itself or to beat with the high-frequency non-modulated carrier wave. Nomenclature varies, but we may call the method 'heterodyne detection' when the scattered wave beats against an external standard wave and 'self-beat spectroscopy' when beats are produced by the various components of the scattered wave amongst themselves (Cummins and Swinney **1970**; Benedek **1969**). In most cases the spectral analysis is performed as a single-channel analysis and is therefore rather inefficient in that at each stage a small amount only of the available information is being used. Recently it has become possible to determine the fluctuations of the photocurrent directly. This is known as 'intensity-fluctuation spectroscopy', and the second-order correlation function (eqn (4.98)) may be determined directly

(Ford, Karasz, and Owen 1970; Foord *et al.* 1970; Camerini-Otero, Pusey, Koppel, Schaefer, and Franklin 1974). Advanced technology allows the measurement to be performed very efficiently by multi-channel techniques in which the auto-correlation function is rapidly obtained. Applications of this technique to solutions of biological macromolecules have been reviewed (Ford **1972**; Cummins **1974**), and many more successful applications may be expected in this rapidly and constantly improving versatile technique. By a judicious choice of experimental technique, fluctuations occurring on time-scales of 1 Hz up to about 10^{15} Hz (the frequency of the light) can be studied. A huge field of study has thus become available.

5

SEDIMENTATION EQUILIBRIUM

5.1. The analytical ultracentrifuge

THE analytical ultracentrifuge has, in recent years, become one of the most versatile and useful instruments in the investigation of synthetic macro-molecules and biological polymers. Of the two basic approaches—namely, the study of transport phenomena and of systems at sedimentation equilibrium—it is the latter which can be analysed by rigorous thermo-dynamic formalism (Williams, van Holde, Baldwin, and Fujita **1958**). Meselson, Stahl, and Vinograd (1957) introduced the analysis of equilibrium sedimentation in a density gradient and thereby considerably increased the scope of the ultracentrifuge in molecular biology. Although the basic differential equation applicable to equilibrium sedimentation remains valid in this situation, great care must be exercised in the interpretation of experi-mental results, both because the solutions are multi-component and because pressure corrections to partial volumes and preferential interaction para-meters may not be negligible. Casassa and Eisenberg (**1964**) showed that, with respect to equilibrium sedimentation, it is possible to achieve considerable simplification, symmetrical presentation with respect to all components, and gain rather than loss of rigour in a compressible system, if, instead of the conventional partial volumes, density derivatives with respect to components of interest ('density increments') under well-specified restrictions are used in the basic equations. This formulation of equilibrium sedimentation has previously been used by Vrij (1959) and by Eisenberg (1962). Here it must be emphasized that, whereas for two-component systems the use of either the classical buoyancy term $(1 - \bar{v}\rho)$ or the density increment $d\rho/dc$ (see Chapter 3) is equally rewarding, for multi-component systems the use of density increments is aesthetically more pleasing and provides a better insight into the nature of the physical phenomena. Thus, for instance, it can be shown (Eisenberg 1967), on a basis of a simple calculation, that it is sufficient to know the distance by which a banded isotopically substituted species is displaced at equilibrium in a density gradient with respect to the position of the corresponding natural isotope, in order to evaluate correct molecular weights from the width of the band. Recent advances in ultracentrifugation theory and practice are summarized conveniently in two conference proceedings (Williams **1963**; Yphantis **1969**).

In addition to Tanford's text on the physical chemistry of macromolecules (**1961**), the more recent intermediate-level physical-biochemistry text of van Holde (**1971**) provides a good background and contains many useful problems. There is also an article by Teller (**1973**) on the characterization of proteins by sedimentation equilibrium in the analytical ultracentrifuge.

5.2. Basic equations for sedimentation in a multi-component system

In a discussion of equilibrium in a gravitational field, it is customary to subdivide the system under consideration into a sequence of contiguous phases, of fixed volume and of infinitesimal thickness, in the direction of the field. This stratagem is employed to uphold the usual thermodynamic convention that a phase is homogeneous in all its properties. It is characteristic of a gravitational potential ϕ that transfer a mass M from a phase α at potential $\phi^{(\alpha)}$ to a different position at potential $\phi^{(\beta)}$ involves an amount of work $M(\phi^{(\beta)} - \phi^{(\alpha)})$ independent of the chemical nature of the matter. The total potential $\tilde{\mu}_i$ of the species i is given by the sum of chemical, gravitational, and electrostatic terms

$$\tilde{\mu}_i = \mu_i + M_i \phi + v_i \mathscr{F} \psi, \tag{5.1}$$

where v_i is the valency (with the appropriate sign) of species i, $\mathscr{F}$ is the Faraday and ψ is the electrostatic potential of the infinitesimal phase. The theory of heterogeneous equilibrium requires that $\tilde{\mu}_i$ be uniform for any component throughout the system, so that

$$d\mu_i + M_i d\phi + v_i \mathscr{F} d\psi = 0. \tag{5.2}$$

We are interested in the equilibrium distribution of electroneutral components and therefore assume that the electroneutrality condition is satisfied locally and no complications arise as a consequence of gradients of electric charge resulting from inequality of the gravitational forces exerted on ionic species of unlike mass. The approximation can be regarded as completely inconsequential in situations attainable in practice. Supporting electrolyte is always present in such concentration that the electroneutrality condition *per se* does not affect the distribution of the polyelectrolyte molecules in the field (Svedberg and Pedersen **1940**; Johnson, Kraus, and Scatchard 1954; Williams *et al.* **1958**)†

† These considerations are equally applicable to equilibrium sedimentation in a density gradient (see Section 5.4) and correct molecular weights, particularly in the very-high molecular-weight range, should be obtained by this method. Yet it was found (Thomas and Pinkerton 1962) that, in the case of DNA in caesium chloride gradients, molecular weights were evaluated by this method which were much too low. Daniel (1969) extended some theoretical considerations of Yeandle (1959) and claimed that charge effects, encountered in sedimentation velocity experiments (see Section 6.3) persist under equilibrium conditions and affect the DNA distribution in equilibrium sedimentation in a density gradient. Schmid and Hearst (1969, 1971) could show by a very careful investigation that equilibrium sedimentation in a density gradient yields correct molecular weights of coliphage DNA and charge effects need not be considered under equilibrium conditions.

Consider eqn (5.2) applied to the electroneutral component 2, the polyelectrolyte molecule PX_Z, suspended in an aqueous medium containing the low-molecular-weight salt XY, component 3. We assume that (as a result of electrostatic interactions) $(1-i)Z$ counter-ions are 'associated' with the polyelectrolyte, which carries an effective charge $-iZ$ rather than its full electronic charge $-Z$ (see Section 2.4 and Appendix 5). We shall see that for our particular purpose i does not have to be defined precisely. We write

$$d\mu_P^* + M_P^* \, d\phi - iZ\mathscr{F} \, d\psi = 0 \qquad (5.3)$$

for the poly-ion, where both μ_P^* and M_P^* are defined here to include the contributions from the $(1-i)Z$ counter-ions 'associated' with the poly-ion and

$$d\mu_X + M_X \, d\phi + \mathscr{F} \, d\psi = 0 \qquad (5.4)$$

for the 'free' univalent positive counter-ion X. We multiply eqn (5.4) by iZ and add it to eqn (5.3) to yield

$$d(\mu_P^* + iZ\mu_X) + (M_P^* + iZM_X) \, d\phi = 0, \qquad (5.5)$$

which is identical with eqn (6.1) of Casassa and Eisenberg (**1964**),

$$d\mu_2 + M_2 \, d\phi = 0, \qquad (5.6)$$

because $\mu_P^* + iZ\mu_X = \mu_P + Z\mu_X = \mu_2$ and $M_P^* + iZM_X = M_P + ZM_X = M_2$, the chemical potential and the molecular weight respectively of the electroneutral polyelectrolyte component 2. The electrostatic potential ψ is eliminated when electroneutral components (defined as above or in any other way) are chosen in an equilibrium experiment. This is why it is therefore not necessary to define i precisely in the case of an equilibrium experiment.

The basic thermodynamic equations for sedimentation in a gravitational field potential,

$$\phi = -\tfrac{1}{2}\omega^2 r^2, \qquad (5.7)$$

have been given by Goldberg (1953); ω is the angular velocity and r is the distance from the centre of rotation (Fig. 5.1). We have, from eqns (5.6), (5.7), and (2.35),

$$M_2\omega^2 r \, dr = RTa_{22} \, dm_2 + RTa_{23} \, dm_3 + \bar{V}_2 \, dP, \qquad (5.8)$$

and a similar equation can be written for component 3

$$M_3\omega^2 r \, dr = RTa_{23} \, dm_2 + RTa_{33} \, dm_3 + \bar{V}_3 \, dP. \qquad (5.9)$$

The Gibbs–Duhem equation for a phase of fixed volume V containing n_J moles of component J at constant temperature T gives the condition

$$V \, dP = \sum_J n_J \, d\mu_J \qquad (5.10)$$

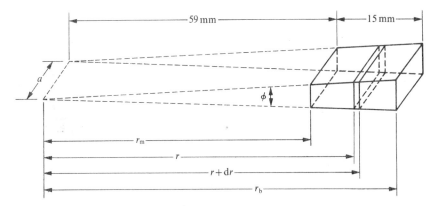

FIG. 5.1. Schematic diagram of a sector-shaped ultracentrifuge cell, at a distance from the axis of rotation corresponding to its position in the rotor. The angle ϕ is generally 4°, but smaller angles are often used. The distance a represents the optical path in the cell, that is, the thickness of the liquid column contained between the quartz windows. (From Schachman **1959**.)

for change of pressure in the vicinity of the phase.† Combination of eqn (5.10) with eqns (5.7) and (5.6), which applies to any electroneutral component J, yields the hydrostatic-pressure condition

$$dP = \rho\omega^2 r\,dr,\qquad(5.11)$$

where

$$\rho = \sum_J \frac{n_J M_J}{V}\qquad(5.12)$$

is just the density of the phase. We now substitute eqn (5.11) in eqns (5.8) and (5.9) and use eqn (3.1) to give

$$\omega^2 r\,dr\,V_m(\partial\rho/\partial m_2)_{P,m_3} = RT(a_{22}\,dm_2 + a_{23}\,dm_3)\qquad(5.13)$$

and

$$\omega^2 r\,dr\,V_m(\partial\rho/\partial m_3)_{P,m_2} = RT(a_{23}\,dm_2 + a_{33}\,dm_3).\qquad(5.14)$$

It should be noted that we are directly using the derivatives $\partial\rho/\partial m_J$ instead of the conventional quantities $M_J\,(1 - \bar{v}_J\rho)$; this procedure will lead to considerable simplification in the equations for sedimentation equilibrium and transport. To calculate the distribution of component 2 we eliminate

† Constant temperature is assumed and variations dT in temperature are disregarded. In practice temperature fluctuations δT in an ultracentrifuge cell may lead to convection currents which in turn may make attainment of sedimentation-equilibrium distribution conditions extremely unlikely. Under these conditions the formation of a minute positive density gradient deriving from the presence of the low-molecular-weight component 3 in the ultracentrifugal field may prove extremely felicitous in stabilizing the essentially unstable system with respect to spontaneous temperature fluctuations.

dm_3 between eqn (5.13) and (5.14) and obtain

$$\frac{\omega^2}{2}\left(\frac{dm_2}{dr^2}\right)^{-1}\left\{\left(\frac{\partial\rho}{\partial m_2}\right)_{P,m_3} - \frac{a_{23}}{a_{33}}\left(\frac{\partial\rho}{\partial m_3}\right)_{P,m_2}\right\} = RT\left(a_{22}-\frac{a_{23}^2}{a_{33}}\right), \quad (5.15)$$

where we have written dr^2 for $2r\,dr$. We note that, from eqn (3.6) and (2.71) the expression in braces in eqn (5.15) equals $(\partial\rho/\partial m_2)_{P,\mu_3}$. We also use the expression eqn (2.39) for the derivative of the osmotic pressure to give

$$\frac{\omega^2}{2}\left(\frac{d\ln m_2}{dr^2}\right)^{-1}\left(\frac{\partial\rho}{\partial m_2}\right)_{P,\mu_3}^* = \frac{d\Pi}{dm_2}\left(1-\frac{\bar{V}_2^*}{V_m}m_2\right), \quad (5.16)$$

where

$$\bar{V}_2^* \equiv \bar{V}_2 - \frac{a_{23}}{a_{33}}\bar{V}_3. \quad (5.17)$$

Eqn (5.16) is formally identical with the equations applicable to a two-component system, provided that proper restrictions in the density increments have been taken into consideration. It may be transformed by some algebraic manipulation† into a particular attractive exact form on the c-concentration scale

$$\frac{\omega^2}{2}\left(\frac{d\ln c_2}{dr^2}\right)^{-1}\left(\frac{\partial\rho}{\partial c_2}\right)_\mu = \frac{d\Pi}{dc_2}. \quad (5.21)$$

Eqn (5.21) holds for every component in the system; thus we can write

$$\frac{\omega^2}{2}\left(\frac{d\ln c_J^{(r)}}{dr^2}\right)^{-1}\left(\frac{\partial\rho}{\partial c_J}\right)_\mu^{(r)} = \left(\frac{d\Pi}{dc_J}\right)^{(r)}, \quad (5.22)$$

---

† To transform eqn (5.16) to the c-concentration scale we write

$$\frac{dc_2}{dr^2} = \frac{dm_2}{dr^2}\left(\frac{\partial c_2}{\partial m_2}\right)_{\text{sed}}.$$

The subscript sed affixed to dc_2/dm_2 and similar derivatives indicates constraint to the conditions of sedimentation equilibrium, i.e. the derivative is to be evaluated with respect to the concentration profile in the centrifugal field. By differentiation of

$$c_2 = m_2 M_2/V_m,$$

$$\left(\frac{\partial c_2}{\partial m_2}\right)_{\text{sed}} = (M_2/V_m)\left\{1-(\partial V_m/\partial m_2)_{\text{sed}}(m_2/V_m)\right\},$$

and

$$\frac{d\ln c_2}{dr^2} = \frac{d\ln m_2}{dr^2}\left\{1-\left(\frac{\partial V_m}{\partial m_2}\right)_{\text{sed}}\frac{m_2}{V_m}\right\}. \quad (5.18)$$

From eqn (2.42) we find

$$\left(\frac{\partial V_m}{\partial m_2}\right)_{\text{sed}} = \bar{V}_2 + \bar{V}_3\left(\frac{\partial m_3}{\partial m_2}\right)_{\text{sed}} - \bar{V}_m\kappa\left(\frac{\partial P}{\partial m_2}\right)_{\text{sed}}$$

and the superscript (r) is a reminder that the variables depend on position r in the centrifugal field. Obviously, an expression of the form of eqn (5.22) can be written for any concentration variable proportional to c_J, such as C_J (eqn (2.4)) and C_u (eqn (2.14)), in particular,

$$\frac{\omega^2}{2}\left(\frac{d\ln C_u}{dr^2}\right)^{-1}\left(\frac{\partial\rho}{\partial C_u}\right)_\mu = \frac{d\Pi}{dC_u}. \tag{5.23}$$

The superscript (r) is understood to be applicable but will not be carried henceforth to avoid cumbersome notation, wherever the dependence of c or other parameters is clearly implied by the nature of the experiment. The eqns (5.21)–(5.23) are exact and completely general for any component among any number of components of any molecular weight, without restrictions to thermodynamic ideality or to incompressibility. The introduction of the osmotic pressure has been done in a formally exact way and establishes a connection with the thermodynamics derivations presented in Chapter 2. Whereas the quantities appearing in these equations are directly measurable for systems with a single macromolecular solute, for instance, and a multiplicity of diffusible components, the validity of the relations is completely independent of any consideration as to whether the osmotic pressure can actually be determined experimentally. The symmetrical form of eqns (5.21)–(5.23) is, in particular, due to the use of the density increments (at constant chemical potentials of components diffusible through a semi-permeable membrane), which are also conveniently measurable in many important practical situations. Pressure effects may be manifested in the dependence of the variables, and in particular $(\partial\rho/\partial c_2)_\mu$, on pressure.

---

and for $(\partial P/\partial m_2)_{\text{sed}}$ we use the hydrostatic-pressure relation (5.11),

$$\left(\frac{\partial P}{\partial m_2}\right)_{\text{sed}} = \rho\omega^2 r\left(\frac{dm_2}{dr}\right)^{-1}$$

We substitute $(\partial m_3/\partial m_2)_{\text{sed}}$ obtained from eqn (5.14) and eqn (5.16) to obtain

$$\left(\frac{\partial V_m}{\partial m_2}\right)_{\text{sed}} = \bar{V}_2^* + \frac{d\Pi}{dm_2}\frac{\bar{V}_m - \bar{V}_2^* m_2}{m_2(\partial\rho/\partial m_2)_{P,\mu_3}}\left\{\bar{V}_3\frac{(\partial\rho/\partial m_3)_{P,m_2}}{a_{33}RT} - \kappa\rho\right\}. \tag{5.19}$$

We also derive, from eqn (3.6),

$$\left(\frac{\partial\rho}{\partial m_2}\right)_{P,\mu_3} - \left(\frac{\partial\rho}{\partial m_2}\right)_\mu = \left(\frac{\partial\rho}{\partial m_3}\right)_{P,m_2}\left\{\left(\frac{\partial m_3}{\partial m_2}\right)_{P,\mu_3} - \left(\frac{\partial m_3}{\partial m_2}\right)_\mu\right\} - \kappa\rho\frac{d\Pi}{dm_2},$$

which with eqns (2.38) and (2.71) yields

$$\left(\frac{\partial\rho}{\partial m_2}\right)_{P,\mu_3} - \left(\frac{\partial\rho}{\partial m_2}\right)_\mu = \left\{\left(\frac{\partial\rho}{\partial m_3}\right)_{P,m_2}\frac{\bar{V}_3}{RTa_{33}} - \kappa\rho\right\}\frac{d\Pi}{dm_2}. \tag{5.20}$$

Substitution of eqns (5.18), (5.19), and (5.20) into eqn (5.16), and use of

$$\frac{d\Pi}{dm_2}\bigg/\left(\frac{\partial\rho}{\partial m_2}\right)_\mu = \frac{d\Pi}{dc_2}\bigg/\left(\frac{\partial\rho}{\partial c_2}\right)_\mu$$

yields eqn (5.21).

5.3. Conventional sedimentation equilibrium in a three-component system

In the practical discussion of equilibrium sedimentation in solutions of biological macromolecules we may conveniently make the somewhat arbitrary distinction between two extreme cases encountered in practice. We refer to the conventional equilibrium method and the more recent density gradient technique, which will be discussed in detail in Section 5.4. In the typical conventional (classical) experiment, a macromolecular solute component 2 (or a mixture of such solutes) is sedimented in a system that in addition to component 1, also contains an additional (or additional) low-molecular-weight solute component 3 (or solutes) at relatively low concentrations, usually not exceeding 1 M and often much lower. These are the usual supporting electrolytes or complex buffer systems employed in the study of polyelectrolytes and biological macromolecules. The characteristics of these materials and the angular velocities ω usually employed in these studies are such that the low-molecular-weight components undergo negligible sedimentation in the absence of macromolecular components, and any redistribution of low-molecular-weight components in the solution at equilibrium results primarily from an interaction with macromolecular solute. Under these circumstances the density ρ^0 of the mixed solvent is essentially constant. In the case of aqueous solutions, with which studies of biological macromolecules are mostly concerned, the effect of pressure on the solvent or on the solute particles may be usually disregarded, except in rare circumstances (see, for instance, Josephs and Harrington (1967) for a study of the pressure-dependent association of myosin to form filaments in the ultracentrifuge). Pressure effects in ultracentrifugation of interacting systems have been discussed by Harrington and Kegeles (**1973**). The concentration of the macromolecular component 2 is finite throughout the liquid column in the ultracentrifuge cell and increases (or decreases if $(\partial\rho/\partial c_2)_\mu < 0$) monotonically away from the centre of rotation. The consequences of this situation lead to the straightforward evaluation of the differential expressions of the previous section for equilibrium sedimentation in a multi-component system.

5.3.1. *Homogeneous macromolecular component*

Consider eqn (5.21), for instance. The osmotic pressure Π can be expanded in a virial series by eqn (1.2). Therefore

$$\frac{\mathrm{d}\ln c_2}{\mathrm{d}r^2} = \frac{\omega^2}{2RT}\left(\frac{\partial\rho}{\partial c_2}\right)_\mu\left(\frac{1}{M_2} + 2A_2 c_2 + 3A_3 c_2^2 + \cdots\right)^{-1} \tag{5.24}$$

and, in the limit of vanishing concentration of component 2,

$$\frac{\mathrm{d}\ln c_2}{\mathrm{d}r^2} = \frac{\omega^2}{2RT}\left(\frac{\partial\rho}{\partial c_2}\right)_\mu M_2. \tag{5.25}$$

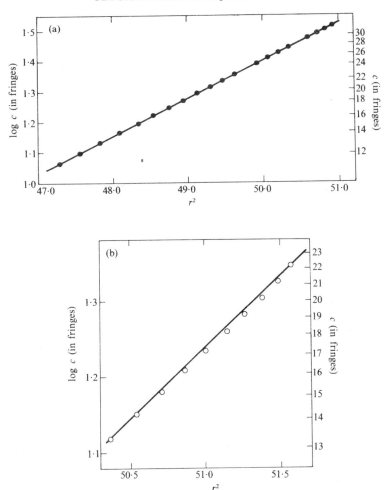

FIG. 5.2. Molecular-weight determinations of proteins by sedimentation equilibrium. The ordinate gives the logarithm of the concentration (in fringes) and the abscissa the square of the distance from the axis of rotation (in cm²). (a) Data for a homogeneous protein, aldolase (Stellwagen and Schachman 1962). (b) Data for an inhomogeneous protein, rabbit pseudo-globulin (Richards and Schachman, unpublished data). (From Schachman 1963.)

If ρ^0 is constant throughout the liquid column then, by eqn (3.9), $(\partial\rho/\partial c_2)_\mu$ is also constant throughout, because all the quantities on the right-hand side of this equation are independent of c_2, at low macromolecular concentration (for the purpose of our argument we need not restrict ourselves to a particular three- or four-component system). Therefore, if we plot the experimental values of $\ln c_2$ against r^2 (Fig. 5.2) then the slope of this linear plot (at low concentrations c_2 and for a monodisperse macromolecular component 2) is proportional to M_2. If the density increment and ω are known, then M_2 may be evaluated.

The use of the differential equation in volume concentration units is convenient because concentrations derived by the optical probes used in the ultracentrifuge (interference, Schlieren, and light-absorption methods) naturally relate to volume concentration units. Because we are at present only interested in the slope of Fig. 5.2 it is quite sufficient to determine any quantity proportional to $c_2^{(r)}$ rather than the absolute value itself. Other features which are also not peculiar to the analysis of the multi-component system, but are identical with the situation for the simple two-component system, involve the case in which the virial coefficients are not negligible (eqn (5.24)) and positive and may be derived from a more refined analysis of the experimental results. Downward curvature would then be expected in the plot of Fig. 5.2. Polydispersity, on the other hand, would lead to upward curvature and the slope at each level r (and in the limit of negligible virial correction) is proportional to the weight-average molecular weight $M_w^{(r)}$† at the position r. The integration of the differential equation for sedimentation equilibrium also proceeds by standard methods applicable to simple two-component systems. The experimental analysis is based on a combination of measurements over a range of velocities and concentrations for various liquid column lengths, whereby it usually becomes possible to separate non-ideality from polydispersity contributions. The case of macromolecular systems in chemical associative equilibrium will be discussed in Section 5.5. In general, both lower (M_n) and higher (M_z) moments of the molecular weight distribution may be obtained (see p. 112 for a discussion of systems comprising heterogeneous macromolecular components).

The use of the density increment $(\partial \rho/\partial c_J)_\mu$ is analogous to the use of the corresponding refractive-index increment in the formulation of the light-scattering equation of multi-component systems. Whereas the refractive-index increment depends on the refractive index of the medium (p. 62), the density increment correspondingly depends on the density of the solution.

---

† We have, in the limit $c_2 \to 0$, from eqn (5.25),

$$dc_J = (\omega^2/RT)r\,dr(\partial \rho/\partial c_2)_\mu M_J c_J .$$

$\sum c_J = c_2$ and we assume that $(\partial \rho/\partial c_2)_\mu$ is independent of the molecular weight of the species and dependent on the chemical nature and the solvent medium only. We now sum over all species

$$d\sum c_J = dc_2 = (\omega^2/RT)r\,dr(\partial \rho/\partial c_2)_\mu \sum M_J c_J ,$$

and, because $M_w = \sum c_J M_J/c_J$,

$$\frac{d\ln c_2}{dr^2} = \frac{\omega^2}{2RT}\left(\frac{\partial \rho}{\partial c_2}\right)_\mu M_w^{(r)} . \tag{5.26}$$

This is similar to the result obtained in light-scattering of polydisperse systems (eqn (4.47)), except that, in equilibrium sedimentation, redistribution of the species occurs and M_w is a function of the position r.

It is thus not surprising that in conventional practice one aims at characterizing a given macromolecular solute by a quantity, such as the partial volume, which is believed not to depend upon the detailed composition of the system. As already discussed in Section 3.2 the apparent quantity ϕ' (eqn (3.12)) has been suggested to replace $\bar{v}_2$ in multi-component systems. Substitution of $(\partial\rho/\partial c_2)_\mu$ from eqn (3.12) in eqn (5.25), for instance, yields

$$\frac{d \ln c_2}{dr^2} = \frac{\omega^2}{2RT}(1 - \phi'\rho)M, \qquad (5.27)$$

which formally resembles the equations for a two-component system. We have seen (Figs 3.2 and 3.3, pp. 57, 58), however, that ϕ' varies with the composition of the system in nucleic-acid solutions (at high concentration of CsCl and NaCl) and in protein solutions in denaturing solvents, such as urea or GuHCl. Edelstein and Schachman (1967) and Thomas and Edelstein (1971) have developed a method (reviewed by Edelstein and Schachman **1973**) for the simultaneous evaluation of apparent partial volumes (ϕ') and molecular weights of proteins by equilibrium sedimentation in a medium consisting in the one case of light and in the other case of heavy water. Preferential interaction coefficients with solvent, which determine $(\partial\rho/\partial c_2)_\mu$ are presumably not significantly affected by the substitution of light by heavy water.

In an additional application of this method Edelstein and Gibson (**1971**) resolved a long-standing controversy known as the 'salt paradox' in haemoglobin studies. This expression has been used to describe the apparent contradiction of the dissociation of haemoglobin into dimers in 2 M NaCl with the maintenance of normal co-operativity and rate of reaction towards ligands. The paradoxical aspects of the situation were based to some extent on an overestimation of the extent of dissociation in 2 M NaCl. Haemoglobin in 2 M NaCl is only slightly dissociated to dimers at the concentrations usually examined and the integrity of the tetramer appears to be obligatory for co-operativity in ligand-binding. Conclusions of a similar nature were also achieved by Kellett (1971) by equilibrium sedimentation and by Noren, Ho, and Casassa (1971) by a light-scattering study and consideration of the multi-component nature of the solutions. The dramatic 'effective' hydration of haemoglobin of 25 per cent, as reported by Edelstein and Gibson, is somewhat misleading if interpreted in terms of physical hydration, as it can be shown that part of this effect is due to exclusion of salt (see the discussion in Section 3.3 on a physical model for binding of small solute molecules to a macromolecular system).

It is possible to use the true partial volume $\bar{v}_2$ in the buoyancy term to cast the equations for sedimentation equilibrium in a three-component system into the conventional form applicable to two-component systems and to define a factor Λ (analogous to the factor Ω, eqn (4.43), defined with respect to refractive-index increments in light-scattering experiments) such that (see eqn (3.9)) for a three-component system

$$\left(\frac{\partial \rho}{\partial c_2}\right)_\mu = (1 - \bar{v}_2 \rho)\left\{1 + \xi_3 \frac{(1 - \bar{v}_3 \rho)^0}{(1 - \bar{v}_2^0 \rho)^0}\right\} \equiv (1 - \bar{v}_2 \rho^0)\Lambda, \qquad (5.28)$$

and substitution of $(\partial \rho/\partial c_2)_\mu$ from the above equation into eqn (5.25) yields

$$\frac{\mathrm{d}\ln c_2}{\mathrm{d}r^2} = \frac{\omega^2}{2RT}(1 - \bar{v}_2 \rho)M^*, \qquad (5.29)$$

where an apparent molecular weight M^* is defined here to equal $M\Lambda$. Substitution of $(\partial \rho/\partial c_2)_\mu$ from eqn (5.28) in eqn (5.24) shows that the virial coefficient in this formulation becomes $A_2^* = A_2/\Lambda$. The magnitude of the correction term depends (compare with eqn (4.43) for the light-scattering correction term Ω) on the value of the preferential absorption parameter ξ_3, on the partial volumes $\bar{v}_3$ and $\bar{v}_2$, and on salt concentration c_3, as it affects the solvent density ρ^0. The factor Λ equals unity (even for strong preferential interactions ξ_3) if $\bar{v}_3 \rho^0$ equals unity.

We can, of course, use the equivalent expression (eqn (3.25)) to define Λ in terms of the interaction parameter ξ_1',

$$\Lambda = 1 + \xi_1' \frac{1 - \bar{v}_1 \rho^0}{1 - \bar{v}_2 \rho^0}. \qquad (5.30)$$

From the discussion following eqn (3.25) it is clear that Λ does not become unity in aqueous polyelectrolyte solutions ($\bar{v}_1$ is approximately unity) in the extrapolation $c_3 \to 0$ ($\rho^0 \to 1$) as, under these conditions, ξ_1' (by eqn (3.26)) increases considerably with decreasing concentration of component 3; the vanishing of $(1 - \bar{v}_1 \rho^0)$ under these conditions is therefore not sufficient to make Λ become unity. Procedures based on the extrapolation to ρ^0 equal to unity are not adequate for obtaining correct molecular weights.

We can now ask questions similar to those asked with respect to osmotic pressure in Section 1.3 and with respect to light-scattering and SAXS in Sections 4.4 and 4.5; namely, which molecular weight is determined in a charged interacting macromolecular system? From eqn (5.25) we have deduced that the slope of the plot of the logarithm of any quantity (ultraviolet absorption, number of fringes) proportional to c_2, versus r^2, is proportional to $(\partial \rho/\partial c_2)_\mu M_2$, and M_2 may be derived if the accessory quantities are known. The slope increases with increase in M_2, and therefore the sensitivity of the method increases as the molecular weight increases. Note that the product $(\partial \rho/\partial c_2)_\mu M_2$ can be written $\{\partial \rho/\partial (c_2/M_2)\}_\mu$, which indicates that the density increment is naturally expressed in terms of an increment due to the number of particles, and not their weight. Considerations presented earlier with respect to molecular-weight determinations by osmotic pressure and light-scattering apply here as well. Molecular weights are obtained in whatever units we choose to express concentrations (see footnote p. 22, for instance, or the discussion on p. 78).

We have shown that the equations derived above for equilibrium sedimentation in a three-component system can be used in the differential form for the evaluation of molecular weights and virial coefficients. No further difficulties arise if we have a heterogeneous macromolecular component 2 characterized by unique values of $\bar{v}_2$ and ξ_3 (and therefore $(\partial \rho/\partial c_2)_\mu$), or if we are dealing with a more complex buffer system, composed of a number of diffusible low-molecular-weight components. If we wish to analyse and integrate the differential equation for equilibrium sedimentation in the manner amply described in the literature pertinent to this field (for the early literature see Svedberg and Pedersen 1940; for more recent work see Goldberg 1953; Williams et al. 1958; Schachman 1959; Baldwin and van Holde 1960; Fujita 1962, 1975; Yphantis 1964; Creeth and Pain 1967; Adams 1968) we must impose a number of restrictions such that: (1) the solutions be incompressible so that partial volumes are independent of pressure; (2) all activity coefficients be independent of pressure; (3) the interaction parameters ξ be independent of concentration of component 2; (4) there be no redistribution of diffusible components in the centrifugal field in the absence of component 2. From assumptions (1), (2), and (4) it follows that the second virial coefficient in eqn (5.24), for instance, is independent of pressure and thus of r. This can be seen from equations developed in Section 2.3. Invariance of the a_{JK} with pressure also implies that the partial volumes are independent of concentration. This is shown by differentiating eqn (A2.4) with respect to m_K and interchange of the order of the differentiation

$$\left\{\frac{\partial}{\partial m_K}\left(\frac{\partial \mu_J}{\partial P}\right)_m\right\}_P = \left\{\frac{\partial}{\partial P}\left(\frac{\partial \mu_J}{\partial m_K}\right)_P\right\}_m = RT\left(\frac{\partial a_{JK}}{\partial P}\right)_m = \left(\frac{\partial \bar{V}_J}{\partial m_K}\right)_P. \quad (5.31)$$

As a result of the assumed constancy of the $\bar{v}_J$ with respect to concentration, the density increment at fixed composition $(\partial \rho/\partial c_2)_{P,m}$ contains no linear dependence on concentration (see eqn (3.5)). The density increment $(\partial \rho/\partial c_2)_\mu$ measured at osmotic equilibrium also assumes a limiting form with no linear dependence on c_2 (eqn (3.27), for instance), provided assumption (3) is valid. Under these conditions then $(\partial \rho/\partial c_2)_\mu$ can be regarded as a constant, to within the same assumptions.

With the four assumptions stated above, eqn (5.24) is directly integrable. To obtain the concentration profile in the cell one further needs an integration constant obtained by introducing the condition of conservation of mass, that the integral of c_2 over the volume of the solution be the same before centrifugation and at equilibrium in the field. The derivations given in the literature for two-component systems can be applied directly to the more complicated systems considered here, since our basic equations are of the same form as those for a binary system.

Whereas the conditions stipulated above might appear rather restrictive at first sight, they are often rather well-fulfilled in conventional equilibrium studies on biological macromolecules in aqueous solutions (conditions in density gradients will be discussed in Section 5.4). Centrifuge speeds in these cases are rather low, as are concentrations of component 2; water is a rather incompressible liquid. Thus compressibility effects and deviations from van't Hoff's law can be small, and redistribution of diffusible solutes in the absence of component 2 practically negligible.

For synthetic polymers in organic solvents the situation is usually much less favourable (Mandelkern, Williams, and Weissberg 1957; Baldwin and van Holde **1960**). Organic solvents are usually much more compressible than water, and, since specific-density increments of organic macromolecules in organic solvents are generally smaller than those of biological macro-molecules in aqueous media, it is necessary to run the centrifuge at con-siderably higher speeds. Effects of compressibility are thus doubly enhanced. Thermodynamic interactions are frequently considerable and it is difficult to make accurate concentration measurements by refractometry or interfero-metry at low enough concentrations of the macromolecular component. Thermodynamic complications are sometimes minimized by working at the Flory theta temperature Θ (Flory **1953**), the temperature at which A_2 vanishes; it is expected that at this temperature the higher virial coefficients also vanish and, at any rate, their significance in affecting the experimental results is much reduced. It is possible, of course, to obtain solutions of some biological macromolecules in selected organic solvents, and the problems mentioned above should then be carefully considered.

5.3.2. *Heterogeneous macromolecular components*

We conclude this discussion on conventional equilibrium in a three-component system by a limited elaboration of the information on molecular-weight averages obtainable if the density increment $(\partial\rho/\partial c_2)_\mu$ is independent of the molecular weight of the (chemically) identical species which make up component 2. We have already seen (eqn (5.26)) that, in the limit $c_2 \to 0$, the weight-average molecular weight $M_w^{(r)}$ is obtained at any level r in the equilibrium distribution of macromolecular solutes (which is not identical with the original molecular-weight distribution before ultracentrifugation), regardless of interactions with diffusible components.

In principle, sedimentation equilibrium measurements also yield higher and lower moments of the solute mass. A hierarchy of integral equations can be derived (Goldberg 1953; Yphantis 1964) from the equilibrium conditions and solved in some circumstances to obtain the number M_n and z-average M_z molecular weights, in addition to M_w, for a multi-component system, polydisperse with respect to the mass of the macromolecular component,

$$M_n = \frac{\sum n_J M_J}{\sum n_J} = \frac{\sum n_J M_J}{n} = \frac{\sum c_J}{\sum (c_J/M_J)} = \frac{c_2}{\sum (c_J/M_J)}, \qquad (5.32)$$

$$M_w = \frac{\sum n_J M_J^2}{\sum n_J M_J} = \frac{\sum c_J M_J}{\sum c_J} = \frac{\sum c_J M_J}{c_2}, \qquad (5.33)$$

$$M_z = \frac{\sum n_J M_J^3}{\sum n_J M_J^2} = \frac{\sum c_J M_J^2}{\sum c_J M_J} = \frac{\sum c_J M_J^2}{M_w c_2}. \qquad (5.34)$$

This process could be continued but in practice experimental data are usually not accurate enough to consider higher averages of M and these will therefore not be discussed. We shall consider here only the case of vanishing concentration c_2 or, equivalently, thermodynamic ideality (that is, measurements close to the Flory theta temperature, wherever this can be properly defined). Non-ideality will be briefly discussed in Section 5.5.

To derive the lowest molecular-weight average M_n we integrate eqn (5.25) for component J in the form

$$\int_{r_m}^{r} \frac{dc_J}{dr} dr = c_J^{(r)} - c_J^{(m)} = L_2 M_J \int_{r_m}^{r} c_J \, dr^2, \qquad (5.35)$$

where $L_2 \equiv \omega^2 (\partial \rho / \partial c_2)_\mu / 2RT$ is assumed to be identical for all Js and r_m is the radius at the solution meniscus. Division by M_J, summation over all J, and re-arrangement leads to

$$M_n^{(r)} = \frac{c_2^{(r)}}{L_2 \int_{r_m}^{r} c_2 \, dr^2 + \sum (c_J^{(m)}/M_J)}, \qquad (5.36)$$

where the sum in the last term of the denominator (equal to $c_2^{(m)}/M_n^{(m)}$) is proportional to the number $n_J^{(m)}$ of solute molecules per unit volume at the meniscus. In general, $M_n^{(r)}$ cannot be evaluated directly, since this sum is unknown. However, if the meniscus concentration may be neglected with respect to the concentration at some arbitrary reference point $r > r_m$ in the solution and the smallest M_J is large enough so that $n_J^{(m)}$ is also negligible, then eqn (5.36) simplifies to the more tractable form

$$L_2 M_n^{(r)} = \frac{c_2^{(r)}}{\int_{r_m}^{r} c_2^{(r)} \, dr^2}. \qquad (5.37)$$

These considerations have been developed (Yphantis 1964) in relation to the high-speed meniscus-depletion method and computational procedures for corrections for non-negligible values of the sum in eqn (5.36) have also been applied (Roark and Yphantis 1969).

We have already derived the value

$$L_2 M_w^{(r)} = \frac{dc_2/dr^2}{c^{(r)}}.$$ (5.26)

To derive $M_z^{(r)}$ we note that eqn (5.25) may be integrated to give the exponential expression

$$c_J^{(r)} = A \exp(L_2 M_J r^2),$$ (5.38)

where the integration constant A can be evaluated if conservation of mass is invoked in a sectorial cell. (A can also be evaluated from $c_J^{(m)}$ at the meniscus r_m, regardless of conservation of mass.) Use of eqn (5.38) in the definition of M_z in eqn (5.34) yields

$$L_2 M_z^{(r)} = \frac{d^2 c/d(r^2)^2}{dc_2/dr^2},$$ (5.39)

and the form of the general expression for the moments M_k (Yphantis 1964) can be derived by inspection of eqns (5.37), (5.26), and (5.39).

Some simple manipulations yield the two expressions

$$\frac{M_w}{M_n} - 1 = \frac{d \ln M_n/dr^2}{L_2 M_n}$$ (5.40)

and

$$\frac{M_z}{M_w} - 1 = \frac{d \ln M_w/dr^2}{L_2 M_w}$$ (5.41)

for measures of the width of the distribution curve of the molecular weight at the position r. The moments $M_z > M_w > M_n$ are also ever-increasing functions of r (for positive L).

To obtain the average molecular weights $\overline{M}$ of the entire solute sample (before redistribution by ultracentrifugation) it is necessary to use integration procedures. For the sector-shaped cell (Fig. 5.1) customarily used in ultra-centrifuge studies we derive, from eqns (5.32)–(5.34), by integrating over the total sector cell from the meniscus r_m to the cell bottom r_b and interchanging the summation sign,

$$\overline{M}_n = \frac{\sum \int c_J \, dr^2}{\sum \int (c_J/M_J) \, dr^2} = \frac{\int c_2 \, dr^2}{\int (c_2/M_n^{(r)}) \, dr^2},$$ (5.42)

$$\overline{M}_w = \frac{\sum \int M_J c_J \, dr^2}{\sum \int c_J \, dr^2} = \frac{\int M_w c_2 \, dr^2}{\int c_2 \, dr^2},$$ (5.43)

$$\overline{M}_z = \frac{\sum \int M_J^2 c_J \, dr^2}{\sum \int M_J c_J \, dr^2} = \frac{\int M_z M_w c_2 \, dr^2}{\int M_w c_2 \, dr^2}.$$ (5.44)

We further consider conservation of mass, by observing that the total solute content proportional to

$$\int_{r_m}^{r_b} \tfrac{1}{2} c_2 \, dr^2$$

is constant during ultracentrifugation, and therefore this integral is equal to $0.5c_{20} \int dr^2 = 0.5c_{20} (r_b^2 - r_m^2)$, where c_{20} is the uniform concentration c_2 before sedimentation. Substitution of the value of M_n, M_w, and M_z from eqns (5.37), (5.26), and (5.39) into the appropriate expressions above yields

$$L_2 \overline{M}_n = \frac{c_{20} (r_b^2 - r_m^2)}{\int_{r_m}^{r_b} \left(\int_{r_m}^{r'} c_2 \, dr^2 \right) dr'^2} \tag{5.45}$$

$$L_2 \overline{M}_w = \frac{2(c_2^{(b)} - c_2^{(m)})}{c_{20} (r_b^2 - r_m^2)}, \tag{5.46}$$

and

$$L_2 \overline{M}_z = \frac{\left(\dfrac{dc}{dr}\right)^{(b)} - \left(\dfrac{dc}{dr}\right)^{(m)}}{c_2^{(b)} - c_2^{(m)}}. \tag{5.47}$$

Furthermore, if the meniscus concentration is negligible, $\overline{M}_w$ equals $M_n^{(b)}$, that is, the weight-average molecular weight of the complete solution is the number-average obtained at the bottom of the cell. Also, if both meniscus concentration and its gradient may be neglected $\overline{M}_z$ equals $M_w^{(b)}$.

As is indicated by eqn (5.24), the criterion for homogeneity of solutes showing ideal-solution behaviour is that a plot of $\ln c$ versus r^2 be linear. For a heterogeneous solute the graph must be convex upward, since M_w increases with increasing r (see eqn (5.41)), if $(\partial \rho / \partial c_2)_\mu$ is positive. However a positive second virial coefficient—and this is the usual circumstance since phase-separation occurs if the virial coefficient becomes appreciable negative (but see Section 5.5 for a discussion of pronounced upward convexity due to macromolecular association) has a qualitatively opposite effect. Thus, apparent constancy of $d \ln c / dr^2$ throughout the centrifuge cell cannot be accepted as decisive evidence of homogeneity, unless it is certain that limiting dilute-solution behaviour adequately describes the system. Rather stringent requirements of experimental precision and freedom from artefacts must be expected to discern slight inflections in the experimental equilibrium curves. These conditions are best met by the use of interference optics (Godfrey and Harrington 1970), but the proper use of absorption optics and a split-beam photoelectric scanner (Schachman and Edelstein 1973), preferably in conjunction with a digital on-line computer data-collector and analyser, may lead to equally rewarding results.

The problem of integrating the differential equations for distribution of a heterogeneous macromolecular solute, when thermodynamic interactions among these components cannot be neglected, or other simplifying assumptions fail, has so far yielded only to solutions of limited applicability—a circumstance not at all surprising, in view of the difficulty of performing the integration under fairly general conditions for systems with only one non-diffusible solute. We shall discuss such a particular example involving molecular-weight heterogeneity and thermodynamic non-ideality in Section 5.5. We shall let it suffice here to reiterate that introduction of density increments formulated to include the interactions between diffusible and non-diffusible solutes still essentially reduces the problem formally to that of a system without diffusible solutes; and therefore, the various available treatments (described above) for a heterogeneous polymer in one solvent can be utilized.

5.3.3. The approach to equilibrium

Archibald (1947) found the differential equations for the distribution of solutes at equilibrium in the centrifugal field to hold in a two-component system, irrespective of attainment of equilibrium, at the top and bottom boundaries of the liquid column. These considerations, derived from the general transport equations for sedimentation diffusion, are based on the kinetic criterion for equilibrium, that there be no net flow through an arbitrary level r; this criterion holds at all times at r_m and r_b. Williams et al. (1958) have shown by the methods of irreversible thermodynamics that the same result is valid for multi-component systems. The differential equations developed above always apply at the boundaries as they do at true equilibria. Archibald's method is known as the approach-to-equilibrium method, and extrapolation of data to the beginning of the experiment, before any redistribution of solutes has occurred, affords an analysis relating directly to the original system. Eqn (5.26) can be written for the meniscus position, at the initial time,

$$\left(\frac{\mathrm{d}\ln c_{20}}{\mathrm{d}r^2}\right)_{r_m} = \frac{\omega^2}{2RT}\left(\frac{\partial\rho}{\partial c_2}\right)_\mu M_\mathrm{w}. \tag{5.48}$$

Hence from c_{20} and its initial gradient at the meniscus, it is possible to obtain M_w of the heterogeneous solute without requirement of explicit evaluation of interactions between diffusible and non-diffusible solutes. The introduction of density gradients, evaluated at fixed chemical potentials of diffusible solutes, does not create new theoretical or experimental difficulties, and additional detailed elaborations of Archibald's methods are not affected by this modification.

5.3.4. *Salt-free polyelectrolyte solutions*

We now digress for a moment to consider equilibrium sedimentation of a salt-free two-component polyelectrolyte solution, the light-scattering properties of which we have discussed in Section 4.6. The differential equation for equilibrium sedimentation (eqn (5.21)) becomes

$$\frac{d \ln c_2}{dr^2} = \frac{\omega^2}{2}(1 - \bar{v}_2 \rho^0)\left(\frac{d\Pi}{dc_2}\right)^{-1} \tag{5.49}$$

in this situation; we also know, from our previous discussion, that we are not allowed to expand the osmotic pressure in a virial series. By eqn (4.72)

$$\Pi = (RTc_2/M_2)(1 + v\phi_p), \tag{5.50}$$

and differentiation with respect to c_2 and substitution into eqn (5.49) leads to

$$\frac{d \ln c_2}{dr^2} = \frac{\omega^2(1 - \bar{v}_2 \rho^0)}{2RT} \frac{M_2}{1 + v\phi_p}. \tag{5.51}$$

Therefore $M_2/(1 + v\phi_p)$ rather than M_2 (eqn (5.25)) is derived by this experiment. We remember that v is the number of charges carried by the polymeric chain and ϕ_p is the practical osmotic coefficient; usually $v\phi_p$ is much larger than unity. If the charge is eliminated, eqn (5.25) is eventually recovered. By eqn (5.51) ϕ_p may be evaluated in similar fashion to the analysis of the light-scattering eqn (4.76). We can write eqn (5.51) in the equivalent form

$$\frac{d \ln C_u}{dr^2} = \frac{\omega^2}{2RT} \frac{M_u - \bar{v}_u \rho^0}{Z^{-1} + \alpha\phi_p}. \tag{5.52}$$

Obviously any concentration unit (refractive index, optical density, etc.) proportional to C_u in the derivative $d \ln C_u/dr^2$ will be equally satisfactory.

5.4. Sedimentation equilibrium in a density gradient

In the other type of sedimentation-equilibrium measurement, introduced a few years ago by Meselson *et al.* (1957) into the study of solutions of biological macromolecules, a 'heavy', simple electrolyte, such as caesium chloride, at very high concentration (typically above 5 M) is run in the ultracentrifuge at such high speeds that at equilibrium there forms an appreciable concentration gradient, and thus a density gradient, from re-distribution of the simple-electrolyte component 3, even in the absence of the macromolecular component 2. Conditions may therefore be chosen to cause $(\partial\rho/\partial c_2)_\mu$ to vanish at some intermediate level r_B (we use B for 'band') in the solution column; dc_2/dr vanishes at r_B according to eqn (5.25).

The concentration gradient is positive for $r < r_B$, where $(\partial\rho/\partial c_2)_\mu > 0$ and negative for $r > r_B$ when $(\partial\rho/\partial c_2)_\mu < 0$; the macromolecular solute 2 is distributed in a band with the maximum concentration at r_B. We shall see that the position of the band relates to partial specific volumes and thermo-dynamic interaction parameters and the width of the band decreases with increasing molecular weight. The purpose of the theory is to provide the quantitative interpretation from the position and width of the band under given experimental conditions.

Overshadowing the interest in the unique elegance of sedimentation equilibrium in a density gradient as a versatile physico-chemical tool, for the investigation of macromolecules so large as to be difficult to investigate by the conventional equilibrium method, is its remarkable usefulness as a biological tool, in particular in the novel way in which it has utilized isotope-labelling methods. The classical experiment in this field, of course, is due to Meselson and Stahl (1958), who showed that the replication of E. coli DNA was semi-conservative by following banding patterns of subsequent generations of density-labelled $[^{15}N]$DNA transferred to the light (^{14}N) isotope medium. The isotopically labelled and non-labelled materials were clearly separated in the equilibrium-sedimentation patterns (Fig. 5.3).

Schildkraut, Marmur, and Doty (1961) pioneered DNA renaturation and hybridization studies, and for a study of banding differences in different caesium salts of deletion mutants in phage lambda we refer to Costello and Baldwin (1972). This list of examples is by no means exhaustive (see Vinograd and Hearst (**1962**) and Hearst and Schmid (1971) for further examples of biological interest). The detailed analysis of equilibrium sedimentation in a density gradient has also been reviewed by Vinograd (**1963**), by Hearst and Schmid (**1973**), and by Szybalski and Szybalski (**1971**) as applied to aqueous nucleic-acid solutions; an example of a study of a protein (bovine serum mercaptalbumin) in six salt solutions (CsCl, CsBr, CsI, KBr, RbBr, and Cs_2SO_4) was reported by Ifft and Vinograd (1966) (see the discussion of proteins in density gradients at sedimentation–equilibrium by Ifft **1973**), and a review of the rather difficult analysis of density-gradient centrifugation of synthetic polymers in a mixture of organic solvents is due to Hermans and Ende (**1964**).

5.4.1. *The position of the macromolecular band in a density gradient*

To establish the equations for equilibrium sedimentation in a density gradient we consider, for the sake of the argument, the simplest case of the three-component system previously discussed. The differential eqn (5.21) applies in this case as well except that ρ^0 and therefore $(\partial\rho/\partial c_2)_\mu$ (by eqn (3.27)) are not constant across the centrifuge cell. The density ρ^0 increases mono-tonically from the meniscus to the bottom of the cell, and the condition for the formation of a band of the macromolecular component, on either side of which c_2 decreases (d ln c_2/dr = 0 at the centre of the band), requires the density increment $(\partial\rho/\partial c_2)_\mu$ to vanish at this position. The buoyancy con-dition therefore becomes $(\partial\rho/\partial c_2)_\mu = 0$ at r_B (the distance from the centre of

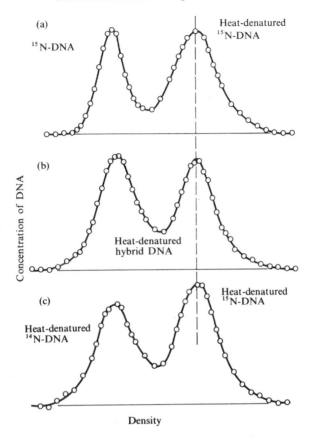

FIG. 5.3. The dissociation of the subunits of *E. coli* DNA upon 'heat denaturation'. Each smooth curve connects points obtained by microdensitometry of an ultraviolet absorption photograph taken after 20 hours of centrifugation in caesium chloride solution at 44 770 r.p.m. The base-line density has been removed by substraction. (a) A mixture of heated and unheated bacterial lysates. Heated lysate alone gives one band in the position indicated. Heating brings about a density increase of 0.016 g ml^{-1} and a reduction of about half in the apparent molecular weight of the DNA. (b) Heated lysate of ^{15}N bacteria grown for one generation in ^{14}N growth medium. Before heat denaturation, the hybrid DNA contained in this lysate forms only one band. (c) A mixture of heated ^{14}N and heated ^{15}N bacterial lysates. The density difference is 0.015 g ml^{-1}. (From Meselson and Stahl 1958.)

rotation to the centre of the band), and therefore (see eqn (3.27) for the three-component system)

$$\rho_B^0 = \frac{1 + \xi_3}{\bar{v}_2^0 + \xi_3 \bar{v}_3},\tag{5.53}$$

where ρ_B^0 is the density of the solvent system (in the absence of component 2) at the position r_B. If the partial specific volumes are known from measurements at the appropriate salt concentration at atmospheric pressure, and their variation with pressure is either taken into consideration, or assumed to be negligible, then obviously knowledge of ρ_B^0 permits the evaluation of ξ_3 at the centre of the band, under the pertinent experimental conditions. It is, of course, also possible to express the buoyancy condition for a three-component system on the basis of eqn (3.25) in terms of preferential inter-action with respect to component 1, and write the equivalent expression

$$\rho_B^0 = \frac{1 + \xi_1'}{\bar{v}_2^0 + \xi_1' \, \bar{v}_1}. \tag{5.54}$$

We already know (see eqn (3.20)) that ξ_1' and ξ_3 are simply related ($\xi_3 = -w_3 \xi_1'$), and the formal relationships, on which eqns (5.53) and (5.54) are based, do not imply anything in terms of molecular mechanisms of component 'binding' and 'solvation', which have been discussed in Section 3.3. Hearst and Vinograd (1961) chose to call $1/\rho_B^0$, of eqn (5.54), $\bar{v}_s$, the partial specific volume of the 'solvated' macromolecule, and Schmid and Hearst (1971) propagate this intuitive motion (see, for instance, Fig. 1 of Schmid and Hearst 1971) by a pictorial representation of the 'solvated' macromolecule. The thermodynamic derivation on which the differential and the integrated equations for equilibrium sedimentation are based (Section 5.3) is completely independent of any assumption relating to molecular processes of 'solvation' or 'ion-binding', and it is therefore possible to analyse this situation without even mentioning these phenomena. In the manner in which $1/\rho_B^0$ is called the partial specific volume of the 'solvated' species, it could, by eqn (5.53), correspondingly be called (with hardly less or more justification) the partial specific volume of the starred components 2* of Casassa and Eisenberg (1960, **1964**). Nothing is gained, neither is anything lost, by either representation, but perhaps some complications and some confusion, which could have been avoided, are created. We shall attempt to analyse the equilibrium sedimentation experiment in a density gradient avoiding all extraneous considerations. In this context $1/\rho_B^0$ is simply the reciprocal of ρ^0 at the centre of the band formed by the macromolecular species, and not the partial specific volume of a 'solvated' or otherwise defined component.

5.4.2. The molecular weight of the macromolecular component

To integrate eqn (5.21) in the simplest possible case for consideration, we first discuss the case of the solution so dilute in component 2 that only the first term M_2^{-1} in the virial-expansion equation (1.2) need be considered. Schmid and Hearst (1969) believe though that, as far as coliphage nucleic acids are concerned, this assumption is not valid and that upward curvature in the plots

$$\frac{1}{M_w^*} \equiv \frac{1}{M_2} + 2A_2 c_2 + 3A_2 c_2^2 + \cdots \tag{5.55}$$

(obtained from experiments undertaken at different nucleic-acid concentrations) indicates that two further terms in the expansion have to be considered.† There is no difficulty, in principle, in including this refinement, and we may disregard it for the time being. To integrate eqn (5.25) we expand $(\partial\rho/\partial c_2)_\mu^0$ about r_B to write

$$\left(\frac{\partial\rho}{\partial c_2}\right)_\mu^0 = \chi\delta + O(\delta^2), \tag{5.56}$$

where δ is $(r - r_B)$ and χ

$$\chi \equiv \left\{ \frac{d}{dr}\left(\frac{\partial\rho}{\partial c_2}\right)_\mu^0 \right\}_{r_B} \tag{5.57}$$

is the gradient of the density increment $(\partial\rho/\partial c_2)_\mu^0$ at r_B (the numerical value of χ is negative for a positive density gradient $d\rho^0/dr$ for the salt). Introducing this result into eqn (5.25) and performing the integration we obtain

$$\ln\left(\frac{c_2}{c_{2B}}\right) = \int^\delta \frac{M_2\,\omega^2}{RT}\{\chi\delta + O(\delta^2)\}(r_B + \delta)\,d\delta$$

$$= \frac{M_2\,\omega^2 r_B \chi}{2RT}\delta^2 + O(\delta^3), \tag{5.58}$$

where c_{2B} is the concentration of component 2 at position r_B. If we can assume that terms of order greater than δ^2 can be neglected (this is a valid assumption for narrow bands of high-molecular-weight nucleic acids but may not apply to the broader bands encountered in the analysis of low-molecular-weight proteins (Ifft and Vinograd 1966), then this is just a gaussian distribution about r_B,

$$c_2 = c_{2B}\exp(-\delta^2/2\sigma^2), \tag{5.59}$$

with the standard deviation

$$\sigma^2 = -\frac{RT}{M_2\,\omega^2 r_B \chi}. \tag{5.60}$$

Consequently, the molecular weight can be obtained unambiguously from the half-width of the gaussian concentration distribution, if the gradient of $(\partial\rho/\partial c_2)_\mu^0$ is known, and nothing need be said explicitly about ξ_3 or about ξ_1'. The form of eqn (5.60) with the definition of χ (eqn (5.57)), demonstrates

† This is the first instance reported in which curvature is claimed in a plot of $1/M_w^*$ against c_2 for DNA solutions. Jamie Godfrey (work recently completed in our laboratory) finds that, in the case of low-molecular-weight DNA ($0\cdot25 < M_w \times 10^{-6} < 1\cdot2$) $1/M_w^*$ is strictly linear with concentration in both light-scattering and sedimentation–equilibrium experiments.

(as has been shown previously with respect to conventional equilibrium sedimentation—Section 5.3) that the molecular weight will be given in whatever units we choose to express the concentration in the density increment. No real difficulties are caused should the bands be non-gaussian (eqn (5.58)) or should it be necessary to keep higher terms in the virial expansion (eqn (5.55)); these problems can be handled by straightforward integrational procedures or numerical analysis of the whole concentration distribution. The major problem that remains is the evaluation of χ, and this can be done in a number of ways. The classical way, which was first developed in Vinograd's laboratory (Hearst and Vinograd 1961; Vinograd and Hearst **1962**), for determining the banding properties of nucleic acids is based on a procedure involving the discussion of preferential solvation and the definition of a solvated molecular volume. We shall show how their procedure relates to the determination of χ, the quantity defined by Casassa and Eisenberg (**1964**).

For the evaluation of χ (eqn (5.57)) we first establish the connection with the work of Hearst and Vinograd, and therefore rewrite eqn (3.25) to read

$$(\partial\rho/\partial c_2)_\mu = (1+\xi_1')(1-\rho^0\bar{v}_{\rm s}),\tag{5.61}$$

where

$$\bar{v}_{\rm s} = \frac{\bar{v}_2^0 + \xi_1'\,\bar{v}_1}{1+\xi_i'}\tag{5.62}$$

has been defined by Hearst and Vinograd (1961) as the partial specific volume of the 'solvated' macromolecule. This separation is only one of many arbitrary separations, and the correct result will be obtained if a consistent procedure is followed throughout.

We next expand the various terms in eqn (5.61) in terms of δ and $r_{\rm B}$, and keep the linear terms only,

$$\xi_1' = \xi_{1\rm B}' + (\mathrm{d}\xi_1'/\mathrm{d}r)_{\rm B}\,\delta,\tag{5.63}$$

$$\bar{v}_{\rm s} = \bar{v}_{\rm sB} + (\mathrm{d}\bar{v}_{\rm s}/\mathrm{d}r)_{\rm B}\,\delta,\tag{5.64}$$

and

$$\rho^0 = \rho_{\rm B}^0 + (\mathrm{d}\rho^0/\mathrm{d}r)_{\rm B}\,\delta.\tag{5.65}$$

Substitution into eqn (5.61), differentiation with respect to δ, setting $(1-\rho_{\rm B}^0\,\bar{v}_{\rm sB})$ equal to zero, and again keeping the linear terms only yields

$$\chi = -\left\{(1+\xi_1')\bar{v}_{\rm s}\left(\frac{\mathrm{d}\rho^0}{\mathrm{d}r}+\frac{\rho^0}{\bar{v}_{\rm s}}\frac{\mathrm{d}\bar{v}_{\rm s}}{\mathrm{d}r}\right)\right\}_{\rm B},\tag{5.66}$$

or, in the Vinograd and Hearst (**1962**) terminology,

$$\chi = -(1+\xi_{1\rm B}')\bar{v}_{\rm sB}\,(\mathrm{d}\rho/\mathrm{d}r)_{\rm eff},\tag{5.67}$$

where the 'effective' density gradient $(d\rho/dr)_{\text{eff}}$ is the sum of the 'physical' density gradient $d\rho^0/dr$ at r_B and a term proportional to the gradient of $\bar{v}_s$, also at r_B. If the value of χ from eqn (5.66) is introduced into eqn (5.60) and we furthermore write M_{sB} for $M_2(1+\zeta'_{1B})$, then the formulation of Hearst and Vinograd for the standard deviation of the band is obtained,

$$\sigma^2 = \frac{RT}{M_{sB}\,\bar{v}_{sB}\,(d\rho^0/dr)_{\text{eff}}\,\omega^2 r_B}. \tag{5.68}$$

To evaluate $(d\rho^0/dr)_{\text{eff}}$ Vinograd and Hearst (**1962**) derive the following expression

$$\left(\frac{d\rho^0}{dr}\right)_{\text{eff}} = \left(\frac{1}{\beta}+\psi\rho^2\right)(1-\alpha)\omega^2 r, \tag{5.69}$$

where

$$\frac{1}{\beta} = \frac{d}{d\ln a_3}\frac{M_3(1-\bar{v}_3\rho^0)}{RT} \tag{5.70}$$

(a_3 is the activity of component 3 and the above expression is derived from the equilibrium distribution of component 3 in the absence of component 2), ψ is the slope in the plot

$$\rho_B = \frac{1}{\bar{v}_{sB}}(1-\psi P_b) \tag{5.71}$$

and is therefore derived from the pressure-dependence of the buoyant density ρ_B, and α is the product

$$\alpha = \left(\frac{\partial\rho_B}{\partial a_1}\right)_P\left(\frac{da_1}{d\rho}\right). \tag{5.72}$$

of the slope of the plot of buoyant density ρ_B against water activity a_1, and the slope of the plot of a_1 against density. In all quantities in the eqns (5.69)–(5.72) pressure-dependence has been considered and the quantities have been reduced to and refer to the value of the parameters at atmospheric pressure. The reader is referred to the work of Vinograd and Hearst and their collaborators for further details and numerical values of the parameters under various experimental conditions.

Because, in the past, the molecular weights obtained from the bandwidths of the equilibrium sedimentation in a density-gradient experiment have been considerably too low (Thomas and Pinkerton 1962), there have been doubts with respect to the value of the parameters derived from the somewhat involved analysis of Vinograd and Hearst. It was gratifying therefore that it can be shown (Eisenberg 1967; Cohen and Eisenberg 1968) by a very simple analysis of the isotope-substitution experiment (see below) that the analysis of Vinograd and Hearst of the performance of the three-component system at equilibrium in a density gradient was essentially correct, including their values of the numerical parameters.

5.4.3. *Isotope substitution calibration*

Vinograd and Hearst (**1962**) remarked that the determination of molecular weights in a buoyant density system involves 'the determination of ξ_i' and the distance of separation caused by incorporation of a known amount of isotope into the macrospecies'. The classical study involving the substitution of the common isotope ^{14}N by ^{15}N in nucleic acids is due to Meselson and Stahl (1958), but substitution by the carbon isotope ^{13}C has also been studied (Meselson and Weigle 1961). Baldwin, Barrand, Fritsch, Goldthwait, and Jacob (1966) described a method for determining relative molecular weights from the buoyant densities of hybrid-labelled and unlabelled DNA dimers. Eisenberg (1967) showed that the evaluation of the distance of separation caused by isotopic substitution into the macrospecies is all that is required for the evaluation of χ (and therefore of M_2), and a knowledge of ξ_1' is not required.

The assumptions underlying the application of the method are that (1) isotopic substitution changes the weight of the macromolecular component but does not affect the molecular volume† and (2) preferential thermodynamic interactions with the solvent mixture are not affected by isotopic substitution. Cohen and Eisenberg (1968) showed that under these assumptions the procedures of Vinograd and Hearst (**1962**) and the isotope-substitution method of Eisenberg (1967) yielded identical results. This conclusion was considerably strengthened by Schmid and Hearst (1971), who greatly extended the study of band-shifts due to isotope substitution and convincingly showed that the low molecular weights of nucleic acids in equilibrium sedimentation in a density gradient previously obtained were not due to the effect of charge, as had been claimed by Daniel (1969) (Poon and Schumaker (1971) also state that by retaining the terms involving the charge of the macromolecule, it is possible to account for most of the concentration-dependence), but could mostly be related to errors arising from the use of film methods in the earlier papers rather than the now ubiquitous photoelectric scanner and the neglect of virial coefficients in the relatively concentrated DNA bands (Schmid and Hearst 1969). Charge effects (see the discussion in Section 5.2) therefore do not play a significant role in determining the equilibrium distribution of polyelectrolyte macromolecules in an ultracentrifugal field.

We denote, as before, by r_B the centre of the band formed by the natural DNA (or other macromolecular system under investigation) and r_B' the

---

† We have ample reason to believe that this is essentially true: in the rather extreme case of H_2O and D_2O, the ratio of the molecular weights is 0·900, while the ratio of molecular volumes is close to unity (0·997).

corresponding position for the DNA fully substituted by ^{15}N. We have (by eqn (3.27)) at r'_B, for the natural DNA,

$$(\partial\rho/\partial c_2)^{(r'_B)}_\mu = \{(1-\bar{v}^0_2\rho^0)-\xi_3(1-v_e\rho^0)\}^{(r'_B)}, \qquad (5.73)$$

and for the labelled species

$$0 = \{(1-\bar{v}^0_2\rho^0/x)-(\xi_3/x)(1-\bar{v}_3\rho^0)\}^{(r'_B)}. \qquad (5.74)$$

Here x is the ratio of the molecular weights of the labelled $(M+\Delta M)$ and natural DNA species and is equal to about $1+(15/4\times441)$ for a DNA species with 50 per cent GC content, that is, 15 nitrogens per 4 nucleotides. From eqns (5.73) and (5.74) we find

$$\left(\frac{\partial\rho}{\partial c_2}\right)^{(r'_B)}_\mu = -\frac{\Delta M}{M} \qquad (5.75)$$

for $(\partial\rho/\partial c_2)_\mu$ of the $[^{14}N]DNA$ at r'_B; $(\partial\rho/\partial c_2)_\mu$ of this natural species at r_B is equal to zero, and therefore χ, the gradient of $(\partial\rho/\partial c_2)_\mu$ between r_B and r'_B, is

$$\chi = -\frac{\Delta M}{M\Delta r}, \qquad (5.76)$$

where Δr is the magnitude of the isotopic shift. The problem is thus solved, and M_2 may be derived by eqn (5.60) from the half-width of the gaussian band (or from a more elaborate formulation, including deviations from gaussian behaviour or consideration of corrections due to virial coefficients), without any knowledge of partial volumes, interaction parameters, and their dependence on pressure, and position r, by means of the above 'internal-calibration' procedure. The method is equally well applicable to other poly-electrolytes and non-ionic polymers in compressible organic-solvent mixtures. The polymers to be used in the calibration procedure are not required to have identical chain lengths or chain-length distribution. Once χ is determined for a given polymer–solvent mixture system under specified experimental conditions molecular weights M_2 may be obtained for all homologous members of the series. It is, of course, not practical to undertake an isotope-substitution calibration for each unknown-molecular-weight determination. Therefore we may express χ in a more practical form,

$$\chi = -\frac{\Delta M}{M\Delta\rho}\left(\frac{d\rho}{dr}\right)^{(r_B)}, \qquad (5.77)$$

where $\Delta\rho$ is now a material constant characteristic of a given DNA solvent system and $(d\rho/dr)^{(r_B)}$ is the solvent density gradient at r_B. We must specify carefully on which density scale $\Delta\rho$ is defined. Meselson and Stahl (1958), by all indications, determined $\Delta\rho$ on the composition density scale and

TABLE 5.1

Values of S† (eqn (5.79)) for DNA‡ salts in various simple salt solutions, at 20 °C; according to Schmid and Hearst (1971)

Salt	$S^{-1} \times 10^{10}$ (g s^2 cm^{-5})	ρ_B^0 (g ml^{-1})
Caesium formate	$4 \cdot 02 \pm 0 \cdot 08$	$1 \cdot 752$
Caesium chloride	$8 \cdot 21 \pm 0 \cdot 17$	$1 \cdot 705$
Caesium trifluoroacetate	$11 \cdot 46 \pm 0 \cdot 02$	$1 \cdot 600$
Caesium bromide	$16 \cdot 4 \ \pm 0 \cdot 02$	$1 \cdot 628$
Caesium sulphate	$19 \cdot 0 \ \pm 0 \cdot 36$	$1 \cdot 426$
Caesium chloride, pH 12	$8 \cdot 08 \pm 0 \cdot 08$	$1 \cdot 763$

† $S = \beta_{\text{eff}}/(1+\Gamma')$, in the nomenclature of Schmid and Hearst.

‡ The buoyant densities were determined with *E. coli* DNA and are adequate, according to Schmid and Hearst, for use in the base composition range (50 ± 25) per cent GC. They also report the temperature-dependence in the range 7–33 °C for the various systems.

therefore $(\mathrm{d}\rho/\mathrm{d}r)^{(r_B)}$ should be the composition density gradient for $\Delta\rho$ reported by them.

The quantity directly determined and reported by Schmid and Hearst (1971) from their isotope-substitution studies of *E. coli* DNA in several caesium salts is (their equation (29))

$$\frac{\Delta M \rho_B^0}{M \Delta r \omega^2 r_B} = \frac{(1+\xi_1')}{\omega^2 r_B}\left(\frac{\mathrm{d}\rho}{\mathrm{d}r}\right)_{\text{eff}} \frac{(1+\xi_1')}{\beta_{\text{eff}}},$$

and, by eqn (5.67) $(\bar{v}_{JB} = 1/\rho_B^0)$, this is equal to

$$\frac{1+\xi_1'}{\beta_{\text{eff}}} = -\left(\frac{\rho_B^0}{\omega^2 r_B}\right)\chi \equiv S^{-1}. \tag{5.78}$$

Substitution of χ from eqn (5.78) into eqn (5.60) yields

$$M_2 = S\frac{RT\rho_B^0}{\sigma^2 \omega^4 r_B^2}, \tag{5.79}$$

where the numerical factor S is derived from the isotopic shift of the DNA band; see Table 5.1 for values of S for nucleic acids in various solvent systems. Schmid and Hearst (1971) estimate that values of S obtained by them from studies with *E. coli* DNA may be used without correction for the evaluation of molecular weights of DNAs in the base composition range of 50 ± 25 per cent GC. If a DNA of an extreme base composition is being studied, suitable corrections of $(1+\xi_1')$ may be estimated from the data of Tunis and Hearst (1968).

5.4.4. Concentration dependence of the width of the band

Schmid and Hearst (1969) found that, in the case of coliphage DNA solutions, the concentration-dependence cannot be neglected and a more elaborate expression than eqn (5.79) has to be used to determine the molecular weight in this instance. We shall follow their treatment in establishing the pertinent equations in the gaussian approximation (higher-order contributions from the dependence on δ will not be considered). We substitute χ from eqn (5.56) into eqn (5.24) and define a quantity

$$L' = -\omega^2 r_B \chi / RT \tag{5.80}$$

to obtain (upon consideration of the virial coefficients $\Gamma_2 = A_2 M_2$ and $\Gamma_3 = A_3 M_2$ only)

$$(1 + 2\Gamma_2 c_2 + 3\Gamma_3 c_2^2)\,d \ln c_2 = -L'M_2 \,\delta \,d\delta. \tag{5.81}$$

Eqn (5.81) is readily integrated to give

$$\ln(c_{2B}/c_2) + 2\Gamma_2(c_{2B} - c_2) + \tfrac{3}{2}\Gamma_3(c_{2B}^2 - c_2^2) = \tfrac{1}{2}L'M_2\,\delta^2 \tag{5.82}$$

We use the simplified notation $c_2^{(\delta)} \equiv c_2$ and $c_2^{(\delta=0)} \equiv c_{2B}$. To evaluate eqn (5.82) we determine the width σ_{app} of the experimental distribution at the concentration

$$c_2 = c_{2B}\exp(-\tfrac{1}{2}) = 0{\cdot}606 c_{2B},$$

and obtain, by referring to

$$c_2 = c_{2B}\exp(-\delta^2/2\sigma_{app}), \tag{5.83}$$

$$\frac{1}{M_{app}} \equiv L'\sigma_{app}^2 = \frac{1}{M_2}(1 + 1{\cdot}576\Gamma_2\,c_{2B} + 1{\cdot}898\Gamma_3\,c_{2B}^2). \tag{5.84}$$

A better utilization of the data is made by the slightly more elaborate use of moments of the distribution. For this treatment we multiply eqn (5.81) by $c_2\,\delta$ to obtain

$$-L'M_2\,c_2\,\delta^2\,d\delta = \delta(1 + 2\Gamma_2 c_2 + 3\Gamma_3 c_2^2)\,dc_2. \tag{5.85}$$

Eqn (5.85) is now integrated, choosing integration limits from $-\infty$ to $+\infty$. This is very reasonable because the concentration c_2 usually drops to zero rapidly on both sides of the band. The entire band is positioned in the cell with essentially zero macromolecular concentration at the meniscus and the bottom. The right-hand side of eqn (5.85) is integrated by parts over these limits and the following result is obtained.

$$L'M_2 \int_{-\infty}^{+\infty} c_2\,\delta^2\,d\delta = \int_{-\infty}^{+\infty} (c_2 + \Gamma_2 c_2^2 + \Gamma_3 c_2^3)\,d\delta. \tag{5.86}$$

Eqn (5.86) is normalized by dividing by

$$\int_{-\infty}^{+\infty} c_2\,d\delta$$

and expressed in a different notation, by the moment relation, to give

$$L'M_2 \langle \delta^2 \rangle = 1 + \Gamma_2 \langle c_2 \rangle + \Gamma_3 \langle c_2^2 \rangle, \qquad (5.87)$$

where the nature of the averages $\langle \delta^2 \rangle$, $\langle c_2 \rangle$, and $\langle c_2^2 \rangle$ is clear from the procedure described; $(\langle \delta^2 \rangle \equiv \int c_2 \delta^2 \, d\delta / \int c_2 \, d\delta$, $\langle c_2 \rangle \equiv \int c_2^2 \, d\delta / \int c_2 \, d\delta$ and $\langle c_2^2 \rangle \equiv \int c_2^3 \, d\delta / \int c_2 \, d\delta)$. For a gaussian distribution Schmid and Hearst (1969) then assume proportionality between $\langle c_2 \rangle^2$ and $\langle c_2^2 \rangle$,

$$\langle c_2^2 \rangle = \frac{2}{\sqrt{3}} \langle c_2 \rangle^2,$$

to give

$$L'\langle \delta^2 \rangle = \frac{1}{M_2} \left(1 + \Gamma_2 \langle c_2 \rangle + \frac{2\Gamma_3}{\sqrt{3}} \langle c_2 \rangle^2 \right) \equiv \frac{1}{M_{app}}. \qquad (5.88)$$

The averages appearing above are obtained by numerical analysis over the whole equilibrium distribution. Since the numerical value of L' is known,

$$L' = \omega^4 r_B^2 / RT \rho_B^0 S, \qquad (5.89)$$

an apparent molecular weight M_{app} may be determined as a function of concentration $\langle c_2 \rangle$.

Schmid and Hearst (1969) believe that the experimental determination of M_{app} and $\langle c_2 \rangle$ (eqn (5.88)) or M_{app} and c_{2B} (eqn (5.84)) are too inaccurate to permit a three-parameter fit of the data, as required by these equations. To obtain a two-parameter fit they introduce the connection between the second and third virial coefficient (eqn (1.5)), and assume special values for g. They thereby obtain a series of linear plots of a function of apparent molecular weight against concentration from which the desired quantity M_2 may be obtained by extrapolation.

5.4.5. *Heterogeneous macromolecular solutes*

Two types of heterogeneity may occur: simple dispersion in molecular weight and variation in partial volume. We have seen that the latter is of particular importance because density gradients provide an extremely selective means for investigating and separating species that vary only very slightly in effective density. This application has yielded much significant information in studies of synthesis and composition of natural and synthetic polynucleotides.

Heterogeneity in molecular weight is readily considered along the lines developed for conventional equilibrium sedimentation in Section 5.3. Meselson *et al.* (1957) have already considered the general situation of a polymer heterogeneous with respect to molecular weight although homogeneous with respect to effective density. Eqns (5.79) or (5.84) or (5.88) then apply for each macromolecular component separately, and the total concentration c_2 is just the sum of the independent gaussian functions for each of the J macromolecular components. The fact that $(\partial \rho / \partial c_J)_\mu$ is identical for each J, and equal to $(\partial\rho/\partial c_2)_\mu$ implies that χ as well as L' is unique for the system and that the gaussian concentration distribution is centred at the same r_B, the symmetrical composite distribution being given by (in the gaussian approximation and in the limit of vanishing macromolecular concentration)

$$\sum_J c_J = c_2 = \sum_J c_{JB} \exp(-\delta^2/2\sigma_J^2), \qquad (5.90)$$

where

$$\sigma_J^2 = -RT/M_J\,\omega^2 r_B \chi = 1/M_J L'. \qquad (5.91)$$

Differentiation of eqn (5.90) with respect to δ^2, and then use of eqn (5.90) again to eliminate the sum of gaussians in the derivative, gives

$$\frac{\mathrm{d}\ln c_2}{\mathrm{d}\delta} = -L'M_w\,\delta, \qquad (5.92)$$

where M_w refers to the value at position δ. The same result can be obtained directly from eqn (5.26) and the linear approximation eqn (5.56) for χ. In principle, the higher molecular weight averages can be obtained from the higher derivatives of the concentration distribution (see Section 5.3) to the extent that this distribution is precisely enough defined. The molecular weights for the whole solute are formed by integrating over the band, the weight average, for example, being given by eqns (5.43)† and (5.92),

$$\overline{M}_w = \frac{\displaystyle\int_{-\infty}^{+\infty} M_w\,c_2\,\mathrm{d}\delta}{\displaystyle\int_{-\infty}^{+\infty} c_2\,\mathrm{d}\delta}$$

$$= -\frac{\displaystyle\int_{-\infty}^{+\infty} \frac{1}{\delta}\left(\frac{\mathrm{d}c_2}{\mathrm{d}\delta}\right)^{(\delta)}\mathrm{d}\delta}{\displaystyle\int_{-\infty}^{+\infty} c_2\,\mathrm{d}\delta} = \frac{1}{L'\sigma^2}, \qquad (5.93)$$

where σ^2 here is the standard deviation of the composite gaussian concentration distribution.

In the density-gradient equilibrium, the concentration c_2 does vanish within the cell, and it is therefore possible to obtain the number-average molecular weight (Meselson *et al.* 1957) as well as the higher averages. The relevant expressions, again in the gaussian approximation are best derived on the basis of the moments defined by Goldberg (1953), and for this particular

† We integrate over $\mathrm{d}\delta = \mathrm{d}r$ rather than over $\delta r^2 = 2r\,\mathrm{d}r$ (as in eqn (5.43) for sectorial cells) because r (and therefore the cross-section of the cell) is considered constant over the relatively narrow bands. The procedure is exact for rectangular cells, and higher-order terms could be added for wider bands in sector-shaped cells.

application in density gradients for a continuous molecular-weight distribution by Hermans and Ende (1963, **1964**). For a discrete distribution of molecular weights we may define the moments

$$\Lambda_t = \sum M_J^t \, c_{J0}.$$ (5.94)

Thus Λ_0 is simply $\sum c_{J0} = c_{20}$, the uniform concentration c_2 before centrifugation; $\Lambda_{-1} = \sum (c_{J0}/M_J)$ and $\Lambda_1 = \sum M_J c_{J0}$; therefore $\Lambda_0/\Lambda_{-1} = \bar{M}_n$, $\Lambda_1/\Lambda_0 = \bar{M}_w$, and so forth. The moments Λ_t are related to the moments of the functions of the local concentration c_2. Thus

$$\sum \int_{-\infty}^{+\infty} c_J \, d\delta = \sum c_{J0} = \Lambda_0$$ (5.95)

and

$$\int_{-\infty}^{+\infty} c_J \delta^2 \, d\delta = c_{JB} \int \delta^2 \exp(-\delta^2/2\sigma_J^2) \, d\delta = (2\pi)^{\frac{1}{2}} \sigma_J^3 c_{JB}.$$ (5.96)

To evaluate eqn (5.96) we require the value of c_{JB}, which is obtained by substituting c_J from eqn (5.90) into eqn (5.97)

$$c_{J0} = \int_{-\infty}^{+\infty} c_J \, d\delta = c_{JB} \int_{-\infty}^{+\infty} \exp(-\delta^2/2\sigma_J^2) \, d\delta$$ (5.97)

and performing the integration, to yield

$$c_{J0} = (2\pi)^{\frac{1}{2}} \sigma_J c_{JB}$$ (5.98)

(a proportionality constant depending on cell dimensions need not be considered, as we shall be interested in the ratios of the defined moments; also see footnote on p. 129 with reference to the integration over c rather than rc for sector-shaped cells).

Substitution of c_{JB} from eqn (5.98) in eqn (5.96), and summation over all Js, yields

$$\int_{-\infty}^{+\infty} c_2 \delta^2 \, d\delta = \sum c_{J0} \sigma_J^2 = \frac{1}{L'} \sum \frac{c_J}{M_J} = \frac{\Lambda_{-1}}{L'}.$$ (5.99)

From eqns (5.95) and (5.99),

$$L'\bar{M}_n = L' \frac{\Lambda_0}{\Lambda_{-1}} = \frac{\int c_2 \, d\delta}{\int_{-\infty}^{+\infty} c_2 \delta^2 \, d\delta} \equiv \frac{1}{\langle \delta^2 \rangle}.$$ (5.100)

In similar fashion we can derive

$$\int_{-\infty}^{+\infty} \frac{1}{\delta}\left(\frac{dc_2}{d\delta}\right)^{(\delta)} d\delta = -L'\Lambda_1.$$ (5.101)

The ratio Λ_1/Λ_0 from eqns (5.101) and (5.95) gives eqn (5.93), as expected.

Not all moments of the distribution can be obtained with an equal degree of accuracy. Since the evaluation of Λ_{-1} for instance, requires integration of $\delta^2 c_2$ over δ, small errors in the tails of c_2 at large values of δ will affect the integration considerably. This becomes worse when Schlieren optics are used because the $dc_2/d\delta$ curve must now be multiplied by δ^3. Interference or absorption optics are therefore preferable to Schlieren optics for the determination of Λ_{-1}. For the determination of Λ_1 the opposite is true because this requires integration of $\delta^{-1} dc_2/d\delta$ and to obtain $dc_2/d\delta$ from c_2 requires differentiation.

So far, these considerations on polydisperse systems have been based on the equations valid for vanishing macromolecular concentration. For finite concentration, the second and third virial coefficients must be taken into account. The correction involved may be considerable unless the polymer concentration is low or the virial coefficients are quite close to zero (use of Θ solvent, for instance, in some specific instances). The macromolecular band will remain symmetrical no matter how much the distribution may differ from a simple superposition of gaussian curves. This is due to the fact that the effect of polymer–polymer interactions is the same at positive and at negative values of δ, as long as the effect of the small difference in solvent composition between these two points remains negligible. Hermans and Ende (1963) have evaluated the 'apparent' moments and the ratio of these moments which represent 'apparent' molecular weights, consisting of the true molecular weights modulated by multiplication with the properly weighted virial-expansion functions.

5.4.6. *Effective density heterogeneity*

Another complication enters if solutes are heterogeneous in effective density ρ_B, that is, if the gradient of $(\partial\rho/\partial c)_\mu$ is not the same for all species. The gaussian distributions for the individual components are then not centred at a common r_B, and the composite band structure may exhibit a variety of forms—symmetrical or skewed unimodal, bimodal (see the discussion above on bimodal bands of isotopically substituted macromolecules), or poly-modal—depending on the distribution of effective densities.

For a homogeneous solute at the dilute-solution limit, a plot of $\log c$ versus δ^2 is a straight line of negative slope. This behaviour is therefore a necessary (but not sufficient) condition to establish homogeneity. Qualita-tively, heterogeneity in molecular weight alone must always result in positive curvature of the plot. In as much as high-molecular-weight species are concentrated, relatively, toward the centre of the band and $d \ln c_2/dr$ is proportional to $M_w^{(r)}$, the slope must become less negative as δ^2 increases. Negative curvature of the plot (or any departure from unimodal band symmetry) is therefore decisive evidence of heterogeneity, with respect to density. Baldwin (1959) has shown that the special case of a solute with uniform molecular weight, but with a gaussian distribution of effective densities, yields a simple gaussian concentration distribution. Thus a molecular weight obtained on an erroneous supposition that the gaussian band necessarily indicates homogeneity would be too low. An experimental resolution of this last ambiguous situation is, however, possible. If the material on either side of the apparent r_B is isolated (in a partition cell) and then rebanded, a skewed distribution will be found if the original material was heterogeneous. It has also been suggested that such density heterogeneity might be detected by comparing the bands found in cells of different shapes. Baldwin (1959) has shown, however, that the differences in concentration profiles in radial and cylindrical cells are likely to be well within the uncertainty of even the most precise measurements. The more complicated situation existing when the solute is heterogeneous, both with respect to density and molecular weight, has been discussed by Hermans (1963a, 1963b, 1969).

As previously mentioned, the study of nucleic acids and other poly-nucleotides has been particularly helped by the development of the density-gradient technique. It has been found possible to form caesium chloride gradients of such selectivity that very small differences in effective density due to differences in base composition or to the isotopic labelling of species can give rise to variations in band-shape or, sometimes, to the separation of discrete bands. While it refers to a possibly rather artificial model, Baldwin's calculation of $c_2^{(s)}$ for material with a gaussian distribution of effective density is important in showing that extremely small deviations from homogeneity can decrease a measured apparent molecular weight by a large factor. For example, Baldwin points out that the apparent molecular weight, about 10^7, obtained from bacteriophage DNA bands (shown in Figure 2 of Meselson and Stahl (1958)) would be too small by a factor of 2 were the standard deviation ρ_B only 0·2 per cent of the mean. It seems quite possible that variation in the composition of DNA from a single organism might be great enough to cause such broadening of the band. In a somewhat different application, Buchdahl, Ende, and Peebles (1961) have discussed the analysis of the distribution of non-ionic polymer species of different stereo-regular structure from band-broadening in density gradients formed with mixtures of two organic solvents (see also Hermans and Ende **1964**).

The precise differential location of peaks of bands in density-gradient equilibrium sedimentation (with reference to the position of known markers) is now commonly used to determine the guanosine and cytosine content of DNA samples to ± 1 per cent GC, corresponding to a change in effective density of 0·001 g ml^{-1} (Sueoka 1959). With DNA, density heterogeneity can also be caused by, in addition to variable base composition, varying degree of unfolding (native and denatured DNA can essentially be separated on a

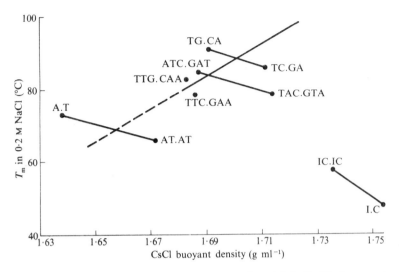

F IG. 5.4. Base composition of synthetic DNAs as a function of their Cs_2SO_4 buoyant-density values. The solid diagonal line represents the values found for a variety of naturally occurring DNAs of different base compositions. (From Wells, Larson, Grant, Shortle, and Cantor 1970.)

density gradient), by incorporation of non-typical bases such a 5-bromouracil, or by incorporation of isotopes. Each component will band at its own buoyant density so that a broader, non-gaussian distribution is obtained, resulting in a convex plot of $\log c_2$ versus δ^2. Wells and Larson (1970, 1972) and Wells, Larson, Grant, Shortle, and Cantor (1970) could show that synthetic DNAs which have the same base composition but different nucleotide sequences (sequence isomers) differ with respect to their thermal coil transition as well as their buoyant densities as determined in CsCl density gradients (Fig. 5.4). Creeth and Pain (**1967**) summarize various approaches suggested towards recognizing and separating weight and density heterogeneity in density-gradient systems.

5.4.7. Conclusions

A particularly appealing use of equilibrium density-gradient centrifugation was made in the study of dyes which bind to DNA by intercalating between successive base-pairs in the Watson–Crick double helix and superhelical DNAs (Bauer and Vinograd 1968, 1970*a*, 1970*b*, **1974**; Wang **1971**). The theory must now involve an additional small molecular component and is easily extended to encompass this case. A thermodynamic analysis of this problem has been presented by Bauer and Vinograd (1969), this being an extension of the earlier development of Hearst and Vinograd (1961) for three-component systems. The review article of Szybalski and Szybalski (**1971**) contains a wealth of references on such problems as instrumentation and techniques, reagents and densities of solutions (CsCl and Cs_2SO_4), calculation of density gradients, base composition, buoyant densities and melting temperatures of nucleic acids, effect of various modifications of nucleic acids (glucosylation, methylation, denaturation and formaldehyde, separation of complementary strands, alkaline density gradients, irradiation, complexing of silver and mercury ions, and interaction with antibiotics and dyes), RNA, ribosomes, and RNA–DNA hybrids, as well as equilibrium density-gradient centrifugation of proteins, nucleoproteins, and poly-saccharides.

Here some aspects have been described of a method whose impact will certainly increase as applications become more frequent.

5.5. Analysis of macromolecular association and non-ideality

5.5.1. Non-ideality and self-association

We have, in Section 2.3 as well as in Appendix IV (p. 230) discussed osmotic pressure and deviations from ideality as expressed in the usual expansion in powers of the concentration in the virial series. Positive virial coefficients derive from volume exclusion, which can be evaluated, and less tractable contributions due to repulsive forces between macromolecules. Furthermore, in charged systems, and in the presence of low-molecular-weight salts, contributions to the virial coefficients deriving from the unequal distribution of ions diffusible across a semipermeable membrane can be evaluated, and are known as Donnan terms.† The contributions of these can be varied over a wide range of values by a choice of simple-salt concentration and valency type of the constituent ions and, particularly in the case of proteins, by variations in the pH. Thus, as we have seen in Section 2.4, if the simple salt is of the binary uni–univalent type then no contribution due to unequal distribution of ions accrues to A_3, and the major contribution is to A_2. A more general expression involving Donnan equilibria of non-symmetrical simple salts has been given by Flory (**1953**) (see also Roark and Yphantis (1971) for a detailed discussion). For 2:1 salts unequal distribution of simple salts leads to $A_3 > 0$ if the co-ion is univalent, $A_3 < 0$ if the counter-ion is univalent, and A_4 equals zero.

If attractive forces dominate then negative contributions to the virial coefficients may lead to a cancelling of A_2 and the higher coefficients in spite of positive volume exclusion; this is the Flory Θ temperature, and has

† We have already extensively discussed the fact that no Donnan term contributes to the first virial coefficient, from which the correct molecular weight may be obtained free of any extraneous assumptions, and in whatever units we wish to express M; the remark of Roark and Yphantis (1971) that 'in the case of the usual definition (component 2 being ... the polyelectrolyte plus its counter-ions), the limiting value of the apparent weight-average molecular weight, as c_2 approaches zero, is less than the defined ideal value' is therefore somewhat surprising. The Donnan effect does not decrease the molecular weight averages from their ideal value, which should be obtained independent of the choice of components.

been observed for highly charged polyelectrolyte solutions (Eisenberg and Woodside 1962; Eisenberg 1966). Usually, upon lowering the temperature or increasing the salt concentration, the virial coefficients become negative and phase-separation occurs, but both upper and lower consolute temperatures may be observed (see Eisenberg and Ram Mohan (1959) for a study on polyvinylsulphonate and Eisenberg and Felsenfeld (1967) for a study (Fig. 2.2, p. 40) of polyriboadenylic acid (poly A)). Positive virial coefficients lead to decreasing apparent molecular weights with increasing concentration. In the case of self-association of the macromolecules, the apparent molecular weights increase with increasing concentration. In practice, both types of effects may contribute significantly. Godfrey and Harrington (1970) have demonstrated that for a myosin preparation undergoing self-association, the apparent molecular weight first increases with increasing concentration due to dimerization, attains a maximum, and then decreases with further increase in concentration, due to the increased contribution of positive virial coefficients at higher concentrations (see Fig. 5.10(a), p. 147).

In any analysis which involves a mixture of interacting macromolecules, chemically identical or of various kinds, in a non-ideal solution, it is not obvious that deviations from ideality are additive or may be simply averaged. We shall consider a specific example, the mixture of two macromolecular components only, to illustrate this problem (Casassa 1960, 1962). We have, in general, for the osmotic-pressure second virial coefficients,†

† We consider here for simplicity a two-component system comprising a heterogeneous neutral component 2 and no diffusible component. For the more general case discussing the proper weighting of virial coefficients in various experimental situations (including light-scattering and sedimentation equilibrium) we refer to Casassa and Eisenberg (**1964**). We have by eqn (2.34), for two components only

$$(V_m^0/m_2)(\mathrm{d}\Pi/\mathrm{d}m_2) \approx \mu_{22},$$

where

$$\mu_2 = \sum x_J \mu_J$$

and the partial derivative μ_{22} of this quantity with respect to m_2 is

$$\mu_{22} = \sum x_J \sum \mu_{JK}(\mathrm{d}m_K/\mathrm{d}m_2) = \sum\sum \mu_{JK} x_J x_K,$$

and the x_J are mole fractions m_J/m_2; $\sum x_J = 1$. We use

$$\mu_J = \mu_J^0 + RT \ln m_J \gamma_J$$

the definition

$$M_n = \sum x_J M_J = \sum m_J M_J/m_2 = c_2 V_m/m_2$$

and the weight fractions y_J

$$y_J = m_J M_J / \sum m_J M_J = w_J/w_2$$

to derive, on the c-concentration scale,

$$\frac{1}{RT}\frac{\Pi}{c_2} = \frac{1}{M_n} + \frac{1}{2}\sum_J\sum_K \frac{\mathrm{d}\ln\gamma_J}{\mathrm{d}c_K}\frac{y_J y_K}{M_J}c_2$$

or, by analogy with eqns (1.10) and (1.11),

$$\frac{1}{RT}\frac{\Pi}{c_2} = \frac{1}{M_n} + \left(\sum_J\sum_K A_{JK} y_J y_K\right)c_2 + \cdots.$$

$$A_2(\text{OP}) = \sum_J \sum_K A_{JK} y_J y_K, \tag{5.102}$$

where y_J is the weight fraction of component J ($y_J = w_J/w_2$; $\sum y_J = 1$), A_{JJ} represents the interaction leading to A_2 of the 'pure' component J, and the A_{JK} are the cross-interaction terms in the mixed system. In light-scattering (we assume equal refractive index for all macromolecular solutes),

$$A_2(\text{LS}) = \sum_J \sum_K A_{JK} M_J M_K y_K \bigg/ \left(\sum_J M_J y_J\right)^2$$

$$= \sum_J \sum_K A_{JK} M_J M_K y_J y_K / M_w^2, \tag{5.103}$$

and in equilibrium sedimentation a related expression applies. For the simple case of two sharp fractions of a synthetic polymer in an organic solvent system, if $M_4 > M_2$ then $A_{22} > A_{44} > 0$ in good solvent systems. Eqn (5.102) simplifies to

$$A_2(\text{OP}) = A_{22} y_2^2 + A_{24} y_2 y_4 + A_{44} y_4^2. \tag{5.104}$$

A_2 is not necessarily a linear function of the weight fraction of either component and may actually go through a maximum if $A_{24} > A_{22} > A_{44}$, or through a minimum if $A_{24} < A_{44} < A_{22}$. The exact nature of the averages, the extension to finite angles of scattering in the case of light-scattering, and the critical values of the interaction parameters have been discussed by Casassa (1960, 1962). The assumption (Blum and Morales 1952) that the cross-coefficient is the geometric mean of the A_{JJ}s,

$$A_{JK}^2 = A_{JJ} A_{KK},$$

is not justifiable, particularly for mixtures of dissimilar proteins, where the intermolecular interactions usually reflect differences more complex than simple inequality in molecular size. In the simplest example of a mixture of two homogeneous macromolecules the system is characterized by three inter-action parameters and therefore at least three systems ($2(n+1)/2$ systems in the general case) with variable composition must be studied if all the A_{JK} are to be found. It is assumed, of course, that the A_{JK} are independent of composition of the non-diffusible solute mixture. Systems might exist that are well behaved in the sense that the osmotic coefficient ϕ approaches unity linearly for any values y_J and y_K, as m_2 becomes very small, yet exhibit a dependence of the A_{JK} on composition. What is required is a reaction between components J and K that is independent of total solute concentration and does not change the total concentration of non-diffusible species (Scatchard, Gee, and Weeks 1954).

As one example to illustrate these problems we refer to the above study of Scatchard et al. (see Casassa and Eisenberg 1964) on the osmotic behaviour

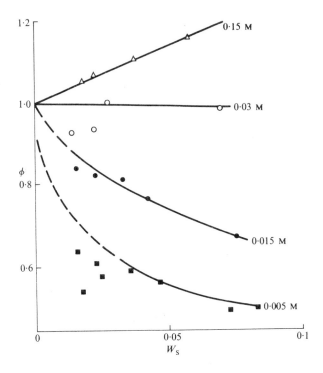

F IG. 5.5. Osmotic coefficient of equimolal mixtures of isoionic serum albumin (sample A6) and γ-globulin (sample G13) in sodium chloride at 25 °C. (From Scatchard, Gee, and Weeks 1954.)

of mixtures of human serum albumin and various γ-globulin fractions. The osmotic coefficient ϕ for an equimolal mixtures of isoionic (electrodialysed) proteins is plotted in Fig. 5.5 for several concentrations of added sodium chloride. At very low salt concentration ϕ is less than unity, shows marked upward curvature, and approaches the limit unity at infinite dilution with an indefinitely steep slope; therefore the second virial coefficient appears negative and indefinitely large. This behaviour is typical of a reversibly associating system, and such a description is physically reasonable in this instance, in as much as titration curves indicate the two species of protein ions to be oppositely charged at the pH of the isoionic mixture. (We recall that the phenomenon of charge fluctuations in protein solutions at low ionic strength (Section 4.7) also leads to attractive forces between macromolecules, and therefore negative apparent virial coefficients.) Although the interaction deduced here is presumably between unlike proteins, polymerization of a single protein species will produce a qualitatively similar effect; see for instance the case of insulin in acid solution (Doty and Edsall 1951), β-casein

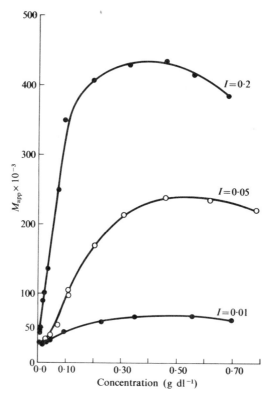

FIG. 5.6. Concentration-dependence of the apparent molecular weight of β-casein at different ionic strengths. Experimental conditions: sodium phosphate buffers (pH 7·0) and ionic strengths indicated with the plots; temperature 21 °C. (From Payens, Brinkhuis, and Van Markwijk 1968.)

(Fig. 5.6) at different ionic strengths (Payens, Brinkhuis, and Van Markwijk 1969), and glutamic acid hydrogenase (Eisenberg and Tomkins 1968) under various experimental conditions.

The observations in Fig. 5.5 indicate that as the amount of salt is increased, the strong electrostatic interaction is progressively suppressed until at concentration above 0·03 M the second virial coefficient becomes positive (an indication of effective intermolecular forces of repulsion) and the osmotic coefficient is linear, or nearly so, over the concentration range for osmotic-pressure measurements. Further measurements on the same two proteins, mixed at different composition ratios, showed that at high salt concentration it is possible to fit the quadratic forms

$$B_2 = B_{22} x_2^2 + 2B_{24} x_2 x_4 + B_{44} x_4^2,$$

where the Bs are virial coefficients on the molal concentration scale (eqn (2.49)) to the experimental data to an accuracy within the experimental uncertainty. The interaction parameters given for this system by Scatchard *et al.* are

$$B_{22} = 300 \quad B_{24} = 385 \quad B_{44} = 350,$$

with subscripts 2 and 4 denoting albumin and globulin respectively. From the molecular weights determined by the osmotic measurements $M_2 = 70\,400$ and $M_4 = 187\,000$ and the B_{JK} we can compute

$$A_{22} = 6{\cdot}05 \times 10^{-5} \quad A_{24} = 2{\cdot}92 \times 10^{-5} \quad A_{44} = 1{\cdot}00 \times 10^{-5}.$$

All the interactions on a molal basis (as given by the B_{JK}) are of the same order of magnitude; hence, the virial coefficient B_2 is not strongly a function of composition of the mixed proteins. However, because of the considerable disparity in the molecular weight of the two proteins, the interactions per unit mass of protein are quite different and the virial coefficient A_2 is markedly dependent on composition.

In the case of a self-associating protein we are not likely to encounter effects as drastic as observed in the interaction described above between two particles of unlike mass and unlike (opposite) charge. It is reasonable to assume that that part of the virial terms depending on charge (the Donnan terms) is independent of mass, and depends mostly on the ratio of charge to mass. This ratio is usually little affected in the process of self-association. Yet, in bulky, globular, or anisotropic proteins, close to the isoelectric point (and therefore carrying a relatively low charge only) a large contribution to the virial coefficients (in solutions of reasonably high ionic strength) is due to volume exclusion proper. As was exemplified in Fig. 2.1 (p. 40) this contribution may depend on the degree of association and only in special cases (as for sufficiently elongated rod-like particles of uniform cross-section, see eqn (2.58), for instance) is the virial contribution between like particles independent of mass.

What is usually determined in the analysis of self-associating systems by light-scattering or equilibrium sedimentation is some average of an apparent molecular weight as a function of concentration (mass per unit volume, or some related quantity). The difficulty of performing a full analysis in terms of association constants and non-ideality corrections usually by far exceeds the experimental accuracy or the availability of sufficient independent experiments. With respect to the association process we must know whether the association is limited or indefinite, whether the association of monomer to n-mers is concerted or proceeds in discrete steps, whether the association constants are identical or assume a range of values. Obviously, rather detailed information is required if one also wishes to account for non-ideality (other than association) in a rational way. Sometimes one is fortunate in that the association reaction can be studied in a concentration range in which the non-ideality corrections are of lesser importance (Godfrey and Harrington

1970; Reisler and Eisenberg 1972); yet, the best that can usually be done is to accept the fact that in most practical cases the non-ideality can be regarded as a correction term only in the over-all analysis and therefore the sweeping simplification is made that the contribution of the non-ideality to the chemical potential of any species is proportional to the mass of the species (Roark and Yphantis 1969, for instance). This assumption requires that the virial coefficients A_2, A_3 and so forth are considered fixed and independent of c, or alternatively the activity coefficients γ (on a mass basis) are independent of the state of association of the system. Further analysis will now proceed on the basis of this simplifying assumption. Solution of the equations for associating systems by curve fitting on the assumption that the non-ideality (limited to A_2) is a fixed parameter may vitiate the physical interpretation of the analysis and lead to an incorrect model for the association process (see Adams (**1967, 1968**); Adams and Lewis (1968), for instance, for ambiguities in the β-lactoglobulin system).

   In associating systems, transport properties are usually affected because of changes in dimensions of the macromolecular aggregates. To the extent to which transport properties, such as sedimentation velocity, for instance (see Chapter 6) can be properly interpreted, information on protein interaction and association may be derived (Cann and Goad **1973**; Gilbert and Gilbert **1973**).

5.5.2. *Analysis of self-association by equilibrium sedimentation*

We shall consider now in some detail the considerations of Roark and Yphantis (1969) on studies of self-associating systems by equilibrium sedimentation. We are interested in the process whereby n-monomeric units (or 'oligomers', if these are composed of a discrete number of subunits) associate reversibly to form discrete n-mers. Thermodynamic characterization of these systems provides information about the enthalpy and entropy of the reaction, in particular if perturbations are applied by alteration of the solvent medium, interactions (sometimes of a regulatory nature) with small molecules, and change of temperature. Equilibrium sedimentation is particularly effective for such an investigation because in contradistinction to osmotic pressure and light scattering which usually yields single averages of the experimental quantities only (but compare the more recent method of scattering with coherent light (Section 4.8)) it expands the molecular-weight scale and allows various moments of the distribution to be obtained. Somewhat similar information can be derived by the recent extensive use of chromatography on gels and absorbing columns (Gordon **1969**; Fischer **1969**; Ackers **1973**; Bernardi **1973**) although these methods are to some extent semi-empirical, rely on calibration procedures with materials of known weight or shape, and may lead to faulty conclusions in the case of materials with aberrant shape, charge, or interactions. Altogether, transport properties (see Chapter 6) determining the flow in solutions or through absorption columns are less amenable to precise interpretation than the evaluation of true equilibrium properties such as equilibrium sedimentation in the ultracentrifuge. By means of the ultracentrifuge it is possible as well to determine the stoichiometry, heterogeneity, and extent of reversibility of the particular self-association reactions of interest in this context. It may be stated in general that if the system can be characterized by a single macromolecular 'thermodynamic' component, then (provided that pressure-dependence in the ultracentrifuge may be ignored) the apparent 'point' molecular weights $M^{(r)}$ determined are functions of c exclusively and a unique curve should be derived from all experiments, independent of the initial 'loading' concentration of the centrifuge cell.

A simple self-associating solute may be described by either set of eqns (5.105) or (5.106) below.

Sequential reactions:

$$M_1 + M_1 \rightleftarrows M_2 \qquad K_{21} = [M_2]/[M_1]^2$$
$$M_2 + M_1 \rightleftarrows M_3 \qquad K_{32} = [M_3]/[M_2][M_1]$$
$$M_3 + M_1 \rightleftarrows M_4 \qquad K_{43} = [M_4]/[M_3][M_1] \qquad (5.105)$$
$$\vdots \qquad\qquad \vdots$$
$$M_{j-1} + M_1 \rightleftarrows M_j \qquad K_{j,j-1} = [M_j']/[M_{j-1}][M].$$

Parallel reactions:

$$2M_1 \rightleftarrows M_2 \qquad K_{21} = [M_2]/[M_1]^2$$
$$3M_1 \rightleftarrows M_3 \qquad K_{31} = [M_3]/[M_1]^3$$
$$4M_1 \rightleftarrows M_4 \qquad K_{41} = [M_4]/[M_1]^4 \qquad (5.106)$$
$$\vdots \qquad\qquad \vdots$$
$$jM_1 \rightleftarrows M_j' \qquad K_{j,1}' = [M_j]/[M_1]^j,$$

where the $[M_j]$ are the activities of the j-mer. If the thermodynamic non-ideality is considered separately, by way of the customary virial coefficients, then we can substitute concentrations for the activities $[M_j]$.

The two descriptions above are equivalent with respect to the equilibrium properties of the system, with

$$K_{j,1} = \Pi K_{j,j-1}.$$

Even though there may be a large number of species present, the solute can be considered as a single thermodynamic component and, as stated above, any molecular-weight average at each level r is uniquely a function of total solute concentration, for a given specified solvent composition and temperature. In the absence of any significant long-range forces, it is possible to expand the ideal weight-average molecular weight, for instance, in a series in powers of the concentration. The first coefficient of this series obviously corresponds to the molecular weight M_1 of the monomer. If all the species are ideal then the coefficients should be functions of the association constants only, although it is by no means clear† that an expansion in integral powers of c is adequate (see eqn (5.125)). In practice it is found that it is also necessary to consider contributions from non-ideality (excluded volume or charge) discussed earlier above. It is usually assumed that the partial specific volumes, or density and refractive-index increments are identical for the various species. The case when the associating solute consists of more than one thermodynamic component has been discussed extensively by Roark and Yphantis (1969) and will not be further discussed here. The precise procedures and computer programs devised by these authors to obtain the number through $(z+1)$ molecular-weight averages are available.

If there are two ideal sedimenting species of molecular weights M_1 and M_2 for instance, and of weight fractions $(1-y(r))$ and $y(r)$ respectively, then the number-average and weight-average molecular weight of point r in the cell can be written as

$$\frac{1}{M_n} = \frac{1-y}{M_1} + \frac{y}{M_2} \qquad (5.108)$$

and

$$M_w = (1-y)M_1 + yM_2 . \qquad (5.109)$$

If y is eliminated from the two expressions above, we obtain an equation

$$M_w = -M_1 M_2 (1/M_n) + M_1 + M_2 . \qquad (5.110)$$

In this particular case a graph of M_w against $1/M_n$ yields a straight line with slope $-M_1 M_2$ and intercept $M_1 + M_2$. In the case of a monomer–j-mer association,

$$M_w = -jM_1^2(1/M_n) + (j+1)M_1 , \qquad (5.111)$$

---

† Stafford and Yphantis (1972) have analysed theoretical power expansions for self-associating systems governed by mass action assuming the solute to be ideal except for this solute–solute interaction. They find that the usefulness of such equations is severely limited by their extremely narrow interval of convergence. The virial equation for the weight-average degree of polymerization X_w of an ideal monomer j-mer system is

$$X_w^{-1} = 1 - (j-1)Kc^{j-1} + 0.5(2j-2)(2j-1)K^2c^{2j-2} - \cdots , \qquad (5.107)$$

and the series diverges when X_w is larger than $1 \cdot 17 – 1 \cdot 28$ (for details see original article). For indefinitely associating systems, with equal successive molar association constants, the effective limit of X_w is $\sqrt{2}$. The linear range of X_w^{-1} as a function of c^{j-1} at best extends to 7 per cent association, a range in which experimental error usually is a large fraction of the change in molecular weights. Complete expressions, such as eqn (5.125) for the monomer–dimer equilibrium, should therefore be used in preference to the empirical expansions in integral powers of the concentration.

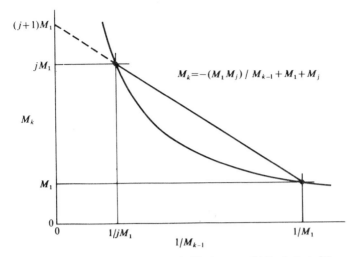

$$M_k = -(M_1 M_j) / M_{k-1} + M_1 + M_j$$

FIG. 5.7. 'Two-species plot' for the system $jA = A_j$. The heavy, solid line is that of the equation; the hyperbola is given by $M_k/M_{k-1} = 1$. Intersections of the hyperbola with the 'two-species line' form the terminal points of the 'two-species line' and give the values of M_1 and M_j. (From Roark and Yphantis 1969.)

at level r and, with respect to the other molecular-weight averages,

$$M_z = -jM_1^2(1/M_n) + (j+1)M_1, \qquad (5.112)$$

and so forth. These equations are valid at all levels r. Fig. 5.7 shows the procedure by which a graphical analysis of the data proceeds. If deviations from linearity of this so-called 'two-species' plot indicate that more than two species are present, then Roark and Yphantis suggest a 'three-species' plot as an extension to the above procedure. Assume that three ideal sedimenting species are present with molecular weights M_1, jM_1, and lM_1, with weight fractions at radius r of $1 - y_j - y_l$, y_j, and y_l respectively. Then

$$\frac{1}{M_n} = \frac{1}{M_1}\left\{1 + \left(\frac{1}{j} - 1\right)y_j + \left(\frac{1}{l} - 1\right)y_l\right\} \qquad (5.113)$$

$$M_w = M_1\left\{1 + (j-1)y_j + (l-1)y_l\right\}, \qquad (5.114)$$

$$M_w M_z = M_1^2\left\{1 + (j^2-1)y_j + (l^2-1)y_l\right\}. \qquad (5.115)$$

From the above three equations, y_j and y_l may be eliminated to yield

$$M_n M_w M_z - aM_n M_w - bM_n + d = 0, \qquad (5.116)$$

where a, b, and d are coefficients which depend only on M_1, j, and l. Differentiation with respect to M_n yields

$$\frac{d(M_n M_w M_z)}{dM_n} = a\frac{d(M_n M_w)}{dM_n} + b, \qquad (5.117)$$

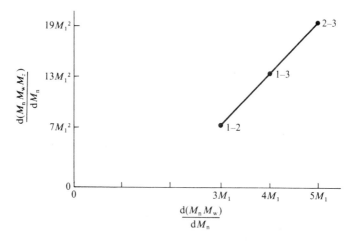

FIG. 5.8. 'Three-species plot' for monomer–dimer–trimer. The 'three-species line' connects the three points where only two species (as indicated) exist. With only three molecular species present the values of the derivatives given on the ordinate and abscissa must lie on this bounded line. (From Roark and Yphantis 1969.)

where $a = (j+l+1)M_1$ and $b = -(j+jl+l)M_1^2$. Thus, in this case, if only three ideal sedimenting species are present $d(M_n M_w M_z)/dM_n$ must be a linear function of $d(M_n M_w)/dM_n$ and this is illustrated in Fig. 5.8 for a monomer–dimer–trimer case. The coefficients of the resulting straight line are sufficient to determine any two of the three quantities M_1, j, and l if the other is known. If the monomer molecular weight M is known, j and l may be found. If there are only two species present, the derivatives of eqn (5.117) will be constant. Again, we refer to Roark and Yphantis (1969) for further elaboration and extensions to more complicated situations.

We now wish to consider the procedure suggested by Roark and Yphantis (1969) for non-ideal systems. From the basic assumption, already discussed earlier, that the contribution of the non-ideality to the chemical potential of any species is proportional to the mass of the species, the activity coefficients of the various species are connected by the relation

$$\ln \gamma_j = j \ln \gamma_1 ,$$

or, in the notation of Scatchard,

$$\beta_{jl} \equiv \partial \ln \gamma_j / \partial m_l ,$$
$$\beta_{jl}/M_j M_l = \beta_{11}/M_1^2 .$$

The non-ideality for the isolated monomer is of the form

$$\beta_{11} = 2A_2 M_1^2 ,$$

which corresponds to eqn (1.11),

$$\ln \gamma = 2A_2 Mc,$$

with A_2 representing the colligative second virial coefficient. Such an expression describes the non-ideality (of a single-species solute) arising from excluded volume with neglect of terms in c^2 and higher. Fortunately, as we have seen before, in the case of a uni–univalent added simple electrolyte, there is no non-ideality arising from Donnan effects contributing to the third virial coefficient and the higher non-even coefficients. The considerations presented above lead to a distinct separation of the effects of association and of other non-ideality, to the extent that it is limited to a contribution to the second virial coefficient only. In fact the procedure of Roark and Yphantis revolves around computational devices designed towards eliminating the term linear in the concentration from the calculated results. To this effect we write

$$\frac{1}{M_w^*} = \frac{1}{M_w} + 2A_2 c, \tag{5.118}$$

where M_w^* is an apparent weight-average molecular weight and no other non-ideality is assumed to contribute to the other terms. Similarly the apparent number-average molecular weight M_n^* is given by

$$\frac{1}{M_n^*} = \frac{1}{M_n} + A_2 c. \tag{5.119}$$

Next a set of moments are derived that are independent of A_2, and therefore of any non-ideality associated with this term. We divide eqn (5.119) by c and differentiate with respect to c^{-1} to obtain the first 'ideal' moment $M_{y1}(c)$,

$$\frac{1}{M_{y1}} \equiv \frac{\mathrm{d}(1/cM_n^*)}{\mathrm{d}(1/c)} = \frac{\mathrm{d}(1/cM_n)}{\mathrm{d}(1/c)} = \frac{2}{M_n} - \frac{1}{M_w}. \tag{5.120}$$

We have used eqn (5.40) to derive the expression on the right-hand side of eqn (5.120). The moment M_{y1} contains no contribution from A_2. Thus, for a non-ideal system (with $A_2 \neq 0$) M_{y1} has the same value as for an ideal system (with $A_2 = 0$).

To derive additional 'ideal' moments, Roark and Yphantis define a new moment M_v, which is related to M_w in the same way that M_w is related to M_n,

$$\frac{1}{M_w} = \frac{\mathrm{d}(c/M_n)}{\mathrm{d}c} \tag{5.121}$$

(this can be derived from eqns (5.26) and (5.40)),

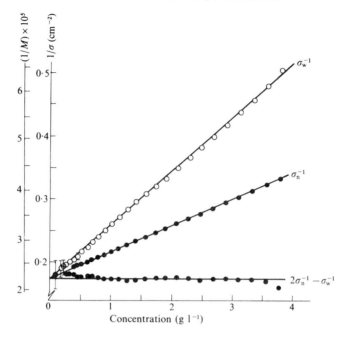

FIG. 5.9. Example of a simple non-ideal system: ovalbumin in 0·1 M acetic acid. The non-ideal behaviour of ovalbumin in acetic acid, 0·5% sucrose (used to form a stabilizing density gradient) and in the absence of salt is shown. Equilibrium ultracentrifugation at 33 450 r.p.m. and at 19 °C. (From Roark and Yphantis 1969.)

$$\frac{1}{M_v^*} = \frac{\mathrm{d}(c/M_w^*)}{\mathrm{d}c} = \frac{1}{M_v} + 4A_2\,c\,. \tag{5.122}$$

We can now find two other 'ideal' moments M_{y2} and M_{y3} from M_w and M_v, respectively (eqn (5.41) is used in this derivation)

$$\frac{1}{M_{y2}} = \frac{\mathrm{d}(1/cM_w^*)}{\mathrm{d}(1/c)} = \frac{\mathrm{d}(1/cM_w)}{\mathrm{d}(1/c)} = \frac{M_z}{M_w^2} = \frac{\mathrm{d}(c/M_{y1})}{\mathrm{d}c_2} \tag{5.123}$$

$(M_z/M_w^2$ also equals $(1/M_w^*)_{\max}$ derived by setting $\mathrm{d}M_w^*/\mathrm{d}c$ equal to zero) and

$$\frac{1}{M_{y3}} = \frac{\mathrm{d}(1/cM_v^*)}{\mathrm{d}(1/c)} = \frac{\mathrm{d}(1/cM_v)}{\mathrm{d}(1/c)} = \frac{M_z}{M_w^3}(M_{z+1} - 3M_z + 3M_w)$$

$$= \frac{\mathrm{d}(c/M_{y2})}{\mathrm{d}c}\,. \tag{5.124}$$

By linear combination of the 'ideal' moments M_{y1}, M_{y2}, and M_{y3} higher virial coefficients may be eliminated. Thus, for instance, the fourth virial coefficient (which may have a significant contribution from the Donnan effect for a highly charged system) may be eliminated, and also the higher virial

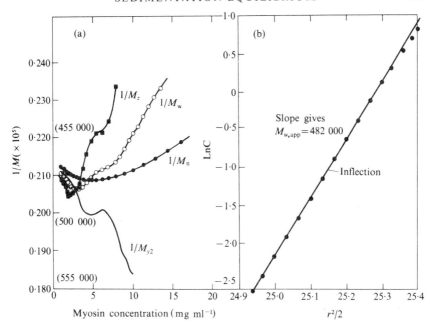

F$_{IG}$. 5.10. (a) Roark and Yphantis computer-program analysis of high-speed sedimentation-equilibrium run of myosin solution with minimal concentration of higher n-mer. The loading concentration was: $2 \cdot 2 \, \text{mg ml}^{-1}$ of myosin in $0 \cdot 5 \, \text{M KCl}$–$0 \cdot 2 \, \text{M PO}_4^{2-}$–$0 \cdot 01 \, \text{M EDTA}$; pH $7 \cdot 3$; $12\,000 \, \text{r.p.m.}$; $6 \, °\text{C}$. Many data points were omitted. (b) Shows $\ln c$ versus r^2 of the data in (a). Concentration is given in millimetres of fringe displacement. (From Godfrey and Harrington 1970.)

coefficients by detailed procedures which follow the recipe described above.

To show the usefulness of this approach, Roark and Yphantis examine an equilibrium ultracentrifugation experiment on a single-species solute—in the absence of association, but with large non-ideality. For ovalbumin in $0 \cdot 1 \, \text{M}$ acetic acid, the Donnan effect is considerable at this pH, with no salt present. The observed values of M_n^{-1}, M_w^{-1} and $M_{y1}^{-1} = 2M_n^{-1} - M_w^{-1}$ are shown in Fig. 5.9, as a function of c. Note that M_n^{-1} and M_w^{-1} are indeed linear with concentration, showing that the nonideality is exclusively related to the second virial coefficient, and M_{y1} is indeed constant and equal to M_1 in this case. The analysis of an associating system (β-lactoglobulin at low pH) is rather more involved, and we refer to the original publication of Roark and Yphantis for a detailed discussion.

A particular instructive example in which a monomer–dimer equilibrium has been resolved by painstaking application of the analytical ultracentrifuge is the study of the myosin system at high ionic strength (Godfrey and Harrington 1970). Fig. 5.10(a) indicates that the reciprocal molecular weight averages M_n^{-1}, M_w^{-1}, and M_z^{-1} first decrease with increasing concentration

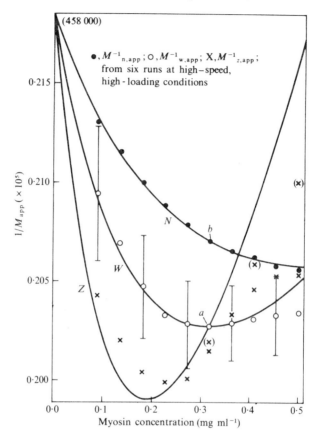

FIG. 5.11. Averaged reciprocal moments versus concentration from 21 high-speed sedimentation-equilibrium runs. Points are experimental (see key). Vertical bars are 95 per cent confidence limits for M_w^{-1} mean values. Solvent was 0.5 M KCl–0.2 M PO_4^{2-}–0.01 M EDTA; pH 7.3; $6\,°C$, 9000–1200 r.p.m.; curves: reversible monomer–dimer association, $M_1 = 458\,000$, $B = 6.60 \times 10^{-6}$ mol dl^{-1} g^{-2}, $k_2 = 9.98$ dl g^{-1}; $Z = M_{z,app}^{-1}$; $W = M_{w,app}^{-1}$; $N = M_{n,app}^{-1}$. (From Godfrey and Harrington 1970.)

(because of the monomer–dimer equilibrium) and then increase with further increase in concentration because of influence of a positive virial coefficient. The reciprocal ideal moment M_{y2}^{-1} (see eqn (5.123)) is free of the influence of the second virial coefficient and decreases continuously; the irregularity in the increasing limb of M_w^{-1} and M_z^{-1} and in M_{y2}^{-1} is presumably due to the formation of higher j-mers and underlines the sensitivity of the method in proper hands. The correct molecular weight of myosin was established in this study to be $458\,000$, and not as believed before. The insensitivity of the usual $\ln c$ versus r^2 plot is clearly apparent from an examination of Fig. 5.10(b). Average reciprocal moments versus concentration from 21 high-

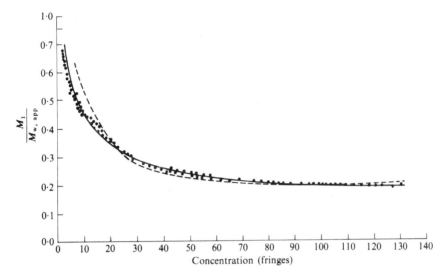

FIG. 5.12. Sedimentation equilibrium of β-lactoglobulin at $16\,^\circ C$ in 0·2 ionic strength acetate buffer (pH 4·61). Comparison of plots of M_1/M_w, against concentration for the monomer–dimer–octamer (dashed line) association having average values ($1\,mol^{-1}$) of $K_2 = 24·1$, $K_5 = 4·0 \times 10^6$, and $BM_1 = 0·014$, with the indefinite association (solid line) having average values ($ml\,mg^{-1}$) of $k = 0·4$ and $BM_1 = 1·6$. The points indicate the observed values. The indefinite association gives a much better description of the experimental data. (From Adams and Lewis 1968.)

speed sedimentation equilibrium runs are shown in Fig. 5.11. The curves are calculated from the equations (Adams and Fujita 1963),

$$c_2 = k_2\, c_1^2,$$

$$c_1 + c_2 = c,$$

$$\frac{1}{M_w^*} = \frac{1}{M_w} + 2A_2\, c,$$

and

$$M_w = \frac{(c_1 + 2c_2)M_1}{c_1 + c_2},$$

which may be combined to yield

$$2/X_w^* = 1 + (1 + 4k_2\, c)^{-\frac{1}{2}} + 2A_2\, M_1\, c \qquad (5.125)$$

(where $X_w^* = M_w^*/M_1$ is apparent-weight-average degree of polymerization), and by a similar procedure equations for M_n^* and M_z^* may be deduced. The parameters M_1, and A_2, and k_2 are derived by extrapolation of any of the curves to $c = 0$ (to obtain M_1) and simultaneous solution of the equations for M_w^* and M_n^*, for instance ($X_n^* = M_n^*/M_1$),

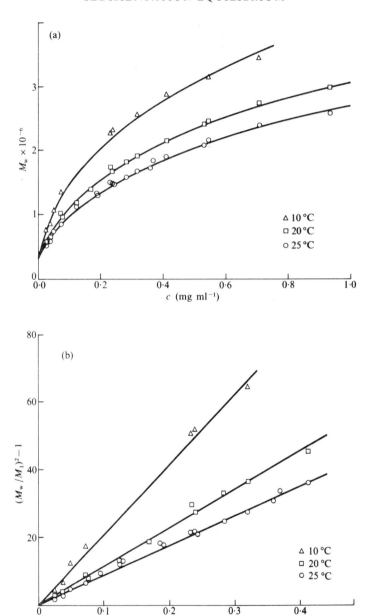

FIG. 5.13. Bovine liver glutamate dehydrogenase in $0.2\,\mathrm{M}$ phosphate buffer saturated with toluene, pH 7, $10^{-4}\,\mathrm{M}$ EDTA; (a) Weight-average molecular weight M_w (from light-scattering measurements) versus concentration; (b) plots of $\{(M_w/M_1)^2 - 1\}$ versus concentration. (From Reisler and Eisenberg 1972.)

$$2/X_n^* = 1 + 2(1 + 4k_2 c)^{-\frac{1}{2}} + A_2 M_1 c, \tag{5.126}$$

on the assumption that A_2 is the same for both expressions. A similar representation of this system from light-scattering results with essentially identical values of the molecular parameters was obtained by Herbert and Carlson (1971).

The analysis of self-associating systems is a delicate undertaking and entails ambiguities which are not always easily avoided. Instructive in this context is the work of Adams and Lewis (1968) who showed (Fig. 5.12) that equilibrium sedimentation results of β-lactoglobulin A in an acetate buffer (pH 4·61) of 0·2 ionic strength are better represented by indefinite association (with unique values for a constant association constant and second virial coefficient A_2) than by a monomer–dimer–octamer association, which Adams and Lewis first believed to apply. We have been able to show that the enzyme glutamate dehydrogenase associates to form long rods of indefinite length (Eisenberg and Tomkins 1968; Reisler, Pouyet, and Eisenberg 1970), rather than finite octamers, as was previously believed (Sund and Weber **1966**; Sund and Burchard 1968). We also showed (Reisler and Eisenberg 1971) that the concept of a unique virial coefficient A_2 in a self-associating system (glutamate dehydrogenase in this specific case) may be inadequate when A_2 is derived by parametrizing the relevant equations on this assumption (Chun and Kim 1969) and other procedures must take account of this limitation. In the case of the glutamate-dehydrogenase systems, it was possible to find conditions (Fig. 5.13) such that the association process overwhelmingly overshadowed non-ideality due to excluded volume or Donnan effects.

5.5.3. *Analysis of indefinite self-association*

In the final paragraphs of this section, we shall discuss the arithmetic inherent in the open-ended indefinite self-association process. We shall assume that the process (see Elias and Bareiss 1967; van Holde and Rosetti 1967; Elias **1972**) is described by a single association constant k (the free energy of addition of each additional monomeric, or oligomeric, unit is independent of the degree of association of the system) and that one value of A_2 characterizes the thermodynamic non-ideality of the system. The latter assumption is not particularly felicitous, but it is universally taken in view of the fact that a more realistic representation introduces parameters which cannot be satisfactorily resolved in a system in which self-association occurs, in addition to thermodynamic non-ideality.†

All thermodynamic non-ideality is expressed in the second virial coefficient. We therefore use concentrations rather than activities in the reaction-scheme eqns (5.105) and (5.106). If we express the equilibrium constant k in units

† See Eisenberg, Josephs, and Reisler (**1976**), who draw attention to an incorrect statement in some of our earlier publications.

$\mathrm{ml\,mg^{-1}}$ then the concentration c_1 ($\mathrm{mg\,ml^{-1}}$) of the ith species is given by

$$c_i = ik^{i-1}c_1^i, \tag{5.127}$$

therefore

$$M_{\mathrm{w}} = \frac{\sum c_i M_i}{c} = \frac{1}{c}(c_1 M_1 + c_2 M_2 + c_3 M_3 + \cdots)$$

$$= \frac{M_1}{c}(c_1 + 2c_2 + 3c_3 + \cdots)$$

and

$$X_{\mathrm{w}} = \frac{c_1}{c}(1 + 4kc_1 + 9k^2c_1^2 + 16k^3c_1^3 + \cdots). \tag{5.128}$$

Now, as $kc_1 < 1,$† eqn (5.128) is given exactly as

$$X_{\mathrm{w}} = \frac{c_1}{c}\frac{1+kc_1}{(1-kc_1)^3}. \tag{5.129}$$

We also have

$$c = \sum c_i = c_1(1 + 2kc_1 + 3k^2c_1^2 + 4k^3c_1^3 + \cdots,$$

$$c = c_1/(1-kc_1)^2, \tag{5.130}$$

hence, substitution of eqn (5.130) in eqn (5.129) yields

$$X_{\mathrm{w}} = \frac{1+kc_1}{1-kc_1}. \tag{5.131}$$

If we now eliminate kc_1 between eqns (5.130) and (5.131), we obtain the simple exact expression

$$X_{\mathrm{w}}^2 = 1 + 4kc$$

† The requirement $kc_1 < 1$ is always true. To derive this we use the probabilistic arguments presented by Flory (1953) in his discussion of random condensation polymerization with equal reactivity of all functional groups. The probability p that a given functional group has reacted is equal to the fraction of all functional groups of this type which have condensed (independent of chain length). Obviously p is smaller than unity. In the self-associating system, no groups have reacted in the monomer, one group in the dimer, two in the trimer ($i-1$) in the i-mer, and so forth. Therefore,

$$p = \frac{\sum\limits_{1}^{\infty}(i-1)c_i/i}{\sum\limits_{1}^{\infty}c_i},$$

and, if we substitute c_i of eqn (5.127),

$$p = \frac{\sum (i-1)k^{i-1}c_1^i}{\sum ik^{i-1}c_1^i} = 1 - \frac{\sum k^{i-1}c_1^i}{\sum ik^{i-1}c_1^i} = kc_1,$$

as is easily verified. The product kc_1 is therefore equal to p and is thus always smaller than unity.

or

$$M_w = M_1 (1+4kc)^{\frac{1}{2}}. \tag{5.132}$$

To calculate X_n we proceed from the definition of $M_n = c/\sum c_J/M_J$ (eqn (5.32)) to find by a calculation similar to that described above

$$X_n^{-1} = 1 - kc_1,$$

from which, by combination with eqn (5.131),

$$2X_n = X_w + 1$$

or

$$2M_n = M_w + M_1. \tag{5.133}$$

Similarly, from the definition of $M_z = \sum c_i M_i^2 / \sum c_i M_i$, we perform the summation to find the correlation $(X_z = M_z/M_1)$

$$2X_z = 3X_w - \frac{1}{X_w}$$

or

$$2M_z = 3M_w - M_1^2/M_w. \tag{5.134}$$

For large degrees of association, we obtain the simple asymptotic relation

$$M_z : M_w : M_n = 3:2:1,$$

which is known as the most probable distribution and is well known from studies of synthetic condensation polymers (Flory 1953).

If non-ideality is considered then we must replace M_w, for instance, in eqn (5.132) by

$$\frac{M_w^*}{1 - 2A_2 M_w^* c} = M_1 (1+4kc)^{\frac{1}{2}}, \tag{5.135}$$

which takes into consideration a correction due to a linear term in c (eqn (5.118)). From the above equation, the limiting slope $d(X_w^* - 1)/dc$ when $c \to 0$ is not equal to $4k$ (as would be the case in the ideal situation) but rather to $4(k - A_2 M_1)$. In favourable cases the correction is small and the indefinite association is amenable to straightforward analysis. From the analysis of the ultracentrifuge results at equilibrium it is, of course, also possible to form the ideal moments M_{y1} or M_{y2}, for instance, of Roark and Yphantis (1969), and thereby to eliminate the effect of the second virial coefficient. For further elaborations and treatment of other situations, we refer to the very extensive literature in this field, a minute fraction of which has been quoted in this chapter.

6

TRANSPORT METHODS

THE discussion of transport methods in this chapter is not exhaustive and refers mainly to some problems which arise because the sedimenting macromolecules carry charges and the solvent is composed of more than one molecular weight component. We shall refer to the sedimentation coefficient s, for instance, as the flow per unit concentration, per unit centrifugal field, in the absence of concentration gradients. We therefore only consider some contributions to the numerical value of s and completely disregard the practical reality of the existence of boundaries, and yet from the shape of boundaries and deviations from the expected ideal shape, some of the more interesting bits of information which the ultracentrifuge can provide, are derived. Such information has been often reviewed (Svedberg and Pedersen **1940**; Schachman **1959**; Fujita **1962**; Williams **1963**; Creeth and Pain **1967**). One of the most interesting aspects concerns the analysis of the sedimentation process in protein interactions and associating systems (Gilbert and Gilbert **1973**; Cann and Goad **1973**). In his classical remarks Gilbert (1955) could show that even from a qualitative analysis of sedimenting boundaries of concentration gradients in mixed interacting systems, it was possible to derive conclusions with respect to the interactions. Yet the complex nature of the flow, the necessity to disregard diffusion, the imperfect knowledge of the frictional coefficients, and other simplifying assumptions, make a quantitative analysis extremely difficult. It is interesting to consider an example extensively discussed by Gilbert and Gilbert (**1973**) in their recent review. Under certain experimental conditions (pH 1·6) bovine β-lacto-globulin A dissociates into two equal subunits, whereas it undergoes an association process to larger aggregates at higher pH (4·65). Gilbert and Gilbert have analysed the data of Armstrong and McKenzie (1967) in terms of a dimer–tetramer–hexamer and closed pseudocubical octamer. Values of s are assumed for the intermediate species, and unequal association constants are fitted for the individual steps. Yet Adams and Lewis (1968) (see Fig. 5.12) believe that their equilibrium sedimentation data for β-lactoglobulin A under associating conditions are better fitted by an indefinite association with a unique intrinsic association constant; the dashed line in their Fig. 5.12 clearly indicates to what extent a simulated curve for a monomer–dimer–octamer association differs from the indefinite association (solid) line. We shall not further discuss this system which has also been extensively described by Timasheff and Townend (1968) who also support the tendency towards the formation of a compact, highly symmetrical, stable octamer at low temperatures, in the pH range 3·8–5·1.

The aim of this chapter will be the analysis of sedimentation and diffusion, and of charge effects, in the component ionic systems, mainly by the methods of irreversible thermodynamics.

6.1. Equations for multi-component systems in the formulation of the thermo-dynamics of irreversible processes

The equations for diffusion and sedimentation in multi-component systems can be derived from a unified point of view by the methods of non-equilibrium thermodynamics. We shall, for convenience of presentation, first discuss the case of non-ionic systems, and in the following section we will then introduce the problems arising when ionic solutions are being investigated. The phenomenological analyses presented here have been developed in the work of Hooyman and his coworkers (1953, 1956) and of Peller (1958). A detailed discussion was presented by Fujita (**1962**). Eisenberg (1962) showed that in multi-component systems comprising a macromolecular solute and a number of low-molecular-weight components, the reasonable simplifying assumption that the total chemical potential of the low-molecular-weight components is uniform throughout the cell leads to less involved and more tractable expressions. Appendix VI (p. 238) provides a basic background for an acquaintance with non-equilibrium thermodynamics, it follows the text of Katchalsky and Curran (**1965**), based on the pioneering contributions of Lars Onsager, Ilya Prigogine, S. R. deGroot, and J. G. Kirkwood.

We write for the dissipation function Φ, which is the entropy production times T (see Appendix VI, eqn (A6.19)) of a component under isothermal conditions (grad $T = 0$) and in the absence of chemical reaction ($j_{ch} = 0$)

$$\Phi = \sum_{k=1}^{n} j_k x_k, \tag{6.1}$$

where the n generalized forces are given by

$$x_k = \nabla(-\tilde{\mu}_k'), \tag{6.2}$$

$$\tilde{\mu}_k' = \mu_k' + \phi = \mu_k' - \tfrac{1}{2}\omega^2 r^2. \tag{6.3}$$

Forces x_k, flows j_k and potentials μ_k' (equal to μ_k/M_k) are all per gram of component k; the average velocity v_k equals j_k/c_k. We consider, for simplicity, one-dimensional radial sedimentation and diffusion, and therefore replace the gradient operator by the derivative d/dr, to obtain for x_k (to simplify the notation, the vectorial nature of the forces and the flows will be omitted in this chapter).

$$x_k = -\frac{RT}{M_k} \sum_{j=2}^{n} a_{kj} \frac{\mathrm{d}m_j}{\mathrm{d}r} - \bar{v}_k \frac{\mathrm{d}P}{\mathrm{d}r} + \omega^2 r, \tag{6.4}$$

where the a_{kj} are defined by eqn (2.17), $\bar{v}_k = \bar{V}_k/M_k$ and the pressure gradient $\mathrm{d}P/\mathrm{d}r$ at mechanical equilibrium is equal to $\rho\omega^2 r$ by eqn (5.11). Coriolis forces (see Fitts **1962**) are assumed to be negligible and are not considered. We rewrite eqn (6.4) in the form

$$x_k = \frac{V_m}{M_k} \left(\frac{\partial \rho}{\partial m_k}\right)_{P,m} \omega^2 r - \frac{RT}{M_k} \sum_{j=2}^{n} a_{kj} \frac{\mathrm{d}m_j}{\mathrm{d}r}, \tag{6.5}$$

where we have used eqn (3.1)

$$V_m(\partial \rho/\partial m_k)_{P,m} = M_k(1 - \bar{v}\rho)$$

for the density increment. The first term in eqn (6.5) can be interpreted as the net sedimenting force, corrected for buoyancy (sedimentation of species k does not occur for $(\partial \rho/\partial m_k)_{P,m}$ equal to zero) whereas the second term corresponds to a diffusion force; at equilibrium x_k is equal to zero, there is no net flow and eqn (5.13) or (5.14) for equilibrium sedimentation are recovered.

The forces in eqn (6.1) are not independent. They are related by an expression similar to the Gibbs–Duhem relation[†]

$$\sum_{k=1}^{n} c_k x_k = 0. \tag{6.6}$$

We utilize eqn (6.6) to express the force acting on the solvent in terms of the forces on the solute

$$x_1 = -\sum_{k=2}^{n} w_k x_k, \tag{6.9}$$

[†] Eqn (6.6) is obtained by multiplying eqn (6.5) by c_k, substituting $M_k(1 - \bar{v}_k \rho)$ for $V_m(\partial \rho/\partial m_k)_{P,m}$ and summing over all components

$$\sum_{k=1}^{n} c_k x_k = \omega^2 r \sum_{k=1}^{n} c_k(1 - \bar{v}_k \rho) - RT \sum_{k=1}^{n} \frac{c_k}{M_k} \sum_{j=2}^{n} a_{kj} \frac{\mathrm{d}m_j}{\mathrm{d}r}. \tag{6.7}$$

1. The first term on the right-hand side of eqn (6.7) is zero because

$$\sum_{k=1}^{n} c_k = \rho \quad \text{and} \quad \sum_{k=1}^{n} c_k \bar{v}_k = 1.$$

2. As for the second term, consider

$$\sum_{k=1}^{n} n_k \mathrm{d}\mu_k = RT \sum_{k=1}^{n} n_k \sum_{j=2}^{n} a_{kj} \mathrm{d}m_j + \sum_{k=1}^{n} n_k \bar{V}_k \mathrm{d}P. \tag{6.8}$$

where w_k is the molality, $w_k = c_k/c_1$. Introducing eqn (6.9) into the expression for the dissipation function (eqn (6.1)) we obtain

$$\Phi = \sum_{k=2}^{n} (j_k - w_k j_1) . x_k \qquad (6.10)$$

$$= \sum_{k=2}^{n} j_k^1 . x_k$$

in which the $(n-1)$ flows j_k are relative to the solvent component. This becomes obvious if we write

$$j_k^1 = c_k \left(\frac{j_k}{c_k} - \frac{j_1}{c_1} \right) = c_k (v_k - v_1), \qquad (6.11)$$

because $j_k = c_k v_k$ (eqn (A6.4)). Detailed formulations and interconnections of the flows j_k with respect to various forces, of either experimental or theoretical significance, are discussed by Fujita (**1962**).

Thus the dissipation function for an n-component system is expressed in terms of $(n-1)$ independent flows and forces. Only for independent diffusional flows can meaningful phenomenological equations be written for which Onsager's reciprocal relations for the equality of the cross-coefficients hold. The measured 'absolute' flows j_k are referred to the walls of the measuring cell. It can be shown (see Katchalsky and Curran **1965**) that for zero-volume flow, and low concentration of solute the two flows j_k and j_k^1 are practically identical. In a binary system the ratio j_2/j_2^1 is equal to the volume fraction of the solvent, which is usually close to unity in dilute solutions; this problem will not be pursued here further.

We can now write the phenomenological equations

$$j_i^1 = \sum_{k=2}^{n} l_{ik} x_k \qquad (6.12)$$

relating the $(n-1)$ independent flows j_i^1 to the $(n-1)$ conjugate forces; the

---

The last term in eqn (6.8) equals $V \, dP$, by the Gibbs–Duhem equation, at constant temperature,

$$\sum_{k=1}^{n} n_k \, d\mu_k - V \, dP = 0.$$

Therefore eqn (6.8) leads to

$$RT \sum_{k=1}^{n} n_k \sum_{j=2}^{n} a_{kj} \, dm_j = 0,$$

$$RT \sum_{k=1}^{n} \frac{c_k}{M_k} \sum_{j=2}^{n} a_{kj} \, dm_j = 0,$$

and

$$\sum_{k=1}^{n} c_k x_k = 0. \qquad \text{Q.E.D.} \qquad (6.6)$$

magnitude of the phenomenological coefficients l_{ik} depends on the units used for the flows and the forces. If we substitute the value of x_k from eqn (6.5) we obtain

$$j_i^1 = V_m \omega^2 r \sum_{k=2}^n \frac{l_{ik}}{M_k} \left(\frac{\partial \rho}{\partial m_k}\right)_{P,m} - RT \sum_{k=2}^n \frac{l_{ik}}{M_k} \sum_{k=2}^n a_{kj} \frac{dm_j}{dr} \qquad (6.13)$$

or, equivalently,

$$j_i^1 = \omega^2 r \sum_{k=2}^n l_{ik}(1 - \bar{v}_k \rho) - RT \sum_{k=2}^n \frac{l_{ik}}{M_k} \sum_{j=2}^n a_{kj} \frac{dm_j}{dr}. \qquad (6.14)$$

In the linear treatment the l_{ik} are not functions of ω or of the forces, so that the phenomenological coefficients are not functions of the generalized forces.

In the special case of isothermal diffusion, in the absence of a centrifugal field, ω is equal to zero and (in the conventional notation of Fick's first law for diffusion)

$$j_i^1 = - \sum_{j=2}^n D_{ij} \frac{dc_J}{dr}, \qquad (6.15)$$

where the set of $(n-1)^2$ diffusion coefficients D_{ij} is defined by

$$D_{ij} \equiv RT \sum_{k=2}^n \frac{l_{ik}}{M_k} a_{kj} \left(\frac{dm_j}{dc_j}\right)_{fl}. \qquad (6.16)$$

The transformation $(dm_j/dc_j)_{fl}$ of the molalities to the more familiar volume concentration units under the conditions specific to this 'flow' experiment proceeds analogously as outlined in the footnote on p. 38 (eqns (2.51)–(2.54)) or for the sedimentation-equilibrium experiment (see footnote on p. 104, eqns (5.18)–(5.20)). An appropriate transformation could be derived for the present case. In the limit of zero concentration of a species j it is possible to write $(dm_j/dc_j)^0 = V_m^0/M_2$. At finite concentrations of species j this will not be entirely correct. We define, purely for aesthetic reasons,

$$a_{kj}(dm_j/dc_j)_{fl} \equiv a'_{kj} \qquad (6.17)$$

and rewrite eqn (6.16) to read

$$D_{ij} \equiv RT \sum_{k=2}^n (l_{ik}/M_k)a'_{kj}. \qquad (6.18)$$

The $(n-1)$ linear eqns (6.18) can be solved for the l_{ik} in terms of the experimentally determinable D_{ij}

$$(RT l_{ik}/M_k)|a'| = \sum_{j=2}^n D_{ij} A'_{kj} \equiv F'_{ik}, \qquad (6.19)$$

where $|a'|$ is the determinant of the a'_{jk} and A'_{kj} is the cofactor† of the element a'_{kj} of $|a'|$.

With these definitions we can rewrite eqn (6.13) to read

$$j_i^1 = \frac{V_m \omega^2 r}{RT|a'|} \sum_{k=2}^{n} F'_{ik} \left(\frac{\partial \rho}{\partial m_k} \right) - \sum_{k=2}^{n} D_{ik} \frac{dc_k}{dr}. \tag{6.20}$$

The sedimentation coefficient of component i may be defined as the relative velocity $(v_i - v_1)$ (which is equal to the flow per unit concentration j_i^1/c_i by eqn (6.11)) per unit centrifugal field, and in the absence of concentration gradients; we therefore have

$$s_i \equiv \frac{j_i^1}{c_i \omega^2 r} = \frac{V_m}{c_i RT|a'|} \sum_{k=2}^{n} F'_{ik} \left(\frac{\partial \rho}{\partial m_k} \right)_{P,m}. \tag{6.21}$$

The diffusion coefficients appear only in the determinants F'_{ik}, defined by eqn (6.19)

The mathematical theory relating to transport phenomena has been summarized by Fujita (**1962**); the experimental determination of diffusivity has been reviewed by Geddes and Pontius (**1960**), Jost (**1960**), Svensson and Thompson (**1961**), Crank and Park (**1968**), and Dunlop, Steel, and Lane (**1972**). On a less specialized basis mention must be made of the discussions in Tanford (**1961**) and van Holde (**1971**). Diffusion coefficients and cross-coefficients for some low-molecular-weight three-component systems have been measured by Dunlop and Gosting (1955, 1959) and Dunlop (1957a, 1957b); an exact solution of the equations for free diffusion in three-component systems with interacting flows has been given by Fujita and Gosting (1956).

6.2. Three-component non-ionic systems

We will now specialize the equations of the preceding section to the simpler case of a non-ionic three-component system, consisting of two solutes, components 2 and 3, and one solvent, component 1.

We write (eqn (6.10)) for the dissipation function

$$\Phi = j_2^1 x_2 + j_3^1 x_3. \tag{6.22}$$

The phenomenological eqns (6.12) are

$$j_2^1 = l_{22} x_2 + l_{23} x_3 \tag{6.23}$$

and

$$j_3^1 = l_{32} x_2 + l_{33} x_3. \tag{6.24}$$

---

† The cofactor A_{jk} of the element a_{jk} of a determinant $|a|$ is $(-1)^{j+k}$ times the determinant formed by striking out the row and column intersecting in a_{jk}; the sign depends on the *positions* of j and of k (even or odd) and not on the label attached to it by the conventions used here with respect to the designations of the various species or components.

We derive x_2 and x_3 from eqn (6.5), restricting ourselves for the moment to the case of pure one-dimensional diffusion ($\omega = 0$), proceeding in direction r; we use the definition, eqn (6.17), for a'_{kj},

$$x_2 = -RT\left(\frac{a'_{22}}{M_2}\frac{dc_2}{dr} + \frac{a'_{23}}{M_3}\frac{dc_3}{dr}\right), \tag{6.25}$$

$$x_3 = -RT\left(\frac{a'_{32}}{M_2}\frac{dc_2}{dr} + \frac{a'_{33}}{M_3}\frac{dc_3}{dr}\right). \tag{6.26}$$

Substitution of x_2 and x_3 into eqns (6.23) and (6.24) and some elementary re-arrangements lead to

$$j_2^1 = -RT\left(\frac{l_{22}}{M_2}a'_{22} + \frac{l_{23}}{M_3}a'_{32}\right)\frac{dc_2}{dr} - RT\left(\frac{l_{22}}{M_2}a'_{23} + \frac{l_{23}}{M_3}a'_{33}\right)\frac{dc_3}{dr} \tag{6.27}$$

and

$$j_3^1 = -RT\left(\frac{l_{32}}{M_2}a'_{22} + \frac{l_{33}}{M_3}a'_{32}\right)\frac{dc_2}{dr} - RT\left(\frac{l_{32}}{M_2}a'_{23} + \frac{l_{33}}{M_3}a'_{33}\right)\frac{dc_3}{dr}. \tag{6.28}$$

In terms of the straight-(D_{22} and D_{33}) and cross-(D_{23} and D_{32}) diffusion coefficients a generalization of Fick's equation for two interdependent diffusional flows yields

$$j_2^1 = -D_{22}\frac{dc_2}{dr} - D_{23}\frac{dc_3}{dr} \tag{6.29}$$

and

$$j_3^1 = -D_{32}\frac{dc_2}{dr} - D_{33}\frac{dc_3}{dr}. \tag{6.30}$$

Comparison of the sets of equations for j_2^1 and j_3^1 reveals the relationships

$$\begin{aligned}
D_{22} &= RT\{(l_{22}a'_{22}/M_2) + (l_{23}a'_{32}/M_3)\}, \\
D_{23} &= RT\{(l_{22}a'_{23}/M_2) + (l_{23}a'_{33}/M_3)\}, \\
D_{32} &= RT\{(l_{32}a'_{22}/M_2) + (l_{33}a'_{32}/M_3)\}, \\
D_{33} &= RT\{(l_{32}a'_{23}/M_2) + (l_{33}a'_{33}/M_3)\}.
\end{aligned} \tag{6.31}$$

These relationships could, of course, have been written down directly from eqn (6.18). The symmetry of the hydrodynamic coefficients (eqn (A6.23))

$$l_{23} = l_{32}$$

does not lead to equality of the cross-diffusion coefficients D_{23} and D_{32}. Neither is the condition of zero hydrodynamic coupling ($l_{23} = 0$) sufficient for the vanishing of D_{23}. Both hydrodynamic (l_{23}) and thermodynamic (a'_{23}, a'_{32}) coupling must vanish for the cross-diffusion coefficients to go to zero. The relation between the diffusion coefficients D_{ij}, the Onsager coefficients l_{ij} and the thermodynamic interaction coefficients a'_{ij} may be represented in matrix form

$$\begin{bmatrix} D_{22} & D_{23} \\ D_{32} & D_{33} \end{bmatrix} = \begin{bmatrix} l_{22}/M_2 & l_{23}/M_3 \\ l_{32}/M_2 & l_{33}/M_3 \end{bmatrix} \begin{bmatrix} RTa'_{22} & RTa'_{23} \\ RTa'_{32} & RTa'_{33} \end{bmatrix}. \qquad (6.32)$$

Solving eqns (6.31) for the l_{ij} we obtain

$$RT|a'|l_{23}/M_3 = -D_{22}a'_{23} + D_{23}a'_{22}, \qquad (6.33)$$

$$RT|a'|l_{32}/M_2 = -D_{32}a'_{33} - D_{33}a'_{32}, \qquad (6.34)$$

which are identical with the solution for the general case (eqn (6.19)).

In the presence of the centrifugal field ($\omega \neq 0$) we can derive the sedimentation coefficients s_2 and s_3 for the three-component system by eqn (6.21). Thus (compare also eqn (6.19)) in terms of the hydrodynamic coefficients, s_2 is given by

$$s_2 = \frac{j_2^1}{c_2\omega^2 r} = \frac{V_m}{c_2}\left\{ \frac{l_{22}}{M_2}\left(\frac{\partial\rho}{\partial m_2}\right)_{P,m_3} + \frac{l_{23}}{M_3}\left(\frac{\partial\rho}{\partial m_2}\right)_{P,m_2}\right\}, \qquad (6.35)$$

and in terms of the diffusion coefficients and thermodynamic parameters

$$s_2 = \frac{V_m}{c_2 RT|a'|}\left\{ F'_{22}\left(\frac{\partial\rho}{\partial m_2}\right)_{P,m_3} + F'_{23}\left(\frac{\partial\rho}{\partial m_3}\right)_{P,m_2}\right\}. \qquad (6.36)$$

Introducing the values of F'_{22} and F'_{23} we obtain

$$s_2 = \frac{V_m}{c_2 RT|a'|}\left\{ \left(\frac{\partial\rho}{\partial m_2}\right)_{P,m_3}(D_{22}a'_{33} - D_{23}a'_{32}) \right.$$
$$\left. + \left(\frac{\partial\rho}{\partial m_3}\right)_{P,m_2}(D_{23}a'_{22} - D_{22}a'_{23})\right\}. \qquad (6.37)$$

6.2.1. Vanishing concentration of the macromolecular component

Eqn (6.37) is an unwieldy expression which can be reduced to a simpler form when $c_2 \to 0$ (Baldwin 1958). In this case D_{23} vanishes since j_2^1 and dc_2/dr go to zero but dc_3/dr remains finite (see eqn (6.29)); $\lim_{c_2\to 0}(D_{23}/c_2)$ equals $(\partial D_{23}/\partial c_2)^0$ evaluated at $c_2 = 0$, by l'Hôpital's rule. Also when $m_2 = V_m c_2/M_2$ goes to zero, a_{22} goes to infinity, but $m_2 a_{22}$ equals unity. All other derivatives a_{ij} stay finite; $\lim_{m_2\to 0} M_2|a| = a_{33}$ and $\lim_{m_2\to 0} m_2|a'| = a'_{33} V_m^0/M_2$. Upon introducing all these simplifying features into eqn (6.37) we obtain

$$s_2 = \frac{V_m^0 D_{22}}{RT}\left(\frac{\partial\rho}{\partial m_2}\right)_{P,m_3}\left[1 + \frac{(\partial\rho/\partial m_3)_{P,m_2}}{(\partial\rho/\partial m_2)_{P,m_3}^0} \right.$$
$$\left. \times \left\{\left(\frac{\partial D_{23}}{\partial m_2}\right)^0\left(\frac{V_m^0}{D_{22}a'_{33}M_2} - \frac{a_{23}}{a_{33}}\right)\right\}\right] \qquad (6.38)$$

which can be written in the more conventional form

$$s_2 = \frac{M_2(1-\bar{v}_2\rho^0)D_{22}}{RT}\left[1+\frac{M_3(1-v_3\rho^0)}{M_2(1-v_2^0\rho^0)}\left\{\left(\frac{\partial D_{23}}{\partial c_2}\right)^0\frac{1}{D_{22}a'_{33}}-\frac{a_{23}}{a_{33}}\right\}\right]. \quad (6.39)$$

This is the expression given by Baldwin (1958). It bears resemblance (if the term in braces is not considered) to the Svedberg equation for two-component systems yet it can still not be properly evaluated unless the magnitude of the derivative $(\partial D_{23}/\partial c_2)^0$ is known. It strictly reduces to the two-component form if the density increment $(\partial\rho/\partial m_3)_{P,m_2}$ is equal to zero; it also reduces to an interesting form if the derivative of the cross-diffusion coefficient with respect to concentration, $(\partial D_{23}/\partial c_2)^0$, vanishes. A more general expression, based on the assumption that (at finite concentrations c_2 as well) grad $\tilde{\mu}_3 = 0$ in the transport equations will now be considered (Eisenberg 1962).

6.2.2. *Consequences of the assumption that grad $\tilde{\mu}_3 = 0$ in the transport equations*

The flow in a centrifugal field of the macromolecular component 2 in a solution containing two or more low-molecular-weight species is described by either eqns (6.12), (6.13), (6.14), or (6.20); the flow j_2^1 is given in terms of the field and all the concentration gradients dc_j/dr. We have seen that the diffusion coefficients are derived from the flow j_2^1 in the absence of the external field, and the sedimentation coefficient s is defined as the velocity per unit field in homogeneous solution (that is, the dc_j/dr are equal to zero; see eqn (6.21) or either (6.35) or (6.37) for the three-component system). In the three-component system considered, C_3 (on a molar basis) is fairly large and C_2 is usually much smaller than C_3; also D_{33} is usually much larger than D_{22} because of the large disparity in size between the macromolecular component 2 and the low-molecular-weight component 3 (we recall that the flows are referred to the solvent component 1). Under these conditions a plausible assumption is that, in the sedimentation experiment, for instance, while the solution just ahead of the boundary is homogeneous with respect to component 2, component 3 (and all other low-molecular-weight components which might be present in the solution) is essentially in equilibrium, that is, $\tilde{\mu}_3$ is constant and x_3, the gradient $-d\tilde{\mu}_3/dr$ (see eqn (6.2)), is equal to zero (similar considerations apply for the diffusion experiment). This assumption leads to a particularly simple result. We now have for the flow j_2^1 from eqn (6.12), with $x_3 = 0$,

$$j_2^1 = l_{22}x_2 \quad (6.40)$$

and x_2 is given, from eqn (6.5), by

$$x_2 = \frac{V_m}{M_2}\left(\frac{\partial\rho}{\partial m_2}\right)_{P,m_2}\omega^2 r - \frac{RT}{M_2}\left(a_{22}\frac{dm_2}{dr}-a_{23}\frac{dm_3}{dr}\right). \quad (6.41)$$

We may now eliminate dm_3/dr from eqn (6.41) by use of eqn (6.5) for x_3, with $x_3 = 0$

$$0 = V_m \left(\frac{\partial \rho}{\partial m_3}\right)_{P,m_2} \omega^2 r - RT\left(a_{32}\frac{dm_2}{dr} - a_{33}\frac{dm_3}{dr}\right).$$

We obtain for x_2 (considering $a_{23} = a_{32}$)

$$x_2 = \omega^2 r \frac{V_m}{M_2}\left\{\left(\frac{\partial \rho}{\partial m_2}\right)_{P,m_3} - \frac{a_{23}}{a_{33}}\left(\frac{\partial \rho}{\partial m_3}\right)_{P,m_2}\right\} - \frac{RT}{M_2}\left(a_{22} - \frac{a_{23}^2}{a_{33}}\right)\frac{dm_2}{dr}, \quad (6.42)$$

or, for the flow j_2^1, and more compactly (see eqns (2.39), (5.15), and (5.16))

$$j_2^1 = \frac{l_{22}\omega^2 r V_m}{M_2}\left(\frac{\partial \rho}{\partial m_2}\right)_{P,\mu_3} - \frac{l_{22} RT|a|}{M_2 a_{33}}\frac{dm_2}{dr}. \quad (6.43)$$

For the sedimentation coefficient s_2 (when dm_2/dr is zero) we derive, from the above equation

$$s_2 = \frac{l_{22} V_m}{c_2 M_2}\left(\frac{\partial \rho}{\partial m_2}\right)_{P,\mu_3} = \frac{V_m}{M_2 f_2'}\left(\frac{\partial \rho}{\partial m_2}\right)_{P,\mu_3}, \quad (6.44)$$

where f_2' is the friction coefficient (c_2/l_{22}) of 1 g of component 2. To transform to the c-, mass per unit volume, concentration scale we use

$$\left(\frac{\partial c_2}{\partial m_2}\right)_{P,\mu_3} = \frac{M_2}{V_m}(1 - c_2 \bar{v}_2^*),$$

where $v_2^* = \bar{V}_2^*/M_2$ (see eqn (5.17)), and obtain

$$s_2 = \frac{(1 - c_2 \bar{v}_2^*)}{f_2'}\left(\frac{\partial \rho}{\partial c_2}\right)_{P,\mu_3}. \quad (6.45)$$

The density increment $(\partial \rho/\partial c_2)_{P,\mu_3}$ is given by (see the analogous derivation of $(\partial \rho/\partial c_2)_\mu$, eqn (3.8))

$$\left(\frac{\partial \rho}{\partial c_2}\right)_{P,\mu_3} = \frac{(1 - \bar{v}_2 \rho) + \zeta_3'(1 - v_3 \rho)}{1 - \bar{v}_2^* c_2}, \quad (6.46)$$

where the interaction parameter $\zeta_3' \equiv (\partial w_3/\partial w_2)_{P,\mu_3}$ and ρ is the density of the solution. Substitution of $(\partial \rho/\partial c_2)_{P,\mu_3}$ into eqn (6.45) yields

$$s_2 = \frac{1}{f_2'}\{(1 - \bar{v}_2 \rho) + \zeta_3'(1 - \bar{v}_3 \rho)\}. \quad (6.47)$$

For the diffusion coefficient D_2,

$$D_2 \equiv D_{22} - D_{23}\frac{a_{32}}{a_{33}}\frac{(dm_2/dc_2)_{P,\mu_3}}{(dm_3/dc_3)_{P,\mu_3}},$$

we obtain (from eqns (6.5), (6.15), and (6.43) at zero field)

$$D_2 = \frac{l_{22}}{M_2} \frac{RT|a|}{a_{33}} \left(\frac{dm_2}{dc_2}\right)_{P,\mu_3} = \frac{l_{22}}{M_2} \frac{RT|a|}{a_{33}} \frac{V_m^2}{V_m - m_2 V_2^*}$$

$$= \frac{l_{22} V_m}{M_2 c_2} \frac{d\Pi}{dm_2}. \tag{6.48}$$

We have specified $(dm/dc_2)_{P,\mu_3}$, rather than the subscript $f\,l$, because of the specific single assumption ($\mu_3 = $ constant) on which the calculation in this section is based; we have also used eqn (2.39) and (5.17) and the relation $c_2 = m_2 M_2 / V_m$.

Division of eqn (6.48) by eqn (6.44) yields the simple expression, valid at finite concentrations of component 2,

$$\frac{s_2}{D_2} = \frac{(\partial\rho/\partial m_2)_{P,\mu_3}}{d\Pi/dm_2}. \tag{6.49}$$

We substitute $(\partial\rho/\partial m_2)_{P,\mu_3}$ in terms of $(\partial\rho/\partial m_2)_\mu$ (eqn (5.20))

$$\left(\frac{\partial\rho}{\partial m_2}\right)_{P,\mu_3} = \left(\frac{\partial\rho}{\partial m_2}\right)_\mu + \frac{d\Pi}{dm_2}\left\{\left(\frac{\partial\rho}{\partial m_3}\right)_{P,m_2} \frac{\bar{V}_3}{RTa_{33}} - \kappa\rho\right\} \tag{6.50}$$

and transform to the c-concentration scale to yield

$$\frac{s_2}{D_2} = \frac{(\partial\rho/\partial c_2)_\mu}{d\Pi/dc_2} + \left\{\left(\frac{\partial\rho}{\partial m_3}\right)_{P,m_2} \frac{\bar{V}_3}{RTa_{33}} - \kappa\rho\right\}$$

$$= \frac{1}{RT}\left(\frac{\partial\rho}{\partial c_2}\right)_\mu \left(\frac{1}{M_2} + 2A_2 c_2 + \ldots\right)^{-1} + \left\{\left(\frac{\partial\rho}{\partial m_3}\right)_{P,m_2} \frac{\bar{V}_3}{RTa_{33}} - \kappa\rho\right\}. \tag{6.51}$$

For reasonably high values of M_2 the second term on the right-hand side of eqns (6.50) and (6.51) (in the latter equation the virial expansion eqn (1.2) has been applied) is always negligible with respect to the first term. At vanishing concentration c_2 we obtain

$$\frac{s_2}{D_2} = \frac{(\partial\rho/\partial c_2)_\mu M_2}{RT}, \tag{6.52}$$

which is an analogue of the Svedberg equation (Svedberg and Pedersen **1940**) for multi-component systems, under the assumption that all low-molecular-weight components are essentially at sedimentation equilibrium; eqn (6.52) is furthermore practically identical with eqns (6.38) or (6.39) if $(\partial D_{23}/\partial c_2)^0$ is taken to be zero.

6.3. Three-component ionic systems

In previous chapters of this book we have been able to show that absolute information on molecular weight, intermolecular interactions, and distribution of mass in charge-carrying macromolecules can be obtained by application of equilibrium studies without explicit consideration of the ionic polyelectrolyte nature of the macromolecules. To be sure, this ionic nature influences the molecular conformation, interactions with other macro-molecules, and interactions with small ions in solution. Yet, for many intents and purposes, and in particular for the applications discussed above, a thermodynamic framework constructed on the basis of choosing components in electroneutral combinations from the ionized species, is adequate to solve the aforementioned problems. When we presently turn to the investigation of transport phenomena it becomes necessary to re-state the problem and to reconsider the question of the extent to which the above conclusions still hold with respect to velocity sedimentation and diffusion measurements, which involve motion of macromolecules in an irreversible process. We shall exclude from our discussion such typical ionic processes as electro-phoresis and conduction, which obviously must involve properties of the single constituent ions, and (at finite concentrations) interactions between them. We shall therefore limit ourselves to the study of phenomena in which, as before, over-all electroneutrality is preserved; our query is restricted to the significance of so-called 'charge effects' which may arise in the transport of electroneutral components after a microscopic separation of the species in the process of flow. As an introduction to the topic it is instructive to consider the related problems in the well-investigated analogous case of simple electrolytes, and to point out over-all resemblances and possibly divergent behaviour when polyelectrolyte macromolecules are involved. The analysis of charge effects in diffusion and sedimentation in simple electrolyte mixtures is summarized in the monographs of Robinson and Stokes (**1959**), Harned and Owen (**1958**), Katchalsky and Curran (**1965**), and Fujita (**1975**). The sedimentation of simple electrolytes does not appear to be a rewarding subject of investigation with the centrifugal fields presently available in commercial instruments and the study of simple electrolytes and low-molecular-weight polymers of relatively high charge is limited to equilibrium studies (Johnson, Kraus, and Scatchard, 1954, 1960; Scatchard **1963; 1966b**).

The effect of charge on the sedimentation of macromolecules has been studied in the early days of the ultracentrifuge by Tiselius (1932) and by Svedberg and Pedersen (**1940**) and by Pedersen (1958). More recently explicit calculations of the effect of charge on sedimentation and diffusion have been presented by Alexandrowicz and Daniel (1963; 1968), Daniel and Alexandrowicz (1963), and Nagasawa and Eguchi (1967). The problem has also been analysed in terms of the formalism of irreversible thermodynamics by Mijnlieff and Overbeek (1962), by Mijnlieff (1962; **1963**), Schoenert (1960), Haase (**1963**), and most recently by Varoqui and Schmitt (1972). We shall attempt to reconcile below the various, often equivalent, procedures presented. We mostly consider (Eisenberg, 1976) the case of a system whose components 2 and 3 are an ionized macromolecule and a simple salt respectively. Whereas in the previous section in this chapter we have used the designation species or component rather loosely, we now recall that, by the definition introduced in Chapter 2, the term species refers to the charged ionic species and the term component applies to electroneutral components formed by considering combination of the ionic species. The simplest system to be considered is, as before, component 1, the principal solvent (water), component 2, a Z-valent polymer PX_Z, and component 3, a simple salt XY, having an ion X in common with the macromolecular component. The 'salt-free' case refers to the two-component system when component 3 is absent. Extension to more complicated systems can be made without introducing new principles.

6.3.1. Simple electrolytes

Both electrical conductance and diffusion in simple electrolytes (Robinson and Stokes 1959) relate to motion of ions under the influence of an external electrical field in the one case, and the gradient of the chemical potential of the electrolyte, in the other. In conduction though the ions of opposite charge move in opposite directions but in diffusion they are constrained by electroneutrality to move in the same direction. In the limit of infinite dilution the motion of ions becomes independent of each other in conduction whereas in diffusion they remain constrained to move with equal speed because of the requirement of electroneutrality. Thus, while the basic mobility and frictional resistance will be similar in both instances, the effects of inter-ionic interactions (classically described by the Debye–Hückel ionic atmosphere) will differ. We shall derive the equation for the diffusion of a simple electrolyte. The aim of the calculation is to indicate how the individual ion-mobility terms derived from electrophoresis or conductance appear in the diffusion equation, and how inter-ionic interaction affects diffusion. We shall then be able to ask whether a similar connection applies in the poly-electrolyte case.

Consider a single uni–univalent electrolyte XY which dissociates into monovalent cations X and anions Y. We may consider the chemical potentials per gram μ'_X and μ'_Y of the ionic species, provided that the final equations will contain the chemical potential μ of the electroneutral electrolyte as a whole. We have

$$\mu' = m_X \mu'_X + m_Y \mu'_Y, \qquad (6.53)$$

where $m_X = M_X/M$ and $m_Y = M_Y/M$ are the numbers of grams of species X and Y upon dissociation of one gram of the electrolyte XY. The forces on the single ions due to the gradient of the chemical potential are $-\mathrm{d}\mu'_X/\mathrm{d}r$ and $-\mathrm{d}\mu'_Y/\mathrm{d}r$ respectively. Because of the unequal mobility of the ions an electric field E arises which exerts on each ion an additional force given by eE and

$-eE$ respectively. These forces, acting on ions of absolute mobility ω'_X and ω'_Y (per gram) produce equal velocity v given by

$$v = \omega'_X \left(\frac{eN_A E}{M_X} - \frac{d\mu'_X}{dr} \right) = -\omega'_Y \left(\frac{eN_A E}{M_Y} + \frac{d\mu'_Y}{dr} \right). \qquad (6.54)$$

The faster ion diffuses ahead, but is slowed down by the field exerted by the slower ion. The opposite effect arises for the slower ion but eventually both move with a common velocity v (the velocity v represents a perturbation of the ordinary molecular thermal motions of the particles). The electrical field can be eliminated from eqns (6.54) to give for v

$$v = - \frac{\omega'_X \omega'_Y}{m_X \omega'_X + m_Y \omega'_Y} \frac{d\mu'}{dr}. \qquad (6.55)$$

We can now write for the flow j at the point where the concentration is c (see eqn (A610)),

$$j = cv = - \frac{\omega'_X \omega'_Y}{m_X \omega'_X + m_Y \omega'_Y} c \frac{d\mu'}{dc} \frac{dc}{dr}, \qquad (6.56)$$

which defines a diffusion coefficient D,

$$D = \frac{\omega'_X \omega'_Y}{m_X \omega'_X + m_Y \omega'_Y} \frac{d\mu'}{d\ln c} \qquad (6.57)$$

in terms of the mobilities ω' of the individual ions and the derivative of the chemical potential μ' of the electroneutral electrolyte. This is known as the Nernst–Hartley relation. The ωs are proportional to the limiting conductance λ^0 of the ions (Robinson and Stokes **1959**; Harned and Owen **1958**) and the limiting diffusion coefficient D_0 at $c = 0$ is therefore well defined. When the concentration dependence is considered it was observed that, for simple electrolytes, the ratio $D/(d\mu'/d\ln c)$ was not concentration independent. Substitution of the conductances λ at finite concentrations for λ^0 led to overcorrection. The problem was solved for simple electrolyte by the realization that the effect of the ionic atmosphere, at finite concentration of ions is different in the case of conduction and of diffusion. Two main effects of the interaction between electric charges of ions have been described: these are known as the 'electrophoretic effect' and the 'relaxation effect'. The electrophoretic effect is due to the fact that when an ion moves through a viscous medium it tends to drag with it some of the surrounding medium. Ions therefore do not move in a stationary medium but against the stream of ions of opposite charge in conductance, and with the stream of ions of opposite charge (moving in the same direction) in diffusion. The electrophoretic effect in simple electrolytes has been calculated by Onsager and Fuoss (1932). The relaxation effects in the conductance of simple electrolytes (Debye and Hückel 1923; Onsager 1927) is due to the fact that as a result of ions moving in opposite directions the ionic atmospheres are deformed, the symmetrical distribution of ions is disturbed, and the central ion experiences a force related to the tendency of the ionic atmospheres to relax to the time-averaged spherical symmetry characteristic of the equilibrium case. In diffusion both ions move in the same direction with the same velocity, and therefore no deformation of ionic atmospheres occur: the relaxation effect is absent. This explains why use of finite conductances of electrolytes to account for the concentration dependence of D over-corrects, as stated above.

A somewhat different situation arises in the study of self-diffusion and tracer-diffusion in electrolyte solutions. In self-diffusion the solute molecules are in a uniform liquid, but the molecules are continuously moving (even in the absence of concentration gradients of solutes) as a result of random thermal motions. Robinson and Stokes (1959) state that 'this process can never be detected because of the indistinguishability of the molecules'. We now know the molecular dynamics of uniform indistinguishable molecules can be detected by a variety of means and the measurement of self-diffusion constants and molecular motions in uniform solutions can, for instance, be investigated by spectral-broadening or time-correlation experiments in light-scattering studies with coherent radiation (Section 5.7). It is thus of considerable importance to properly characterize the factors contributing to self-diffusion in uniform systems. A closely related subject concerns diffusion in mixtures of isotopic species, or tracer-diffusion when an isotopically labelled ion of one kind in very small amount diffuses in a large excess of electrolyte. Since mixtures of isotopic species behave practically ideally thermodynamically, the gradient of chemical potential is ideal and the driving force for inter-diffusion of isotopic species arises solely from the contribution to the free energy of the ideal entropy of mixing. In tracer-diffusion the movement of the tracer ions is not tied to that of the ions of opposite sign. The electrophoretic effect may be neglected since the concentration of the radioactive species is very low. However, the relaxation effect of the ionic atmosphere may be important, as in distinction to diffusion in a concentration gradient, the reference tracer ion is moving relative to a background of non-diffusing ions, and therefore the symmetry of its ionic atmosphere may be disturbed.

6.3.2. *Charge effects in sedimentation and diffusion of polyelectrolyte solutions*

An early theoretical attempt to characterize the sedimentation of systems of charged macromolecules is due to Pedersen (1958). He observes that if charged macromolecules are sedimented, the higher sedimentation tendency of the macromolecules as contrasted to that of the slower sedimenting counter-ions results in a microscopic separation of charge between the bottom of the cell and the macromolecular boundary. This separation establishes an electric field $E = \mathrm{d}\psi/\mathrm{d}r$ in the intervening column of solution, which slows down the macromolecular ion and speeds up the counter-ions. Both ions move with equal intermediate velocity. This is called the 'primary charge effect'. In diffusion, on the other hand, the small counter-ions diffuse faster than the large macro-ions and pull the latter after them. Thus, whereas in sedimentation the charge effect slows down the large ions (as opposed to an equivalent non-charged particle) in diffusion the contrary effect is observed. We shall see below that a much debated point concerns the question whether or not the primary charge effect vanishes at infinite dilution of macromolecules.

We have thus concluded that as a result of acquiring an electrical charge a macromolecule is slowed down in a sedimentation field and accelerated in diffusion. With increasing concentration of simple salt the charges on the macromolecules are screened, the sedimentation coefficient increases and the diffusion coefficient decreases. This is known as the 'primary salt effect'. Do these coefficients ever approach the values for uncharged macromolecules when simple salt concentration increases 'to infinity'? We must distinguish here between almost rigid (globular or multi-helical) undeformable macromolecules and (mostly chain-like) macromolecules whose conformations are appreciably affected by ionic strength. In the first case we might indeed approach (by extrapolation to high ionic strength) the sedimentation and diffusion coefficients of the uncharged species—in the second case we shall be faced with an inextricable mixture of charge and conformation effects.

The 'secondary charge effect' arises from unequal mobilities and sedimentation coefficients of the ions of the simple-electrolyte component 3. It is therefore less fundamental in mixed polyelectrolyte–electrolyte solutions and can be minimized or eliminated by choosing a supporting electrolyte such as sodium chloride, for instance, in which both cation and anion have nearly identical sedimentation coefficients.†

We refer to Tables 6.1 and 6.2, taken from Pedersen (1958), in which the sedimentation constants of cations and of anions, calculated from conductances, are tabulated. Fig. 6.1, also taken from Pedersen (1958), schematically summarizes the charge and salt effects.

Although the charge effects in the sedimentation and diffusion of multi-component polyelectrolyte systems have been extensively investigated both

---

† Sometimes though the specific nature of an experiment may preclude such a choice (consider a sedimentation study in a density gradient for instance, in which the supporting electrolyte, say caesium chloride, has been used for considerations relating to the formation of the density gradient) and in such an instance the secondary charge effect must be taken into consideration in the interpretation of the experimental results.

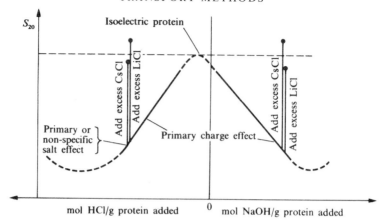

F I G. 6.1. Schematic diagram showing the influence of the various salt and charge effects on the sedimentation coefficient. (From Pedersen 1958.)

on theoretical and on experimental grounds in the last 20 years, yet the problem cannot be considered solved in a satisfactory way. It appears to the critical observer that transport properties in these complex systems have not been treated with the rigour with which the equilibrium properties have been interpreted and the experimental data on well-defined systems are far from being extensive as the previously mentioned diffusion studies on simple electrolytes. A simple problem, for instance, which has not been solved in unequivocal terms, is whether combination of the sedimentation and diffusion coefficients (in the manner in which this is undertaken for binary systems in the Svedberg equation) leads to a well-defined value for the molecular weight, at all macromolecular concentrations or only in the limit of infinite dilution.

In the classical approach to the sedimentation problem of charged species (first extensively discussed in Pedersen (1958)) the effect is calculated by which the sedimentation of the macromolecular ion is retarded by the electrostatic field set up between the meniscus and the bottom of the ultra-centrifuge cell (under non-equilibrium conditions) by the unequal mobilities of the ions constituting the various electroneutral components. Electro-neutrality requires the ions to move together (in electroneutral combinations) and therefore no net current flows in the ultracentrifuge cell.† Pedersen explicitly introduced the electrophoretic mobilities of the ions to account for the retardation of the macro-ion in the electrostatic field associated with the sedimentation velocity experiment of charged species, but apparently

† Under conditions of sedimentation equilibrium re-adjustment of the concentrations of the solutes leads to vanishing of the electrostatic potential (Robinson and Stokes **1959**). Sedi-mentation equilibrium can therefore be considered exclusively for the electroneutral components without reference to the electrostatic field (see Section 5.2).

TABLE 6.1

Sedimentation constants in aqueous solution, for cations at 25 °C, in Svedberg units, calculated from limiting equivalent conductivities (from Pedersen 1958)

Ion	$\lambda_{25°C}$	M	$\bar{V}$	$s_{25°C}$
NH_4^+	73·55	18·04	18·0	0·001
Li^+	38·68	6·94	−0·9	0·033
Mg^{2+}	53·05	24·32	−20·7	0·128
Na^+	50·10	23·00	−1·4	0·131
K^+	73·50	39·10	8·8	0·239
Ba^{2+}	63·63	137·36	−12·1	0·511
Rb^+	77·81	85·48	13·8	0·599
Cs^+	77·26	132·91	21·2	0·927
Tl^+	74·7	204·39	14·8	1·522

TABLE 6.2

Sedimentation constants in aqueous solutions for anions at 25 °C, in Svedberg units, calculated from limiting equivalent conductivities (from Pedersen 1958)

Ion	$\lambda_{25°C}$	M	$\bar{V}$	$s_{25°C}$
$CH_3CO_2^-$	40·9	59·04	41·5	0·078
F^-	55·4	19·00	−2·2	0·126
Cl^-	76·35	35·46	18·0	0·144
HCO_3^-	44·5	61·02	23·5	0·180
CO_3^{2-}	69·3	60·01	−1·7	0·230
HPO_4^{2-}	(52·3)	95·98	8·3	0·246
NO_3^-	71·46	62·01	29·3	0·252
$H_2PO_4^-$	(44)	96·99	29·4	0·320
$B_4O_7^{2-}$	(44·9)	155·28	(17·1)	0·333
SO_4^{2-}	80·02	96·07	16·4	0·343
ClO_4^-	67·36	99·46	46·4	0·385
Br^-	78·14	79·92	24·9	0·462
IO_3^-	(40·0)	174·92	27·7	0·633
I^-	(76·84)	126·91	36·5	0·747

could account only for part of the effect. Alexandrowicz and Daniel (1963, 1968) argued that because of electrostatic interactions between the macro-ions and the small counter-ions (see Appendix 5, p. 232) the retardation effect becomes smaller still, yet the failure of Pedersen to account for the retardation effect is attributed to the fact that introduction of explicit electrophoretic mobilities is not justified in velocity sedimentation. Thus, whereas in electrophoresis the two oppositely charged ions move in opposite directions, in sedimentation motion of both ions is directed by the buoyancy and the direction of the field. Alexandrowicz and Daniel eliminate the actual mobilities from the equations of motion, as will be shown below. Starting from their basic assumptions a different result (to be described below) will be reached in our calculation. The effect of the ion atmosphere on the diffusion coefficients of charged rod-like macromolecules and hence on the spectrum of light scattered from such a solution (see Section 4.7) was investigated by Stephen (1971) in a model based on the Debye–Hückel linearization procedure.

A more systematic approach that deals with the combined problem of sedimentation and diffusion of charged species uses the methods of ir-reversible thermodynamics. A rather formidable analysis by this approach is due to Mijnlieff and Overbeek (1962) and Mijnlieff (1962); and we must refer to Mijnlieff (**1963**) for a comprehensive summary of this work. More recently Varoqui and Schmitt (1972) have reformulated this problem in simpler terms and have also calculated friction coefficients of charged species for the rod-like polyelectrolyte model (see Appendix 5). They claim dis-agreement with the earlier conclusion of Pedersen and of Alexandrowicz and Daniel that the primary charge effect in sedimentation disappears at vanishing concentration of the macro-ion species, but the disagreement is difficult to resolve in view of the fact that the results are not expressed in easily comparable form. The earlier authors claim that charge effects due to the (in principle measurable) electrostatic potential between the meniscus and bottom of the ultracentrifuge cell disappears at vanishing concentration of the sedimenting charged species. This may indeed be true. Varoqui and Schmitt, on the other hand, calculate the effect of charge on the friction coefficients, which persists at all reasonable dilutions at which measure-ments with polyelectrolyte systems have meaning (see Appendix 5). This limiting charge effect was ignored by Pedersen who assumed that at 'infinite' dilution the counter-ions to the macro-ion are spread over the whole volume of the solution, and was absorbed by Alexandrowicz and Daniel into an 'effective charge' parameter. Unfortunately, many problems remain. Fric-tional coefficients depend both on the radius of the ionic atmosphere and on the shape of the macro-ion coils (see Nagasawa and Eguchi 1967) and macromolecules of perfectly known and well-defined rigid shape are not readily available. We must also consider the problem of the coupling between the motion of the macro-ion and the ions composing the atmosphere, for which no complete solution has been provided. In sedimentation the motion of the sedimenting species is at zero concentration gradient. The macro-ion sediments because of its large size; the counter-ions in the atmosphere are much smaller and would not be 'dragged' along were it not for the electro-neutrality requirement. If the coupling between macro-ion and atmosphere is tight then the frictional resistance of the ions in the atmosphere must be considered (Alexandrowicz and Daniel assume that 'bound' counter-ions do not contribute to the frictional resistance at all). On the other hand, in the case of less-tight coupling we can visualize the macro-ion as moving through the homogeneous solution, leaving some of its own counter-ions behind and picking up the complement required for electroneutrality from the macro-ions sedimenting from the slice of solution just ahead in the field. A reduced contribution to the frictional resistance by the counter-ions would be expected in this case. In diffusion the analysis would consider a process occurring in a concentration gradient, whereas self-diffusion, as already mentioned, occurs in homogeneous solution. Another difficulty concerns the evaluation of the hydrodynamic properties of macromolecular coils with excluded volume (see Eirich **1956**) and the extent to which these coils are freely draining or shield the motion of small ions or solvent molecules; for space-filling globular macromolecules, hydrodynamic uncertainties may arise from the odd shape of the protein, for instance, or ill-defined hydration layers (this was discussed already many years ago in the classical monograph of Cohen and Edsall **1943**).

The difficulties enumerated above need not lead to abandonment of the use of sedimentation and diffusion for the characterization of charged species. At high enough concentrations of salt, the radius κ_{DH}^{-1} of the Debye–Hückel ionic atmosphere is small when compared to the dimensions of the bulky macromolecules, and with judicious choice of a simple salt system (to avoid secondary charge phenomena) the effects of charge in sedimentation and diffusion may be reduced to a small contribution. The quantitative discussion to follow should be helpful towards the design of critical experimental procedures. In particular, extensive variation of counter- and co-ions at fixed ionic concentrations has not been fully exploited.

6.3.3. *Reformulation of the Alexandrowicz–Daniel calculation*

Following the basic concept of Svedberg and Pedersen, Alexandrowicz, and Daniel (1963, 1968) 'regard the actual velocity of each ion in sedimentation as composed of two virtual velocities, namely a sedimentation velocity which would be obtained under the isolated action of the external centrifugal field $\omega^2 r$ and an electrophoretic velocity which would be obtained under the isolated action of the internally created field $d\psi/dr$'. The hypothetical velocities are expressed in their explicit form as forces divided by frictions, and not as electrophoretic mobilities, as was proposed by Pedersen. For the familiar system PX_Z, XY (P is a Z-valent negative ion, X and Y are positive counter- and negative co-ions respectively,

$$v_P = \overline{M}_P^* \omega^2 r f_P^{-1} + (iZef_P^{-1})\,d\psi/dr, \tag{6.58}$$

$$v_X = \overline{M}_X \omega^2 r f_X^{-1} - (ef_X^{-1})\,d\psi/dr, \tag{6.59}$$

$$v_Y = \overline{M}_Y \omega^2 r f_Y^{-1} + (ef_Y^{-1})\,d\psi/dr, \tag{6.60}$$

where

$$\overline{M}_j \equiv M_j(1 - \bar{v}_j \rho),$$
$$\overline{M}_P^* = \overline{M}_P + (1 - i)Z\overline{M}_X.$$

i is an effective charge parameter (see Section 5.2) which may at this point be considered as a formal device and need not be defined precisely presently; f_P, f_X, and f_Y are the frictional coefficients per mole of the ionic species P*, X, and Y.†

We modify eqns (6.58)–(6.60) by multiplying both sides of the equations for v_P, v_X, and v_Y by the corresponding charge and concentration, that is, $-iZeC_P$, eC_X, and $-eC_Y$ respectively. The sum of the left-hand sides of these modified equations yields

$$eC_X v_X - eC_Y v_Y - iZeC_P v_P = 0, \qquad (6.61)$$

because of the assumption of zero current flow. From the sum of the right-hand side of these equations we find (electroneutrality is observed at all points, $C_X = C_Y + iZC_P$)

$$\frac{d\psi}{dr} = \frac{\omega^2 r}{e} \frac{(\overline{M}_X f_X^{-1} - \overline{M}_Y f_Y^{-1})C_Y + (\overline{M}_X f_X^{-1} - \overline{M}_P^* f_P^{-1})C_P iZ}{(f_X^{-1} + f_Y^{-1})C_Y + (f_X^{-1} + iZ f_P^{-1})C_P iZ} \qquad (6.62)$$

for $d\psi/dr$; this expression for $d\psi/dr$ is now substituted into eqn (6.58) and the sedimentation coefficient

$$s_P \equiv v_P/\omega^2 r$$

evaluated. We also introduce the buoyant molecular weights and the concentrations of the electroneutral species,

$$\overline{M}_2 = \overline{M}_P^* + iZ\overline{M}_X = M_2(1 - \bar{v}_2\rho),$$
$$\overline{M}_3 = \overline{M}_X + \overline{M}_Y = M_3(1 - \bar{v}_3\rho),$$
$$C_2 = C_P = C_u/Z,$$
$$C_3 = C_Y,$$

to find ($f_P \overline{M}_2^{-1} = f_u \overline{M}_u^{-1}$),

$$\frac{1}{s_P} = \frac{f_P}{\overline{M}_2} + \frac{i^2}{\overline{M}_u} \frac{C_u}{(f_X^{-1} + f_Y^{-1})C_3 + if_X^{-1}C_u} \bigg/ 1 - \frac{\overline{M}_3}{\overline{M}_u} \frac{i}{f_Y} \frac{C_3}{(f_X^{-1} + f_Y^{-1})C_3 + if_X^{-1}C_u}. \qquad (6.63)$$

Eqn (6.63), which is significantly different from the expressions derived by Alexandrowicz and Daniel assumes some interesting and simple limiting forms.

Consider first the case $\overline{M}_3 = 0$ discussed by Ziccardi and Schumaker (1971); this case arises if component 3 is chosen so that $(1 - v_3\rho)$ effectively vanishes; Ziccardi and Schumaker suggest tetramathylammonium chloride

---

† These frictional coefficients represent the average frictional resistance of P*, X, and Y with respect to the solvent mixture; proper frictional cross coefficients between the various species in solution will be considered below in the formulation of the problem by the methods of irreversible thermodynamics.

for this purpose. If $\overline{M}_3$ vanishes then the denominator of eqn (6.63) becomes unity and the expression reduces to

$$\overline{M}_3 = 0; \quad \frac{1}{s_P} = \frac{f_P}{\overline{M}_2} + \frac{i^2}{\overline{M}_u} \frac{C_u}{(f_X^{-1} + f_Y^{-1})C_3 + if_X^{-1}C_u}. \tag{6.64}$$

Eqn (6.64) may be easily analysed (see Ziccardi and Schumaker 1971) and an interesting result is that upon extrapolation to vanishing concentration C_u the limiting value of the sedimentation coefficient is given in terms of the properties of the macromolecular component only.

A very important question concerns the limiting value of s_P, as C_u vanishes, in the general case. We shall therefore develop eqn (6.63) exactly through the linear term in C_u. The result, which is easily obtained is given by

$$\frac{1}{s_P} = \frac{f_P}{\overline{M}_2 - iZ\overline{M}_3(1 + f_Y f_X^{-1})^{-1}}$$

$$+ \frac{C_u}{C_3} \frac{i^2 f_Y}{\overline{M}_u(1 + f_Y f_X^{-1}) - i\overline{M}_3} \left\{ 1 - \frac{\overline{M}_3 f_u f_X^{-1}}{\overline{M}_u(1 + f_Y f_X^{-1}) - i\overline{M}_3} \right\} + \dots \tag{6.65}$$

We need not worry about the complicated form of the term linear in C_u. The interesting term is the limiting value of s_P^{-1} which assumes an even more significant form when $f_Y = f_X \equiv f_{X,Y}$ and the secondary charge effect disappears. We then obtain from eqn (6.65),

$$\frac{1}{s_P} = \frac{f_P}{\overline{M}_2 - \tfrac{1}{2}iZ\overline{M}_3} + \frac{C_u i^2}{C_3(2\overline{M}_u - i\overline{M}_3)} \left\{ f_{X,Y} - \frac{\overline{M}_3 f_P}{(2\overline{M}_2 - iZ\overline{M}_3)} \right\}. \tag{6.66}$$

We recall that i was introduced at the beginning of this discussion as an unspecified effective charge parameter. The only other assumption in this calculation was that of zero net current and electroneutrality. If $\tfrac{1}{2}i$ here be identified with the thermodynamic distribution coefficient Γ (see Section 2.4) then, after some elementary transformations based on equations available in Chapters 2 and 3, the following extremely interesting result is obtained,

$$s_P^0 = \frac{\overline{M}_2 - \Gamma Z\overline{M}_3}{f_P} = \frac{M_2(\partial \rho/\partial c_2)_\mu}{f_P}, \tag{6.67}$$

which is identical with eqn (6.47) derived for non-ionic systems by the methods of irreversible thermodynamics, on the assumption that $\nabla\tilde{\mu}_3 = 0$ ($f_P/M_2 \equiv f_2'$, the frictional coefficient per gram of component 2). It is interesting that this result has been obtained on a simple model assuming only zero net current and electroneutrality, and a tentative identification of the model parameter i with the thermodynamic quantity 2Γ. We disagree with the limiting form of s_P obtained by Alexandrowicz and Daniel†

---

† They find $s_P^0 = \overline{M}_P^*/f_P$, where $\overline{M}_P^* = M_P^*(1 - \bar{v}_P^*\rho)$ is the buoyant weight of the charged species, rather than $s_P^0 = \{\overline{M}_2 - \tfrac{1}{2}iZ\overline{M}_3\}/f_P$, as derived here, which involves the buoyant weight of neutral components only.

and further believe that the exact value of i applicable to the transport experiment, and its equivalence with 2Γ, should be thoroughly re-investigated by re-evaluation of existing experimental data, or by newly designed experiments.

The equivalence or non-equivalence of the formal charge parameters i (and its identification with the quantity derived from equilibrium studies) derived from various transport experiments (sedimentation, diffusion, conductance, and electrophoresis) should therefore be submitted to further scrutiny.

From eqn (6.66) we also learn that the concentration-dependence of s_P (due to charge effects) is diminished with increasing C_3. On the other hand, i (or Γ) may significantly increase with increasing C_3 (see Cohen and Eisenberg (1968), and Eisenberg (**1974**), for the behaviour of mixed DNA–simple-salt solutions), and we are therefore facing a situation in which s_P^0 may decrease with increasing C_3 in addition to changes of the frictional coefficient f_P (resulting from changes in molecular size and shape) under these conditions.

In all the derivations presented here, the classical non-ionic concentration-dependence of s_P, of the form $(1 - kC)$ has been disregarded.

The last test of eqn (6.63) concerns the salt-free case when C_3 goes to zero. We easily derive the classical result

$$s_P = \frac{\overline{M}_2}{f_P + iZf_X}, \tag{6.68}$$

which indicates that in this case the frictional resistance f_2 of the macromolecular component is the sum of the frictional resistance f_P of the polyion and iZ times the frictional resistance of the counter-ions; s_P in this case, as is well known, is rather low. The measurement of the sedimentation (as well as the diffusion) coefficient in salt-free polyelectrolyte solutions is extremely precarious because of boundary instabilities and errors due to convection. It is also extremely difficult to render a polyelectrolyte solution completely salt-free. Some of these difficulties have been pointed out by Auer and Alexandrowicz (1969) in their study of the sedimentation, diffusion, and osmotic pressure of NaDNA in salt-free solution and by Nagasawa and Fujita (1964), who investigated the diffusion of polystyrenesulphonic acid and its sodium salt in the absence of added salt. Other work in this field is referred to in these papers.

We now consider the problem of isothermal diffusion for the same system PX_Z, XY discussed above. For this process we write for the velocities v_j of the ionic species (in analogy to eqns (6.58)–(6.60)),

$$v_P = -f_P^{-1}(d\mu_P^*/dr) + iZef_P^{-1}(d\psi/dr), \tag{6.69}$$

$$v_X = -f_X^{-1}(d\mu_X/dr) - ef_X^{-1}(d\psi/dr), \tag{6.70}$$

$$v_Y = -f_Y^{-1}(d\mu_Y/dr) + ef_Y^{-1}(d\psi/dr), \tag{6.71}$$

where, we recall (see Section 5.2),

$$\mu_P^* = \mu_P + (1-i)Z\mu_X.$$

As before, we multiply eqns (6.69)–(6.71) by $-iZeC_P$, eC_X, and $-eC_Y$ respectively, sum, and set the sum of the left-hand side terms equal to zero; we also introduce electroneutrality, $C_X = C_Y + iZC_P$. The effective charge parameter i in diffusion could conceivably be different from the parameter used in velocity sedimentation, but we are not concerned with this aspect now.

Performing these operations we find

$$e\frac{d\psi}{dr} = \frac{\left\{\dfrac{(d\mu_Y/dr)}{f_Y} - \dfrac{(d\mu_X/dr)}{f_X}\right\}C_Y + \left\{\dfrac{(d\mu_P^*/dr)}{f_P} - \dfrac{(d\mu_X/dr)}{f_X}\right\}iZC_P}{(f_X^{-1} + f_Y^{-1})C_Y + (iZf_P^{-1} + f_X^{-1})iZC_P}. \tag{6.72}$$

We introduce $d\psi/dr$ from the above expression into eqn (6.69) for v_P, consider

$$d\mu_2 = d\mu_P^* + iZ\,d\mu_X$$

and

$$d\mu_3 = d\mu_X + d\mu_Y,$$

and evaluate

$$D_2 = -v_P(d\ln C_2/dr)^{-1}.$$

The result is ($C_P \equiv C_2$, $C_Y \equiv C_3$)

$$D_2 = \frac{1}{f_P\left(\dfrac{d\ln C_2}{dr}\right)}\frac{\dfrac{d\mu_2}{dr} - \dfrac{d\mu_3}{dr}\dfrac{iZC_3}{f_Y}\left\{(f_X^{-1}+f_Y^{-1})C_3 + \dfrac{iZ}{f_X}\right\}^{-1}}{1 + \dfrac{i^2Z^2}{f_P}C_2\left\{(f_X^{-1}+f_Y^{-1})C_3 + \dfrac{iZ}{f_X}C_2\right\}^{-1}}. \tag{6.73}$$

For the purpose of practical evaluation we may now consider the special condition, already discussed, that in the mixed polyelectrolyte–simple-salt system μ_3 is constant and $d\mu_3/dr$ vanishes.† If we introduce this condition into eqn (6.73) we obtain

$$\frac{1}{D_2}\frac{d\mu_2}{d\ln C_2} = f_P + \frac{i^2Z^2C_2}{(f_X^{-1}+f_Y^{-1})C_3 + iZf_X^{-1}C_2}, \tag{6.74}$$

where (see eqns (1.9) and (1.10))

$$\frac{1}{RT}\frac{d\mu_2}{d\ln C_2} = 1 + \frac{d\ln y_2}{d\ln C_2} = 1 + 2A_2M_2c_2 + \ldots.$$

At vanishing concentration C_2,

$$D_2 = RT/f_P. \tag{6.75}$$

† It is advisable to perform the classical diffusion experiment across a phase boundary consisting of a polyelectrolyte solution in dialysis equilibrium with the solution of the simple salt.

If the frictional coefficient f_P is identical for diffusion and sedimentation it may be eliminated between eqns (6.75) and (6.67), to yield a Svedberg-type equation akin to eqn (6.52), derived for the non-ionic case.

In the salt-free case $C_3 = 0$ and eqn (6.73) reduces to

$$\frac{1}{D_2}\frac{\mathrm{d}\mu_2}{\mathrm{d}\ln C_2} = f_P + iZf_X,$$

which is a well-known result for salt-free polyelectrolyte solutions and may be considered in conjunction with eqn (6.68) for the sedimentation coefficient.

For an analysis of conductance, transference numbers, electrophoresis, relaxation and electrophoretic effects, diffusion, and liquid junction potentials in salt-free polyelectrolyte solutions, we refer to the discussion by Katchalsky, Alexandrowicz, and Kedem (**1966**).

6.3.4. *Sedimentation and diffusion coefficients of polyelectrolytes by the methods of irreversible thermodynamics*

We first consider the system PX_Z, XY in terms of the three linearly independent flows J_P^1, J_Y^1, and J_X^1, taken with respect to the solvent, component 1, in terms of the gradients of the total chemical potentials (including gravitational and electrical terms (see eqn (5.1)) of the ionic species, $\tilde{\mu}_P$, $\tilde{\mu}_Y$, and $\tilde{\mu}_X$; it is convenient to use flows, forces, concentrations and electrical charges *per mole* in this section ($J_k = j_k/M_k$, $X_k = x_k M_k$ and $L_{ik} = l_{ik}/M_i M_k$)

$$-J_P^1 = L_{PP}\,\mathrm{grad}\,\tilde{\mu}_P + L_{PY}\,\mathrm{grad}\,\tilde{\mu}_Y + L_{PX}\,\mathrm{grad}\,\tilde{\mu}_X$$
$$-J_Y^1 = L_{YP}\,\mathrm{grad}\,\tilde{\mu}_P + L_{YY}\,\mathrm{grad}\,\tilde{\mu}_Y + L_{YX}\,\mathrm{grad}\,\tilde{\mu}_X \qquad (6.76)$$
$$-J_X^1 = L_{XP}\,\mathrm{grad}\,\tilde{\mu}_P + L_{XY}\,\mathrm{grad}\,\tilde{\mu}_Y + L_{XX}\,\mathrm{grad}\,\tilde{\mu}_X$$

The dissipation function (eqn (A6.19))

$$\Phi = -J_P^1\,\mathrm{grad}\,\tilde{\mu}_P - J_Y^1\,\mathrm{grad}\,\tilde{\mu}_Y - J_X^1\,\mathrm{grad}\,\tilde{\mu}_X. \qquad (6.77)$$

With these definitions the system is well determined and the phenomenological coefficients satisfy the Onsager reciprocal relations ($L_{ik} = L_{ki}$) (see Appendix 6, p. 245) and we therefore have six independent coefficients. Fluxes with respect to the solvent are not usually measurable, and it is therefore preferable to transform these fluxes to a more convenient reference frame. We choose the frame fixed with respect to the local centre of volume which (see Fujita **1962**) moves with a velocity v^V,

$$v^V = \sum v_k \bar{V}_k C_k, \qquad (6.78)$$

where v_k is the velocity of species k with respect to the frame fixed to the cell and the summation is over all species. The flows J_k^V with respect to the centre of volume frame are related to the flows J_k (relative to the cell) by

$$J_k^V = C_k(v_k - v_k^V) = J_k - C_k v^V, \qquad (6.79)$$

and, with use of eqn (6.78),

$$J_k^V = J_k - C_k \sum \overline{V}_i J_i. \qquad (6.80)$$

Substitution of eqn (6.11) into eqn (6.80) demonstrates that we also have

$$J_k^V = J_k^1 - C_k \sum \overline{V}_i J_i^1, \qquad (6.81)$$

where the summation now does not include the solvent ($J_1^1 = 0$); the last equation will be used in our transformation of flows in this section.

We now transform eqns (6.76) to three alternate flows: J_Y^V, J_P^V and total electrical current J_{el} (which we will eventually set equal to zero); subsequently we will also assume the mean volume velocity to be zero for low concentrations of solutes or if the partial molar volumes do not depend on concentrations (deGroot, Mazur and Overbeek 1952; Kirkwood, Baldwin, Dunlop, Gosting, and Kegeles 1960) and the total volume flow is zero. Under these conditions J_k^V will be approximated by J_k.

The matrix M transforming the old flows of eqn (6.76) to the new flows is (see eqn (6.81) for the flows of matter)

$$M = \begin{bmatrix} 1 - C_P \overline{V}_P & -C_P \overline{V}_Y & -C_P \overline{V}_X \\ -C_Y \overline{V}_P & 1 - C_Y \overline{V}_Y & -C_Y \overline{V}_X \\ -v\mathscr{F} & -\mathscr{F} & \mathscr{F} \end{bmatrix} \qquad (6.82)$$

and the new flows are

$$\begin{aligned} J_P^V &= (1 - C_P \overline{V}_P)J_P^1 - C_P \overline{V}_Y J_Y^1 - C_P \overline{V}_X J_X^1, \\ J_Y^V &= -C_Y \overline{V}_P J_P^1 + (1 - C_Y \overline{V}_Y)J_Y^1 - C_Y \overline{V}_X J_X^1 \\ J_{el} &= \mathscr{F}(-vJ_P - J_Y + J_X). \end{aligned} \qquad (6.83)$$

To obtain the new forces X_k associated with these fluxes we take into account the invariance of the dissipation function when expressed in either the new forces–fluxes system or in the original system. The general relation between forces satisfying this requirement is given by (see Fitts **1962**)

$$X_{\text{new}} = -(\tilde{M}^{-1})X_{\text{old}}, \qquad (6.84)$$

where $\tilde{M}^{-1}$ is the transpose of the inverse of the matrix M defined in eqn (6.82). The new forces X_P, X_Y, and X_{el} associated to J_P^1, J_X^1, and J_{el} written explicitly as functions of the $\nabla \bar{\mu}_k$s are

$$X_2 \equiv X_P = -\frac{1}{C_1 \overline{V}_1}\{(1 - C_3 \overline{V}_3)\nabla\bar{\mu}_2 + C_3 \overline{V}_2 \nabla\bar{\mu}_3\},$$

$$X_3 \equiv X_Y = -\frac{1}{C_1 \overline{V}_1}\{C_2 \overline{V}_3 \nabla\bar{\mu}_2 + (1 - C_2 \overline{V}_2)\nabla\bar{\mu}_3\}, \qquad (6.85)$$

$$X_{el} = -\frac{\nabla\bar{\mu}_X}{\mathscr{F}} - \frac{\overline{V}_X}{\mathscr{F}C_1 \overline{V}_1}(C_2 \nabla\bar{\mu}_2 + C_3 \nabla\bar{\mu}_3).$$

Since $\nabla\tilde{\mu}_2$ and $\nabla\tilde{\mu}_3$ correspond to the total chemical potential of the electroneutral salt (no electrical forces are involved in $\nabla\tilde{\mu}_3$ and $\nabla\tilde{\mu}_2$) and only quantities corresponding to electroneutral components appear in X_P^V and X_Y^V, we may identify

$$J_2^V \equiv J_P^V; \quad X_2 \equiv X_P$$

and

$$J_3^V \equiv J_Y^V; \quad X_3 \equiv X_Y.$$

Eqns (6.85) for the X_k are identical with the equations for the set of forces χ, ψ, and ϕ of Mijnlieff and Overbeek (**1962**) and Mijnlieff (1962). In their procedure (see Mijnlieff 1963, his eqn 3), the total potential $\bar{\mu}$ is split into terms depending on concentration, pressure, and ultracentrifugal and electrostatic fields respectively (see eqns (5.1) and (5.7)).

For our further deliberations we approximate the flows J_k^V by the experimental flows J_k with respect to a frame of reference fixed to the cell and also note that, at low concentrations of solutes $(1 - C_2\,\overline{V}_2)$, $(1 - C_3\,\overline{V}_3)$, and $C_1\,V_1$ are close to unity and the terms in C_2 and C_3 vanish. Under these conditions the forces of eqns (6.85) assume the simple forms

$$
\begin{aligned}
X_2 &= -\nabla\tilde{\mu}_2 \\
X_3 &= -\nabla\tilde{\mu}_3, \\
X_{el} &= -\nabla\tilde{\mu}_X/\mathscr{F},
\end{aligned}
\tag{6.86}
$$

which is the form used by Varoqui and Schmitt (1972). Caution has to be exercised with respect to this simplification because, whereas the case of vanishing concentration C_2 is often realized, the concentration C_3 of the added simple salt may be quite high in a given experimental situation.

With the newly defined flows and forces we may write the phenomenological equations

$$
\begin{aligned}
J_2 &= L_{22}X_2 + L_{23}X_3 + L_{2e}X_{el}, \\
J_3 &= L_{32}X_2 + L_{33}X_3 + L_{3e}X_{el}, \\
J_{el} &= L_{e2}X_2 + L_{e3}X_3 + L_{ee}X_{el}.
\end{aligned}
\tag{6.87}
$$

We next apply the condition of zero current $(J_{el} = 0)$ and substitute the electrical force X_{el} in J_2 and J_3 to obtain the final system of phenomonological equations for the transport of electroneutral components

$$
\begin{aligned}
J_2 &= \mathscr{L}_{22}X_2 + \mathscr{L}_{23}X_3, \\
J_3 &= \mathscr{L}_{32}X_2 + \mathscr{L}_{33}X_3,
\end{aligned}
\tag{6.88}
$$

where the coefficients

$$
\begin{aligned}
\mathscr{L}_{22} &= L_{22} - \frac{L_{e2}^2}{L_{ee}}, \\
\mathscr{L}_{23} &= L_{23} - \frac{L_{e2}L_{e3}}{L_{33}}.
\end{aligned}
\tag{6.89}
$$

Both the L_{ij} and the $\mathscr{L}_{ij}$ satisfy the Onsager relations, and the system at zero current is therefore defined by three phenomenological coefficients only. It should be noted that in the phenomenological equations formulated by Fujita (1962) for ionic systems, the Onsager relations for the coefficients are not obeyed.

Varoqui and Schmitt (1972) relate the phenomenological coefficients from eqns (6.88) and (6.89) to frictional coefficients by the formulation of Spiegler (1958). In a quasi-stationary state the applied forces acting on a particle at constant speed are opposed by all frictional forces exerted on the particle by the surrounding medium, the total force acting on the particle being equal to zero. For particle P, for instance,

$$\nabla\tilde{\mu}_P = F_{PX} + F_{PY} + F_{P1}. \tag{6.90}$$

The frictional force F_{ij} refers to the interaction of 1 mol of particle i with all particles j in its vicinity. From this definition derives the relationship

$$C_i F_{ij} = C_j F_{ji}. \tag{6.91}$$

The frictional force is proportional to the relative velocities of particles i and j

$$F_{ij} = -f_{ij}(v_i - v_j). \tag{6.92}$$

f_{ij} is the interparticle friction coefficient and v_i and v_j are the mean time-averaged velocities of i and j; if the flows are referred relative to the solvent ($v_1 = 0$), the following equations are obtained

$$\begin{aligned}
-\nabla\tilde{\mu}_P &= f_{PX}(v_P - v_X) + f_{PY}(v_P - v_Y) + f_{P1} v_P, \\
-\nabla\tilde{\mu}_Y &= f_{YX}(v_Y - v_X) + f_{YP}(v_Y - v_P) + f_{Y1} v_Y, \\
-\nabla\tilde{\mu}_X &= f_{XY}(v_X - v_Y) + f_{XP}(v_X - v_P) + f_{X1} v_X.
\end{aligned} \tag{6.93}$$

Eqns (6.93) are solved for the velocities v_i, these are multiplied by the concentrations C_i to give the macroscopic fluxes J_i and a set of equations similar to eqns (6.76) is obtained. By identification, Varoqui and Schmitt obtain the relationship between the phenomenological and the friction coefficients. They derive two limiting cases. For excess salt and vanishing polymer concentration

$$C_3 \gg C_2, \ \mathscr{L}_{22} = \frac{C_2}{f_{P1} + (C_3/C_2)(f_{YP} + f_{XP})} = \frac{C_2}{f_{P1} + f_{PY} + f_{PX}},$$

$$\begin{aligned}
\mathscr{L}_{23} &= \frac{C_3(f_{YP} + f_{XP}) - \nu C_2 f_{X1}}{(f_{Y1} + f_{X1})\{f_{P1} + (C_3/C_2)(f_{YP} + f_{XP})\}} \\
&= \frac{C_2(f_{PY} + f_{PX} - \nu f_{X1})}{(f_{Y1} + f_{X1})(f_{P1} + f_{PY} + f_{PX})}.
\end{aligned} \tag{6.94}$$

The second form of the phenomenological coefficients is obtained by the use of eqns (6.91) and (6.92).

For the case of zero salt

$$C_3 = 0, \quad \mathscr{L}_2 = \frac{C_2}{f_{P1} + v f_{X1}},$$

$$\mathscr{L}_{23} = 0. \tag{6.95}$$

For sedimentation in a centrifugal field we use eqns (6.35) and (3.1) and substitute

$$l_{ik} = \mathscr{L}_{ik} M_i M_k$$

to derive

$$s_2 = \frac{\overline{M}_2 - \overline{M}_3 \{ v - (f_{PX} + f_{PY})/f_{X1} \} \{ 1 + (f_{Y1}/f_{X1}) \}^{-1}}{f_{P1} + f_{PY} + f_{PX}}, \tag{6.96}$$

which is identical with the limiting form of eqn (6.65) if the interparticle frictions f_{PX} and f_{PY} (not considered in the previous derivation) are set equal to zero and only the particle–solvent frictions f_{P1}, f_{Y1}, and f_{X1} are considered ($v = iZ$).

For the case of zero salt we find

$$C_3 = 0, \quad s_2 = \frac{\overline{M}_2}{f_{P1} + v f_{X1}}, \tag{6.97}$$

which is identical with eqn (6.68). A similar correspondence with the previously derived equations applies for the expressions for the diffusion coefficients.

Is it possible to evaluate the interparticle frictions f_{PX} and f_{PY} and to evaluate their relative importance with respect to f_{P1}? In principle they are measurable by way of the measurement of self-diffusion coefficients of small ions with the help of radioactive tracer ions. Varoqui and Schmitt (1972), for instance, obtain

$$D'_X = \frac{RT}{f_{XY} + f_{X1} + f_{XX}},$$

$$D_X = \frac{RT}{f_{XP} + f_{XY} + f_{X1} + f_{XX}}, \tag{6.98}$$

where D'_X and D_X are the self-diffusion coefficients at a given salt concentration in the absence and in the presence of the polyelectrolyte component, respectively. It is assumed that the values of f_{XY}, f_{X1}, and f_{XX} are unaffected by the addition of the polyelectrolyte. A similar expression is obtained for D'_Y and D_Y. On the basis of these relations we have

$$f_{XP} = \frac{RT}{D'_X} \left(\frac{D'_X}{D_X} - 1 \right),$$

$$f_{YP} = \frac{RT}{D'_Y} \left(\frac{D'_Y}{D_Y} - 1 \right). \tag{6.99}$$

In the absence of salt the counter-ion mobility may be determined with accuracy even at low polyelectrolyte concentrations. In the presence of excess salt D'_Y/D_Y and D'_X/D_X become close to unity as C_2 decreases and therefore the limiting coefficients f_{XP} and f_{YP} cannot be determined with any accuracy and no such results are available.

The self-diffusion coefficients of small ions in polyelectrolyte solutions have been evaluated theoretically (Lifson and Jackson 1962; Jackson and Coriell 1963, 1964; Coriell and Jackson 1963; Manning 1967, 1969a) although both the classical experimental results (Huizenga, Grieger, and Wall 1950; Wall and Grieger 1952; Wall, Grieger, Huizenga, and Doremus 1952) in this field, as well as the theoretical interpretation of the exchange times of counter-ions, have been subject to controversy (see Gottlieb (1971) for an experimental re-investigation and the short communications of Jackson, Lifson, and Coriell (1969) and Manning (1969b) for a discussion of the theoretical aspects). A more detailed discussion and references to more recent experimental investigations are given in the review by Manning (**1972**). The topic is beyond the scope of this book, in which the discussion has been limited to the properties of electroneutral components and has not covered in depth the transport properties of charged ionic species. A summary of elementary polyelectrolyte theory of equilibrium properties is given in Appendix 5 (p. 232) and the transport theories of polyelectrolytes (see Manning **1972**) are based on simple extensions of these ideas to non-equilibrium systems.

7

VISCOSITY

7.1. Introduction

VISCOSITY in liquids is a very complicated and incompletely evaluated phenomenon. It arises from energy dissipation as a result of molecular motion and interaction in flow. When we say incompletely evaluated, we do not mean from the purely phenomenological aspects, according to which the fluid is considered to constitute an incompressible continuum, subject to the well established laws of classical fluid mechanics, a field of research which has in recent years experienced a great deal of renewed interest. We mean rather that viscosity is incompletely evaluated from the point of view of molecular theory, which aims at a quantitative interpretation of viscous flow on the basis of detailed molecular structure and interactions.† It is a fortunate, though by no means trivial, feature of suspensions or solutions of macro-molecules in solvents consisting of small molecules, that valuable information on macromolecular structure and interactions may be derived from viscosity measurements on such systems. It is permissible, when considering systems made up of molecules of such dissimilar size, to consider the solvent, or suspending medium, to be a continuum and to relate the extra energy dissipated in viscous flow (and the related viscosity increase) due to the presence of the large molecules to molecular parameters and interactions between the macromolecules. An early and successful example of such an investigation is Einstein's theory developed in 1905, for the viscosity of suspensions of non-interacting rigid spheres. This has been extended more recently to interacting rigid spheres and to particles carrying electrical charges. Further developments include the viscosity increments of rigid prolate and oblate ellipsoids of rotation, of rigid rods, and of deformable particles. A more complicated case, but still amenable to theoretical analysis, is exemplified in the chain-like macromolecules whose configurations are continuously changing as a result of thermal motion and freedom of rotation around molecular bonds; in the 1930s Staudinger had already recognized the value of viscosity measurements in characterizing certain properties of long-chain molecules. Much more experimental and theoretical work has

---

† Bondi (1956), in his discussion of theories of viscosity of liquids, states that a rigorous approach based on continuum mechanics and molecular theory is 'so complicated as to preclude application to other than simple monoatomic liquids'.

accumulated since. If we recognize that most macromolecules of biological interest, such as globular and rod-like proteins, denatured proteins, poly-peptides, viruses, nucleic acids, polynucleotides, and others can be satisfactorily represented by one of the above models, then the usefulness of viscosity measurement towards the aim of increasing our understanding of these macromolecular systems immediately becomes apparent.

A further point, sometimes overlooked in biophysical studies but well known to the rheologist, is that additional parameters are required, in well-defined experiments, to characterize the flow of complex biological fluids such as protoplasm, blood, and mucus (the classical observation is the Weissenberg effect, by which it is shown that upon stirring viscoelastic fluids, a tendency is observed for the fluids to climb up the stirring-rod). We would like to point out in this chapter some of the basic features of the hydro-dynamic theory required for the design of such experiments. These ideas have been applied very recently (Shafer, Laiken, and Zimm 1974; Shafer 1974) to study the radial migration of very large DNA molecules in concentric-cylinder flow. Shafer *et al.* have suggested that this radial velocity depends on the $\frac{5}{2}$ power of the molecular weight and can be used for molecular weight separations in systems comprising bacterial and eukaryotic chromosomal DNA.

For the purpose of definition, we now consider Newton's theory of linear viscosity, which is based on the hypothesis 'that the resistance which arises from the lack of slipperiness of the parts of the liquid, other things being equal, is proportional to the velocity with which the parts of the liquid are separated from one another'. Assume (Fig. 7.1) two parallel infinite planes at distance d; plane 1 is stationary and plane 2 is moving with respect to plane 1 with a fixed velocity v; the space between the two planes is filled with a Newtonian liquid for which the shear viscosity η is a constant defined by

$$S_{12} = \eta\kappa, \qquad (7.1)$$

where $\kappa = v/d$ is the velocity gradient, or rate of shear (in s^{-1}) and S_{12} is the shearing stress (in dyn cm^{-2}), that is, the force per unit area in the direction of the moving plate. The flow is assumed to be laminar and there is no slip at the walls; therefore the first layer of liquid adhering to the stationary plane is at rest. The velocity changes linearly with distance x^1 and the layer of liquid adhering to the upper plate moves with the velocity v.[†]

The process described above is known as simple shear. It may be likened to the sliding of a pack of rigid cards. More fundamentally[‡] we now consider

[†] In the case of simple liquids, to be defined below, the condition of no slip is always satisfied even in the case of fluids, such as mercury, which do not wet the boundary walls.

[‡] For an elementary discussion of this and similar processes see Reiner (**1960a**); more advanced discussions, using the elements of tensor analysis are Reiner (**1960b**) and chapters in Feynman, Leighton, and Sands (**1963**).

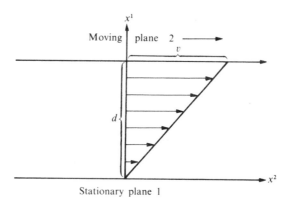

FIG. 7.1. Simple shearing flow between infinite planes. Velocity profile of simple fluid.

an imaginary spherical element in our liquid (Fig. 7.2(a)) at rest; the axes at 45° to the direction of flow are called the principal axes of deformation. In simple shear (Fig. 7.2(b)) the sphere under consideration is deformed into an ellipsoid, the principal axes of deformation being rotated through the angle shown. Fig. 7.2(c) shows that the same result may be obtained by pure shear (that is, extension of one and contraction of the other principal axis, without rotation) and a subsequent rotation. Simple shear can always be decomposed into a pure deformation followed by a rotation; in addition, in certain types of flow, translation has to be considered. The two most important classes of viscometric flows realizable to within certain approximations in the laboratory are laminar (telescopic) flow in pipes (Poiseuille flow) and rotational flow between concentric cylinders (Couette flow).

   As mentioned earlier, we are not interested in the viscosity of the fluid itself, but rather in the viscosity increase due to additional energy dissipation when a macromolecule is suspended in a given solvent medium; the rate of work done in overcoming frictional resistance is equal to $\eta\kappa^2$ per unit volume, and therefore additional energy dissipation leads to an increase in viscosity. How does this additional energy dissipation come about? In the absence of a suspended particle, the most general fluid motion in a viscometric flow consists of translation, rotation, and deformation. If we suspend a rigid spherical particle, large with respect to the solvent molecules making up the flowing medium but small with respect to the dimensions of the instrument, in the field of flow it will disturb the original flow. Neither translation nor rotation (in the special case of a spherical rigid particle) lead to additional energy dissipation as long as the particle follows the specified movement of the liquid. On the other hand, the additional boundary condition that the liquid adhere to the walls of the particle, provides the

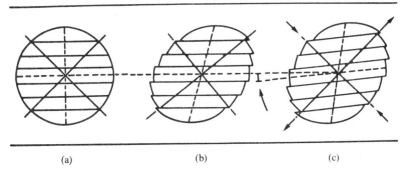

FIG. 7.2. Model sphere in fluid between parallel planes; (a) unstrained sphere, at rest; (b) ellipsoid produced by simple shear; (c) equivalence of simple shear to pure shear followed by rotation. The principal axes of deformation (full lines) remain at right-angles after deformation. In pure shear their direction in space remains unaltered, in simple shear they are rotated through the angle shown. (From Reiner **1960**.)

required mechanism. The rigid sphere cannot deform, as the liquid sphere it replaces would, and disturbance of the deformation process in the suspension medium leads to a viscosity increase by additional energy dissipation. In dilute non-interacting systems the energy dissipation is a simple sum of the energy dissipated by the individual particles. In mathematical terms, Einstein's equation represents a solution of Stokes's approximation (for slow motions) of the Navier–Stokes equations of hydrodynamics. This is not to be confused with the classical solution by Stokes for the translational resistance encountered by a rigid sphere in steady slow motion in a viscous medium.†

The analysis presented above can be extended to particles of different geometrical shapes; in the case of anisotropic particles rotary Brownian motion has to be considered. The viscosity will always be higher except in those cases where the introduction of the macromolecules, by some molecular mechanism, destroys loose structures which were present in the suspending liquid before its introduction. In the case of deformable particles, it can be shown by suitable tensorial analysis in elasticity theory that the particle experiences tension and compression at right-angles, at 45° (at slow rates of flow) with respect to the lines of flow. An analysis of energy dissipation and related viscosity increase occurring in this situation is somewhat more involved than in the case of the rigid particles.

We have previously remarked that the viscosity of the solvent medium is generally Newtonian, that is, it is constant and independent of the rate

† For a precise mathematical statement of the qualitative ideas presented above we refer to *Fluid mechanics* by Landau and Lifshitz (**1959**); an excellent early discussion on the viscosity of solutions of macromolecules (as the problem presented itself at the threshold of the era in which organic macromolecules were recognized as well-defined colloid particles) is given by Guth and Mark (**1933**).

of shear. Many polymer systems show non-Newtonian behaviour, that is, the viscosity becomes a function of the rate of shear. We are now ready to understand in a qualitative way a few mechanisms for non-Newtonian behaviour in dilute solutions of macromolecules. As mentioned above, excess energy is dissipated per particle, due to either a rotational or deformational mechanism. Particle interaction may lead to further dissipation of energy, that is, additional viscosity increase. If particle interaction is of such a nature that labile structures are formed which are stable at rest, but are disrupted during flow, the viscosity will decrease with increasing rate of shear. This is known as *structural viscosity* and may be quite often eliminated by appreciably decreasing the concentration. A class of non-Newtonian behaviour which persists to the limit of zero concentration can be attributed to the individual particles. Rigid particles, in laminar flow, rotate with a period proportional to the reciprocal of the rate of shear. A spherical particle, during rotation, will offer the same resistance to flow, independent of the orientation of the particle. Not so an anisotropic particle, an ellipsoid of rotation, or a rod. Less energy will be expended if the particle lies at an angle close to the direction of flow, rather than at right angles to it. While still rotating, as in the case of the isotropic particle, the anisotropic particle will tend to spend more time in orientations in which it encounters less hydrodynamic resistance. Thermal motion, manifesting itself as rotary Brownian diffusion, will act against the orientating action of the hydrodynamic field. At high rates of shear anisotropic particles will spend most of the time in oriented configurations. This phenomenon, which represents an 'orientation' mechanism for the dependence of viscosity on rate of shear, can be directly visualized between crossed polarizers in the birefringence-of-flow method (Edsall **1943**; Peterlin **1956**; Harrington **1967**). When the flow is stopped the anisotropic particles re-assume random configurations as the result of thermal motion. The time of relaxation τ of the orientation is inversely proportional to the rotary diffusion constant θ, which decreases with increase in anisotropy. A parameter α is defined by the ratio κ/θ; at values $\alpha \ll 1$ the orientation of particles is essentially random, the solution is not birefringent, and the flow is Newtonian. When α becomes commensurate with unity and increases beyond unity, the solutions become birefringent and the viscosity decreases with increasing rate of shear. It may reach a limiting value if the particles are completely oriented. In the case of deformable particles and chain-like macromolecules both relaxation of orientation and of deformation is involved and it can again be shown that orientation of the deformed particles at high enough values of α may lead to a decrease of viscosity with increasing rate of shear. In some special situations the non-Newtonian intrinsic viscosity may pass through a minimum and then increase with increasing rate of shear (Bianchi and Peterlin 1968).

In the determination of viscosity one distinguishes between η, the dynamic

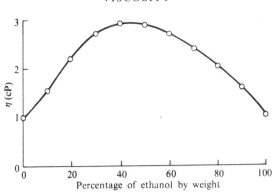

FIG. 7.3. Dynamic viscosity η of mixture of water and ethanol, at 20 °C. (From Bingham and Jackson 1918.)

viscosity, and $v = \eta/\rho$, the kinematic viscosity; ρ is the density of the fluid. The dynamic viscosity is expressed in c.g.s. units in dyn s cm^{-2}, g cm^{-1} s^{-1}, or poises (P); the centipoise (cP) is 0·01 P (the viscosity of water is 1 cP at 20·20 °C). The kinematic viscosity is expressed in cm^2 s^{-1} or stokes. Sometimes, in investigations involving macromolecular solutes, it is necessary to use mixed solvents. The reader is warned that, while in many cases, involving mostly non-polar solvents, the viscosity varies monotonically with composition from one pure solvent to the other, the behaviour is much more complex in the case of mixtures of polar solvents. A typical case is exemplified by the mixture of ethyl alcohol and water; Fig. 7.3 shows typical data taken from the work of Bingham and Jackson (1918). Special consideration must be given to systems involving preferential absorption of one of the solvents on to the macromolecular component, leading to a local change in solvent composition and viscosity in the vicinity of the macromolecule.

We now proceed to define a few quantities which are of interest in the interpretation of the viscosity increase resulting from the introduction of macromolecular particles into a given solvent medium. The relative viscosity η_{rel},

$$\eta_{rel} \equiv \eta/\eta_0, \tag{7.2}$$

where η is the viscosity of the solution and η_0 that of the pure solvent. Further, the specific viscosity η_{sp} is given by

$$\eta_{sp} \equiv \frac{\eta - \eta_0}{\eta_0} = \eta_{rel} - 1, \tag{7.3}$$

and the intrinsic viscosity $[\eta]$ is given by

$$[\eta] \lim_{c \to 0} \frac{\eta_{sp}}{c}, \tag{7.4}$$

where η_{sp}/c is known as the reduced viscosity. None of these quantities have the dimension of viscosity and therefore their designations as viscosities are, strictly speaking, misleading. The terminology viscosity number for η_{sp}/c and limiting viscosity number, Staudinger index, for $[\eta]$, as approved by the International Union of Pure and Applied Chemistry (IUPAC) (1952) has not found general acceptance. Further confusion exists with respect to the concentration units which sometimes are given in $g\,ml^{-1}$, $g\,dl^{-1}$ or, particularly in polyelectrolyte work (where a well-defined equivalent repeating unit may be recognized), in equivalents l^{-1}. To avoid confusion it is always advisable when quoting $[\eta]$ data to append the relevant units which, in keeping with the concentration units used, may be either $ml\,g^{-1}$, $dl\,g^{-1}$, or l equivalent^{-1}.

Using the definitions just given (and by hydrodynamic theory), Einstein's classical expression for the viscosity of a dilute suspension of rigid spheres is formulated as

$$\eta_{sp} = 2 \cdot 5\phi, \tag{7.5}$$

where ϕ is the volume fraction of the spheres; obviously η_{sp}/c, or rather $[\eta]$ (as particle–particle interactions have not been taken into account in Einstein's treatment) is a constant, independent of the size of the spheres. Staudinger's equation for the viscosity of solutions of chain-like coils, as modified by Mark (**1938**) and by Houwink (1940), is

$$[\eta] = KM^a, \tag{7.6}$$

where K and a are constants depending on a given homologous polymer solvent system at a given temperature. The exponent a in the original Staudinger equation was believed to be unity and is now known to vary between 0·5 and about 0·9 for flexible molecules and to assume values greater than unity for more rigid types of structure.

The concentration dependence of η_{sp}/c may usually be expressed in a power series in the concentration

$$\eta_{sp}/c = [\eta] + k[\eta]^2 c + \cdots, \tag{7.7}$$

where k is a dimensionless constant, of the order of 0·4–0·6 for most chain-like polymer systems; it is known as the Huggins constant (Huggins 1942).

We conclude with a general remark on the non-Newtonian character of dilute solutions of polymers. We have stated that the viscosity of the solvent is constant, but that the viscosity contribution due to a suspension of rigid ellipsoids, for example, may depend on the rate of shear. Theoretical curves for the dependence of $[\eta]$ upon κ for rigid ellipsoids of rotation have been computed (Scheraga 1955) from rigorous hydrodynamic equations. The full lines in Fig. 7.4 represent the ratio $[\eta]^\kappa/[\eta]^0$ of the shear-dependent intrinsic viscosity over its value at zero rate of shear, as a function of κ, for a rigid

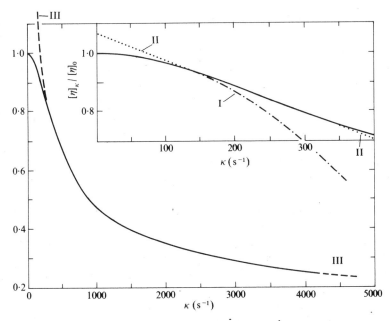

FIG. 7.4. Ratio of $[\eta]$ at rate of shear κ to $[\eta]$ at $\kappa = 0$ for rigid prolate ellipsoid of rotation of axial ratio $p = 300$ and rotary diffusion constant $\theta = 70\,\mathrm{s}^{-1}$. Full line, theoretical curve (Scheraga 1955). I, correct quadratic limiting law $(1 - 3\cdot4 \times 10^{-6}\kappa^2)$, for $\kappa < 140\,\mathrm{s}^{-1}$. II, linear approximation $(1\cdot065 - 9\cdot1 \times 10^{-4}\kappa)$, for $100 < \kappa < 400\,\mathrm{s}^{-1}$. III, reciprocal square-root approximation $(0\cdot2 + 5\cdot97 \times 10^{-2}\kappa^{\frac{1}{2}})^{-1}$, for $\kappa > 300\,\mathrm{s}^{-1}$. (From Eisenberg 1957.)

prolate ellipsoid of rotation of axial ratio $p = 300$, length $L = 7400\,\text{Å}$, and rotary diffusion constant $\theta = 70\,\mathrm{s}^{-1}$. It is seen that at a rate of shear of about $1000\,\mathrm{s}^{-1}$ $[\eta]$ drops to half its value at zero rate of shear. Over the same range of κ the viscosity η of a very dilute suspension of these ellipsoids varies to a much smaller extent; if, at a given concentration $\eta_{\mathrm{rel}} = 1\cdot1$ and $\eta_{\mathrm{sp}} = 0\cdot1$ in the limit or vanishing rate of shear, at $\kappa \approx 1000\,\mathrm{s}^{-1}$ the corresponding values would be $\eta_{\mathrm{rel}} = 1\cdot05$ and $\eta_{\mathrm{sp}} = 0\cdot05$. The relative viscosity, and therefore the viscosity of the solution, thus only decreases by 5 per cent, whereas η_{sp} drops to one half. The purpose of our argument is to show that even in situations in which $[\eta]$ varies strongly with rate of shear, the actual solutions, at low enough concentrations, deviate only very slightly from Newtonian behaviour. Obviously, as the concentration (and with it η_{rel}) increases, departures from Newtonian behaviour become more pronounced.

No attempt will be made in the following to cover the extensive literature, exhaustively reviewed, on the general field of viscosity and its measurement. The problem of viscometry is extensively treated in the monograph of Barr (**1931**) and the early work on the viscosity and viscometry of colloids is discussed by Philippoff (**1942**). An exhaustive discussion of instrumental methods is given by Umstätter (**1952**); articles of special interest on theories and applications of modern rheology are by Riseman and Kirkwood (**1956**) on the statistical mechanical theory of irreversible processes in solutions of macromolecules, by Frisch and Simha (**1956**) on the viscosity of colloidal suspensions and macromolecular solutions, by Zimm (**1960**) on the normal-coordinate method for polymer chains in dilute solutions, and by Conway and Dobry–Duclaux (**1960**) on the viscosity of suspensions of electrically charged particles and solutions of polymeric electrolytes.

In relation to interpretation of viscosity data in dilute polymer solutions we also mention the articles of Cerf (**1959**) on the dynamics of solutions of macromolecules in a velocity field, of Yang (**1961**) on the viscosity of macro-molecules in relation to molecular conformation and of Kurata and Stockmayer (**1963**) on the intrinsic viscosities and unperturbed dimensions of long-chain molecules. The measurement of the viscosity of nucleic acid solutions has been discussed by Zimm (**1971**) and by Uhlenhopp and Zimm (**1973**) and of dilute polymer solutions in general by van Oene (**1968**). Reference is also made to Flory (**1953**), Tanford (**1961**), and van Holde (**1971**) for valuable discussions of the application of viscosity studies to solution of synthetic and biological macromolecules.

Protein molecules (in particular proteins composed of anisotropic subunits or capable of associating to form high-molecular-weight aggregates) often exhibit complex shapes, which precludes interpretation of viscosity or sedimentation data by exact hydrodynamic theory. In such instances success has been achieved by modelling such proteins by macroscopic bodies and evaluation of frictional parameters by hydrodynamic similarity experiments. Successful applications to biological macromolecules include studies on tobacco mosaic virus (Haltner and Zimm 1959), bacteriophages (Douthart and Bloomfield 1968), glutamate dehydrogenase and its associated forms (Reisler and Eisenberg 1970; Reisler, Pouyet, and Eisenberg 1970; and Eisenberg and Reisler 1971), and myosin dimers (Burke and Harrington 1971, 1972). Attempts to calculate rotational frictional coefficients of particles of complicated shape have been reviewed by Bloomfield (**1968**).

7.2. Viscometric flows

7.2.1. Continuum theory and simple fluids

The following discussion makes reference to a treatment of the continuum theory of viscoelastic fluids of Coleman and Noll (1959, 1961); the theory has been presented with less mathematical machinery than the original work in a monograph on viscometric flows of non-Newtonian fluids by Coleman, Markovitz, and Noll (**1965**), which also contains many historical references on viscosity studies. The main conclusions only are presented here and the interested reader is referred to the original articles for mathematical details and proof. Certain steady-flow problems, of interest to the biophysicist, can be solved assuming Noll's definition of a fluid and of incompressibility. We will refer in particular to simple shearing flow, flow through a capillary pipe (Poiseuille flow), and flow between two concentric cylinders (Couette flow). The solutions obtained are in terms of three unspecified real functions of one variable and depend on the particular material only; they are called 'material functions'. These functions are simply related and are independent of the type of flow used in their determination. Conversely, if the three material functions are known, the complete stress and velocity profiles can be predicted for all the flows specified above. We shall, in the following, mainly be concerned with one of these material functions, in order to give meaning to the important concept of non-Newtonian, or 'shear-dependent' viscosity. The other two functions, which are related to the so-called 'normal stress' coefficients will not be investigated here.

The stress $S(t)$ at a material point X in a body at time t is determined by the past history of the motion in an arbitrarily small neighbourhood of X. For most materials of interest in physical chemistry $S(t)$ is determined at X by the history, up to time t, of only the first spatial gradient F at X of the displacement function; the deformation gradient $F(\tau)$ for X at any time τ is a second-order tensor.† Substances for which the history of the deformation gradient determines the stress have been called 'simple materials'. The relationship between the history of the deformation gradient and the stress tensor is established by a functional‡ which in general depends on which configuration of the material is taken as reference in computing the deformation gradient. If the functional does not depend on the configuration used as reference configuration for the computation of $F(\tau)$ at X, then X is a material point of a 'simple fluid'. It follows that a simple fluid is an isotropic material and furthermore every configuration of a simple fluid is undistorted. In mathematical language and for isochoric (volume-preserving) motion, that is, for an incompressible fluid, the relationship is expressed by a constitutive equation.§

The stress in an incompressible fluid is determined by the history of the

---

† The components of a tensor are vectors. In the most general case a second-order tensor is specified by three vectors, or nine numbers. A vector is a first-order tensor and is specified by three numbers. A scalar number may be referred to as a zero-order tensor. No special notation for vectors or tensors will be used in this chapter.

‡ A functional is a function whose arguments are functions and whose values may be tensors; the stress tensor at time t is taken as a functional of the history of the deformation gradient up to time t, which may in turn be regarded as a tensor-valued function of a time variable τ.

§ *Constitutive equations* are relations between entities that describe a physical process. For instance, 'the shearing stress is a linear function of the rate of shear' is a constitutive equation defining Newton's theory of linear viscosity; $PV = nRT$ is a constitutive equation defining an ideal gas. Constitutive equations should be clearly distinguished from *field equations* which express general principles of physics, and are applicable to all materials; for example, conservation of mass, of energy, and so forth.

motion only up to a scalar pressure P. The tensor T

$$T = S + PI \qquad (7.8)$$

is called the extra stress, and I is the identity tensor.

In isochoric (volume-preserving) motion of an incompressible fluid body, the velocity field $v(x, t)$ satisfies the relation

$$\nabla . v = 0 \qquad (7.9)$$

(x being the position occupied by the material point X at time t) throughout the body at all time t. One also assumes in considering special flow problems in incompressible fluids that the body forces g (per unit mass) have a single-valued potential

$$g = -\nabla\psi. \qquad (7.10)$$

The modified pressure ϕ is defined by

$$\phi = P + \rho\psi, \qquad (7.11)$$

where ρ is the density of the fluid; ϕ coincides with P in the absence of body forces. The dynamical equations take the form

$$\nabla . T - \nabla\phi = \rho\dot{v}, \qquad (7.12)$$

where

$$\dot{v} = \dot{v}(x, t) = \frac{\mathrm{d}}{\mathrm{d}t} v(x, t)$$

is the acceleration field at x at time t.

7.2.2. Simple shearing flow

The concepts introduced above will now be applied to simple shearing flow of an incompressible fluid. The flow is defined by assuming that in some Cartesian coordinate systems x^1, x^2, x^3 the velocity field $v(x) = v^1$, v^2, v^3 has the form

$$
\begin{aligned}
v^1 &= 0, \\
v^2 &= v(x^1), \\
v^3 &= 0,
\end{aligned}
\qquad (7.13)
$$

The velocity field v is independent of t (steady flow) and satisfies eqn (7.9). In simple shearing flow, as defined above, and without any further assumptions or approximation, Coleman and Noll show that the components of

$T(t)$ have the form

$$\|T(t)\| = \begin{Vmatrix} T_{11} & T_{12} & 0 \\ T_{21} & T_{22} & 0 \\ 0 & 0 & T_{33} \end{Vmatrix}, \quad T_{12} = T_{21}, \tag{7.14}$$

$$T_{11} + T_{22} + T_{33} = 0, \tag{7.15}$$

where the T_{ij} are functions of the velocity gradient, or the rate of shear κ

$$\kappa = \frac{dv(x^1)}{dx^1} \tag{7.16}$$

alone. The components T_{ij} of the extra stress may be expressed in terms of three independent functions of κ,

$$T_{12} = \tau(\kappa), \quad T_{11} - T_{33} = \sigma_1(\kappa), \quad T_{22} - T_{33} = \sigma_2(\kappa), \tag{7.17}$$

and for the components S_{ij} of the stress tensor $S(t)$ we have

$$S_{12} = S_{21} = \tau(\kappa), \quad S_{11} - S_{33} = \sigma_1(\kappa), \quad S_{22} - S_{33} = \sigma_2(\kappa). \tag{7.18}$$

The functions τ, σ_1, and σ_2 do not depend on which Cartesian coordinate system is used to obtain the simple velocity field (eqn (7.13)). These functions thus depend only on the material and not on the direction in which the material is being sheared. For this reason, τ, σ_1, and σ_2 are called material functions. It also follows from isotropy that

$$\tau(-\kappa) = -\tau(\kappa) \quad \sigma_i(\kappa) = \sigma_i(-\kappa) \tag{7.19}$$

that is τ must be an odd function and σ_1 and σ_2 are even functions.

The 'shear dependent' non-Newtonian viscosity can be identified with $\tau(\kappa)/\kappa$,

$$\eta(\kappa) = \frac{\tau(\kappa)}{\kappa}, \tag{7.20}$$

and it follows from eqn (7.19) that η must be an even function of κ. If approximations based on Taylor expansions of η, σ_1, and σ_2 in the neighbourhood of $\kappa = 0$ are used to fit experimental data, only even powers of κ can occur.

For the special case of incompressible perfect fluids

$$\tau(\kappa) = \tau_1(\kappa) = \tau_2(\kappa) = 0 \tag{7.21}$$

for all κ. For incompressible Newtonian fluids,

$$\tau(\kappa) = \kappa\eta, \\ \sigma_1(\kappa) = \sigma_2(\kappa) = 0 \tag{7.22}$$

for all κ; that is, the viscosity function (eqn (7.20)) is a constant larger than zero, τ is linear in κ, and the normal stress differences shown in eqn (7.18) are zero.

Consider now simple shearing flow between an infinite plane 1 at rest and an infinite plane 2 moving with constant speed v, at distance d, parallel to plane 1. The position of the coordinate systems is defined in Fig. (7.1) (p. 186); the x^3-axis, not shown in the Figure, is in plane 1. The usual boundary conditions stating that the fluid adheres to the walls, that is, the absence of slip, is

$$v(0) = 0, \quad v(d) = v. \tag{7.23}$$

The modified pressure ϕ, defined in eqn (7.18) is assumed to have no gradient in the direction of flow,

$$\partial\phi/\partial x^2 = 0. \tag{7.24}$$

It was shown above that for simple shearing flow, the extra stress T_{ij} are functions of κ alone; thus by eqn (7.16) the T_{ij} can vary with the x^1 coordinate only. The dynamical equations eqn (7.12) reduce to

$$\frac{\partial T_{11}}{\partial x^1} + \frac{\partial\phi}{\partial x^1} = 0,$$

$$\frac{\partial T_{12}}{\partial x^1} + \frac{\partial\phi}{\partial x^2} = 0, \tag{7.25}$$

$$\frac{\partial\phi}{\partial x^3} = 0.$$

These differential equations are satisfied only if

$$T_{12} = b, \tag{7.26}$$

$$\phi = T_{11} - c, \tag{7.27}$$

where b and c are constants.

From eqns (7.26) and (7.17) it follows that $\kappa = \tau^{-1}(b)$ is constant; τ has a single-valued strictly increasing odd inverse τ^{-1} in an interval close to $\kappa = 0$. From eqns (7.16) and the boundary conditions eqn (7.23),

$$v(x^1) = (v/d)x^1, \tag{7.28}$$

$$\kappa = v/d, \tag{7.29}$$

and, according to eqn (7.18),

$$S_{12} = \tau(v/d). \tag{7.30}$$

Since S_{12} equals the tangential force per unit area that must be applied to the moving plane 2 in order to produce the flow, eqn (7.30) gives a physical meaning to the material function τ; it is proven that S_{12} depends on τ only and is independent of the other material functions. It follows from eqns (7.29),

(7.17), and (7.15) that all the components T_{ij} of T must be constant. Hence by eqn (7.27) the modified pressure ϕ is a constant. Using eqns (7.11) and (7.8) we find

$$S_{11} = c - P\psi. \qquad (7.31)$$

If the potential ψ of the body forces is known, then a measurement of the normal force per unit area on the moving plane determines the value of the constant c. Eqns (7.25) and (7.18) yield

$$S_{11} - S_{33} = \sigma_1(v/d), \quad S_{22} - S_{33} = \sigma_3(v/d), \qquad (7.32)$$

and thus give a physical meaning to the material function σ_1 and σ_2. Finally, the following expression is found for the matrix of the stress tensor:

$$\|S\| = \begin{Vmatrix} c - \rho\psi & \tau(v/d) & 0 \\ \tau(v/d) & c - \rho\psi + \sigma_2(v/d) - \sigma_1(v/d) & 0 \\ 0 & 0 & c - \rho\psi - \sigma_1(v/d) \end{Vmatrix}. \qquad (7.33)$$

It is quite obvious that flow between two infinite planes cannot be realized in the laboratory. Coleman and Noll show that there are several other steady-flow problems, of practical importance that can be solved exactly without neglect of inertia for incompressible fluids, and the resulting stress and velocity profiles related by the same material functions τ, σ_1, and σ_2. We shall consider in the following only Poiseuille flow and Couette flow, which is a special case of helical flow, that is, flow between two concentric cylinders, which may or may not rotate with respect to each other. Measurements may be performed in suitable combinations to yield the three material constants from whichever set of experiments is most suitable from a practical point of view. Here again, the basic equations refer to infinite pipes (in Poiseuille flow) or to infinite concentric cylinders (in Couette flow) and the experimentalist is faced with the problem of accounting for end effects in a suitable way.

7.2.3. Poiseuille flow

We consider a steady flow of an incompressible simple fluid in an infinite circular pipe of radius R and use cylindrical coordinates (Fig. 7.5) labelled

$$r = x^1, \quad z = x^2, \quad \theta = x^3, \qquad (7.34)$$

with the z-axis coincident with the axis of the pipe. We have Poiseuille flow if, in the above coordinate system, the components of the velocity field have the form

$$\begin{aligned} v^r &= 0, \\ v^z &= v(r), \\ v^\theta &= 0, \end{aligned} \qquad (7.35)$$

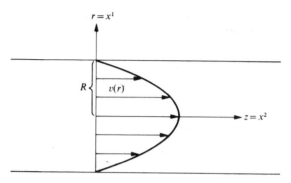

$$r = x^1$$

$$R \{ \quad v(r) \qquad\qquad z = x^2$$

FIG. 7.5. Poiseuille flow. Parabolic velocity profile of Newtonian liquid.

and if the fluid adheres to the wall,

$$v(R) = 0. \tag{7.36}$$

If we solve the dynamical eqns (7.12) for this case, considering that the shearing stress S_{rz} must be continuous at the centre of the pipe (that is for $r = 0$), we find

$$S_{rz} = -\tfrac{1}{2}ar, \tag{7.37}$$

where a, which is also called the driving force, is the applied force per unit volume in the direction of flow.† If there are no body forces, then a reduces to the pressure head per unit length. If the only body force is gravity acting in the direction of flow, and if there is no pressure head, then a is simply the specific weight of the fluid.

For the velocity gradient‡ we have

$$\kappa = \frac{dv(r)}{dr}, \tag{7.38}$$

and, from eqns (7.18) for $S_{12} = S_{rz} = \tau(\kappa)$, eqns (7.37) and (7.38), and since τ is an odd function,

$$\kappa = g(F), \tag{7.39}$$

where we have designated the shearing stress S_{rz} by F and by $-g(F)$ the inverse of τ, $\tau^{-1}(F)$.

The above equation, together with the boundary condition (eqn (7.36))

† Elementary considerations, assuming telescopic flow, immediately show that the shearing stress S_{rz} equals the ratio between the applied force $-\pi r^2 La$ and the area $2\pi rL$ of an imaginary cylinder of length L, at radius r. Coleman and Noll prove, without special assumptions, that such a flow exists. This may appear trivial to the experimentalist but is not so as can be seen from the analysis of flow between a cone and a plate, which cannot exist without secondary flows except at very slow motions, when inertia may be neglected.

‡ Poiseuille flow, as well as simple shearing flow, is rectilinear, that is, the fluid particles travel in straight trajectories. Thus no distinction has to be made between velocity gradient and rate of shear.

determines the velocity profile

$$v(r) = -\int_r^R g(\tfrac{1}{2}ar)\,dr. \tag{7.40}$$

The volume discharge Q per unit time through a cross-section of the pipe is

$$Q = 2\pi \int_0^R v(r)r\,dr. \tag{7.41}$$

After integration by parts (see also Krieger and Maron (1952) and Hermans (**1953**)) and use of eqns (7.36) and (7.39), we find

$$Q = \frac{8\pi}{a^3} \int_{F=0}^{F_m} F^2 g(F)\,dF, \tag{7.42}$$

where $F_m = -\tfrac{1}{2}aR$ is the maximum shearing stress at the capillary wall. Thus, if the material function $\tau(\kappa) = F$ is known, we can predict, for pipe flow, the dependence of the rate of discharge Q on the driving force a. Again it is seen that Q depends on τ only and not on the other material functions. Eqn (7.42) is easily inverted

$$g(F_m) = -\frac{1}{\pi a^2 R^3}\frac{d}{da}\{a^3 Q(a)\}. \tag{7.43}$$

If $Q = Q(a)$ has been measured, eqn (7.43) may be used to calculate the material function τ.

The matrix of the physical components of the stress tensor, in the cylindrical coordinate system, has the form

$$\|S\| = \begin{Vmatrix} S_{rr} & S_{rz} & 0 \\ S_{zr} & S_{zz} & 0 \\ 0 & 0 & S_{\theta\theta} \end{Vmatrix}, \tag{7.44}$$

and for the evaluation of the normal stresses, we refer to the papers of Coleman and Noll. They ascribe the tendency of a stream of an incompressible viscoelastic fluid to swell upon efflux from a pipe to both a dependence of S_{rr} on r and a lack of equality between S_{rr} and S_{zz}. They also suggest a direct experimental way of determining the material constant σ_1, without neglect of inertia. Considering a steady flow of an incompressible simple fluid between two fixed coaxial circular cylinders of radii R_1 and $R_2 (R_1 < R_2)$, the difference $S_{rr}(R_2) - S_{rr}(R_1)$ in radial thrust per unit area on the inner and outer cylinders, which is a measurable quantity, is determined by the material constant σ_1 only. In the case of a Newtonian fluid, as mentioned above in eqns (7.22) the normal stresses are equal to zero, and the viscosity function $\eta(\kappa)$ is a constant. Eqn (7.40) is then readily integrated (with the use of $g(F) = F/\eta$) to yield the normal parabolic profile for a Newtonian fluid (Fig. 7.5),

$$v(r) = (R^2 - r^2)a/4\eta. \tag{7.45}$$

In similar fashion eqn (7.42) is integrated to give for the volume discharge per unit time

$$Q = \pi a R^4/8\eta, \tag{7.46}$$

which is the well-known Hagen–Poiseuille equation.

For the practical evaluation of shear-dependent viscosity, independent of instrument constants, Krieger and Maron (1952) describe the following procedure. Define an apparent fluidity

$$\phi_{app} = 8Q/\pi R^4 a, \tag{7.47}$$

which is the reciprocal of the apparent viscosity, and from Hagen–Poiseuille's formula eqn (7.46) coincides with the true fluidity in the case of a Newtonian fluid. Combination of eqns (7.42) and (7.47) gives

$$\phi_{app} = \frac{4}{F_m^4} \int_{F=0}^{F_m} F^2 g(F)\,dF, \tag{7.48}$$

and use of Leibnitz's rule to differentiate with respect to F_m under the definite integral gives

$$\frac{1}{\eta(\kappa_m)} \equiv \frac{g(F_m)}{F_m} = \phi_{app}\left(1 + \tfrac{1}{4}\frac{d\ln\phi_{app}}{d\ln F_m}\right). \tag{7.49}$$

The second term in parenthesis on the right-hand side of eqn (7.49) permits a precise and straightforward determination of the shear-dependent viscosity $\eta(\kappa_m)$ from apparent fluidity data ϕ_{app} taken at various values of the shearing stress F_m at the capillary wall. A plot of $g(F_m)$ against F_m is independent of instrumental constants, and therefore it should be possible to superimpose all such curves for a given polymer system. These two variables have been called (Reiner **1960a, b**) consistency variables. Obviously from eqn (7.49), ϕ_{app} is also independent of the dimensions of the instrument.

Suppose we are interested in the relative viscosities η_{rel} for a series of solutions of a polymer at various concentrations. In Poiseuille flow, at fixed driving force a, $g(F_m)$ will vary in the series, but F_m will be constant. Following Yang (**1961**) we focus our attention on

$$\eta_{rel}(F_m) = \eta(F_m)/\eta_0, \tag{7.50}$$

where η_0 is the viscosity of the Newtonian solvent. For a driving force a, a given instrument and a given effluent volume V, $Q = V/t$, η_{rel} is related to the effluent times t and t_0 by

$$\eta_{rel}(F_m) = \frac{t}{t_0}\left(1 - \tfrac{1}{4}\frac{d\ln(at)}{d\ln a}\right)^{-1}, \tag{7.51}$$

as, for the Newtonian solvent, the term $\ln\phi_{app}/d\ln F_m$ equals zero. The correction term in eqn (7.51) may be evaluated from a plot of $\ln at$ versus $\ln a$.

In polymer work one is mostly interested in the intrinsic viscosity $[\eta]$. The following development, leading to the determination of $[\eta]$, is due to Hermans (**1953**). We have, from eqns (7.4) and (7.7),

$$\eta(F) = \eta_0(1 + [\eta]^F c + \cdots), \tag{7.52}$$

and, taking reciprocals,

$$\frac{1}{\eta(F)} = \frac{1}{\eta_0}(1 - [\eta]^F c - \cdots). \tag{7.53}$$

We rewrite eqn (7.42) in the form

$$\frac{1}{t} = \frac{8\pi}{Va^3}\int_{F=0}^{F_m} dF\,\frac{F^3}{\eta(F)}, \tag{7.54}$$

where we have used $Q = V/t$ and, from eqns (7.39) and (7.20), $\eta(F) = F/g(F)$. We next substitute eqn (7.53) into eqn (7.54) to give

$$\frac{1}{t} = \frac{8\pi}{Va^3}\int_{F=0}^{F_m}\frac{dF\,F^3}{\eta_0} - \frac{8\pi}{Va^3}\int_{F=0}^{F_m}\frac{dF\,F^3}{\eta_0}[\eta]^F c + \cdots. \tag{7.55}$$

As the viscosity η_0 of the solvent is a constant, the first term on the right-hand side of eqn (7.55) may be integrated; use of the value of $F_m = -\tfrac{1}{2}aR$, and the Hagen–Poiseuille eqn (7.46) then yields

$$\frac{1}{t} = \frac{1}{t_0} - \frac{\pi ac R^4}{2V\eta_0 F_m^4}\int_0^{F_m} dF\,F^3[\eta]^F + \cdots. \tag{7.56}$$

In the limit of zero concentration, an experimentally measurable quantity E can now be defined

$$E \equiv \lim_{c\to 0}\frac{1}{ac}\left(\frac{1}{t_0} - \frac{1}{t}\right) = \frac{\pi R^4}{2V\eta_0 F_m^4}\int_{F=0}^{F_m} dF\,F^3[\eta]^F. \tag{7.57}$$

Differentiation under the integral, in similar fashion as demonstrated when passing from eqn (7.48) to eqn (7.49), then leads to

$$[\eta]^{F_m} = at_s E\left(1 + \tfrac{1}{4}\frac{d\ln E}{d\ln a}\right). \tag{7.58}$$

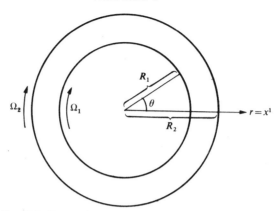

FIG. 7.6. Couette flow between concentric cylinders.

From eqn (7.57),

$$\lim_{c \to 0} \frac{t - t_s}{t_s c} = at_s E, \qquad (7.59)$$

which is equal to $[\eta]^{F_m}$ only if E is independent of a.

7.2.4. Couette flow

Consider a steady flow of an incompressible simple fluid between coaxial cylinders of radii R_1 and R_2 $(R_1 < R_2)$; the inner and outer cylinders are assumed to rotate with constant angular velocities Ω_1 and Ω_2. We use cylindrical coordinates (Fig. 7.6) with the z-axis coincident with the axis of the cylinders and label the coordinates

$$r = x^1, \quad \theta = x^2, \quad z = x^3. \qquad (7.60)$$

The physical components of the velocity field are assumed to have the form

$$v^r = 0, \quad v^z = 0, \quad v^\theta = r\omega(r), \qquad (7.61)$$

that is, in distinction to helical flow in general, the motion is in circles[†] and the velocity has no component in the z-direction; ω has the dimension of angular velocity. The boundary conditions, expressing adherence of the fluid to the walls are

$$\omega(R_1) = \Omega_1, \quad \omega(R_2) = \Omega_2. \qquad (7.62)$$

It can be shown without special assumptions (Coleman and Noll 1959) that

---

[†] Unlike simple shearing and Poiseuille flow, where the motion is rectilinear, velocity gradient and rate of shear are not synonymous. The rate of shear equals the velocity gradient, minus a rotation (Reiner **1960a**).

in Couette flow the velocity profile obeys the equation

$$\frac{d\omega(r)}{dr} = (1/r)g(F), \tag{7.63}$$

where the rate of shear $g(F)$ is the inverse of τ, $\tau^{-1}(F)$, F is the shearing stress

$$F = \frac{M}{2\pi r^2}, \tag{7.64}$$

and M is the torque per unit height required to maintain the relative motion of the two cylinders. Integration of eqn (7.63) yields

$$\Omega_2 - \Omega_1 = \tfrac{1}{2} \int_{F(R_2)}^{F(R_1)} (1/F)g(F)\,dF. \tag{7.65}$$

The matrix of the physical components of the stress tensor for Couette flow has the following form

$$\|S\| = \begin{Vmatrix} S_{rr} & 0 & S_{r\theta} \\ 0 & S_{zz} & 0 \\ S_{\theta r} & 0 & S_{\theta\theta} \end{Vmatrix}. \tag{7.66}$$

In the above equation $S_{r\theta} = S_{\theta r} = F$; Coleman and Noll give exact expressions for S_{rr} and for $S_{rr} - S_{zz}$ and $S_{\theta\theta} - S_{zz}$. If the potential of the body forces is independent of r, they show that the difference $S_{rr}(R_2) - S_{rr}(R_1)$ of the normal stresses at the outer and inner cylinders (which is a measurable quantity), can be related to the sum of three separable integrals, involving the centrifugal forces and the material constants σ_1 and σ_2 respectively. From a combination of various types of experiments, in well-defined viscometric flows, all three material constants (τ, σ_1, and σ_2) characteristic of a given simple fluid, can be completely evaluated without any approximation.

We now return to the main object of our discussion, that is, the experimental evaluation of the shear-dependent viscosity $\eta(\kappa)$ from Couette flow. Consider the special case in which the inner cylinder remains at rest, while the outer cylinder rotates with constant angular velocity Ω. Eqn (7.65) with the boundary condition $\omega(R_1) = 0$, $\omega(R_2) = \Omega$ now becomes

$$\Omega = \tfrac{1}{2} \int_{F_2}^{F_1} \frac{1}{F} g(F)\,dF. \tag{7.67}$$

If the gap between the two cylinders is very small $(R_2 - R_1)/R_1 \ll 1$, $g(F)$ may be considered constant and eqn (7.67) may be approximated by

$$\Omega \approx (R_2 - R_1/R_1)g(F). \tag{7.68}$$

We now wish to calculate the viscosity η from an experimental determination of $M = M(\Omega)$. In the case of a Newtonian fluid the viscosity

$\eta = F/g(F)$ is constant and eqn (7.67) may be integrated to yield

$$\Omega = \frac{M}{4\pi\eta}\left(\frac{1}{R_1^2} - \frac{1}{R_2^2}\right). \tag{7.69}$$

This is known as the Margules equation. To calculate the shear-dependent viscosity $\eta(\kappa)$ we follow the procedure of Krieger and Elrod (1953) and Krieger and Maron (1954). We differentiate eqn (7.67) with respect to $\ln F_1$ to obtain the difference equation

$$2\frac{d\Omega}{d\ln F_1} = g(F_1) - g(F_2). \tag{7.70}$$

Define a function $h(F_1) = 2\,d\Omega/d\ln F_1$ and further define a quantity $s = R_2/R_1$. From eqn (7.70),

$$\begin{aligned}
h(F_1) &= g(F_1) - g(s^{-2}F_1), \\
h(s^{-2}F_1) &= g(s^{-2}F_1) - g(s^{-4}F_1), \\
h(s^{-4}F_1) &= g(s^{-4}F_1) - g(s^{-6}F_1),
\end{aligned} \tag{7.71}$$

and so forth. Since $s > 1$ and $g(0) = 0$,

$$\sum_{n=0}^{\infty} h(s^{-2n}F_1) = g(F_1). \tag{7.72}$$

The sum in eqn (7.72) is slowly converging and may be evaluated by using the Euler–MacLaurin sum formula to yield the final asymptotic expression for the rate of shear at the inner stationary cylinder.

$$\begin{aligned}
g(F_1) &= \frac{\Omega}{\ln s}\left\{1 + \ln s\,\frac{d\ln\Omega}{d\ln F_1} + \frac{(\ln s)^2}{3\Omega}\frac{d^2\Omega}{d(\ln F_1)^2} - \frac{(\ln s)^4}{45\Omega}\frac{d^4\Omega}{d(\ln F_1)^4} + \cdots\right\} \\
&= \frac{\Omega}{\ln s}\left\{1 + m\ln s + \tfrac{1}{3}(m\ln s)^2 + \frac{(\ln s)^2}{3}\frac{dm}{d\ln F_1} + \cdots\right\},
\end{aligned} \tag{7.73}$$

where $m = d\ln\Omega/d\ln F_1$ and s is an instrumental constant; m is unity for a Newtonian fluid.

The bracketed term in eqn (7.73) is a power series in $\ln s$; therefore the smaller the value of s (that is, smaller clearance between the two cylinders) the sooner will it be possible to break off the power series. Krieger and Elrod have shown that usually a knowledge of m is sufficient and it is not necessary to perform a second graphical differentiation to obtain $dm/d\ln F_1$. This will certainly be true in dilute solutions of macromolecules which usually do not exhibit large deviations from Newtonian behaviour. If, following Krieger and Maron, we define an apparent fluidity ϕ_s

$$\phi_s = \frac{4\pi R_1^2 R_2^2 \Omega}{M(R_2^2 - R_1^2)} = 2\left/F_1\left(1 - \frac{1}{s^2}\right)\right., \tag{7.74}$$

whence

$$m = 1 + \frac{d \ln \phi_s}{d \ln F_1}, \qquad (7.75)$$

then it can be shown that, to a good approximation,

$$\frac{g(F_1)}{F_1} = \phi_s \left\{ 1 + k_1 \frac{d \ln \phi_s}{d \ln F_1} + k_2 \left(\frac{d \ln \phi_s}{d \ln F_1} \right)^2 \right\}, \qquad (7.76)$$

where

$$k_1 = (s^2 - 1)(1 + \tfrac{2}{3} \ln s)/2s^2$$

and

$$k_2 = \ln s(s^2 - 1)/6s^2.$$

For a Newtonian fluid of viscosity η, $\phi_s = 1/\eta$ and $d \ln \phi_s/d \ln F_1 = 0$; $g(F_1)$ and F_1 are the consistency variables for Couette flow and a plot of these quantities should be superimposable with a plot of $g(F_m)$ against F_m from Poiseuille flow. In general though ϕ_s, as can be seen from eqn (7.76) will depend on s, in distinction to ϕ_{app}, defined in Poiseuille flow, which is independent of instrumental constants. Krieger and Elrod have shown experimentally that a composite plot of $g(F_m)/F_m$ against F_m from capillary measurements (eqn (7.48)) and $g(F_1)/F_1$ against F_1 from concentric cylinder measurements (eqn (7.76)) yields a unique curve for a non-Newtonian fluid (GR–S rubber latex containing 62·2 per cent solids by weight).

If, as is usually the case in dilute solution work, η_{rel} is required, and the solvent is Newtonian, then it is easily seen that by combining eqns (7.76) and (7.69) for the same instrument and at a given value of Ω,

$$\eta_{rel}(F_1) = \left(\frac{M}{M_s} \right) \left\{ 1 + k_1 \frac{d \ln(\Omega/M)}{d \ln M} + k_2 \left(\frac{d \ln(\Omega/M)}{d \ln M} \right)^2 \right\}^{-1} \qquad (7.77)$$

Here, similarly as in the eqn (7.51) for capillary flow, the leading term is a calculated value (M/M_s) and the correction term is obtained from a graphical differentiation of a plot of $\ln (\Omega/M)$ against $\ln M$; in distinction to eqn (7.57), eqn (7.77) is not exact but involves breaking off a power series at a suitable point. It can be shown at hand of theoretical examples for extreme cases of solutions of a highly anisotropic particles investigated in a rotational cylinder instrument of suitable dimensions, that this procedure is completely justified.

7.2.5. Laminar and turbulent flow conditions

The equations for Poiseuille and Couette flow arrived at in the previous sections are valid only in the case of steady, laminar flow. They break down with onset of turbulence. The problem of turbulence *per se* is outside the province of the biophysicist in the study of dilute solutions of macro-molecules; it may be of interest in the study, for instance, of the flow of complex biological fluids under extreme conditions of flow. (It is of historical interest that Poiseuille's investigations were prompted by his interest in the flow of blood.) Such flows may well be turbulent but their investigation is outside the scope of this book. What is needed here is a criterion for evaluating the range of experimental conditions in which laminar flow exists and the establishment of critical flow parameters, at which the onset of turbulence is to be expected.

In discussing the problem of turbulence we have first to consider the type of flow under investigation, that is, flow in pipes, flow between concentric cylinders, or flow past solid bodies. As the largest dimensions of our suspended macromolecules will almost always be much smaller than the smallest dimension of the instrument (see Lifson (1956) for an exception to this case), we can limit ourselves to a discussion of the first two situations, that is, we can assume that the same stability conditions for either Poiseuille or Couette flow will apply, both in the absence and in the presence of low concentrations of dissolved macromolecules.† For each type of flow, we have to establish a rule which makes the criterion for critical flow conditions independent of the dimensions of the instrument. In the flow of in-compressible fluids the kinematic viscosity $v = \eta/\rho$, the velocity v of the main stream, and a linear dimension l of the instrument determine the flow. From these quantities one dimensionless quantity only can be formed, called the Reynolds number (Re),

$$(Re) = \rho v \, l/\eta \, . \tag{7.78}$$

The law of similarity, due to Reynolds, states that flows of the same type are similar if they have the same Reynolds number. Thus the establishment of a critical Reynolds number for a given type of flow permits the estimation of the onset of turbulence, if the dimensions of the instrument are known. At small (Re), small perturbations arising in a steady flow decrease with time; the flow is stable. At values of (Re) larger than the critical value, the flow becomes unstable with respect to such perturbations. Knowledge of the critical Reynolds number for a given type of flow permits the estimation of the onset of turbulence, if the dimensions of the instrument are known. Sometimes more than one transition region exists, the lower one of which may correspond to a region of turbulent but stable and well-reproducible flow. The critical (Re) will, in general, depend on the type of flow, and the complex mathematical problem of stability has not been completely solved.

† This is not always so in more concentrated systems, as can be seen from the discussion of so-called structural turbulence in Philippoff's monograph (1942). Unfortunately, in such cases, the distinction between structural viscosity and structural turbulence is rather difficult to achieve.

All that is known is the experimentally determined range of critical (Re) for different types of flow. Experimental investigations under laminar flow conditions should be undertaken under conditions well removed from this critical range.

In the study of dilute aqueous solutions of biological polymers, or in solvents having a value of v close to that of water, turbulence in capillary viscometers is seldom a problem. The critical (Re) for capillary flow,

$$(Re) = 2Rv\rho/\eta, \qquad (7.79)$$

has been found to have a lower limit of about 2000. From the Hagen–Poiseuille law, for a Newtonian fluid v_{max} at the centre of the capillary equals $2Q/\pi R^2$. In a typical capillary instrument $R = 2{\cdot}25 \times 10^{-2}$ cm and $Q \approx 10^{-2}$ cm^3 s^{-1} for water at 20 °C; $v_{max} \approx 17{\cdot}5$ cm s^{-1}. If the above values, and the ratio $\rho/\eta \approx 10^2$ s cm^{-2} for water at this temperature, are introduced into eqn (7.79), it is found that $(Re) \approx 56$ for this case, that is well below the critical range for onset of turbulence. Thus, in capillary instruments, unless a special problem involving very high Reynolds numbers is being investigated, turbulence will not be a cause of error. We should be aware though that, in poorly designed instruments, turbulence may occur at the extremities of the capillary. This will be propagated to some extent into the capillary, eventually disappearing if flow conditions in the capillary are stable; such a disturbance is in the nature of an end effect and can be minimized by suitable design and evaluated, together with other correction terms, by calibration with liquids of known v, at different values of the pressure head.

In the case of concentric-cylinder measurements the situation is less favourable. We refer to the theoretical work of Taylor (1936) and the experimental observations of Mooney and Ewart (1934) and Jerrard (1950). The experimental arrangement in which the outer cylinder is rotating is more favourable than that in which the inner cylinder is rotating (see Fig. 7.7) for the velocity distribution across the annular gap in both cases; this is due to the fact that in the former case the distribution of the centrifugal forces stabilizes the motion of the fluid.

For inner rotating cylinders, the flow, according to Taylor, is stable for values of Ω of the cylinder $\Omega < \Omega_c$;

$$\Omega_c^2 = \frac{\pi^4 v^2 (R_1 + R_2)}{2PR_1^2 \, \Delta R^3}, \qquad (7.80)$$

which for values $\Delta R/R_1 \ll 1$ equals 0·057. For outer rotating cylinders Ω_c is much higher and is given in the form of curves. For experimental data we $\left.\begin{array}{l}\\ \\\end{array}\right\}$ p 208

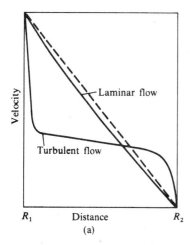

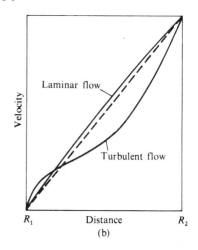

FIG. 7.7. Velocity profile in laminar and turbulent flow between concentric cylinders; (a) inner cylinder rotating; (b) outer cylinder rotating. (From Jerrard 1959.)

where $\Delta R = R_2 - R_1$ and P is a constant,

$$P = 0.0571\left(1 - 0.652\frac{\Delta R}{R_1}\right) + 0.00056\left(1 - 0.652\frac{\Delta R}{R_1}\right)^{-1}, \qquad (7.81)$$

from p. 207 →

refer to the work of Jerrard and to the work of Mooney and Ewart who have shown (Fig. 7.8) that in a plot of rate of shear against shearing stress, in an instrument in which the inner cylinder is rotating, the onset of turbulence can be easily visualized, in that the slope of the curve changes in the critical range. An experimental investigation (Eisenberg 1957a) with an instrument with *outer* rotating cylinder has shown that turbulence, for water at 25 °C, is observed in the range of Ω_c predicted by Taylor for the case of the *inner* rotating cylinder. With a gap $\Delta R = 0.1$ cm, $R_1 = 1.9$ cm, the critical rate of shear was observed to be $150\,\mathrm{s}^{-1}$ and with a gap $\Delta R = 0.2$ cm, $R_1 = 1.8$ cm, it decreased to $25\,\mathrm{s}^{-1}$; it also was found to be strictly proportional to the viscosity of the fluid. The investigation referred to above was not aimed at a study of hydrodynamic stability in Couette flow; therefore conditions to be satisfied in such a study, such as for instance ensuring very high smoothness of the cylinders and freedom from vibrations, were not taken. The investigation was rather aimed at establishing practical limits of laminar flow in a particular instrument used in the study of non-Newtonian behaviour in dilute solution work at low rates of shear. The observation that the values of the critical rate of shear are within the range in which experimental determinations with Couette instruments are usually performed in such

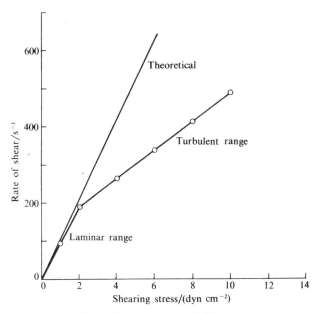

FIG. 7.8. Laminar and turbulent flow of water at 22 °C between concentric cylinders; inner cylinder rotating. (From Mooney and Ewart 1934.)

studies, points to the fact that, unlike in capillary work, great precautions should be taken in this case to ensure that measurements are performed in the laminar range. It is relatively easy though to establish the laminar range for a given instrument and a given Newtonian solvent by analysing a flow curve, such as shown in Fig. 7.8. A more sensitive test is to establish the range of Ω over which M/Ω (see eqn (7.69)) is indeed constant in the case of the Newtonian solvent. With onset of turbulence M/Ω will usually increase due to additional energy dissipated in turbulent flow. Such experimental stability studies can be extended to systems comprising macromolecules, but known to exhibit Newtonian behaviour in this experimental range. If non-Newtonian behaviour is expected the study becomes more difficult as the decrease in viscosity with increasing rate of shear in such systems will generally oppose the apparent increase due to turbulent flow. The useful range of the instrument may be ascertained by superimposing flow curves obtained with different size clearances between the two cylinders. Parallel studies of the same systems in both capillary and rotational cylinder instruments are highly recommended, as we have seen that the correctly evaluated shear dependent viscosity may be obtained by either method.

7.3. Approximations to viscometric flows

Viscometric flows permit a complete derivation of the shear-dependent viscosity. In practice, however, viscometric flows cannot be completely realized. One is faced with the problem of dealing with experimental arrangements which are, to some extent, approximations to viscometric flows only. Some of these approximations are practical experimental difficulties, which can in principle be overcome if the trouble involved in designing more sophisticated experimental set-ups is warranted. Thus, for instance, it is certainly possible, though usually not done, to keep the pressure head in Poiseuille flow absolutely constant. Even though an extraneous constant pressure device is used, the hydrostatic pressure head in the capillary viscometer usually changes during the course of one experiment, leading to a slight variation in the total pressure head; it is possible to program the outside pressure source in such a way as to compensate for this change, but this certainly complicates the experimental design (see Fujita and Homma (1955) who designed such a device). More often one is satisfied with applying a correction which then constitutes an approximation to the viscometric flow. Fortunately, in biophysical work we are not interested in absolute viscosities but rather in viscosity ratios, determined under similar experimental conditions leading to such quantities as η_{sp}/c and $[\eta]$. This circumstance somewhat eases the problem of applying suitable correction terms. If the pressure head is very small, and we aim at an extrapolation to zero rate of shear, it has been suggested that a capillary viscometer with continuously variable head is used. This again constitutes an approximation to Poiseuille flow, specifically involving the use of viscometric-flow equations under non-steady flow conditions, amounting to a neglect of inertia. That this method still constitutes a useful experimental tool is due to the fact that the velocity field while not steady, is changing rather slowly.

There exist other approximations to viscometric flows which cannot be easily eliminated. Here we refer in particular to the fact that neither infinitely long pipes, nor infinitely long cylinders are available in practice. One way of getting around the difficulty is by performing the experiments in instruments of different length and suitable extrapolation to infinite length. Again, while this is the best approach in the determination of absolute viscosities, for the determination of viscosity ratios it is usually sufficient to apply approximate corrections for end effects, and to design instruments in such a way that the approximate nature of these corrections may be safely neglected. Also, although we have continuously stressed that the difficulties arise mostly in connection with the determination of the shear-dependent viscosity, it should be remembered that many macromolecular systems, particularly at low concentrations, exhibit Newtonian behaviour; in such situations it is very often sufficient to clearly establish that the viscosity is indeed constant, independent of the rate of shear, or becomes constant within experimental error at low rates of shear (that is, for a low enough value of $\alpha = \kappa/\theta$). The measurement of viscosity ratios of Newtonian fluids can always be performed more easily and more precisely, than if shear-dependent viscosities are involved. On the other hand, even if η_{sp}/c or $[\eta]$ depend strongly on the rate of shear, the solutions themselves at low enough concentrations corresponding to values of η_{rel} close to unity do not deviate strongly from Newtonian flow behaviour. While no exact theories corresponding to the analysis of viscometric flows exist to account for the transition from the idealized experiment to the practical case, it is hoped that errors involved in approximations to viscometric flows will show up only as second-order corrections in the evaluation of η_{sp}/c and $[\eta]$.

7.3.1. *Poiseuille flow*

The driving force. If the driving force is constant, the flow in the capillary is steady, and the exact equations developed previously apply. In practice the driving force may change slightly during the course of one experiment and it is necessary to assume that the ensuing inertial effects are negligible in the derivation of the equation of flow. The changes in driving force are mainly due to the change in the hydrostatic head of the fluid itself. If an additional outside pressure source is used, which is many times larger than the pressure due to the hydrostatic head, then variations due to a change in hydrostatic head will be of a much smaller order than if the liquid is allowed to fall under gravity only. In both cases an effective head can be defined, corresponding to a constant head which (in the case of Newtonian liquid) would give the same rate of flow. Equations and factors, depending on the geometry of the bulbs from which the liquid is discharged and into which it is flowing, have been given (see the monograph by Dinsdale and Moore **1962**). The evaluation of such effective heads is important in the absolute measurement of the viscosity of Newtonian liquids. In dilute solution work, in which only viscosity ratios and derived quantities are required, it is not necessary to know the exact distribution of the driving force as long as both solution and solvent are Newtonian and the experiment is run in such a way that the effective head (which need not be evaluated) is the same for both systems. Considering the fact that the density of the solution is slightly different from that of the solvent, a density correction (Tanford 1955; Eisenberg and Casassa 1960) which is easily evaluated, has to be applied. In the case of non-Newtonian solutions the situation is more complicated and it is suggested that so-called multi-bulb viscometers in which the solutions are discharged from a series of bulbs with successively lower levels, be used only for a rough indication of establishing non-Newtonian behaviour. At high rates of shear non-Newtonian behaviour in Poiseuille flow is best investigated in viscometers to which a constant outside source of pressure is attached, whereas at low and vanishing rates of shear the viscometer with continuously variable pressure head is recommended.

The density correction. The density correction referred to above is evaluated in the following way for a Newtonian fluid. We refer to the case in which the liquid is flowing under the influence of gravity only ($a = \rho g h/L$, where h is the hydrostatic head and L is the length of the capillary). The relative viscosity, from the Hagen–Poiseuille eqn (7.53), is given by

$$\eta_{\text{rel}} \equiv \frac{\eta}{\eta_0} = \frac{\rho t}{\rho_0 t_0}. \tag{7.82}$$

At low concentrations, the density ρ of the solution may be expanded in a Taylor series in the concentration c, around the density ρ of the solvent

$$\rho = \rho_0 + \left(\frac{\partial \rho}{\partial c}\right)^0 c, \tag{7.83}$$

with neglect of higher terms. In a two-component system $(\partial \rho/\partial c)^0$, for which we usually may write $(\rho - \rho_0)/c$, is well defined and equals $1 - \bar{v}\rho$, where $\bar{v}$ is the partial specific volume of the solute. In a multi-component system (Casassa and Eisenberg **1964**) $(\partial \rho/\partial c)^0$ will depend to some extent on the way in which the dilution is performed, that is, either at constant concentration or at constant chemical potential (by equilibrium dialysis) of the non-macro-molecular components. If we combine eqns (7.82) and (7.83) and use the definition of η_{sp}/c, eqn (7.6), we easily obtain

$$\frac{\eta_{\text{sp}}}{c} = \frac{t - t_0}{t_0 c} + \frac{1}{\rho}\left(\frac{\partial \rho}{\partial c}\right)^0 \frac{t}{t_0}. \tag{7.84}$$

In the limit of zero concentration $t \to t_0$ and

$$[\eta] = \lim_{c \to 0}\left(\frac{t - t_0}{t_0 c}\right) + \frac{1}{\rho}\left(\frac{\partial \rho}{\partial c}\right)^0. \tag{7.85}$$

The second term on the right-hand side of eqn (7.85) thus does not vanish in the limit of $c \to 0$; it is more important the lower the intrinsic viscosity and may be neglected when the intrinsic viscosity is very high. Tanford (1955) has shown that for bovine serum albumin at $25\,°C$ in $0.01\,\text{M KCL}$ the density correction in eqn (7.85) amounts to about 8 per cent of the first term. It is important also in the investigation of a polymer homologous series when the functional relationship eqn (7.6) between the intrinsic viscosity and the molecular weight is to be established down to very low values of the molecular weight. Thus (Eisenberg and Casassa 1960) $[\eta]$ of the potassium salt of polyvinylsulphonic acid of molecular weight $52\,000$ at $25°$ in $0.5\,\text{M KCL}$ is $14.16\,\text{ml g}^{-1}$; it is obtained by adding $(1/\rho^0)(\partial \rho/\partial c)^0 \approx 0.55$ to the experimentally determined first term on the right-hand side of eqn (7.85).

Continuously variable pressure head. The investigation of non-Newtonian

Inner cross-section s

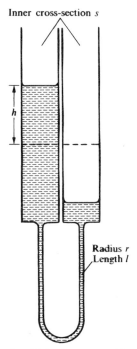

Radius r
Length l

FIG. 7.9. Schematic drawing of capillary viscometer with continuously variable head.

solutions at low rates of shear in capillary instruments is best performed in an instrument with continuously variable pressure head, considering the fact that very low constant rates of shear cannot be maintained in a capillary viscometer. As mentioned above, however, this method represents only an approximation to a viscometric flow, as inertial effects due to the slowly variable force are not considered in the fundamental equations of flow. Such measurements should therefore be compared with measurements in a Couette viscometer (in which constant low rates of shear may be maintained) in order to establish the validity of the method. The method is certainly useful in the range $\alpha = \kappa/\theta \ll 1$ in which dilute solutions of macromolecules exhibit very close approximation to Newtonian behaviour.

Consider (Fig. 7.9) a capillary of length L and radius R connected to two precision-bore cylindrical tubes of inner cross section s. Claesson and Lohmander (1961) use fairly wide tubes, to eliminate surface tension effects, and an extremely precise method to measure changes in level. The driving force at time t is given by

$$a = \frac{2\rho g h}{L},$$ (7.86)

where g is the gravitational constant and h is the height (at time t) in the left tube over the level in the final position at rest. The volume Q flowing through the capillary cross-section in unit time is related to the change in level by

$$Q \equiv \frac{dV}{dt} = -\frac{dh}{dt}. \tag{7.87}$$

Eqn (7.87) is now combined with eqn (7.42) to yield

$$-\frac{dh}{dt} = \frac{8\pi}{sa^3} \int_0^{F_m} dF\, F^2\, g(F). \tag{7.88}$$

For a Newtonian liquid $\eta = F/g(F)$ is constant and eqn (7.88) may be integrated to yield

$$-\frac{dh}{dt} = \frac{\pi a R^4}{8s\eta}, \tag{7.89}$$

where we have used $F_m = \frac{1}{2}aR$. Substitution of the value of a from eqn (7.86) yields

$$-\frac{d\ln h}{dt} = \frac{\pi R^4 \rho g}{4sL}\phi, \tag{7.90}$$

that is, for a Newtonian liquid, a plot of $\ln h$ against time is a straight line, the slope of which may be used to evaluate the fluidity $\phi = 1/\eta$ of the liquid. If the liquid is non-Newtonian we define an apparent fluidity ϕ_{app} by eqn (7.50) and combine this with eqn (7.49), which relates the apparent fluidity to the shear-dependent viscosity in Poiseuille flow. We obtain

$$\frac{1}{\eta(F_m)} = -\frac{q(F_m)}{B\rho}\left(1 + \frac{1}{4q^2}\frac{dq(F_m)}{dt}\right), \tag{7.91}$$

where, for convenience, we have designated $d\ln h/dt$ at h (corresponding to a shearing stress F_m at the wall of the capillary $F_m = (\rho g R/L)h$) by $q(F_m)$ and by B the instrumental constant $\pi R^4 g/4sL$. In dilute polymer solutions at low rates of shear, as already mentioned, the departures from Newtonian behaviour are very small and a plot of $\ln h$ versus t shows very slight curvature only. Maron and Belner (1955) have described a procedure for the precise evaluation of q; the evaluation of the second derivative dq/dt is not always required. This was also concluded by Hermans (1958) and Hermans and Hermans (1959) in their studies on the viscosity of dilute solutions of deoxyribonucleic acid, using an instrument of this type.

If $\eta_{rel}^{F_m}$ is required, and the solvent is Newtonian ($q_0 = $ constant, $dq_0/dt = 0$) we have

$$\eta_{rel}^{F_m} \equiv \frac{\eta(F_m)}{\eta_0} = \frac{\rho q_0}{\rho_0\, q(F_m)}\left(1 + \frac{1}{4q^2}\frac{dq}{dt}\right)^{-1}. \tag{7.92}$$

If the second term in brackets can be neglected then

$$\eta_{rel}^{F_m} = \frac{\rho}{\rho_0} \frac{(d \ln h/dt)_0}{(d \ln h/dt)_{F_m}},$$ (7.93)

this though is tantamount with equating $1/\phi_{app}$ with the true shear-dependent viscosity.

Adsorption effects. It appears reasonable to assume that in the measurement of very dilute solutions, adsorption of dissolved macromolecules on the surface of the capillary may lead to erroneous results in the determination of η_{sp}/c and $[\eta]$, in particular as very fine capillaries are used in the study of very dilute solutions to increase the flow times and achieve a more accurate determination of η_{sp} when η becomes very close to η_0. This effect is not reduced as c decreases and the polymer and reference solutions become more similar to each other. Quite on the contrary this effect, which does not depend on hydrodynamic disturbances of the flow in the viscometer, becomes more troublesome at low concentrations. On *a priori* grounds one would expect a downward curvature in the plot of η_{sp}/c versus c as a result of polymer adsorption. Actually, the opposite was found in a number of instances (Takeda and Endo 1956; Streeter and Boyer 1954) and Fig. 7.10 shows an example described by Reisler and Eisenberg (1970) for solutions of the associating enzyme, glutamate dehydrogenase. Öhrn (1955, 1958) assumes that a layer of thickness b of polymer molecules adsorbed to the surface of the capillary reduces its effective radius from R to $R-b$. On this assumption, for Newtonian solutions flowing under their own weight, the Hagen–Poiseuille equation yields

$$\eta_{rel} = \frac{\rho t}{\rho_0 t_0} \left(\frac{R-b}{R} \right)^4 \approx \frac{\rho t}{\rho_0 t_0} \left(1 - \frac{4b}{R} \right),$$ (7.94)

as $b \ll R$. As can be easily deduced

$$\frac{\eta_{sp}}{c} = \left(\frac{\rho t}{\rho_0 t_0} - 1 \right) \frac{1}{c} - \frac{\rho t}{\rho_0 t_0} \frac{4b}{R} \frac{1}{c}.$$ (7.95)

The second term on the right-hand side of eqn (7.95) increases with decrease in c (when $\rho \rightarrow \rho_0$ and $t \rightarrow t_0$), as long as b remains constant. It can be shown by the use of capillaries with different radii, or by actual study of the adsorption layer in polymer solutions on glass (Tuijnman and Hermans 1957) that values of b required to obtain a 'normal' plot of η_{sp}/c against c by the use of eqn (7.95), in very dilute solutions, can be obtained for a given polymer–solvent system. If we accept the value given by Öhrn (1955) that $b \approx 10^{-5}$ cm for a sample of polystyrene (molecular weight $\approx 0.5 \times 10^6$) in toluene ($[\eta] \approx 150$ ml g^{-1}), then at a concentration of $c = 2 \times 10^{-4}$ g ml^{-1}, in a capillary with $R = 2.25 \times 10^{-2}$ cm, the second term on the right-hand

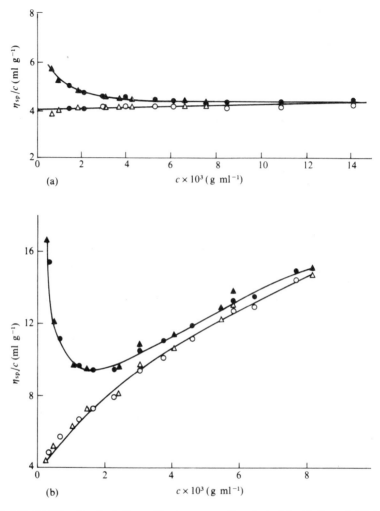

FIG. 7.10. (a) Viscosity of solutions of bovine serum albumin, in 0·2 M NaCl, at 10 °C, in two viscometers; filled points, uncorrected results; non-filled points, results corrected for adsorption. (From Reisler and Eisenberg 1970.) (b) Viscosity of solutions of bovine liver glutamate dehydrogenase in 0·2 M Na$_2$-PO$_4$ buffer, pH 7, 10^{-4} M EDTA, at 10 °C in two viscometers; symbols as in (a). (From Reisler and Eisenberg 1970.)

side of eqn (7.95) is about 9, and therefore represents a considerable correction to η_{sp}/c, which is very close to $[\eta]$ at this concentration; $\eta_{rel} \approx 1·03$ for the example quoted. If this correction, which corresponds to an extrapolation $R \to \infty$ is made, we may recover the downward curvature in a plot of η_{sp}/c versus c, which is due to adsorption *per se*. It is fortunately usually not necessary to perform experiments in the very dilute range in

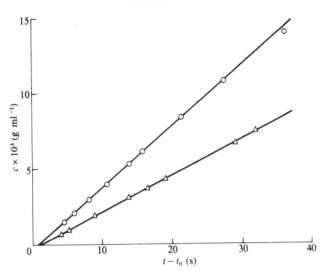

FIG. 7.11. Flow times $t - t_0$ of solutions of bovine serum albumin, at $10\,^\circ$C, in two viscometers (From Reisler and Eisenberg 1970).

which the 'abnormal' behaviour reported above becomes noticeable; as a rule experimental data may be reliably extrapolated from a higher concentration range ($1\cdot05 < \eta_{\mathrm{rel}} < 1\cdot30$). We should be most careful when extrapolating from a range in which a slight upturn of the curve may simulate a curve with different slope and lead to a wrong intercept. It is wise to check whether the Huggins constant k (eqn (7.7)) has a reasonable value.

The best way to test for adsorption, and other instrumental errors as well, is to perform measurements in at least two viscometers having a different capillary radius. In Couette instruments the effect is far less serious both because the clearance between the cylinders is usually larger ($0\cdot1$–$0\cdot2$ cm) than capillary radii and also because ΔR appears in the Margules equation (7.69) raised to the first and not to the fourth power as in the Hagen–Poiseuille law.

Reisler and Eisenberg (1970) find that, in dilute solutions of proteins, a convenient procedure is to plot the flow-times t versus the protein concentration (Fig. 7.11). Extrapolation to zero concentration (which is assumed to be linear at low concentrations) then yields a value for the flow time at $c = 0$ which is different from the flow time of the pure solvent system in the same viscometer. Use of the extrapolated (rather than the measured) values of t_0 in the evaluation of η_{sp}/c then leads to plots with normal curvature (Fig. 7.10). The role of the adsorption layer in capillaries in precision viscometry has been recently thoroughly reinvestigated by Priel and Silberberg (1970) and by Priel, Sasson, and Silberberg (1973) on the basis of a series of extremely precise experiments in dilute solutions of polystyrene in toluene and cyclohexane.

7.2.2. Couette flow

End effects. We have seen above that in Poiseuille flow end effects can be considerably reduced by suitable design of instruments; under such conditions both Newtonian and non-Newtonian flow behaviour can be analysed with confidence. Rotational cylinder viscometers, which are far less accurate and usually more complicated than well-designed capillary instruments, are obviously most useful in the study of non-Newtonian solutions. Our discussion here will be directed towards the problem of accounting for end effects in Couette flow and of designing instruments in which these effects are reduced to a minimum; it will be seen that practical considerations of design make it virtually impossible to reduce end effects in Couette flow to negligible proportions.

A purely mechanical way of eliminating end effects in rotational cylinder instruments is by the use of stationary guard rings. While providing a satisfactory solution of the problem these instruments are mechanically complicated, and difficult to assemble, to align, and to clean. The alternative approach is by evaluating the contribution due to suitably shaped extremities. Such calculations neglect inertia and secondary flows and therefore fall within the class of approximations to viscometric flows.

Consider (Fig. 7.12) a stationary cylinder of radius R_1 and height h suspended in a cup of radius R_2, rotating with angular velocity Ω. The distance between the bottom of the inner cylinder and the cup is designated by l; the same value of l is taken for the distance between the top of the inner cylinder and the rotating cover of the cup. The gap is filled with the liquid under investigation. The viscous drag experienced by the inner cylinder will have contributions from the stress on cylindrical surface, from the stress on the bottom and top surface, and furthermore there will be an edge effect due to the fact that the stress distribution at the extremities does not correspond to that of infinitely long rotating cylinders or infinitely large rotating plates. It is customary to consider these end effects in terms of an increase Δh of the effective length h of the inner cylinder. The total torque $T = M(h + \Delta h)$, in the case of a Newtonian fluid, is then assumed to be given by the Margules equation (7.69),

$$T = \frac{4\pi\Omega\eta(h + \Delta h)}{(1/R_1^2) - (1/R_2^2)}. \tag{7.96}$$

The value of Δh will, in general, depend upon R_1, R_2, h, and l. If, for large enough values of the dimensionless parameter h/R_1, Δh becomes independent of h, then one may obtain Δh from a linear relationship between T and h (all other parameters being kept constant); in other words, the entrance

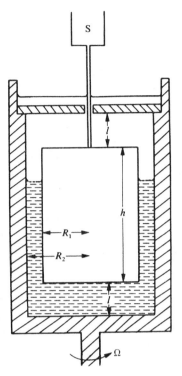

FIG. 7.12. Schematic drawing (not to scale) of concentric cylinder viscometer with flat ends; S, suspension and torque registering device.

perturbations do not overlap and an appreciable zone of true viscometric Couette flow exists. Lillie (1930) has shown experimentally that h must exceed a minimum value to make Δh independent of h. It is possible in the case of major interest, of a non-Newtonian fluid, to obtain the apparent fluidity ϕ_s (see eqn (7.74)) by eliminating the effects of the ends as explained above, and from ϕ_s the true shear-dependent viscosity may then be obtained by eqn (7.76).

The theoretical value of Δh has been evaluated by Oka (**1960**) for the situation under consideration. We have, for a Newtonian fluid,

$$\frac{\Delta h}{h} = \tfrac{1}{4}\frac{R_1^2}{hl}\left\{1-\left(\frac{R_1}{R_2}\right)^2\right\}\left\{1+\frac{2l}{\pi R_1^4 \eta \Omega}(T_1'+T_2')\right\}, \tag{7.97}$$

where the first term in braces is due to the torque on the bottom and top of the inner cylinder and T_1' and T_2' respectively are the torques due to the end effects at the cylindrical and at the planar edges; the contribution of the thin suspension rod or wire is neglected. Oka gives explicit expressions for T_1' and T_2' in the form of infinite series with coefficients which are functions of the non-dimensional parameters R_1/R_2, h/R_2, and l/R_2. For values of R_1/R_2 close to unity, and suitable values of the other parameters, we may approximate eqn (7.97) by

$$\frac{\Delta h}{h} = \frac{1}{2}\frac{R\Delta R}{hl},\qquad (7.98)$$

where $R \sim R_1 \sim R_2$; if we, for example, make $R_1/R_2 = 0.95$, $h/R = 5$, $l/\Delta R = 10$, which are reasonable proportions for a rotational cylinder instrument, then the increase in torque due to the ends is of the order of 1 per cent only. Whereas $\Delta h/h$ in the study of the relative viscosity of Newtonian fluids will not depend on the viscosity of the fluid but on instrumental constants only, this may not be true in the case of non-Newtonian fluids, for which this treatment does not apply. The error introduced in the study of 'slightly' non-Newtonian solutions, in which as already mentioned our main interest resides, may be well within experimental error, as we have shown above that the torque due to extremities may be reduced to a small fraction of the torque on the cylindrical sides by suitable instrumental design. The influence of the ends may be further reduced by removing the top cover and creating a free surface either above the top of the inner cylinder or below it (see dotted line in Fig. 7.12); in the latter case the exact height of the liquid in the gap between the cylinder and the cup is rather difficult to establish, although in principle it affords a rather simple way of observing T as a function of h.

Another method of circumventing the problem of the end effect in Couette flow has been developed by Mooney and Ewart (1934), who designed the conicylindrical viscometer. We will analyse here a form of the instrument (Fig. 7.13) in which the cup and cover are given a cylindrical shape and the inner cylinder terminates at both ends by rather flat cones. The torque due to the extremities, for a Newtonian fluid, is given by (Braun 1951)

$$T_c = \frac{4\pi R_1^3}{3}\eta\Omega\left\{\frac{\sin\alpha}{\cos^2\alpha} - \ln\tan\left(\frac{\pi}{4}-\frac{\alpha}{2}\right)\right\}^{-1},\qquad (7.99)$$

which for small values of the angle α reduces to approximately

$$T_c \approx \frac{4\pi R^3}{3}\eta\Omega.\qquad (7.100)$$

Under these conditions the rate of shear is nearly uniform in the conical gap and is given by $\Omega/\alpha \approx \Omega R/d$; thus, if we make $d = \Delta R$, we ensure nearly constant rate of shear over both cylindrical and conical regions of the inner cylinder. If the torque from eqn (7.100) is combined with that due to the cylindrical surface and the result expressed in the form given by eqn (7.96),

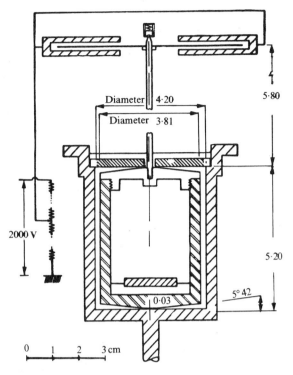

F ɪ ɢ. 7.13. Schematic drawing of rotation viscometer with cylindrical rotating cup and conicylindrical inner stationary cylinder; and with electrostatic restoring torque (From Eisenberg and Frei 1954).

we obtain, for small angles

$$\frac{\Delta h}{h} \approx \tfrac{2}{3}\frac{R}{h}.$$

If we consider the example previously examined for flat ends, where we assumed $h/R = 5$, then we see that an appreciable part of the torque ($\tfrac{2}{15}$—as compared with unity for the cylindrical portion) is contributed by the conical ends; the condition $R_1/R_2 = 0.95$ in the example quoted fixes $\alpha \approx \Delta R/R$ at 0·05 rad (that is at less than 3°). To reduce the contributions from the conical regions further it would be necessary to increase h/R such as to make the dimensions of the instrument highly impractical. We may conclude thus, that, while for the absolute determination of the viscosity of a Newtonian fluid there seems to be a certain advantage in designing a rotational instrument such as to make the rate of shear nearly constant everywhere in the gap between the cup and the inner cylinder, this advantage is to a large extent lost in the case of the determination of non-Newtonian viscosity. Owing to the

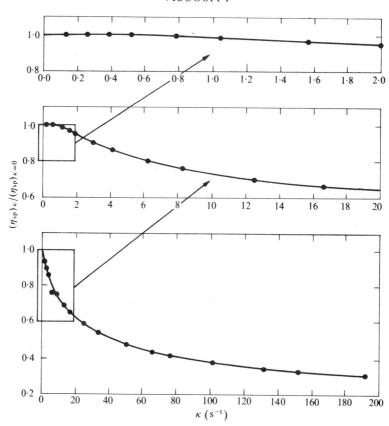

FIG. 7.14. Normalized specific viscosities $(\eta_{sp})_\kappa/(\eta_{sp})_{\kappa=0}$ versus rate of shear κ, for solutions of calf thymus DNA; $c_{DNA} = 5 \times 2 \times 10^{-5} \, \text{g ml}^{-1}$, $c_{NaCl} = 10^{-3} \, \text{M}$, at 25 °C. (From Eisenberg 1957a.)

large contribution of the extremities, we cannot use eqn (7.76) for instance to transform apparent fluidities ϕ_s into true shear-dependent viscosities, as an appreciable portion of the torque does not arise from a viscometric flow. It is obviously possible to arrive at an estimate of the error involved by varying h in the conicylindrical design (and by a plot of T/Ω against h and suitable manipulation of the equations), and thereby separating the contributions due from the cylindrical and conical regions of the instrument, in the case of a slightly non-Newtonian solution.

Eisenberg and Frei (1954) designed, and Frei, Treves, and Eisenberg (1957) improved, the design of a precision rotation viscometer with electrostatic restoring torque for the study of low-viscosity liquids in the centipoise range, at low and intermediate rates of shear. Eisenberg (1957a) used this instrument to study the viscosity behaviour of polyelectrolyte and (1957b) DNA solutions

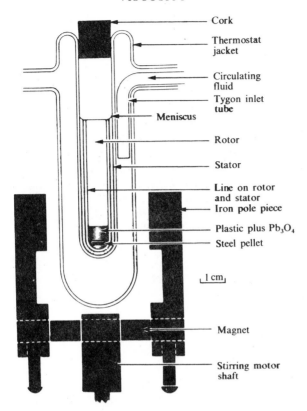

Cork

Thermostat jacket

Circulating fluid

Tygon inlet tube

Meniscus

Rotor

Stator

Line on rotor and stator

Iron pole piece

Plastic plus Pb_3O_4

Steel pellet

⌊1 cm⌋

Magnet

Stirring motor shaft

FIG. 7.15. Floating rotor viscometer of Zimm and Crothers (1962). The time per rotation of the rotor, driven by the field from the rotating magnet, is proportional to the viscosity of the liquid. (From Zimm **1971.**)

at low and medium rates of shear. It could be demonstrated (Fig. 7.14) that the dependence of η_{sp} on the rate of shear follows the limiting behaviour theoretically predicted (see Fig. 7.4 for curves calculated for an elongated rigid prolate ellipsoid of rotation). The limiting law is quadratic, which gives a limiting zero slope in the representation against the rate of shear; with increasing rate of shear the curves in Figs 7.14 and 7.4 are concave down, go through an inflection and assume a concave-up shape.

On realizing that for the measurement of the viscosity of solutions of DNA which has a very high molecular weight a simple instrument is required, Zimm and Crothers (1962) designed a rotation viscometer (Fig. 7.15) constructed of glass and plastic tubing in which the inner rotor floats, suspended on the upper solution meniscus (see also Zimm **1971** and Uhlenhopp and Zimm **1973**). Rotation is imparted by magnetically coupling a metal plug in the rotor to a rotating magnet. The rotor is self-centring in this novel suspension.† Surface tension and end effects in this ingenious instrument do not impede the accurate measurement of relative viscosities in DNA solution at extremely low rates of shear at which the viscosity of high molecular weight DNA is shear independent. The Zimm–Crothers instrument fails in the study of protein solutions in which solid surface films (absent in the case of DNA solutions) disturb the motion of the rotor. To circumvent the problems of solid surface films, Gill and Thompson (1967) designed the Cartesian diver rotating viscometer, in which the rotor, instead of floating from the meniscus, is submerged (with some loss of self-centring capacity) into the solution by exerting pressure directly on the solution from above. An air bubble trapped inside the rotor is compressed until the rotor becomes neutrally buoyant and remains suspended in solution; film problems are avoided since no surface is under shear. Further improvements to this viscometer (Chapman, Klotz, Thompson, and Zimm 1969; Klotz and Zimm 1972a, 1972b; Massa 1973) showed that, if an optical polarizing system is attached to the Cartesian diver viscometer, sudden stopping of the driving torque and measurement of the elastic recoil enabled the performance of a retardation-time experiment from which molecular weights can be estimated by considerations, developed by these authors (the recoil is due to the fact that during flow the shear force deforms or stretches the DNA molecules; when the field is turned off the inner cylinder rotates in the opposite direction due to relaxation of the previously stretched molecules). This method is believed to be useful for molecular weights of DNA at least as high as 10^{10} daltons, and therefore useful to study native and denatured DNA in total lysates of bacterial and eukaryotic cells. We have already referred to more recent application of the method (Shafer *et al.* 1974; Shafer 1974) to the inward radial migration of large DNA molecules, and the possibility of DNA fractionation by this procedure.

† For additional references, as well as improvements to the basic design of Zimm and Crothers, including a modification to operate at variable rate of shear see Melsheimer (1972), and for an automatic recording device see Pruniell and Neimark (1971).

APPENDIXES

Appendix 1. Deviations from electroneutrality

THE following considerations are from Guggenheim (**1967**, Chapter 8). The charge on a proton is given by

$$e \approx 1{\cdot}6 \times 10^{-19}\,\text{C}.$$

With 1 mol of electrons is associated a charge of

$$6 \times 10^{23} \times 1{\cdot}6 \times 10^{-19} = 9{\cdot}6 \times 10^{4}\,\text{C\,mol}^{-1}.$$

Let us consider a single phase, spherical in shape, with radius $r = 1\,\text{cm}$, surrounded by vacuum. We assume that this phase, instead of satisfying the condition of electroneutrality,

$$\sum_i n_i v_i = 0$$

(n_i is the number of ions of type i and charge v_i) contains an excess of $10^{-10}\,\text{mol}$ of charge of valency $+1$; this is too small a quantity to be chemically determined. Most, if not all the excess electrical charge will accumulate on the surface. The electrical potential ψ of a charged sphere, in vacuum, is given by

$$\psi \approx 9 \times 10^{9}\,Q/r,$$

where Q is the charge of the sphere, $9{\cdot}6 \times 10^{-6}\,\text{C}$, and r is $0{\cdot}01\,\text{m}$. The potential ψ is therefore $8{\cdot}6 \times 10^{6}\,\text{V}$. We conclude then that a small departure from electroneutrality too small to be chemically detected would lead to enormous electrostatic potentials. Potential differences of single volts, or even smaller, arising across semipermeable membranes, originate from insignificant deviations from electroneutrality indeed. Bulk phases may therefore be considered to obey the electroneutrality condition in all situations of practical interest.

Appendix 2. The chemical potential and some related thermodynamic quantities

We shall, in the following, briefly review a number of basic thermodynamic relationships, which are rigorously derived in thermodynamic texts (Guggenheim **1967**).

The first principle expresses conservation of energy

$$w + q = \Delta U,$$

where w is work done on the system, q is heat absorbed by the system (zero in an adiabatic process) and U is the energy of the system (dU is the change of U in an infinitesimal process). Changes in the entropy S, an extensive property, are given in an infinitesimal process by

$$dS = d_e S + d_i S,$$

where i refers to the change inside the system and e characterizes the interaction with surroundings.

$$d_e S = q/T,$$

where q is the heat absorbed from surrounding at the absolute temperature T. The second law of thermodynamics states that

$$d_i S > 0 \text{ for a natural change, } dS > q/T,$$

and

$$d_i S = 0 \text{ for a reversible change, } dS = q/T,$$
$$w^\alpha = -P^\alpha dV^\alpha,$$

where P^α is the pressure and V^α is the volume of phase α, on which work w^α is done. A phase is a homogeneous part of a thermodynamic system. For a reversible change in a closed phase

$$dU = T dS - P dV,$$

and for an open phase we have the Gibbs equation

$$dU = T dS - P dV + \sum_i \mu_i dn_i,$$

$$\mu_i = (\partial U/\partial n_i)_{S,V,n}.$$

(A2.1a)

μ_i is the chemical potential of the (independently variable) species i of which there are n_i moles; we shall use subscript n to indicate that all n except n_i with respect to which the differentiation is performed are kept constant.

Other thermodynamic potentials, in addition to the energy U are the Helmholtz (free energy) function $F = U - TS$,

enthalpy $H = U + PV$,
Gibbs (free energy) function $G = F + PV$.

For infinitesimal processes

$$dF = -S dT - P dV + \sum_i \mu_i dn_i,$$

(A2.1b)

$$dH = T dS + V dP + \sum_i \mu_i dn_i,$$

(A2.1c)

$$dG = -S dT + V dP + \sum_i \mu_i dn_i.$$

(A2.1d)

We express thermodynamic functions in terms of chosen thermodynamic potentials, for example, in terms of $G(T, P, n_i)$,

$$\mu_i = (\partial G/\partial n_i)_{P,T,n}, \tag{A2.2}$$

or

$$V = (\partial G/\partial P)_{T,n}.$$

We define partial molal quantities with respect to any extensive property, such as the volume V, for instance, by

$$\bar{V}_j \equiv (\partial V/\partial n_j)_{P,T,n} = \left(\frac{\partial}{\partial n_j}\left(\frac{\partial G}{\partial P}\right)_{T,n}\right)_{P,T,n} \tag{A2.3}$$

$$= \left(\frac{\partial}{\partial P}\left(\frac{\partial G}{\partial n_j}\right)_{P,T,n}\right)_{T,n}$$

$$= \left(\frac{\partial \mu_j}{\partial P}\right)_{T,N}. \tag{A2.4}$$

We write, for the most general change of volume in a mixture of i electro-neutral species or components

$$dV = (\partial V/\partial T)_{P,n}\,dT + (\partial V/\partial P)_{T,n}\,dP + \sum_i \bar{V}_i\,dn_i.$$

At constant pressure and temperature V is homogeneous of the first degree in the n_i and the $\bar{V}_i$ are homogeneous of zero degree in the n_i. This means that if the amount of the phase is increased at constant composition of the phase, the volume increases in the same ratio; we have

$$V = \sum_i n_i \bar{V}_i \tag{A2.5}$$

at constant T and P, and thereby state a useful property of partial molal volumes. The partial molal volume $\bar{V}_i$ may be derived from the experimentally determined apparent molal volume $\phi_i = \Delta V/n_i$ (at constant P, T, and $n_j \neq n_i$) by

$$\bar{V}_i = \phi_i + n_i(d\phi_i/dn_i).$$

From the integrated relations (obtained from eqn (A2.1a)) by considering that the energy U is a homogeneous function of the first degree in the extensive variables S, V, and n_i,

$$U = TS - PV + \sum_i \mu_i n_i,$$

$$G = \sum_i \mu_i n_i,$$

we obtain by differentiation

$$dG = \sum_i \mu_i\,dn_i + \sum_i n_i\,d\mu_i$$

and derive by substitution of eqn (A2.1) the Gibbs–Duhem equation

$$S \, \mathrm{d}T - V \, \mathrm{d}P + \sum_i n_i \, \mathrm{d}\mu_i = 0. \tag{A2.6}$$

Equilibrium conditions may be expressed in different ways. For constant temperature and pressure $\mathrm{d}T = 0$, $\mathrm{d}P = 0$, $\mathrm{d}G = 0$; for given T and P, G is minimum. For hydrostatic equilibrium across a semipermeable membrane

$$P^\alpha = P^\beta.$$

Equilibrium distribution between two phases requires

$$\mu_i^\alpha = \mu_i^\beta$$

for species i permeable through a membrane, but

$$P^\alpha \neq P^\beta$$

in this case and

$$\mu_j^\alpha \neq \mu_j^\beta$$

for species j not permeable through the membrane.

The name of chemical potential for the μ_i derives from the fact that each chemical species tends to move from a phase where its potential is higher to another phase where its potential is lower. Based on considerations of statistical thermodynamics of open systems, we may define the absolute activity

$$\lambda_i = \exp(\mu_i / RT).$$

R is the gas constant and T is the absolute temperature;

$$\mu_i = RT \ln \lambda_i. \tag{A2.7}$$

In mixtures containing more than one component μ_i^0 refers to a properly defined standard state (the value of μ_i for the pure component for instance, at 1 atm, or alternatively at infinite dilution)

$$\mu_i^0 = RT \ln \lambda_i^0 \tag{A2.8}$$

and

$$a_i = \lambda_i / \lambda_i^0 \tag{A2.9}$$

is the relative activity, or activity.

In osmotic equilibrium we have in the simplest case two non-reacting components 1 (the solvent) and 2 (the solute); they are separated by a membrane permeable to 1 but not to 2. For the two phases at equilibrium $T^\alpha = T^\beta$, $P^\alpha \neq P^\beta$ (the osmotic pressure $\Pi = P^\alpha - P^\beta$, with component 2 restricted to phase α) and $\mu_1^\alpha = \mu_1^\beta$; if other components permeable through the membrane were present, then for all those $\mu_i^\alpha = \mu_i^\beta$. To derive the equation for the osmotic pressure we consider the pure solvent phase ($\mu_1^\beta = \mu_1^0$) and the solution phase ($\mu_1^\alpha = \mu_1$) at the same values of T and P. To achieve osmotic equilibrium we raise μ_1 to μ_1^0 by increasing the pressure P on phase α. Mathematically this is expressed by integration of eqn (A2.4), $\overline{V}_1 = (\partial \mu_1 / \partial P)_{T, n_i}$,

$$\Pi \overline{V}_1 = \mu_1^0 - \mu_1 \qquad (A2.10)$$

on the assumption that $\overline{V}_1$ is independent on P in the small pressure range from P to $P + \Pi$ (P is usually atmospheric pressure and Π for dilute solutions is of the order of a few millimetres or centimetres of water). We show in Chapter 2 how the value of μ_1 is related to molecular properties of the solute 2.

Appendix 3. Statistical ensembles and fluctuations

The object of statistical mechanics is to calculate equilibrium properties of macroscopic systems from molecular properties (Hill **1960**). The procedure followed in the ensemble method of Gibbs, which is based on postulates connecting the time-average of a mechanical variable (pressure, energy, volume, number of molecules) with the ensemble average of the same variable. The ensemble average of a given variable is derived by considering a large number of systems, each constructed to be a replica on a thermo-dynamic (macroscopic) level of the actual thermodynamic system whose properties are under investigation. The treatment is then extended to include non-mechanical variables, such as temperature and entropy, by comparing statistical-mechanical and thermodynamic equations. For the purpose of our discussion of the phenomenon of light-scattering (see Chapter 4) we shall be interested not only in the mean values of the mechanical variables, but also in the extent to which they fluctuate around their mean values.

In the micro-canonical ensemble we are concerned with an isolated system with given independent variables V and number of molecules N (N represents a set $N_1, N_2 \ldots$ if the system is multi-component).

The number of states (the degeneracy) associated with a given energy level $U(N, V)$ is $\Omega(N, V, U)$ and the entropy is given by

$$\ln \Omega = \beta TS, \qquad (A3.1)$$

where $\beta = 1/kT$ and k is Boltzmann's constant. The canonical ensemble has fixed volume V, fixed number of molecules, and is immersed in a large heat bath at temperature T. The canonical ensemble partition function $Q(N, V, T)$ is given by

$$Q = \sum \Omega(N, V, U) \exp\{-\beta U(N, V)\}, \qquad (A3.2)$$

where the summation is over all energy levels. The characteristic relation of Q to the thermodynamic functions is

$$\ln Q = \beta(TS - U) = -\beta F. \qquad (A3.3)$$

The grand canonical ensemble has fixed volume V, is in a large heat bath, and is open with respect to molecules in the system. The grand canonical partition function $\Xi(V, \mu, T)$ is given by

$$\Xi = \sum_{U,N} \Omega(N, V, U) \exp\{-U(N, V)\} \exp \beta N \mu$$
$$= \sum_{N} Q(N, V, T) \exp \beta N \mu. \tag{A3.4}$$

The characteristic relation of Ξ to the thermodynamic function is

$$\ln \Xi = \beta(TS - U + N\mu) = \beta PV. \tag{A3.5}$$

The ensemble of interest to the evaluation of light-scattering in a multi-component system is (Stockmayer 1950) a modified grand canonical partition function $Z(T, P, \mu)$ corresponding to a system in statistical equilibrium with surroundings in which constant values of T, P and chemical potentials μ (exclusive of the chemical potential μ_1 of the principal solvent, component 1) are maintained. The system is open to all molecules other than component 1. We have

$$Z = \sum_{U,V,N_i \neq 1} \Omega \exp\{-\beta(U + PV - \sum_{i \neq 1} N_i \mu_i)\}, \tag{A3.6}$$

and the characteristic function is

$$\ln Z = \beta(TS - U - PV + \sum_{i \neq 1} N_i \mu_i) = -\beta N_1 \mu_1. \tag{A3.7}$$

The thermodynamic functions calculated in statistical mechanics are independent of the ensemble used in the calculation. Fluctuations of mechanical variables though, depend on the environment (and therefore the corresponding ensemble) dictated by the nature of the experiment. The probability of a fluctuation from equilibrium values in a thermodynamic system is usually negligible and need not be considered. Yet we are interested in the topic of light-scattering which can be analysed explicitly in terms of fluctuations. If a system is closed and isothermal (the canonical ensemble) there will be fluctuations in P and V but not in N and V (since these are prescribed and fixed). In the grand canonical ensemble T, V, and μ are fixed and fluctuations in the number N of molecules or in P may be considered. We shall show in Chapter 4 how fluctuations in concentrations, in volume, and in a combination of both can be calculated for the ensemble at constant T, P and chemical potentials of the components (excepting μ_1 of the principal solvent).

Appendix 4. The virial expansion in imperfect gases and polymer solutes

It is instructive to compare the pressure of an imperfect gas with the osmotic pressure of macromolecular solutes. The perfect gas law $P = \rho_n kT$, usually valid at high temperatures, may be replaced by the two parameter van der Waals equation

$$(P + a\rho_n^2)(1 - b\rho_n) = \rho_n kT \tag{A4.1}$$

of the imperfect gas; ρ_n is the number of molecules per millilitre ($\rho_n = cN_A/M$), b is 4 times the volume occupied by each molecular sphere (the so-called excluded volume) and ρ_n^2 is the force per unit surface, or pressure, to be added to the outside pressure as a result of the molecular attraction. The van der Waals equation has a rigorous statistical-mechanical foundation (Hill **1960**), a discussion of which is outside the scope of this book. The pressure of an imperfect gas may be expanded in powers of ρ_n,

$$P/\rho_n kT = B_1 + B_2\rho_n + B_3\rho_n^2 + \dots, \tag{A4.2}$$

akin to the osmotic-pressure expansion eqn (1.1); B_1 equals unity and we recover the ideal gas law if all higher virial coefficients $B_2, B_3, \dots$ vanish. By expanding the van der Waals equation (A.1) in powers of ρ_n it is possible to show that

$$B_2 = b - (a/kT), \quad \text{and} \quad B_3 = b^2. \tag{A4.3}$$

At high temperatures, or low attractive forces, $b > a/kT$; upon lowering the temperature a temperature may be reached where $b = a/k\Theta$; Θ is the characteristic, or Boyle, temperature, at which the second virial coefficient vanishes. We may write the virial expansion in the form

$$P/\rho_n kT = 1 + b\left(1 - \frac{\Theta}{T}\right)\rho_n + b^2\rho_n^2 + \dots. \tag{A4.4}$$

We show, in Fig. A4.1 the behaviour: (a) of the real gas, at high temperatures with positive virial coefficients; (b) of the Boyle gas; and (c) of the ideal gas with B_2 and all virial coefficients respectively equal to zero. The case (d) has $T < \Theta$, with negative virial coefficients (with T decreasing further we reach the critical temperature T_c, phase separation and condensation; at the critical temperature $dP/d\rho_n = 0$ and $d^2P/d\rho_n^2 = 0$).

The molecular-weight determination of the gas hinges on the fact that for all gases the limit $P/\rho_n kT$ against n equals unity; thus from the limit we find ρ_n the number of molecules per millilitre. The shapes of the curves in Fig. A4.1 teach us about the excluded volume and forces of interaction between molecules.

In the case of polymer solutions the osmotic pressure Π substitutes the pressure of the gas P, and Θ is known as the characteristic Flory, or theta, temperature (Flory **1953**). The analogy with the gas is complete and the molecular weight may be determined in all cases in which the virial expansion is justified. We have mentioned in Chapter 1 that this is also possible (Hill **1960**) in the case of a charged polyelectrolyte in a solution containing simple salts.

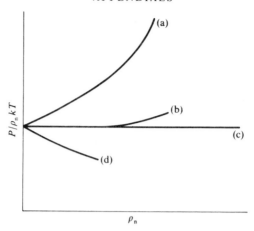

F I G. A4.1. Virial expansion of reduced pressure $P/\rho_n kT$ of dilute gas versus particle density ρ_n; (a) real gas, high temperature, positive virial coefficients; (b) Boyle gas, $A_2 = 0$, higher virial coefficients positive; (c) ideal gas, all virial coefficients vanish; (d) $T_c < T < \Theta$, negative virial coefficients.

Appendix 5. Some aspects of polyelectrolyte theory

In this appendix we shall discuss properties arising from the interaction of the electrical charges residing on biological macromolecules with small mobile counter- and co-ions in solution. By virtue of the high density of fixed charges polynucleotide chains for instance are typical polyelectrolytes over a wide range of pH values. Around neutrality the charge is due to the phosphate groups only, and at low extreme pH values ionization of the purine and pyrimidine bases may provide additional electrical charge. Barely a year after the publication of the Debye–Hückel inter-ionic attraction theory of simple electrolytes, Linderstrøm-Lang (1924) presented the first quantitative interpretation of the influence of electrostatic charge on the properties of globular proteins. For the last 25 years continuous effort has been invested in studying the properties of synthetic coiling poly-electrolytes, and the present status of this field was well summarized in a recent encyclopedia article (Armstrong and Strauss **1969**) two reviews (Crescenzi **1968**; Manning **1972**) and a book (Oosawa **1971**); properties of some biological polyelectrolytes have been discussed in a book edited by Veis (**1970**). The polyelectrolyte properties of polynucleotide chains are particularly pronounced and closely related to the properties of synthetic coiling polyelectrolytes. The well-defined geometry of the stiff DNA double helix, for instance, has led to the often-repeated use of DNA as model substance for the testing of polyelectrolyte theories applicable to stiff coils which are almost rod-like in nature (the literature survey in this Appendix is not complete).

Theories for the polyelectrolyte behaviour of coiling macromolecules have originally been based, with rather limited success, on the concept of either a sphere occupying the domain excluded by the macromolecule and penetrable to small ions, or on coiled chain models. Fuoss, Katchalsky, and Lifson (1951) and independently Alfrey, Berg, and Morawetz (1951) laid the foundation for what was to become the most successful model to date for the study of the properties of polyelectrolyte systems. The cylindrical-rod cell model is based on the assumption that over limited distances along the chain electrical charges are arranged in a linear array with well-defined charge density, a characteristic parameter of the system. Cylindrical symmetry is observed and the distribution of the small ions in the electrostatic field of the macromolecular rod (assumed to be of infinite length) is calculated by suitable application of the Poisson–Boltzmann equation. Exact solutions have been given in the salt-free case (Fuoss *et al.* 1951; Alfrey *et al.* 1951) and the energy and derived quantities have been evaluated (Lifson and Katchalsky 1954). In the presence of added salt Alexandrowicz and Katchalsky (1963) solved the Poisson–Boltzmann equation by an approximation technique; their work has been extensively reviewed Katchalsky *et al.* **1966**; Katchalsky **1971**). Gross and Strauss (**1966**) presented a numerical solution of the Poisson–Boltzmann equation and also utilized the concept of site binding (of ions to the macromolecules) to account for the deviation of certain properties from the expected behaviour. A fair amount of controversy has been generated in the efforts devoted to the understanding of polyelectrolyte behaviour and interest remains unabated (Manning **1972**).

We now present the main results pertaining to interactions between small ions and charged macromolecules in a novel interpretation of the cylindrical-rod model due to Manning (1969*a*). With a few exceptions his results agree with the results previously discussed. The interest arises in that a simple and intuitively attractive picture emerges from Manning's basic assumptions and that other important results may become apparent in further work (Manning **1972**). The validity though of these basic assumptions has not been conclusively established.

To obtain limiting laws for polyelectrolytes akin to the Debye–Hückel limiting law of simple electrolytes it is necessary to refer to the state of infinite dilution at which poly-ions are infinitely far apart from each other and complete dissociation of counter-ions has been achieved. This state is of no practical interest for highly charged polyelectrolytes because no measurements can be undertaken at the very low concentrations required to approximate this state. However, it was assumed that a state of 'infinite dilution' appropriate to polyelectrolyte solutions, over a wide range of poly-ion concentrations is well approximated by a model system in which all polyelectrolyte chains are represented by infinitely long cylinders. This introduces logarithmic potentials which persist to infinity, and adequately describe the behaviour of real solutions at low experimentally accessible concentrations. It can then be postulated that a critical charge density ξ_{crit} exists on the cylinder at which counter-ions associate with ('condense' on) the surface of the cylinder so that the net charge density in dilute solutions is maintained at the critical value. Thus as long as the charge density ξ is below the critical value no counter-ions remain in the domain of the poly-ion at 'infinite' dilution (Oosawa **1971**), but when this value is exceeded a fraction of counter-ions condense such that the value of ξ_{crit} is maintained. The charge density ξ is defined by

$$\xi = e|\beta|/DkT, \qquad (A5.1)$$

where $\beta = e/b$ is the charge per unit length of cylinder (b is the distance between charged groups on the infinitely thin cylinder)—in the present discussion and in view of the fact that dilute solutions only are discussed, the finite radius of the polyelectrolyte backbone is not considered; D is the relative permittivity and ξ_{crit} is equivalent to the Bjerrum length for ion-pair formation in the classical theory of simple electrolyte solutions (Harned and Owen **1958**). For univalent fixed charges, co- and counter-ions, ξ_{crit} is found to be equal to unity. This latter statement is derived in the Manning formulation from an observation by Onsager (as quoted by Manning 1969*a*) that the phase integral for a line charge with point counter-ions diverges at the lower limit if $\xi > \xi_{crit}$. For $\xi < \xi_{crit}$ the Debye–Hückel approximation is believed to apply in the limits of infinite dilution; this remains true even when (by stoichiometry) $\xi > \xi_{crit}$ because by condensation the actual value of ξ is always reduced to its critical value by counter-ion condensation and neutralization of $(1 - \xi^{-1})$ of the poly-ion charge. All interactions between remaining uncondensed small ions and the charged poly-ion (on which some of the counter-ions are condensed) can then be treated in the Debye–Hückel approximation. At infinite dilution the bulk relative permittivity D, rather than some effective value, should be used. For water at 25°C ($D = 78.5$) the critical value $\xi = 1$ corresponds to a charge spacing b of 7·14 Å. For DNA, $b = 1·7$ Å, therefore the condition $\xi > 1$ (ξ is equal to 4·2) applies, and condensation of ions always occurs.

For the case of $\xi < 1$ of a mixed aqueous polyelectrolyte uni–univalent salt solution the potential $\psi(\rho)$ (Manning 1969*a*) at a distance ρ from the line charge (taken along the z-axis) is given by a superposition of screened Coulomb potentials from infinitesimal segments of length dz:

$$\psi(\rho) = \frac{\beta}{D} \int_{-\infty}^{+\infty} \frac{\exp\{-\kappa_{DH}(\rho^2 + z^2)^{\frac{1}{2}}\}}{(\rho^2 + z^2)^{\frac{1}{2}}} \, dz$$
$$= (2\beta/D)K_0(\kappa_{DH}\rho), \qquad (A5.2)$$

where $K_0(\kappa_{DH}\rho)$ is the zeroth-order modified Bessel function of the second kind; κ_{DH} is the Debye–Hückel screening parameter (κ_{DH}^{-1} is the radius of

the ionic atmosphere in the Debye–Hückel ionic interaction theory (see
Harned and Owen **1958**). The function $K_0(\kappa_{DH}\rho)$ tends to the asymptotic
limit $-\ln \kappa_{DH}\rho$ as $\kappa_{DH}\rho \to 0$; therefore when ρ tends to zero the potential
at the position of the line charge due to the mobile ions is $-(2\beta/D)\ln \kappa_{DH}$.
The excess free energy $f^{exc}\,dz$ associated with the segment dz of the line
charge is obtained by a 'charging' process from zero charge ($\beta = 0$) up to
the charge $\beta\,dz$,

$$f^{exc}\,dz = -(\beta^2/D)\ln \kappa_{DH}\,dz. \qquad (A5.3)$$

The total excess free energy F^{exc} of the solution of volume V containing N_p
polyelectrolyte molecules of length L is $F^{exc} = f^{exc}LN_p$, which transforms to

$$F^{exc}/VkT = -\xi C_u \ln \kappa_{DH}, \qquad \xi < 1. \qquad (A5.4)$$

In this calculation the charging process was applied to the fixed ions only
and the contribution of mobile ions was shown to be (Manning and Zimm
1965) of higher order in κ_{DH}, and therefore neglected.

The activity of mobile ions follows by differentiation with respect to

$$\ln \gamma_i = \left\{\frac{\partial(F^{exc}/VkT)}{\partial n_i}\right\}_{T,V,n_{j\neq i}}$$
$$= -\tfrac{1}{2}\xi\lambda C_u/\kappa_{DH}^2,$$
$$i = 1, 2, \quad \xi < 1, \qquad (A5.5)$$

where $\lambda = 4\pi e^2/DkT$. For the three-component system PX$_Z$, XY the screening parameter κ_{DH}^2 equals $\lambda(C_x+C_y)$; mobile ions only are taken into consideration. Eqn (A5.5) can be rewritten as

$$\ln \gamma_\pm = \ln \gamma_i = -\tfrac{1}{2}\xi X(X+2)^{-1},$$
$$i = x, y, \quad \xi < 1, \qquad (A5.6)$$

where $\gamma_\pm$ is the mean activity coefficients of mobile ions, x and y refer to
the counter- and co-ion respectively and $X = C_u/C_3$ is the ratio of polyelectrolyte equivalent to added simple-salt concentration ($C_3 = C_y$,
$C_u + C_3 = C_x$). In salt-free solutions ($X \to \infty$) the activity coefficient $\gamma_{x,p}$ of
the counter-ions equals

$$\ln \gamma_{x,p} = -\tfrac{1}{2}\xi; \quad \xi < 1. \qquad (A5.7)$$

The osmotic coefficient ϕ, which is the ratio of the osmotic pressure to its
ideal value, is defined in terms of the excess part of the osmotic pressure Π^{exc}

$$\Pi^{exc} = kT(\phi-1)(C_x+C_y) = -(\partial F^{exc}/\partial V)_{T,N_p,N_x,N_y},$$
$$(\partial \kappa_{DH}/\partial V)_{N_i} = -\kappa_{DH}/2V, \qquad (A5.8)$$

and differentiation of eqn (A5.4) yields

$$\phi = 1-\tfrac{1}{2}\lambda X(X+2)^{-1}, \quad \xi < 1, \qquad (A5.9)$$

and in salt-free solutions

$$\phi_p = 1 - \tfrac{1}{2}\xi, \quad \xi < 1, \tag{A5.10}$$

in agreement with the result of Lifson and Katchalsky (1954).

The Donnan distribution coefficient

$$\Gamma^c = \lim_{C_u \to 0} (C_3 - C_3')/C_u \tag{A5.11}$$

was shown by Gross and Strauss (**1966**) to be given by

$$\Gamma^c = -\frac{0\cdot 5 + C_3'(\partial \ln \gamma_\pm/\partial C_u)_{C_u \to 0}}{1 + C_3'(\partial \ln \gamma_\pm'/\partial C_3')}$$
$$\approx -0\cdot 5 - C_3'(\partial \ln \gamma_\pm/\partial C_u)_{C_u \to 0}. \tag{A5.12}$$

The approximation improves as C_3' decreases. Differentiation of $\ln \gamma_\pm$ in eqn (A5.6) yields

$$\Gamma^c = \tfrac{1}{2}(\tfrac{1}{2}\xi - 1), \quad \xi < 1, \tag{A5.13}$$

in agreement with the results of Gross and Strauss (**1966**); here Γ^c is due to Donnan exclusion only and therefore approaches $(M_2/M_3) E_3$ as $C_3 \to 0$ (see Section 3.3). Experimentally Γ^c may be identified with $(M_2/M_3)\xi_3$ at very low concentrations and negligible binding of component 3.

The case $\xi > 1$ is of much greater interest, since in polynucleotide and DNA solutions, for instance, this condition almost certainly applies. We must distinguish between 'real' and 'effective' values; ξ refers to the real values as given by eqn (A5.1). However, when the real value of ξ exceeds unity, the effective value will equal unity since condensed counter-ions will neutralize the fraction $(1 - \xi^{-1})$ of the poly-ion charge. Similarly, while the real (stoichiometric) concentration of counter-ions is $(C_u + C_3)$, the effective value for uncondensed counter-ions is $\xi^{-1}C_u + C_3$; the value C_3 is unchanged. As an example we calculate the salt exclusion parameter Γ^c (eqn (A5.11)). Because of the effective equivalent polyelectrolyte concentration $\xi^{-1}C_u$, we have

$$C_3 - C_3' = \xi^{-1}C_u \Gamma^c(1), \tag{A5.14}$$

where $\Gamma^c(1)$ corresponds to a polyelectrolyte concentration with $\xi = 1$. We set $\xi = 1$ in the Debye–Hückel approximation eqn (A5.13) to find $\Gamma^c(1) = \tfrac{1}{4}$. Comparison of eqn (A5.14) and (A5.11) with the value $\Gamma^c(1) = \tfrac{1}{4}$ yields

$$\Gamma^c = (4\xi)^{-1}, \quad \xi > 1, \tag{A5.15}$$

in agreement with the result of Gross and Strauss (**1966**) obtained from the numerical solution of the Poisson–Boltzmann equation.

The other coefficients are obtained by similar considerations which will not be detailed further. Thus it is found that the activity γ_x of counter-ions

$$\gamma_x = (\xi^{-1}X + 1)(X - 1)\exp\{-\tfrac{1}{2}\xi^{-1}X/(\xi^{-1}X + 2)\}, \quad \xi > 1, \tag{A5.16}$$

which reduces in the salt-free case to

$$\gamma_{x,p} = \xi^{-1} e^{-\frac{1}{2}}, \quad \xi > 1. \tag{A5.17}$$

The activity coefficient of the co-ion is given by

$$\gamma_y = \exp\{-\tfrac{1}{2}\xi^{-1}X/(\xi^{-1}X+2)\}, \quad \xi > 1, \tag{A5.18}$$

and the square of the mean activity of mobile ions is given by

$$\gamma_{\pm}^2 = (\xi^{-1}X+1)(X+1)^{-1}\exp(-\xi^{-1}X/\xi^{-1}X+2). \tag{A5.19}$$

The osmotic coefficient ϕ equals

$$\phi = (\tfrac{1}{2}\xi^{-1}X+2)/(X+2), \quad \xi > 1, \tag{A5.20}$$

and, in salt-free solutions,

$$\phi_p = (2\xi)^{-1}, \quad \xi > 1, \tag{A5.21}$$

in agreement with the result of Lifson and Katchalsky (1954).

The notion of condensed and uncondensed counter-ions and the often used concepts of 'bound' and 'free' counter-ions are not freely interchangeable. From the assumption that 'free' counter-ions do not interact with the macro-ions it is concluded that in salt-free solutions the osmotic coefficient ϕ_p should equal the counter-ion activity coefficient $\lambda_{x,p}$ as both are equal to the fraction of 'free' ions. From the limiting laws though for $\xi > 1$ it is found that, in salt-free solutions, the fraction of uncondensed monovalent counter-ions is ξ^{-1}, the osmotic coefficient is $\tfrac{1}{2}\xi^{-1}$ and the counter-ion activity coefficient is $0.61\,\xi^{-1}$. These differences result in the way in which the Debye–Hückel interaction between uncondensed ions and macro-ions affects the various derivatives.

Additional earlier conclusions based on the concept of free ions state that additivity rules hold for colligative properties in mixed polyelectrolyte–simple-salt systems, due to the fact that contributions to the free energy of polyelectrolyte and simple salt are independent of each other and additive. The limiting laws developed by Manning show that the contribution of uncondensed counter-ions originating from the polyelectrolyte and from the added salt cannot be separated. By coincidence the limiting law for the osmotic coefficient coincides with the additivity rule for this quantity, but this does not apply in the case of the activity coefficients.

A number of interesting correlations can be deduced from the above considerations, the best known of which (borne out by experimental results), for all values of ξ, are

$$\Gamma^c = -\tfrac{1}{2}\phi_p \tag{A5.22}$$

and

$$\phi(C_u + 2C_3) = \phi_p C_u + 2C_3, \tag{A5.23}$$

which we have previously used.

Appendix 6. Non-equilibrium thermodynamics

We shall present here a brief discussion of the principles of non-equilibrium thermodynamics, in the context of our discussion of transport phenomena (isothermal diffusion and sedimentation) in Chapter 6. For a more detailed discussion, pertinent references, and proofs of the statements presented in this appendix we refer to the monographs of Fitts (**1962**) and of Katchalsky and Curran (**1965**) on this topic, in which most considerations presented here are elaborated.

In a quasi-equilibrium (or quasi-static) process the external parameters define the state of the system completely and the thermodynamic potentials (see Appendix 2) are functions of state. To extend these considerations to non-equilibrium processes treatments for systems in a state of flow were developed. The function used to distinguish between reversible and irreversible processes is the entropy S, which is a total differential only for quasi-static processes ($dS = dq/T$, where q, as before, is the heat absorbed by the system at the temperature T). In an adiabatic system, enclosed by walls which prevent exchange of both matter and thermal energy between the system and its surroundings, the change in internal energy (for both reversible or irreversible processes) is a total differential, independent of the manner in which the change was brought about. In a reversible adiabatic process the entropy remains constant since $dq = 0$, and therefore $dS = 0$.

An irreversible adiabatic process, on the other hand, is accompanied by an increase in entropy, which can be evaluated if the set of external parameters for the initial and final states are known. To assign entropy values for the intermediate states during the irreversible process we assume that the entropy is a unique function of external and internal parameters respectively, whatever the energy and work content of the system. The same distribution of internal parameters, for a given set of external parameters, can be reached in several ways. The entropy however is determined only by the configuration, the set of local parameters that fully characterize the state of the system at a given moment, no matter by what path, expenditure of work or changes in energy this configuration was achieved. The value of the entropy increase of a real system can thus be compared to the corresponding well-defined entropy increase in a reversible process.

Consider, for example, the concentration distribution in an ultracentrifuge cell at equilibrium, under the influence of an external field (see Chapter 5). The system is characterized by a given configuration (with concentrations increasing from cell meniscus to cell bottom) and energy. If we now remove the external constraints the configuration can be maintained momentarily although the energy is affected. The same configuration can, in principle, be achieved in an irreversible diffusion process, in the absnece of external constraints. We can therefore look upon the external parameters as a device permitting us to achieve the entropy, characteristic of each stage in an irreversible process, by constructing a series of successive equilibrium states, to simulate the entropy increase accompanying the irreversible process. The additional external parameters x_k that have to be applied in order to maintain the non-equilibrium distribution of the internal parameters ξ_k in a state of equilibrium establish a field of forces whose potential energy is

$$- \sum_{k=1}^{n} x_k \xi_k ;$$

it can be shown that the change in entropy in an irreversible process is

$$T\,\mathrm{d}S = \mathrm{d}q - \sum_{k=1}^{n} x_k\,\mathrm{d}\xi_k .$$

For an adiabatic process $\mathrm{d}q = 0$ and

$$T\,\mathrm{d}S = - \sum_{k=1}^{n} x_k\,\mathrm{d}\xi_k . \tag{A6.1}$$

Eqn (A6.1) expresses $\mathrm{d}S$ as a function of the internal and external parameters that make S measurable. The entropy increases in any spontaneous process. The time rate of increase in entropy $\mathrm{d}S/\mathrm{d}t$ as a function of rate of change $\mathrm{d}\xi_k/\mathrm{d}t$ in the internal parameters is given by

$$\frac{\mathrm{d}S}{\mathrm{d}t} = - \sum_{k=1}^{n} \frac{x_k}{T} \frac{\mathrm{d}\xi_k}{\mathrm{d}t}, \tag{A6.2}$$

which can be looked upon as a general representation of entropy production in irreversible processes, by a sum of products of generalized forces x_k/T and internal flows $\mathrm{d}\xi_k/\mathrm{d}t$.

In an isothermal natural process the entropy of the system increases more than can be accounted for by absorption of entropy from the surroundings. We have

$$\mathrm{d}S = \mathrm{d}_e S + \mathrm{d}_i S,$$

where the internal production of entropy $\mathrm{d}_i S$ is positive-definite, as already seen in Appendix 2. It is greater than zero for all irreversible processes and equal to zero for reversible changes. On the other hand, $\mathrm{d}_e S$ may be either positive or negative depending on the entropy exchange with the surroundings. In an adiabatic process $\mathrm{d}_e S = 0$ and at equilibrium no entropy is created and $\mathrm{d}_i S = 0$. These considerations hold not only for the system as a whole but for all parts of the system.

The flows treated in non-equilibrium thermodynamics may be scalar, such as those of chemical reactions (which will not be considered here) or vectorial (such as diffusion, sedimentation, electric current, and others) which have specified directions in space. The flow vector $j_i(x, y, z, t)$ in a continuous system is defined here as the number of grams g_i passing unit area in unit time perpendicular to the area A

$$j_i = \frac{1}{A} \frac{dg_i}{dt}.\tag{A6.3}$$

Alternatively, if the average velocity of the particles of type i is v_i, and their local concentration c_i ($g\,ml^{-1}$), then the local flow of substance i at each point in space is also given by

$$j_i = c_i v_i.\tag{A6.4}$$

For flows and areas of arbitrary mutual orientation we define the differential flux $d\phi_i$ through the area element dA by the scalar product

$$d\phi_i = j_i.dA.$$

For a volume V of arbitrary shape enclosed by an area A,

$$\phi_i = \int_A d\phi_i = \int_A j_i.dA,$$

where the integration is performed over the surface A. The limit of ϕ_i/V for $V \to 0$ is known as the divergence of the flow j_i, $\nabla.j_i$, and assumes well-defined values at all points in space (in Cartesian coordinates the divergence, a scalar quantity, is simply the sum of the partial derivatives of the components of the flow vector with respect to the three coordinates). Positive values of $\nabla.j_i$ indicates net outflow of species i at the given location in space, or a source of material at this point; if $\nabla.j_i < 0$ the point represents a sink for species i, and at points where $\nabla.j_i = 0$ species i is neither accumulated nor removed. According to Gauss the volume integral of $\nabla.j_i$ is related to the surface integral of j_i by

$$\int_V \nabla.j_i dV = \int_A j_i dA.$$

We can now state a number of conservation laws at all points of a system, which are derived from the above consideration. We thus have

$$\partial\rho/\partial t = -\nabla.j_m,\tag{A6.5}$$

$$\partial c_i/\partial t = -\nabla.j_i,\tag{A6.6}$$

$$\partial\rho_e/\partial t = -\nabla.j_e,\tag{A6.7}$$

where the $\partial/\partial t$ indicate local derivatives (at fixed x, y, z) with respect to time, ρ is the density, ρ_e is the energy density and j_m and j_e are the flow of total mass and energy. Non conservative systems can be included by the addition of suitable terms. Thus

$$dc_i/dt = -\nabla.j_i + v_i j_{ch},$$

where $j_{ch} = d\xi/dt$ is the rate of chemical change per unit volume and v_i is the stoichiometric coefficient for the ith component.

In terms of the local entropy density s_v, the entropy per unit volume, the total entropy is

$$S = \int_V s_v \, dV,$$

and the change in total entropy with time is given by

$$\frac{dS}{dt} = \int_V \frac{\partial s_v}{\partial t} \, dV.$$

We may divide this into an entropy flow j_s related to $d_e S$

$$\frac{d_e S}{dt} = -\int_A j_s \, dA = -\int_V \nabla . j_s \, dV,$$

and a positive entropy production term

$$\frac{d_i S}{dt} = \int_V \sigma \, dV.$$

Thus for any local change

$$\partial s_v/\partial t = -\nabla . j_s + \sigma. \tag{A6.8}$$

In the stationary, or steady, state, processes all properties of the system are independent of time. Yet flows continue to occur in these systems and entropy is therefore produced. The time-independence of all properties leads to the vanishing of the partial differentials of ρ, c_i, ρ_e, and s_v with time. Under these conditions $\nabla . j_i$ vanishes for conservative properties and the flow j_i is constant (at equilibrium, on the other hand, all flows vanish as well). For non-conservative steady flow $\partial s_v/\partial t$ must be zero because the external and internal parameters do not change with time; however the divergence of the entropy flow does not vanish,

$$\nabla . j_s = \sigma,$$

and the entropy created at any point must be removed by a flow of entropy at that point. At equilibrium both $\nabla . j_s$ and σ vanish. A steady state cannot be maintained in an adiabatic system since the entropy produced by irreversible processes is not exchanged with the environment; the only time-invariant state achievable in an adiabatic system is that of equilibrium.

Forces which may cause thermodynamic flows may be the affinity of a chemical reaction (a scalar force which is not considered here), differences in chemical potential, hydrostatic pressure, temperature, centrifugal, or electrical fields. All the latter are vectorial forces to which spatial charac-teristics must be assigned. To go from scalar potential fields to vectorial forces we use the gradient operation. Thus for instance, in the case of the chemical potential μ_i' (per gram of component i; $\mu_i' \equiv \mu_i/M_i$) the driving force x_i

$$x_i \equiv -\nabla \mu_i' = -(\partial \mu_i'/\partial n), \tag{A6.9}$$

where the direction n corresponds to the direction of maximum decrease in μ_i' and $d\mu_i'/dn$ is a measure of the local density of equipotential surfaces. In Cartesian coordinates,

$$\nabla \mu_i' = i\frac{\partial \mu_i'}{\partial x} + j\frac{\partial \mu_i'}{\partial y} + k\frac{\partial \mu_i'}{\partial z}.$$

In situations of interest to topics discussed in this book μ_i' usually depends on a single coordinate and, in the ultracentrifuge cell, for instance, the force is simply given by

$$x_i = -(\partial \mu_i'/\partial r).$$

x_i is a force per gram of species i operating in the direction in which the change in chemical potential is greatest.

In a similar fashion the electric force X_{el} per unit charge causing a current is related to the local potential $\psi(r)$ by

$$X_{el} = -\nabla\psi.$$

The over-all 'thermodynamic force' between two points equals $r_u\Delta\mu_i$, the difference in chemical potentials between the two points; likewise the electromotive force E between two points is given by $\Delta\psi$.

In simple diffusion in a binary solution, a single flow j_2 of solute is related to a velocity v_2 by the linear relationship to the driving force for diffusion, $\nabla(-\mu_2')$,

$$j_2 = c_2 v_2 = -\omega_2' c_2 \nabla \mu_2', \tag{A6.10}$$

where ω_2' is the velocity per unit force or mobility of a gram of solute component 2 in the medium; $\omega_2 = 1/f_2'$, and f_2' is the frictional coefficient per gram of component 2. Differentiation of eqn (1.9) for the ideal case ($y = 1$) yields (at constant temperature and pressure)

$$\nabla \mu_2' = (RT/M_2 c_2)\nabla c_2$$

or

$$j_2 = -(RT/M_2)\omega_2'\nabla c_2 = -D_2 \nabla c_2, \tag{A6.11}$$

where D_2 is the diffusion constant ($RT\omega_2'/M_2$ or $RT/M_2 f_2'$ by Einstein's equation) in the above form of Fick's first law for diffusion; non-ideality corrections and diffusion in multi-component systems are discussed in Chapter 6. The phenomenological coefficient l_2 which relates the flow j_2 to the force x_2,

$$j_2 = l_2 x_2 = -l_2 \nabla \mu_2', \tag{A6.12}$$

is equal to $c_2 \omega_2'$ and is therefore a function of concentration; yet l_2 is not a function of the force or of the flow. The translational frictional coefficient per particle $f_2' M_2 / N_A$ for a spherical particle of radius r, in a medium of viscosity η, is determined by Stokes law to be equal to $6\pi r \eta$. Appropriate expressions are available for other types of particles.

The next task is to express the local entropy production σ for a continuous system in which irreversible processes are occurring, in terms of suitable flows and generalized forces. To do this it is assumed that small parts of the system may be considered to be in equilibrium and characterized by well-defined values of T, P, and μ_i. The non-equilibrium thermodynamics which is summarized here is thus concerned with processes which are not far from equilibrium; gradients of the intensive parameters T, P, and μ_i are not excessive, and linear relationships are adequate to describe the behaviour of the system. This is not the place to discuss the fundamental aspects of non-equilibrium thermodynamics, suffice it to say that justification for its use is based on the adequate representation of the experimental results. This restriction limits the usefulness of this discipline, when compared to equilibrium thermodynamics. On the other hand, most processes likely to be encountered in biology are away from equilibrium, and a deeper understanding of non-equilibrium phenomena is essential; a non-linear theoretical approach is the next step. Within the more limited context of this book, it may be stated that transport phenomena, which in multi-component systems are best interpreted by the methods of non-equilibrium thermodynamics, sometimes provide information on biological macromolecules (from the frictional parameters, for instance) which cannot be obtained by way of the stricter formal discipline of equilibrium thermodynamics.

The local entropy production in a continuous system is given by

$$T \frac{\partial s_v}{\partial t} = \frac{\partial q_v}{\partial t} - \sum_{i=1}^{n} \mu_i' \frac{\partial c_i}{\partial t}, \tag{A6.13}$$

where s_v and q_v are the local concentration (per unit volume) of entropy and the heat increment respectively. For a volume element participating in a flow process we write the total differential for any quantity α

$$\frac{d\alpha}{dt} = \frac{\partial \alpha}{\partial t} + v \nabla \alpha, \tag{A6.14}$$

which indicates that the properties of the volume element change not only with time but also with position. Therefore,

$$T \frac{ds_v}{dt} = \frac{dq_v}{dt} - \sum_{i=1}^{n} \mu_1' \frac{dc_i}{dt}. \tag{A6.15}$$

Use of eqns (A6.8) and (A6.6), as well as

$$\partial q_v / \partial t = -\nabla \cdot j_q, \tag{A6.16}$$

for the local heat flow j_q in eqn (A6.15) and some elementary rearrangements yields for the local entropy production

$$\sigma = j_q \nabla \left(\frac{1}{T} \right) + \sum_{i=1}^{n} j_i \nabla \left(-\frac{\mu_i'}{T} \right) + j_{\text{ch}} \frac{A}{T}, \tag{A6.17}$$

where $A = -\sum v_i \mu_i$ is the affinity of the chemical reaction considered here. Eqn (A6.17) shows that σ may be written

$$\sigma = \sum_{i=1}^{n} j_i x_i, \tag{A6.18}$$

in the form of a sum of products of flows j_i with conjugated forces x_i; the force corresponding to the heat flow j_q, for instance, is $\nabla(1/T)$ and to the flow of matter j_i, $\nabla(-\mu_i'/T)$. Although the choice of flows and forces is to some extent arbitrary correct dimensionality must be preserved and the entropy production must be independent of any transformation of flows and forces. Some further algebraic vector manipulations allow σ, or rather T, known as the dissipation function Φ, to be formulated as

$$\Phi = j_s \nabla(-T) + \sum_{i=1}^{n} j_i \nabla(-\mu_i') + j_{\text{ch}} A, \tag{A6.19}$$

where j_s is the entropy flow

$$T j_s = j_q - \sum_{i=1}^{n} \mu_i' j_i \tag{A6.20}$$

and the forces conjugated to the flows assume a slightly different form. The derivations given by Katchalsky and Curran (**1965**) assume that the system is in mechanical equilibrium (thereby excluding viscous flow in a velocity gradient field) and that no external forces act on the system. In the case of electrochemical systems containing electrolytes, eqns (A6.17) and (A6.19) for σ and for Φ can be used unchanged provided that the chemical potential μ_i is substituted by the sum of the chemical, gravitational, and electrostatic potentials

$$\tilde{\mu}_i = \mu_i + M_i \phi + v_i \mathscr{F} \psi$$

defined in Chapter 5 (eqn (5.1)).

We have indicated earlier that in irreversible processes (diffusion in a binary solution was chosen as an example) reasonably close to equilibrium flows are proportional to forces (the flow per unit force is a mobility) or alternatively forces are proportional to flows (the force required to maintain unit flow represents the resistance to flow); heat flow (Fourier's law) or the flow of electricity (Ohm's law) are other examples of straight linear connections. In other instances phenomena are coupled, a typical example being the thermoelectric phenomenon (the Seebeck effect), where a gradient of electric potential is established in a bimetal when a temperature gradient is maintained (the opposite phenomenon is the Peltier effect). In Chapter 6 we are concerned with coupling of flows of various independent components in a multi-component solution. To analyse the behaviour of systems with coupled flows it is necessary to write down the set of phenomenological equations in their most general form

$$j_i = \sum_{k=1}^{n} l_{ik} x_k \qquad (i = 1, 2, 3, \ldots, n).$$ (A6.21)

Here the l_{ii} coefficients, the diagonal elements of the matrix of the phenomenological coefficients, represent the proportionality between the independent flows j_i and their conjugate forces x_i. The coupling, or cross-coefficients l_{ik} represent the (assumed) linear relationship between flows and non-conjugated forces. The related inverse relationship

$$x_i = \sum_{k=1}^{n} r_{ik} j_k \qquad (i = 1, 2, 3, \ldots, n)$$ (A6.22)

can also be set up where the r_{ik} now represent resistances, or frictions, rather than the l_{ik} which are generalized conductances, or mobilities.

We shall not be interested in flows of chemical reactions and will therefore not be concerned with the coupling between quantities of various tensorial orders (scalars with vectors for instance). The most celebrated statement in non-equilibrium thermodynamics is due to Onsager (1931) who could show by statistical arguments that in some cases, and as long as flows and forces are properly chosen in accord with eqn (A6.18), the matrix of phenomenological coefficients is symmetric, that is

$$l_{ik} = l_{ki} \qquad (i \neq k).$$ (A6.23)

The above relationship serves to reduce the number of unknown coefficients when a number of coupled flows and forces are involved, but they also enable the prediction of correlations in a variety of experimental conditions. From the requirement that the entropy production σ be positive it is possible to show that the straight coefficients $l_{ii} \geqslant 0$ and furthermore

$$l_{ii} l_{jj} \geqslant l_{ij}^2.$$ (A6.24)

BIBLIOGRAPHY

(a) Books and general reviews

THESE are indicated in text in bold numerals of year of publication.

ACKERS, G. K. (1973). Studies of protein ligand binding by gel permeation techniques. *Meth. Enzym.* **27** D, 441.

ADAMS, Jr., E. T. (1967). Analysis of self-associating systems by sedimentation–equilibrium experiments, *Fractions*. Beckman Instruments, Palo Alto, California, No. 3, 1.

——(1968). Molecular weights and molecular weight distributions from sedimentation–equilibrium experiments. In *Characterization of macromolecular structure*, p. 84. National Academy of Sciences, Washington, D.C.

—— FUJITA, H. (1963). Sedimentation equilibrium in reacting systems. In *Ultracentrifugal analysis in theory and experiment* (ed. J. W. Williams), p. 119. Academic Press, New York.

ANFINSEN, C. B. (1964). On the possibility of predicting tertiary structure from primary sequence. In *New perspectives in biology* (ed. M. Sela), p. 42. Elsevier, Amsterdam.

ARMSTRONG, R. W. and STRAUSS, U. P. (1969). Polyelectrolytes. In *Encyclopedia of polymer science and technology*, vol. 10, p. 781. Interscience, New York.

BALDWIN, R. L. and VAN HOLDE, K. E. (1960). *Sedimentation of high polymers, Adv. Polymer Sci.* **1**, 451.

BARR, G. (1931). *A monograph of viscometry*. Oxford University Press, New York.

BAUER, W. and VINOGRAD, J. (1974). Circular DNA. In *Basic principles in nucleic acid chemistry* (ed. P. O. P. Ts'o), vol. 2, p. 265. Academic Press, New York.

BEEMAN, W. W., KAESBERG, P., ANDEREGG, J. W., and WEBB, M. B. (1957). Size of particles and lattice defects. *Handb. Phys.* **32**, 321.

BENEDEK, G. B. (1969). *Optical mixing spectroscopy, with applications to problems in physics, chemistry, biology and engineering*. In 'Polarisation, matiere et rayonnement', p. 49. Presses Universitaires de France, Paris.

BERNARDI, G. (1973). Chromatography of proteins on hydroxyapatite. *Meth. Enzy.* **27** Pt D, 471.

BERRY, G. C. and CASASSA, C. R. (1970). Thermodynamic and hydrodynamic behavior of dilute polymer solutions, *Macromol. Revs* **4**, 1.

BLOOMFIELD, V. A. (1968). Hydrodynamic studies of structure of biological macromolecules. *Science, N.Y.* **161**, 1212.

BONDI, A. (1956). Theories of viscosity. In *Rheology* (ed. F. R. Eirich), vol. 1, p. 321. Academic Press, New York.

CANN, J. R. and GOAD, W. B. (1973). Measurement of protein interactions mediated by small molecules using sedimentation velocity. *Meth. Enzym.* **27**D, 296.

CASASSA, E. F. and EISENBERG, H. (1964). Thermodynamic analysis of multicomponent systems. *Adv. Protein Chem.* **19**, 287.

CERF, R. (1959). La dynamique des solutions de macromolecules dans un champ de vitesses. *Adv. Polymer Sci.* **1**, 382.

CHU, B. (1974). Laser light scattering, *Chemical and biochemical applications*, vol. 1. Academic Press, New York.

COHEN, E. J. and EDSALL, J. T. (1943). *Proteins, amino acids and peptides*. Reinhold Publishing Corporation, New York.

COLEMAN, B. D., MARKOVITZ, H., and NOLL, W. (1966). *Viscometric flows of non-Newtonian fluids.* Springer-Verlag, New York.

CONWAY, B. E. and DOBRY-DUCLAUX, A. (1960). Viscosity of suspensions of electrically charged particles and solutions of polymeric electrolytes. In *Rheology* (ed. F. R. Eirich), vol. 3, p. 83. Academic Press, New York.

CRANK, J. and PARK, G. S. (eds) (1968). *Diffusion in polymers,* Academic Press, New York.

CREETH, J. M. and PAIN, R. H. (1967). The determination of molecular weights of biological macromolecules by ultracentrifuge methods, *Progr. Biophys. mol. Biol.* **17,** 217.

CRESCENZI, V. (1968). Some recent studies of polyelectrolyte solutions, *Adv. Polymer Sci.* **5,** 358.

CUMMINS, H. Z. (1974). Applications of light beating spectroscopy to biology. In *Photon correlation and light beating spectroscopy* (eds H. Z. Cummins and E. R. Pike), p. 285. Plenum Press, New York.

—— and PIKE, E. R. (eds) (1974). *Photon correlation and light beating spectroscopy.* Plenum Press. New York.

—— SWINNEY, H. L. (1970). Light beating spectroscopy. *Progr. Opt.* **8,** 133.

DAVIDSON, N. (1962). *Statistical mechanics.* McGraw-Hill, New York.

DINSDALE, A. and MOORE, F. (1962). *Viscosity and its measurement.* Chapman and Hall, London.

DOTY, P. and EDSALL, J. T. (1951). Light scattering in protein solutions, *Adv. Protein Chem.* **6,** 35.

DUNLOP, P. J., STEEL, B. J., and LANE, J. E. (1972). Experimental methods for studying diffusion in liquids, gases, and solids. In *Physical methods of chemistry, Part IV* (eds A. Weissberger and B. W. Rossiter), p. 205. Wiley–Interscience, New York.

DURST, R. A. (ed.) (1969). *Symposium on ion selective electrodes.* U.S. Government Printing Office. Washington.

EDELSTEIN, S. J. and GIBSON, Q. H. (1971). Weights and rates in hemoglobin. Absence of cooperativity in the deoxy-dimer. In *Probes of structure and function of macromolecules and membranes,* vol. 2 (eds B. Chance, T. Yonetani, and A. S. Mildvan), p. 417. Academic Press, New York.

—— SCHACHMAN, H. K. (1973). Measurement of partial specific volume by sedimentation equilibrium in H_2O–D_2O solutions. *Meth. Enzym.* **27D,** 83.

EDSALL, J. T. (1943). Rotary Brownian movement. The shape of protein molecules as determined from viscosity and double refraction of flow. In *Proteins, Amino Acids and Peptides* (ed. E. J. Cohn and J. T. Edsall), p. 506. Reinhold, New York.

—— WYMAN, J. (1958). *Biophysical Chemistry,* Vol. 1, Academic Press, New York.

EIGEN, M. and DEMAEYER, L. (1973). Theoretical basis of relaxation spectrometry. In *Techniques of chemistry,* vol. 6, part 2 (eds A. Weissberger and G. Hammes), p. 63. Wiley–Interscience, New York.

EIRICH, F. E. (ed.) (1956). *Rheology,* vol. 1. Academic Press, New York.

EISENBERG, H. (1971). Light scattering and some aspects of small angle X-ray scattering. In *Procedures in nucleic acid research,* vol. 2 (eds G. L. Cantoni and D. R. Davies), p. 137. Harper and Row, New York.

—— (1974). Hydrodynamic and thermodynamic studies. In *Basic principles in nucleic acid chemistry,* vol. 2 (ed. P. O. P. Ts'o), p. 171. Academic Press, New York.

—— (1974a). Light scattering intensity studies in multicomponent solutions of biological macromolecules. In *Photon Correlation and light beating spectroscopy* (eds H. Z. Cummins and E. R. Pike), p. 551. Plenum Press. New York.

—— JOSEPHS, R. and REISLER, E. (1976). Glutamate dehydrogenase, *Adv. Protein Chem.*

30 (in press).

ELIAS, H. G. (1972). The study of association and aggregation via light scattering. In *Light scattering from polymer solutions* (ed. M. B. Huglin), p. 397. Academic Press, New York.

FEYNMAN, R. P., LEIGHTON, R. B., and SANDS, M. (1963). *The Feynman lectures on physics*, Addison–Wesley, Reading, Massachusetts.

FINCH, J. T. and HOLMES, K. C. (1967). Structural studies of viruses. In *Methods in virology*, vol. 3 (eds K. Marmorosch and H. Koprowski), p. 351. Academic Press, New York.

FINDLAY, A. (1953). *Introduction to physical chemistry* (*4rd edn*). Longmans, Green and Company, London.

FISCHER, L. (1969). An introduction to gel chromatography. In *Laboratory techniques in biochemistry and molecular biology* (eds T. S. Work and E. Work), vol. 6, p. 151. North-Holland, Amsterdam.

FITTS, D. D. (1962). *Nonequilibrium thermodynamics*, McGraw-Hill, New York.

FLEURY, P. A. and BOON, J. P. (1973). Laser light scattering in fluid systems. *Adv. chem. Phys.* **24**, 1.

FLORY, P. J. (1953). *Principles of polymer chemistry*. Cornell University Press, Ithaca, New York.

—— (1969). *Statistical mechanics of chain molecules*. Interscience Publishers, New York.

FORD, Jr. N. C. (1972). Biochemical applications of laser Rayleigh scattering, *Chemica Scripta* **2**, 193.

FRISCH, H. L. and SIMHA, R. (1956). The viscosity of colloidal suspensions and macro-molecular solutions. In *Rheology*, vol. 1 (ed. F. R. Eirich), p. 525. Academic Press, New York.

FUJITA, H. (1962). *Mathematical theory of sedimentation analysis*, Academic Press, New York.

—— (1975). *Foundations of ultracentrifugal analysis*. Wiley, New York.

GEDDES, A. L. and PONTIUS, R. B. (1960). Determination of diffusivity. In *Physical methods of organic chemistry*, part II (ed. A. Weissberger), p. 895. Interscience, New York.

GILBERT, L. M. and GILBERT, G. A. (1973). Sedimentation velocity measurements protein association. *Meth. Enzym.* **27D**, 273.

GORDON, A. H. (1969). Electrophoresis of proteins in polyacrylamide and starch gels. In *Laboratory techniques in biochemistry and molecular biology*, vol. 1 (eds T. S. Work and E. Work), p. 1. North-Holland Publishing Company, Amsterdam.

GROSS, L. M. and STRAUSS, U. P. (1966). Interactions of polyelectrolytes with simple electrolytes. I. Theory of electrostatic potential and Donnan equilibrium for a cylindrical rod model: the effect of site binding. In *Chemical physics of ionic solutions* (eds B. E. Conway and R. G. Barradas), p. 361. Wiley, New York.

GUGGENHEIM, E. A. (1936). In *A commentary on the scientific writings of J. W. Gibbs* (eds F. G. Donnan and A. Haas), Yale University Press, New Haven.

—— (1967). *Thermodynamics* (5th edn). North-Holland, Amsterdam.

GUIDOTTI, G. (1973). Osmotic pressure. *Meth. Enzym.* **27D**, 256.

GUINIER, A. and FOURNET, G. (1955). *Small angle scattering of X-rays*. Wiley, New York.

GUTH, E. and MARK, H. (1933). Die Viskosität von Lösungen, besonders von Lösungen Hochmolekularer Stoffe. *Ergebn. exakt. Naturw.* **12**, 115.

HAASE, R. (1963). Diffusion and sedimentation in multicomponent systems. In *Ultracentrifugal analysis* (ed. J. W. Williams), p. 13. Academic Press, New York.

HARNED, H. S. and OWEN, B. B. (1958). *The physical chemistry of electrolyte solutions*. Reinhold, New York.

HARRINGTON, R. E. (1967). Flow birefringence. In *Encyclopedia of polymer science and technology*, vol. 7, p. 100. Interscience, New York.

HARRINGTON, W. F. and KEGELES, G. (1973). Pressure effects in ultracentrifugation of interacting systems. *Meth. Enzym.* **27D**, 306.

HEARST, J. E. and SCHMID, C. W. (1973). Density gradient sedimentation equilibrium. *Meth. Enzym.* **27D**, 111.

HERMANS, J. J. (1953). Dilute solutions of flexible chain molecules. In *Flow properties of disperse systems*, p. 199. North-Holland, Amsterdam.

—— ENDE, H. A. (1964). Density-gradient centrifugation. In *Newer methods of polymer characterization* (ed. Bacon Ke), p. 525. Interscience, New York.

HILL, T. L. (1960). *An introduction to statistical thermodynamics*, Addison–Wesley, Reading, Massachusetts.

IFFT, J. B. (1973). Proteins in density gradients at sedimentation equilibrium. *Meth. Enzym.* **27D**, 120.

JOST, W. (1960). *Diffusion in solids, liquids and gases*, Academic Press, New York.

KATCHALSKY, A. (1971). Polyelectrolytes. *Pure appl. Chem.* **26**, 327.

——, ALEXANDROWICZ, Z., and KEDEM, O. (1966). Polyelectrolytes solutions, *Chemical Physics of Ionic Solutions* (eds B. E. Conway and R. G. Barradas), p. 295. Wiley, New York.

——, CURRAN, P. F. (1965). *Nonequilibrium thermodynamics in biophysics*. Harvard University Press, Cambridge, Massachusetts.

KERKER, M. (1969). *The scattering of light and other electromagnetic radiation*. Academic Press, New York.

KORNBERG, A. (1974). *DNA synthesis*, W. H. Freeman, New York.

KRATKY, O., LEOPOLD, H., and STABINGER, H. (1973). The determination of the partial volume of proteins by the mechanical oscillator technique. *Meth. Enzym.* **27D**, 98.

——, PILZ, I. (1972). Recent advances and application of diffuse X-ray small-angle scattering on biopolymers in dilute solutions. *Q. Rev. Biophys.* **5**, 481.

KUNTZ, Jr. I. D. and KAUZMANN, W. (1974). Hydration of proteins and polypeptides, *Adv. Protein Chem.* **28**, 239.

KURATA, M. and STOCKMAYER, W. H. (1963). Intrinsic viscosities and unperturbed dimensions of long chain molecules. *Adv. Polymer Sci.* **3**, 196.

LANDAU, L. D. and LIFSHITZ, E. M. (1959). *Fluid mechanics*. Pergamon Press, London.

LEWIS, G. N. and RANDALL, M. H. (1961). *Thermodynamics* (2nd edn, revised by K. S. Pitzer and L. Brewer). McGraw-Hill, New York.

MANNING, G. S. (1972). Polyelectrolytes, *Ann. Rev. phys. Chem.* **23**, 117.

MARK, H. (1938). *Der feste Körper*. Hirzel, Leipzig.

McINTYRE, D. and GORNICK, F. (eds) (1964). *Light scattering from dilute polymer solutions*. Gordon and Breach, New York.

MIJNLIEFF, P. F. (1963). Effects of charge on the sedimentation, the diffusion and the sedimentation equilibrium of colloidal electrolytes. In *Ultracentrifugal analysis* (ed. J. W. Williams), p. 81. Academic Press, New York.

MORAWETZ, H. (1975). *Macromolecules in solution* (2nd revised edn). Interscience Publishers.

OKA, S. (1960). The principles of rheometry. In *Rheology*, vol. 3 (ed. F. R. Eirich), Academic Press, New York.

OLIVER, C. J., PIKE, E. R., and VAUGHAN, J. M. (1973). Non-critical Rayleigh scattering from pure liquids. In *Coherence and quantum optics* (eds L. Mandel and E. Wolf), p. 457. Plenum Press, New York.

OOSAWA, F. (1971). *Polyelectrolytes*. Dekker, New York.

OVERBEEK, J. TH. G., VRIJ, A., and HUISMAN, H. F. (1963). Light scattering by electrolyte solutions containing charged colloidal particles. In *Electromagnetic scattering* (ed. M. Kerker), p. 321. Pergamon Press, Oxford.

PECORA, R. (1972). Quasielastic light scattering from macromolecules. *Ann. Rev. Biophys. Bioeng.* **1**, 257.

PESSEN, H., KUMOSINSKI, T. F., and TIMASHEFF, S. N. (1973). Small angle X-ray scattering. *Meth. Enzym.* **27D**, 151.

PETERLIN, A. (1956). Streaming and stress birefringence. In *Rheology*, vol. 1 (ed. F. R. Eirich), p. 615. Academic Press, New York.

PETICOLAS, W. L. (1972). Inelastic laser light scattering from biological and synthetic polymers. *Adv. Polymer Sci.* **9**, 286.

PHILIPPOFF, W. (1942). *Viskosität der Kolloide*. Theodor Steinkopff, Dresden; reprinted by J. W. Edwards, Ann Arbor (1944).

PITTZ, E. P., LEE, J. C., BABLOUZIAN, B., TOWNEND, R., and TIMASHEFF, S. N. (1973). Light scattering and differential refractometry. *Meth. Enzym.* **27D**, 209.

PROCK, A. and McCONKEY, G. (1962). *Topics in chemical physics*. Elsevier, Amsterdam.

RECHNITZ, G. A. (1975). Membrane electrode probes for biological systems. *Science N.Y.* **190**, 234.

REINER, M. (1960a). *Deformation, strain, and flow*. H. K. Lewis and Company, London.

—— (1960b). *Lectures on theoretical rheology*. Interscience, New York.

RISEMAN, J. and KIRKWOOD, J. G. (1969). The statistical mechanical theory of irreversible processes in solution of macromolecules. In *Rheology*, vol. 1 (ed. F. R. Eirich), p. 495. Academic Press, New York.

ROBINSON, R. A. and STOKES, R. H. (1959). *Electrolyte solutions*. Butterworths, London.

SCATCHARD, G. (1963). Basic equilibrium theory. In *Ultracentrifugal analysis* (ed. J. W. Williams), p. 105. Academic Press, New York.

—— (1966a). Water; a Review. *Fedn. Proc. Fedn. Am. Socs. exp. Biol.* **25**, 954.

—— (1966b). The osmotic pressure, light scattering and ultracentrifuge equilibrium of polyelectrolyte solutions. In *Chemical physics of ionic solutions* (eds B. E. Conway and R. G. Barradas), p. 347. Wiley, New York.

SCHACHMAN, H. K. (1959). *Ultracentrifugation in biochemistry*. Academic Press, New York.

——, EDELSTEIN, S. J. (1973). Ultracentrifuge studies with absorption optics and a split beam photoelectric scanner. *Meth. Enzym.* **27D**, 3.

SCHMATZ, W., SPRINGER, T., SCHELTEN, J., and IBEL, K. (1974). Neutron small-angle scattering, experimental techniques and applications. *J. appl. Cryst.* **7**, 96.

SERRIN, J. (1959). Mathematical principles of classical fluid mechanics. *Handb. Phys.* **8**, 125.

STUHRMANN, H. B. (1974). Neutron small-angle scattering of biological macromolecules in solution. *J. appl. Cryst.* **7**, 173.

SUND, H. and WEBER, K. (1966). Die Quartärstruktur der Proteine, *Angew. Chem.* **78**, 217; *Angew. Chem. int. edn*, **5**, 231.

SVEDBERG, T. PEDERSEN, K. O. (1940). *The ultracentrifuge*. Oxford University Press, London.

SVENSSON, H. and THOMPSON, T. E. (1961).Translational diffusion methods in protein chemistry, *A laboratory manual of analytical methods of protein chemistry* (eds P. Alexander and R. J. Block), vol. 3, p. 57. Pergamon Press, London.

SZYBALSKI, W. and SZYBALSKI, E. H. (1971). Equilibrium density gradient centrifugation. In *Procedures in nucleic acid research*, vol. 2 (eds G. L. Cantoni and D. R. Davies), p. 311. Harper and Row, New York.

TANFORD, C. (1961). *Physical chemistry of macromolecules*. Wiley, New York.

TELLER, D. C. (1973). Characterization of proteins by sedimentation equilibrium in the analytical ultracentrifuge. *Meth. Enzym.* **27D**, 346.

TIMASHEFF, S. N. (1963). The application of light scattering and small-angle X-ray scattering to interacting biological systems. In *Electromagnetic scattering* (ed. M. Kerker), p. 337. Pergamon Press, Oxford.

—— (1970). Protein–solvent interactions and protein conformation, *Accounts chem. Res.* **3**, 62.

——, TOWNEND, R. (1970). Light scattering. In *Physical principles and techniques of protein chemistry*. Part B (ed. S. J. Leach), p. 147. Academic Press, New York.

TOMBS, M. P. and PEACOCKE, A. R. (1974). *The osmotic pressure of biological macro-molecules*, Clarendon Press, Oxford.

UHLENHOPP, E. L. and ZIMM, B. H. (1973). Rotating cylinder viscometers. *Meth. Enzym.* **27D**, 483.

UMSTÄTTER, H. (1952). *Einführung in die Viskometrie und Rheometrie*. Springer Verlag, Berlin.

VAN HOLDE, K. E. (1971). *Physical biochemistry*. Prentice–Hall, Englewood Cliffs, New Jersey.

VAN OENE, H. (1968). Measurement of the viscosity of dilute polymer solutions. In *Characterization of macromolecular structure*, p. 353. Publication 1573, National Academy of Sciences, Washington, D.C.

VEIS, A. (ed.) (1970). *Biological polyelectrolytes*. Dekker, New York.

VINOGRAD, J. (1963). Sedimentation equilibrium in a buoyant density gradient. *Meth. Enzym.* **6**, 854.

——, HEARST, J. E. (1962). Equilibrium sedimentation of macromolecules and viruses in a density gradient. *Prog. Chem. org. nat. Products* **20**, 372.

WANG, J. C. (1971). Use of intercalating dyes in the study of superhelical DNAs. In *Procedures in nucleic acid research*, vol. 2 (eds G. L. Cantoni and D. R. Davies), p. 407. Harper and Row, New York.

WATSON, J. D. (1970). *Molecular biology of the gene* (2nd edn)' W. A. Benjamin, New York.

WILLIAMS, J. W. (ed.) (1963). *Ultracentrifugal analysis in theory and experiment*. Academic Press, New York.

——, VAN HOLDE, K. E., BALDWIN, R. L., and FUJITA, H. (1958). The theory of sedimentation analysis. *Chem. Rev.* **58**, 715.

YANG, J. T. (1961). The viscosity of macromolecules in relation to molecular conformation. *Adv. Protein Chem.* **16**, 323.

YEH, Y. and KEELER, R. N. (1969). A new probe for reaction kinetics—the spectrum of scattered light, *Q. Rev. Biophys.* **2**, 315.

YPHANTIS, D. A. (ed.) (1969). *Advances in ultracentrifugal analysis. Ann. N.Y. Acad. Sci.* **164**, 1.

ZIMM, B. H. (1960). The normal coordinate method for polymer chains in dilute solution. In *Rheology*, vol. 3 (ed. F. R. Eirich), p. 1. Academic Press, New York.

—— (1971). Measurement of viscosity of nucleic acid solutions. In *Procedures in nucleic acid research*, vol. 2 (eds G. L. Cantoni and D. R. Davies), p. 245. Harper and Row, New York.

(b) **Specific journal references**

ADAMS, Jr., E. T. and LEWIS, M. S. (1968). Sedimentation equilibrium in reacting systems. VI. Some applications to indefinite self-associations. Studies with β-lactoglobulin A. *Biochemistry* **7**, 1044.

ALEXANDROWICZ, Z. (1959). The correlation between activities of polyelectrolytes, measured by the light-scattering and osmotic methods. *J. Polymer Sci.* **40**, 91.

—— (1960). Results of osmotic and of Donnan equilibria measurements in poly-methacrylic acid–sodium bromide solutions. Part II. *J. Polymer Sci.* **43**, 337.

——, DANIEL, E. (1963). Sedimentation and diffusion of polyelectrolytes. Part I. Theoretical description. *Biopolymers* **1**, 447.

—— —— (1968). On the limiting sedimentation coefficients of polyelectrolytes. *Biopolymers* **6**, 1500.

——, KATCHALSKY, A. (1963). Colligative properties of polyelectrolyte solutions in excess of salt, *J. Polymer Sci.* **A-1**, 3231.

ALFREY, Jr., T., BERG, P. W., and MORAWETZ, H. (1951). The counter-ion distribution in solutions of rod-shaped polyelectrolytes. *J. Polymer Sci.* **7**, 543.

ARCHIBALD, W. J. (1947). A demonstration of some new methods of determining molecular weights from the data of the ultracentrifuge. *J. phys. Colloid Chem.* **51**, 1204.

ARMSTRONG, J. M. and McKENZIE, H. A. (1967). A method for modification of carboxyl groups in proteins: its application to the association of bovine β-lactoglobulin A. *Biochim. biophys. Acta.* **147**, 93.

AUER, H. E. and ALEXANDROWICZ, Z. (1969). Sedimentation, diffusion, and osmotic pressure of sodium DNA in salt-free solution. *Biopolymers* **8**, 1.

BALDWIN, R. L. (1958). Molecular weights from studies of sedimentation and diffusion in three-component systems. *J. Am. chem. Soc.* **80**, 496.

—— (1959). Equilibrium sedimentation in a density gradient of materials having a continuous distribution of effective densities. *Proc. natn. Acad. Sci. U.S.A.* **45**, 939.

——, BARRAND, P., FRITSCH, A., GOLDTHWAIT, D. A., and JACOB, F. (1966). Cohesive sites on the deoxyribonucleic acids from several temperate coliphages, *J. molec. Biol.* **17**, 343.

BAUER, W. and VINOGRAD, J. (1968). The interaction of closed circular DNA with intercalative dyes. I. The superhelix density of SV40 DNA in the presence and absence of dye. *J. molec. Biol.* **33**, 141.

—— —— (1969). A thermodynamic theory for interacting systems at equilibrium in a buoyant density gradient: the reaction between a small molecular species and a buoyant macromolecule. *Ann. N.Y. Acad. Sci.* **164**, 192.

—— —— (1970*a*). Interaction of closed circular DNA with intercalative dyes. II. The free energy of superhelix formation in SV40 DNA, *J. molec. Biol.* **47**, 419.

—— —— (1970*b*). The interaction of closed circular DNA with intercalative dyes. III. Dependence of the buoyant density upon superhelix density and base composition, *J. molec. Biol.* **54**, 281.

BERNE, B. J. and GINIGER, R. (1973). Electrophoretic light scattering as a probe of reaction kinetics. *Biopolymers* **12**, 1161.

BIANCHI, V. and PETERLIN, A. (1968). The upturn effect in the non-Newtonian intrinsic viscosity of polymer solutions—IV. *Eur. Polym. J.* **4**, 515.

BINGHAM, E. C. and JACKSON, R. J. (1918). *Bull. Bur. Stand., Wash.* **14**, 59.

BLAKE, C. C. F., KOENIG, D. F., MAIR, G. A., NORTH, A. C. T., PHILLIPS, D. C., and SARMA, V. R. (1965). Structure of hen egg-white lyzozyme: a three-dimensional Fourier synthesis at 2 A resolution. *Nature, Lond.* **206**, 757.

BLUM, J. J. and MORALES, M. F. (1952). Light scattering of multicomponent macro-molecular systems, *J. chem. Phys.* **20**, 1822.

BRAUN, I. (1951). Exact formulas for plate and cone viscometer. *Bull. Res. Coun. Israel* **1**, 126.

BRINKMAN, H. C. and HERMANS, J. J. (1949). The effect of non-homogeneity of molecular weight on the scattering of light by high polymer solutions. *J. chem. Phys.* **17**, 574.

BUCHDAHL, R., ENDE, H. A., and PEEBLES, L. H. (1961). Detection of structural differences in polymers in a density gradient established by ultracentrifugation, *J. phys. Chem.* **65**, 1468.

BULL, H. E. and BREESE, K. (1970). Water and solute binding by proteins. I. Electrolytes. II. Denaturants. *Archs. Biochem. Biophys.* **137**, 299; ibid. **139**, 93.

BURKE, M. and HARRINGTON, W. F. (1971). Geometry of the myosin dimer. *Nature, Lond.* **233**, 140.

———— (1972). Geometry of the myosin dimer in high-salt media. II. Hydrodynamic studies on macromolecules of myosin and its rod segments. *Biochemistry* **11**, 1456.

CAMERINI-OTERO, R. D., PUSEY, P. N., KOPPEL, D. E., SCHAEFER, D. E., and FRANKLIN, R. M. (1974). Intensity fluctuation spectroscopy of laser light scattered by solutions of spherical viruses, R17, Q Beta, BSV, PM2 and T7. Diffusion coefficients, molecular weight, solvation and particle dimension. *Biochemistry* **13**, 960.

CASASSA, E. F. (1956). The conversion of fibrinogen to fibrin. XVIII. Light scattering studies of the effect of hexamethylene glycol on thermodynamic interactions in fibrinogen solutions. *J. phys. Chem.* **60**, 926.

—— (1960). On the determination of thermodynamic interactions in solutions of mixtures of two polymer fractions. *Polymer* **1**, 169.

—— (1962). Effect of heterogeneity in molecular weight on the second virial coefficient of polymers in good solvents. *Polymer* **3**, 625.

——, EISENBERG, H. (1960). On the definition of components in solutions containing charged macromolecular species, *J. phys. Chem.* **64**, 753.

———— (1961). Partial specific volumes and refractive index increments in multi-component systems. *J. phys. Chem.* **65**, 427.

CHAPMAN, JR., R. E., KLOTZ, L. C., THOMPSON, D. S., and ZIMM, B. H. (1969). An instrument for measuring retardation times of deoxyribonucleic acid solutions. *Macromolecules* **2**, 637.

CHUN, P. W. and KIM, S. J. (1969). Determination of the equilibrium constants of associating protein systems. IV. The application of the weight average partition coefficient to analysis of BM_1 nonideality term (as applied to bovine liver L-glutamate dehydrogenase). *Biochemistry* **8**, 1633.

CLAESSON, S. and LOHMANDER, V. (1961). Non-Newtonian flow of macromolecular solutions studied by capillary viscometry with a millionfold change in the velocity gradient, *Makromolek Chem.* **44-6**, 461.

COHEN, G. and EISENBERG, H. (1968). Deoxyribonucleate solutions: sedimentation in a density gradient, partial specific volumes, density and refractive index increments, and preferential interactions. *Biopolymers* **6**, 1077.

COLEMAN, B. D. and NOLL, W. (1959). On certain steady flows of general fluids. *Archs. ration. Mech. Analysis* **3**, 289.

———— (1961). Recent results in the continuum theory of viscoelastic fluids, *Ann. N.Y. Acad. Sci.* **89**, 672.

COREY, R. B. and PAULING, L. (1953). Fundamental dimensions of polypeptide chains, *Proc. R. Soc.* **B141**, 10.

CORIELL, S. R. and JACKSON, J. L. (1963). Potential and effective diffusion constant in a polyelectrolyte solution, *J. chem. Phys.* **39**, 2418.

COSTELLO, R. C. and BALDWIN, R. L. (1972). The net hydration of phage lambda. *Biopolymers* **11**, 2147.

COTTON, J. P., DECKER, D., BENOIT, H., FARNOUX, B., HIGGINS, J., JANNINK, G., OBER, R., PICOT, C., and DES CLOIZEAUX, J. (1974). Conformation of polymer chains in the bulk. *Macromolecules* **7**, 863.

CUMMINS, H. Z., CARLSON, F. D., HERBERT, T. J., and WOODS, G. (1969). Translational and rotational diffusion constants of tobacco mosaic virus from Rayleigh line widths. *Biophys. J.* **9**, 518.

DANIEL, E. (1969). Equilibrium sedimentation of a polyelectrolyte in a density gradient of a low-molecular weight electrolyte. I. DNA in CsCl. *Biopolymers* **7**, 359.

——, ALEXANDROWICZ, Z. (1963). Sedimentation and diffusion of polyelectrolytes. Part II. Experimental studies with poly-L-lysine hydrohalides. *Biopolymers* **1**, 473.

DEBYE, P. (1915). Zerstreuung von Röntgenstrahlen. *Annln Physik* [4] **46**, 809.

—— (1944). Light scattering in solutions. *J. appl. Phys.* **15**, 338.

—— (1947). Molecular weight determination by light scattering, *J. phys. Colloid Chem.* **51**, 18.

——, HÜCKEL, E. (1923). Zur Theorie der Elektrolyte. I. Gefrierpunktserniedrigung und verwandte Erscheinungen. *Phys. Z.* **24**, 185.

DEGROOT, S. R., MAZUR, P., and OVERBEEK, J. TH. G. (1952). Nonequilibrium thermodynamics of the sedimentation potential and electrophoresis. *J. chem. Phys.* **20**, 1825.

DONNAN, F. G. (1911). Theorie der Membrangleichgewichte und Membranpotentiale bei Vorhandensein von nicht dialysierenden Elektrolyten. *Z. Elektrochem.* **17**, 572.

DOTY, P. and STEINER, R. F. (1952). Macro-ions. I. Light scattering theory and experiments with bovine serum albumin. *J. chem. Phys.* **20**, 85.

DOUTHART, R. J. and BLOOMFIELD, V. A., Rotational frictional coefficients of macroscopic models of T2 bacteriophage. *Biochemistry* **7**, 3912.

DUNLOP, P. J. (1957a). A study of interacting flows in diffusion of the system raffinose–KCl–H_2O at 25 °C. *J. phys. Chem.* **61**, 994.

—— (1957b). Interacting flows in diffusion of the system raffinose–urea–water. *J. phys. Chem.* **61**, 1619.

——, GOSTING, L. J. (1955). Interacting flows in liquid diffusion: expressions for the solute concentration curves in free diffusion, and their use in interpreting Gouy diffusiometer data for aqueous three-component systems, *J. Am. chem. Soc.* **77**, 5238.

——, GOSTING, L. J. (1959). Use of diffusion and thermodynamic data to test the Onsager reciprocal relation for isothermal diffusion in the system NaCl–KCl–H_2O at 25 °C. *J. phys. Chem.* **63**, 86.

DUPONT, Y., GABRIEL, A., CHABRE, M., GULIK-KRZYWICKI, T., and SCHECHTER, E. (1972). Use of a new detector for X-ray diffraction and kinetics of the ordering of lipids in *E. coli* membranes and model systems. *Nature, Lond.* **238**, 331.

EDELSTEIN, S. J. and SCHACHMAN, H. K. (1967). The simultaneous determination of partial specific volumes and molecular weights with microgram quantities. *J. biol. Chem.* **242**, 306.

EINSTEIN, A. (1910). Theorie der Opaleszenz von homogenen Flüssigkeiten und Flüssigkeitsgemischen in der Nähe des kritischen Zustandes. *Annln Phys.* [4] **33**, 1275.

Eisenberg, H. (1957a). Viscosity behavior of polyelectrolyte solutions at low and medium rates of shear. *J. Polymer Sci.* **23**, 579.

—— (1957b). Viscosity of dilute solutions of preparations of deoxyribonucleic acid at low and medium rates of shear. *J. Polymer Sci.* **25**, 257.

—— (1962). Multicomponent polyelectrolyte solutions. Part I. Thermodynamic equations for light scattering and sedimentation. *J. chem. Phys.* **36**, 1837.

—— (1966). Multicomponent polyelectrolyte solutions. Part IV. Second virial coefficient in mixed polyvinylsulfonate KCl systems near the theta temperature. *J. chem. Phys.* **44**, 137.

—— (1967). Molecular weights from equilibrium sedimentation in a density gradient. *Biopolymers* **5**, 681.

——, CASASSA, E. F. (1960). Aqueous solutions of salts of poly(vinylsulfonic acid). *J. Polymer Sci.* **47**, 29.

—— COHEN, G. (1969). An interpretation of the low-angle X-ray scattering of DNA solutions. *J. molec. Biol.* **37**, 355 (1968); erratum, ibid, **42**, 607.

——, FELSENFELD, G. (1967). Studies of the temperature-dependent conformation and phase separation of polyriboadenylic acid solutions at neutral pH. *J. molec. Biol.* **30**, 17.

—— FREI, E. H. (1954). Precision rotation viscometer with electrostatic restoring torque for the centipoise range. *J. Polymer Sci.* **14**, 417 see also, *Bull. Res. Counc. Israel* **3**, 442.

—— POUYET, J. (1954). Viscosities of dilute solutions of a partially quaternized poly-4-vinylpyridine at low gradients of flow. *J. Polymer Sci.* **13**, 85.

———— (1976). Sedimentation in the ultracentrifuge and diffusion of macromolecules carrying electrical charges, *Biophys. Chem.* (in press).

——, RAM MOHAN, G. (1959). Aqueous solutions of polyvinylsulfonic acid. Phase separation and specific interactions with ions, viscosity, conductance and potentiometry. *J. phys. Chem.* **63**, 671.

——, REISLER, E. (1971). Angular dependence of scattered light, rotary frictional coefficients, and distribution of sizes of associated oligomers in solutions of bovine liver glutamate dehydrogenase. *Biopolymers* **10**, 2363.

——, TOMKINS, G. M. (1968). Molecular weight of subunits, oligomeric and associated forms of bovine liver glutamate dehydrogenase. *J. molec. Biol.* **31**, 37.

——, WOODSIDE, D. (1962). Multicomponent polyelectrolyte solutions, Part 2. Excluded volume study of polyvinylsulfonate alkali halide systems. *J. chem. Phys.* **36**, 1844.

ELIAS, H. G. and BAREISS, R.(1967). Assoziation von Makromolekulen. *Chimia*, **21**, 53.

ELSON, E. L. and MAGDE, D. (1974). Fluorescence correlation spectroscopy. I. Conceptual basis and theory. *Biopolymers* **13**, 1.

EWART, R. H., ROE, C. P., DEBYE, P., and McCARTNEY, J. R. (1946). The determination of polymeric molecular weights by light scattering in solvent–precipitant systems. *J. chem. Phys.* **14**, 687.

FOORD, R., JAKEMAN, E., OLIVER, C. J., PIKE, E. R., BLAGROVE, R. J., WOOD, E., and PEACOCKE, A. R. (1970). Determination of diffusion coefficients of haemocyanin at low concentration by intensity fluctuation spectroscopy of scattered laser light. *Nature, Lond.* **227**, 242.

FORD, N. C., KARASZ, F. E., and OWEN, J. E. M. (1970). Rayleigh scattering from polystyrene solutions. *Discuss. Faraday Soc.* **49**, 228.

FREI, E. H., TREVES, D., and EISENBERG, H. (1957). Improved rotation viscometer for the study of low viscosity liquids at low and intermediate rates of shear. *J. Polymer Sci.* **25**, 273.

FUJIME, S. (1970). Quasi-elastic light scattering from solutions of macromolecules. II. Doppler broadening of light scattered from solutions of semi-flexible polymers, F-actin. *J. phys. Soc. Japan* **29**, 751.

FUJITA, H. and GOSTING, L. J. (1956). An exact solution of the equations for free diffusion in three-component systems with interacting flows, and its use in evaluation of the diffusion coefficients. *J. Am. chem. Soc.* **78**, 1099.

——, HOMMA, T. (1955). Non-Newtonian viscosities in dilute aqueous solutions of sodium carboxymethylcellulose. *J. Polymer Sci.* **15**, 277.

FUOSS, R. M., KATCHALSKY, A., and LIFSON, S. (1951). The potential of an infinite rod-like molecule and the distribution of the counter-ions. *Proc. natn. Acad. Sci. U.S.A.* **37**, 579.

GABRIEL, A. and DUPONT, Y. (1972). A position sensitive proportional detector for X-ray crystallography. *Rev. scient. Instrum.* **43**, 1600.

GILBERT, G. A. (1955). *Discuss. Faraday Soc.* **20**, 68.

GILL, S. J. and THOMPSON, D. S. (1967). A rotating Cartesian diver viscometer, *Proc. natn. Acad. Sci. U.S.A.* **57**, 562.

GODFREY, J. E. and HARRINGTON, W. F. (1970). Self association in the myosin system at high ionic strength. 2. Evidence for the presence of a monomer–dimer equilibrium. *Biochemistry* **9**, 894.

GOLDBERG, R. J. (1953). Sedimentation in the ultracentrifuge. *J. phys. Chem.* **57**, 194.

GOTTLIEB, M. H. (1971). On the rates of exchange between free and bound counter-ions in polyelectrolyte solutions. I. Electroosmotic flows during determinations made by an electrical transference method. *J. phys. Chem.* **75**, 1981, 1985, 1990.

GRUNWALD, E., LOEWENSTEIN, A., and MEIBOOM, S. (1957). Rates and mechanism of protolysis of methylammonium ion in aqueous solution studied by proton magnetic resonance. *J. chem. Phys.* **27**, 630, 641 (1957).

GUINIER, A. (1939). Diffraction of X-rays at very small angles—application to the study of ultramicroscopic phenomena. *Annln Phys.* **12**, 161.

HADE, E. P. K. and TANFORD, C. (1967). Isopiestic compositions as a measure of preferential interactions of macromolecules in two-component solvents. Application to proteins in concentrated aqueous cesium chloride and guanidine hydrochloride. *J. Am. chem. Soc.* **89**, 5034.

HALL, C. E. and SLAYTER, H. S. (1959). The fibrinogen molecule, its size, shape and mode of polymerization. *J. biophys. biochem. Cytology* **5**, 11.

HALTNER, A. J. and ZIMM, B. H. (1959). Rotational friction coefficients of models of tobacco mosaic virus and the size of the virus particle. *Nature, Lond.* **184**, 265.

HEARST, J. E. (1965). Determination of the dominant factors which influence the net hydration of native sodium deoxyribonucleate. *Biopolymers* **3**, 57.

——, SCHMID, C. W. (1971). Sedimentation equilibrium in a density gradient. *Pure appl. Chem.* **26**, 513.

——, VINOGRAD, J. (1961). A three-component theory of sedimentation equilibrium in a density gradient. *Proc. natn. Acad. Sci., U.S.A.* **47**, 999.

HERBERT, T. J. and CARLSON, F. D. (1971). Spectroscopic study of the self-association of myosin. *Biopolymers* **10**, 2231.

HERMANS, Jr., J. (1958). Solution properties of deoxyribonucleic acid. Ph.D. Thesis, Leyden.

——, HERMANS, J. J. (1959). Solution properties of deoxyribonucleic acid (DNA). I. Hydrodynamic behavior. *J. phys. Chem.* **63**, 170.

HERMANS, J. J. (1949). Light scattering by charged particles in electrolyte solutions. *Rec. Trav. chim.* **68**, 859.

—— (1963a), Density gradient centrifugation of a mixture of polymers differing in molecular weight and specific volume, *J. Polymer Sci. C* **1**, 179.

—— (1963b). Information regarding both molecular-weight distribution and density distribution in a polymer subjected to density-gradient centrifugation. *J. chem. Phys.* **38**, 597.

—— (1969). The application of density gradient centrifugation to the problem of compositional distribution in polymers, *Annls N.Y. Acad. Sci.* **164**, 122.

—— ENDE, H. A. (1963). Density gradient centrifugation of a polymer-homologous mixture, *J. Polymer Sci., C* **1**, 161.

——, LEVINSON, S. (1951). Some geometrical factors in light-scattering apparatus, *J. opt. Soc. Am.* **41**, 460.

HOLLEY, R. W., APGAR, J., EVERETT, G. A., MADISON, J. T., MARQUISEE, M., MERRILL,

J. H., PENSWICH, J. R., and ZAMIR, A. (1965). *Science, N.Y.* **147**, 1462.

HOOYMAN, G. J. (1956). Thermodynamics of diffusion in multicomponent systems. *Physica* **22**, 751, 761.

——, HOLTAN, H., MAZUR, P., and DEGROOT, S. R. (1953). Thermodynamics of irreversible processes in rotating systems. *Physica* **19**, 1095.

HOUWINK, R. (1940). Zusammenhang zwischen viskometrisch und osmotisch bestimmten Polymerisationsgraden bei Hochpolymeren. *J. prakt. Chem.* **157**, 15.

HUGGINS, M. L. (1942). The viscosity of dilute solutions of long-chain molecules. IV. Dependence on concentration. *J. Am. chem. Soc.* **64**, 2716.

HUIZENGA, S. R., GRIEGER, P. F., and WALL, F. T. (1950). Electrolytic properties of aqueous solutions of polyacrylic acid and sodium hydroxide. II. Diffusion experiments using radioactive sodium. *J. Am. chem. Soc.* **72**, 4228.

IFFT, J. B. and VINOGRAD, J. (1966). The buoyant behavior of bovine serum mercapt-albumin in salt solutions at equilibrium in the ultracentrifuge. II. Net hydration, ion binding, and solvated molecular weight in various salt solutions. *J. phys. Chem.* **70**, 2814.

IMAI, N. and EISENBERG, H. (1966). Multicomponent polyelectrolyte solutions. Part III. Determination of activity of KCl in potassium polyvinylsulfonate solutions by use of a cation-sensitive glass electrode. *J. chem. Phys.* **44**, 130.

INOUE, H. and TIMASHEFF, S. N. (1972). Preferential and absolute interactions of solvent components with proteins in mixed solvent systems. *Biopolymers* **11**, 737.

INTERNATIONAL UNION OF PURE AND APPLIED CHEMISTRY (1952). Report on nomenclature in the field of macromolecules. *J. Polymer Sci.* **8**, 257.

ISHIHARA, A. and HAYASHIDA, T. (1951). Theory of high polymer solutions. I. Second virial coefficient for rigid ovaloids model. II. Special forms of second osmotic coefficient. *J. phys. Soc. Japan* **6**, 40, 46.

JACKSON, J. L. and CORIELL, S. R. (1963). Effective diffusion constant in a polyelectrolyte solution. *J. chem. Phys.* **38**, 959.

—— —— (1964). On associated ions in polyelectrolytes and trapped Brownian trajectories. *J. chem. Phys.* **40**, 1460.

——, LIFSON, S., and CORIELL, S. R. (1969). Association times of counter-ions to poly-electrolytes in solution. *J. chem. Phys.* **50**, 5045.

JAENICKE, R. and LAUFFER, M. A. (1969). Determination of hydration and partial specific volume of proteins with the spring balance. *Biochemistry* **8**, 3077.

JERRARD, H. G. (1950). Turbulence in apparatus for measurement of streaming double refraction. *J. appl. Phys.* **21**, 1007.

JOHNSON, J. S., KRAUS, K. A., and SCATCHARD, G. (1954). Distribution of charged polymers at equilibrium in a centrifugal field. *J. phys. Chem.* **58**, 1034.

—— —— —— (1960). Activity coefficients of silicotungstic acid; ultracentrifugation and light scattering. *J. phys. Chem.* **64**, 1867.

——, SCATCHARD, G., and KRAUS, K. A. (1959). The use of interference optics in equilibrium ultracentrifugations of charged systems. *J. phys. Chem.* **63**, 787.

JOSEPHS, R. and HARRINGTON, W. F. (1967). Evidence for an unusual pressure dependence in an associating system. Sedimentation studies on myosin. *Proc. natn. Acad. Sci. U.S.A.* **58**, 1587.

KAYE, W. and HAVLIK, A. J. (1973). Low angle laser light scattering—absolute calibration, *Appl. Opt.* **12**, 541; *Polymer Lett.* **9**, 695 (1971).

KELLETT, G. L. (1971). Dissociation of hemoglobin into subunits, *J. molec. Biol.* **59**, 401.

KIM, S. H., SUDDATH, F. L., QUIGLEY, G., MCPHERSON, A., SUSSMAN, J. L., WANG, A. H. J., SEEMAN, N. C., and RICH, A. (1974). Three dimensional tertiary structure of yeast phenylalanine transfer RNA. *Science, N.Y.* **185**, 435.

KIRKWOOD, J. G., BALDWIN, R. L., DUNLOP, P. J., GOSTING, L. J., and KEGELES, G. (1960). Flow equations and frames of reference for isothermal diffusion in liquids. *J. chem. Phys.* **33**, 1505.

——, GOLDBERG, R. J. (1950). Light scattering arising from composition fluctuations in multi-component systems. *J. chem. Phys.* **18**, 54.

——, SHUMAKER, J. B. (1952). The influence of dipole moment fluctuations on the dielectric increment of proteins in solutions. *Proc. natn. Acad. Sci., U.S.A.* **38**, 863.

——, TIMASHEFF, S. N. (1956). The effect of ionization on the light scattering of isoionic proteins. *Archs Biochem. Biophys.* **65**, 50.

KIRSTE, R. G., KRUSE, W. A., and SCHELTEN, J. (1972). Die Bestimmung des Trägheits radius von Polymethylmethacrylat im Glasszustand durch Neutronenbeugung. *Makromol. Chem.* **162**, 299.

KLOTZ, L. C. and ZIMM, B. H. (1972a). Retardation times of deoxyribonucleic acid solutions. II. Improvements in apparatus and theory. *Macromolecules* **5**, 471.

—— —— (1972b). Size of DNA determined by viscoelastic measurements: results on bacteriophages, *Bacillus subtilis and Escherichia coli. J. molec. Biol.* **72**, 779.

KOEPPEL, G. (1967). Elektronmikroskopische Untersuchungen zur Gestalt und zum Makromolekularen Bau des Fibrinogenmoleküls und der Fibrin Fasern. *Z. Zellforsch. mikrosk. Anat.* **77**, 443.

KRATKY, O., LEOPOLD, H., and STABINGER, H. (1969). Dichtemessungen an Flüssigkeiten und Gasen auf 10^{-6} g/cm^3 bei 0·6 cm^3 Präparatvolumen. *Z. angew. Phys.* **27**, 273.

KRATOHVIL, J. P. and DELLICOLLI, H. T. (1970). Measurement of the size of micelles: the case of sodium taurodeoxycholate, *Fedn. Proc. Fedn Am. Socs exp. Biol.* **29**, 1335.

KRIEGER, I. M. and ELROD, H. (1953). Direct determination of the flow curves of non-Newtonian fluids. II. Shearing rate in the concentric cylinder viscometer. *J. appl. Phys.* **24**, 134.

——, MARON, S. H. (1952). Direct determination of the flow curves of non-Newtonian fluids. *J. appl. Phys.* **23**, 147.

—— —— (1954). Direct determination of the flow curves of non-Newtonian fluids. III. Standardized treatment of viscometric data. *J. appl. Phys.* **25**, 72.

LAUFFER, M. A. (1964). Polymerization–depolymerization of tobacco mosaic virus protein. II. Theory of protein hydration. *Biochemistry* **3**, 731.

LEDERER, K. (1972). Small angle X-ray scattering measurements with dilute solutions of fibrinogen. *J. molec. Biol.* **63**, 315.

——, FINKELSTEIN, A. (1970). Hydrodynamic study of fibrinogen molecular models to test their compatibility with data from the ultracentrifuge and viscosity measurements. *Biopolymers* **9**, 1553.

——, SCHURZ, S. (1972). High shear rate viscosity measurements with dilute solutions of bovine fibrinogen. *Biopolymers* **11**, 1989.

LIFSON, S. (1956). On the viscosity of polymer solutions in fine capillaries. *J. Polymer Sci.* **20**, 1.

——, JACKSON, J. L. (1962). On the self-diffusion of ions in a polyelectrolyte solution. *J. chem. Phys.* **36**, 2410.

——, KATCHALSKY, A. (1954). The electrostatic free energy of polyelectrolyte solutions. II. Fully stretched macromolecules. *J. Polymer Sci.* **13**, 43.

LILLIE, H. R. (1930). The Margules method of measuring viscosities modified to give absolute values. *Phys. Rev.* **36**, 347.

LINDERSTRØM-LANG, K. (1924). The ionization of proteins. *C. r. Trav. Lab. Carlsberg* **15**, No. 7.

LOEWENSTEIN, A. and MEIBOOM, S. (1957). Rates and mechanism of protolysis of di- and trimethylammonium ions studied by proton magnetic resonance. *J. chem. Phys.* **27**, 1067.

MAGDE, D., ELSON, E. L., and WEBB, W. W. (1972). Thermodynamic fluctuations in a reacting system-measurement by fluorescence correlation spectroscopy. *Phys. Rev. Letts.* **29**, 705.

—— —— —— (1974). Fluorescence correlation spectroscopy. II. An experimental realization. *Biopolymers* **13**, 29.

MANDELKERN, L., WILLIAMS, L. C., and WEISSBERG, S. G. (1957). Sedimentation equilibrium of flexible chain molecules. *J. phys. Chem.* **61**, 271.

MANNING, G. S. (1967). Molecular theory of counter-ion conductivity and self-diffusion in polyelectrolyte solutions. *J. chem. Phys.* **47**, 2010.

—— (1969a). Limiting laws and counter-ion condensation in polyelectrolyte solutions. III. An analysis based on the Mayer ionic solution theory. *J. chem. Phys.* **51**, 924, 934, 3249.

—— (1969b). Reply to comment of Jackson, Lifson and Coriell. *J. chem. Phys.* **50**, 5045.

——, ZIMM, B. H. (1965). Cluster theory of polyelectrolyte solutions. I. Activity coefficients of the mobile ion, *J. chem. Phys.* **43**, 4250.

MARON, S. H. and BELNER, R. S. (1955). Low shear capillary viscometer with continuously varying pressure head. *J. appl. Phys.* **26**, 1457.

MASSA, D. J. (1973). Flow properties of high-molecular-weight DNA solutions, viscosity, recoil and longest retardation time. *Biopolymers* **12**, 1071.

MEIBOOM, S., LOEWENSTEIN, A., and ALEXANDER, S. (1958). Studies of protolysis kinetics of ammonium ion in aqueous solutions by proton magnetic resonance technique. *J. chem. Phys.* **29**, 969.

MELSHEIMER, J. (1972). Ein Rotationsviskosimeter zur Bestimmung des Viskositäts-verlaufes bei sehr kleinen Geschwindigkeitsgefällen. *Kolloid Z.Z. Polymere* **250**, 97.

MESELSON, M. and STAHL, F. W. (1958). The replication of DNA in *Escherichia Coli*, *Proc. natn. Acad. Sci. U.S.A.* **44**, 671.

——, STAHL, F. W., and VINOGRAD, J. (1957). Equilibrium sedimentation of macro-molecules in density gradients. *Proc. natn. Acad. Sci. U.S.A.* **43**, 581.

——, WEIGLE, J. J. (1961). Chromosome breakage accompanying genetic recombination in bacteriophage. *Proc. natn. Acad. Sci. U.S.A.* **47**, 857.

MIJNLIEFF, P. F. (1962). Sedimentation and diffusion of colloidal electrolytes. Equations for the molecular weight. *Proc. K. ned. Akad. Wet.*, **B65**, 334, 343, 355, 364.

——, OVERBEEK, J. TH. G. (1962). Sedimentation and diffusion in a solution of two electrolytes, as described by irreversible thermodynamics. *Proc. K. ned. Akad. Wet.* **B65**, 221.

MOONEY, M. and EWART, R. H. (1934). The conicylindrical viscometer. *Physics* **5**, 350.

NAGASAWA, M. and EGUCHI, Y. (1967). The charge effect in sedimentation. I. Poly-electrolytes, *J. phys. Chem.* **71**, 880.

——, FUJITA, H. (1964). Diffusion of a polyelectrolyte in aqueous solution in the absence of salt. *J. Am. chem. Soc.* **86**, 3005.

NEUGEBAUER, T. (1943). *Berechnung der Lichtzerstreuung von Fadenkettenlösungen. Annln phys.* [5]**42**, 509.

NORÉN, I. B. E., HO, C., and CASASSA, E. F. (1971). A light scattering study of the effect of sodium chloride on the molecular weight of human adult hemoglobin. *Biochemistry* **10**, 3222.

OBER, R., COTTON, J. P., FARNOUX, B. and HIGGINS, J. S. (1974). Calculation of neutron diffraction pattern by polymer chains in the bulk state. *Macromolecules* **7**, 634.

ÖHRN, O. E. (1956). Preliminary report on the influence of adsorption on capillary dimensions of viscometers. *J. Polymer Sci.* **17**, 137; see also ibid. **19**, 199 (1956).

—— (1958). Precision viscometry of extremely dilute solutions of high polymers. *Arkiv. Kemi* **12**, 397.

ONSAGER, L. (1927). Zur Theorie der Elektrolyte. *Phys. Z.* **28**, 277.

—— (1931). Reciprocal relations in irreversible processes. I. *Phys. Rev.* **36**, 400; II, ibid. **38**, 2265.

——, FUOSS, R. M. (1932). Irreversible processes in electrolytes. Diffusion, conductance, and viscous flow in arbitrary mixtures of strong electrolytes. *J. phys. Chem.* **36**, 2689.

OOI, T. (1958). Light scattering from multi-component systems, *J. Polymer Sci.* **28**, 459.

OTH, A. and DOTY, P. (1952). Macro-ions. II. Polymethacrylic acid. *J. phys. Chem.* **56**, 43.

PAYENS, T. A. J., BRINKHUIS, J. A., and VAN MARKWIJK, B. W. (1969). Self-association in non-ideal systems, combined light scattering and sedimentation measurements in β-casein solutions. *Biochem. Biophys. Acta* **175**, 434.

PECORA, R. (1968). Spectral distribution of light scattered from flexible coil molecules. *J. chem. Phys.* **49**, 1032.

PEDERSEN, K. O. (1958). On charge and specific ion effects on sedimentation in the ultracentrifuge, *J. phys. Chem.* **62**, 1282.

PELLER, L. (1958). Sedimentation in multicomponent systems, *J. chem. Phys.* **29**, 415.

PERLMANN, G. E. and LONGSWORTH, L. G. (1948). The specific refractive increment of some purified proteins. *J. Am. chem. Soc.* **70**, 2719.

POON, P. H. and SCHUMAKER, V. N. (1971). Concentration dependence in three-component systems in sedimentation equilibrium in buoyant density gradients. *Biopolymers* **10**, 2071.

PRIEL, Z., SASSON, M., SILBERBERG, A. (1973). Method for determining the time of flow in a capillary viscometer with an absolute accuracy of 3×10^{-6}. *Rev. scient. Instrum.* **44**, 135.

——, SILBERBERG, A. (1970). Determination of adsorbed layer thickness by precision viscometry. *ACS Polymer Preprints* **11**, 1405.

PRUNIELL, A. and NEIMARK, J. (1971). An automatic recorder for the Zimm–Crothers viscometer. *Analyt. Biochem.* **42**, 202.

RAYLEIGH, Lord (J. W. Strutt) (1871). On the light from the sky, its polarization and colour. *Phil. Mag.* [4], **41**, 107, 274; On the scattering of light by small particles. Ibid. 447.

REISLER, E., HAIK, Y., and EISENBERG, H. Partial specific volumes and interaction parameters of bovine serum albumin in aqueous guanidine hydrochloride solutions (to be published).

——, EISENBERG, H. (1969). Interpretation of equilibrium sedimentation measurements of proteins in guanidine hydrochloride solutions. Partial volumes, density increments and the molecular weight of the subunits of rabbit muscle aldolase. *Biochemistry* **9**, 4572.

—— —— (1970). Studies on the viscosity of solutions of bovine liver glutamate dehydrogenase and on related hydrodynamic models; effect of toluene on enzyme association. *Biopolymers* **9**, 877.

—— —— (1971). Bovine liver glutamate dehydrogenase association and dependence of association on temperature. *Biochemistry* **10**, 2659.

—— —— (1972). Solubility of toluene in bovine liver glutamate dehydrogenase solutions and enhancement of enzyme association. *Biochem. Biophys. Acta* **258**, 351.

——, POUYET, J., and EISENBERG, H. (1970). Molecular weights, association and frictional resistance of bovine liver glutamate dehydrogenase at low concentrations. Equilibrium and velocity sedimentation, light scattering studies and settling experiments with macroscopic models of the enzyme oligomer: *Biochemistry* **9**, 3095.

RIS, H. and CHANDLER, B. C. (1963). *Cold Spring Harbor Symp. quant. Biol.* **28**, 2.

ROARK, D. E. and YPHANTIS, D. A. (1969). Studies of self-associating systems by equilibrium ultracentrifugation. *Ann. N.Y. Acad. Sci.* **164**, 245.

—— —— (1971). Equilibrium centrifugation of nonideal systems. The Donnan effect in self-associating systems. *Biochemistry* **10**, 3241.

ROBERTUS, J. D., LADNER, J. E., FINCH, J. T., RHODES, D., BROWN, R. S., CLARK, B. F. C., and KLUG, A. (1974). Structure of yeast phenylalanine t-RNA at 3 Å resolution. *Nature, Lond.* **250**, 546.

SADRON, C., POUYET, J., FREUND, A. M., and CHAMPAGNE, M. (1965). Repliement des doubles hélices de DNA dans les complexes nucléoprotéiques. *J. Chim. phys.* **62**, 1187.

SCATCHARD, G. (1946). Physical chemistry of protein solutions. I. Derivation of the equations for the osmotic pressure. *J. Am. chem. Soc.* **68**, 2315.

——, BATCHELDER, A. C., and BROWN, A. (1946). Preparation and properties of serum and plasma proteins. VI. Osmotic equilibria in solutions of serum albumin and sodium chloride. *J. Am. chem. Soc.* **68**, 2320.

——, BREGMAN, J. (1959). Physical chemistry of protein solutions. VIII. The effect of temperature on the light scattering of serum albumin solutions. *J. Am. chem. Soc.* **81**, 6095.

——, GEE, A., and WEEKS, J. (1954). Physical chemistry of protein solutions. VI. The osmotic pressures of mixtures of human serum albumin and λ-globulins in aqueous sodium chloride. *J. phys. Chem.* **58**, 783.

SCHACHMAN, H. K. (1963). The ultracentrifuge: problems and prospects. *Biochemistry* **2**, 887.

SCHELTEN, J., SCHLECHT, P., SCHMATZ, W., and MAYER, A. (1972). Neutron small angle scattering of hemoglobin. *J. Biol. Chem.* **247**, 5436.

SCHERAGA, H., (1955). Non-Newtonian viscosity of solutions of ellipsoidal particles. *J. chem. Phys.* **23**, 1526.

SCHILDKRAUT, C. L., MARMUR, J., and DOTY, P. (1961). The formation of hybrid DNA molecules and their use in studies of DNA homologies. *J. molec. Biol.* **3**, 595.

SCHMID, C. W. and HEARST, J. E. (1969). Molecular weights of homogeneous coliphage DNA's from density-gradient sedimentation equilibrium. *J. molec. Biol.* **44**, 143.

—— —— (1971). Density-gradient sedimentation equilibrium of DNA and the effective density gradient of several salts. *Biopolymers* **10**, 1901.

SCHOENERT, H. (1960). Diffusion and sedimentation of electrolytes and non-electrolytes in multicomponent systems. *J. phys. Chem.* **64**, 733.

SCHURR, J. M. and SCHMITZ, K. S. (1973). Rotational relaxation of macromolecules determined by dynamic light scattering. I. Tobacco mosaic virus. *Biopolymers* **12**, 1021.

SHACK, J., JENKINS, R. J., and THOMPSETT, J. M. (1952). The binding of sodium chloride and calf thymus desoxypentose nucleic acid. *J. biol. Chem.* **198**, 85.

SHAFER, R. H. (1974). Radial migration of DNA molecules in cylindrical flow. II. The non-draining model and possible applications to fractionation. *Biophys. Chem.* **2**, 185.

——, LAIKEN, N., and ZIMM, B. H. (1974). Radial migration of DNA molecules in cylindrical flow. I. Theory of free-draining model. *Biophys. Chem.* **2**, 180.

SHOGENJI, H. (1953). Light scattering in electrolyte solutions. *Busseiron kenk-yu*. **62,** 1.

SHULTZ, A. R. and STOCKMAYER, W. (1969). Consideration of the asymptotic behavior of the reciprocal light scattering function for polymer molecular weight distribution moment determination. *Macromolecules* **2,** 178.

SPIEGLER, K. S. (1958). Transport processes in ionic membranes. *Trans. Faraday Soc.* **54,** 1408.

STAFFORD III, W. F. and YPHANTIS, D. A. (1972). Virial expansions for ideal self-associating systems. *Biophys. J.* **12,** 1359.

STELLWAGEN, E. and SCHACHMAN, H. K. (1962). *Biochemistry* **1,** 1056.

STEPHEN, M. J. (1971). Spectrum of light scattered from charged macromolecules in solution. *J. chem. Phys.* **55,** 3878.

STEVENS, C. L. and LAUFFER, M. A. (1965). Polymerization–depolymerization of tobacco mosaic virus protein. IV. The role of water. *Biochemistry* **4,** 31.

STOCKMAYER, W. H. (1950). Light scattering in multicomponent systems. *J. chem. Phys.* **18,** 58.

STRAUSS, U. P. and ANDER, P. (1962). Molecular dimensions and interactions of lithium polyphosphate in aqueous lithium bromide solutions. *J. phys. Chem.* **66,** 2235.

——, WINEMAN, P. L. (1958). Molecular dimensions and interactions of long-chain polyphosphates in sodium bromide solutions. *J. Am. chem. Soc.* **80,** 2366.

STREETER, D. J. and BOYER, R. F. (1954). Viscosities of extremely dilute polystyrene solutions. *J. Polymer Sci.* **14,** 5.

STUHRMANN, H. B. (1973). Comparison of the three basic scattering functions of myoglobin with those from the known crystalline state. *J. molec. Biol.* **77,** 363.

SUEOKA, N. (1959). A statistical analysis of deoxyribonucleic acid distribution in density gradient centrifugation. *Proc. natn. Acad. Sci., U.S.A.* **45,** 1480.

SUND, H. and BURCHARD, W. (1968). Sedimentation coefficient and molecular weight of beef liver glutamate dehydrogenase at the microgram and the milligram level. *European J. Biochem.* **6,** 202.

TAKEDA, M. and ENDO, R. (1956). Viscosity of dilute polyvinyl chloride solution. *J. phys. Chem.* **60,** 1202.

TANFORD, C. (1955). Intrinsic viscosity and kinematic viscosity. *J. phys. Chem.* **59,** 798.

TAYLOR, G. I. (1936). Fluid flow between rotating cylinders. II. Distribution of velocity between concentric cylinders when outer one is rotating and inner one is at rest. *Proc. R. Soc. A***157,** 568.

THOMAS, C. A. and PINKERTON, T. (1962). Sedimentation equilibrium studies on intact and fragmented bacteriophage DNA. *J. molec. Biol.* **5,** 356.

THOMAS, J. O. and EDELSTEIN, S. J. (1971). Molecular weights and volumes from density perturbation ultracentrifugation, application to aldolase and deoxyribonucleic acid polymerase in solutions of guanidine hydrochloride. *Biochemistry* **10,** 477.

TIMASHEFF, S. N., DINTZIS, H. M., KIRKWOOD, J. G., and COLEMAN, B. D. (1955). Studies of molecular interaction in isoionic protein solutions by light scattering. *Proc. natn. Acad. Sci., U.S.A.* **41,** 710.

——, INOUE, H. (1968). Preferential binding of solvent component to proteins in mixed water–organic solvent systems. *Biochemistry* **7,** 2501.

——, TOWNEND, R. (1968). β-Lactoglobulin as a model of subunit enzymes. *Protides Biol. Fluids Proc. Colloq.* **16,** 33.

TISELIUS, A. (1932). The effect of charge on the sedimentation velocity of colloids, especially in the ultracentrifuge. *Kolloid Z.* **59,** 306.

TUNIS, M. J. B. and HEARST, J. E. (1968). On the hydration of DNA. II. Base composition dependence of the net hydration of DNA. *Biopolymers* **6,** 1345.

TUIJNMAN, C. A. F. and HERMANS, J. J. (1957). Precision viscometry of polyvinyl acetate in toluene. *J. Polymer Sci.* **25**, 385.

VAN HOLDE, R. E. and ROSSETTI, G. P. (1967). A sedimentation equilibrium study of the association of purine in aqueous solutions. *Biochemistry* **6**, 2189.

VAROQUI, R. and SCHMITT, A. (1972). Limiting sedimentation and diffusion coefficients of polyelectrolytes. The charge effect. *Biopolymers* **11**, 1119.

VRIJ, A. (1959). Dissertation. Utrecht, Netherlands.

——, OVERBEEK, J. TH. G. (1962). Scattering of light by charged colloidal particles in salt solutions. *J. Colloid Sci.* **17**, 570.

WALL, F. T. and GRIEGER, P. F. (1952). Theory of ion exchange for polyelectrolytes undergoing electrolyte transference. *J. chem. Phys.* **20**, 1200.

—— ——, HUIZENGA, J. R., and DOREMUS, R. H. (1952). Electrolytic properties at polyacrylic acid and sodium hydroxide. III. The rate of sodium ion exchange between polyacrylate and free sodium ions. *J. Chem. Phys.* **20**, 1207.

WALLACE, T. P., VOLOSIN, M. T., DELUMYEA, R. G., and GINGELLO, A. D. (1972). Evaluation of methods for determining the refraction correction for light-scattering photometers. *J. Polymer Sci.* **A-2, 10**, 193.

WARE, B. R. and FLYGARE, W. H. (1972). Light scattering in mixtures of BSA, BSA dimers, and fibrinogen under the influence of electric fields. *J. Coll. Interf. Sci.* **39**, 670.

WELLS, R. D. and LARSON, J. E. (1970). Studies on the binding of actinomycin D to DNA and DNA model polymers. *J. molec. Biol.* **49**, 319.

—— —— (1972). Buoyant density studies on natural and synthetic deoxyribonucleic acids in neutral and alkaline solutions. *J. biol. Chem.* **247**, 3405.

——, GRANT, R. C., SHORTLE, B. E., and CANTOR, C. R. (1970). Physicochemical studies on polydeoxyribonucleotides containing defined repeating nucleotide sequences. *J. molec. Biol.* **54**, 465.

YEANDLE, S. (1959). Effect of electric field on equilibrium sedimentation of macromolecules in a density gradient of caesium chloride. *Proc. natn. Acad. Sci., U.S.A.* **45**, 184.

YPHANTIS, D. A. (1964). Equilibrium ultracentrifugation of dilute solutions. *Biochemistry* **3**, 297.

ZERNICKE, F. (1918). Etude théorique et experimentale de l'opalescence critique. *Archs néerl. Sci. (IIIA)* **4**, 74.

ZICCARDI, R. and SCHUMAKER, V. (1971). Charge effects in sedimentation of polyelectrolytes. *Biopolymers* **10**, 1701.

ZIMM, B. H. (1946). Application of the methods of molecular distribution to solutions of large molecules. *J. chem. Phys.* **14**, 164.

—— (1948). The scattering of light and the radial distribution function of high polymer solutions. *J. chem. Phys.* **16**, 1093.

——, CROTHERS, D. M. (1962). Simplified rotating cylinder viscometer for DNA. *Proc. natl. Acad. Sci. U.S.A.* **48**, 905.

NAME INDEX

SUBJECT INDEX